GREAT BRITAIN
MOUNTAIN BIKING

TOM FENTON & ANDY McCANDLISH

Vertebrate Publishing
www.v-publishing.co.uk

Great Britain Mountain Biking
The best trail riding in England, Scotland and Wales

 First published in 2014 by Vertebrate Publishing.

Vertebrate Publishing
Crescent House, 228 Psalter Lane, Sheffield S11 8UT.
www.v-publishing.co.uk

Photography by John Coefield, Benjamin Haworth, Tom Hutton and Andy McCandlish.
Cover photo by Andy McCandlish.

A CIP catalogue record for this book is available from the British Library.

ISBN: 978-1-906148-51-5

  All maps reproduced by permission of Ordnance Survey on behalf of The Controller
of Her Majesty's Stationery Office. © Crown Copyright 100025218.

 Design by Nathan Ryder, production by Jane Beagley.
Vertebrate Graphics Ltd.
www. v-graphics.co.uk

Printed in China.

Contents

Southern England

Northern England

Wales

Scotland

The idea behind this book

Got a bike? Want to go away for the weekend? Not sure where?

This book can help you. It gives you ideas where to ride your bike in the UK. It tells you what each area is like, when to visit and provides you with all the information you need for a weekend's riding there.

More importantly, it suggests rides in each area. There is a map and full directions for a decent day ride, typical to that area and more than likely the route we'd pick if we were to ride there tomorrow. It should fill the Saturday of your weekend away. When you're done, this guide will tell you where we'd eat, drink and where we'd stay.

Come Sunday, depending on your fitness and time restraints, you might be looking for more of the same or you might be looking for something shorter. That's where the **More Riding** suggestions come in. Depending on the size of the area you're visiting, they'll give you a suitable range of different ideas for further rides in that region.

We've taken the liberty of assuming that you've got a decent level of fitness and know what you're doing on a bike. Basically, if you're like us – keen mountain bikers – then this book is aimed at you.

Have fun!

How to use this book

Fingers crossed, it's pretty self-explanatory. Read the introductions, look at the pictures and find somewhere you like the sound of. Check the information box, figure out where to stay and where to eat and which map to buy. Look at the route, plot it on a map and go and ride it. Come back grinning and repeat the process the following weekend.

The **More Riding** routes are a touch more complicated. Grab the relevant map (see the ride info. box) and find the starting point. From there, check the next place listed in the instructions, find it on the map and look for the most logical way to link the two (example from Urra Moor ride, page 141):

The Route » Clay Bank – road south to NZ 572033 – Urra Moor – Bloworth Crossing – Ouse Gill Head – West Gill Head – West Gill – road near Low Mill – north to Monket House – **Ouse Gill Head – Cockayne** – SE 609963 – Slape Wrath Moor – **East Bank Plantation – BW north around Urra Moor via NZ 581021** – Clay Bank

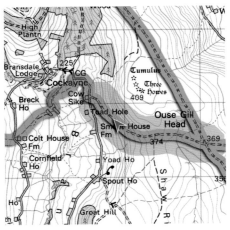
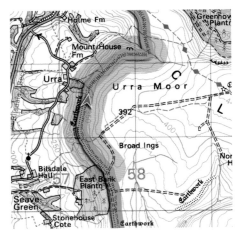

Grades

We've graded the routes blue, red or black – in a similar manner to that used in other Vertebrate guides and at trail centres around the UK. These grades consider technicality, length, strenuousness, navigation and remoteness. So a blue route could be a long, but easy and straightforward cruise, while a black could be a much shorter technical challenge.

Blue = Easy   **Red = Medium**   **Black = Hard**

Blue routes are generally short and within the reach of most riders, even newcomers. They're the kind of route you might pick on for a short day or when they weather's foul. Reds are a little harder, as you might expect. They're going to be longer and more technical – the sort of thing most riders will enjoy. Black routes, meanwhile, are going to be memorable. They might be highly technical or they might be massive routes through remote areas. Either way, they're probably going to demand endurance and technical ability – they're challenges to work up to. The grades are based on average conditions – good weather, not too wet and not too muddy. In a drought, routes will feel easier, in the dark depths of a British summer, harder.

Directions and accuracy

While every effort has been made to ensure accuracy within the directions and measurements in this guide, things change and we are unable to guarantee that every detail will be correct. Please treat stated distances as guidelines. Please exercise caution if a direction appears at odds with the route on the ground. A comparison between map and direction should see you on the right track.

Rights of Way

Countryside access in England and Wales hasn't been particularly kind to cyclists, although things are definitely improving. We have a 'right of way' on bridleways (blue arrows) and byways (red). This doesn't mean we have **the** right of way, just that we're allowed to ride there – give way to walkers and horse riders. (Either stop completely or slow right down.) We're also allowed to ride on green lanes and some unclassified roads, although the only way to determine which are legal and which aren't is to check with the local authority. Obviously, cycle routes are also in! Everything else is out of bounds unless the landowner says otherwise.

Scottish riders, meanwhile, enjoy one of the best access arrangements in the world. Essentially, you can ride virtually anywhere you like, provided you do so **responsibly**. This basically means that you need to respect the countryside and other users. So, leave gates as you find them, don't drop litter, give way to walkers, and so on. Equally importantly, consider what you're riding over and try to avoid soft or boggy ground with a fragile and easily damaged surface. All points that should also be considered by riders south of the border!

What sort of bike should I be riding?

Short answer: it doesn't matter, as long it works and you enjoy riding it – especially for longer or more remote routes. A £99 supermarket-special probably isn't ideal. You won't be going uphill fast if your gears seize but you may be going downhill quicker than planned if your brakes don't work. Pump the tyres up and check that nothing is about to fall off, rattle loose or wear through.

Obviously, bikes these days have got pretty good. If you can afford it, a decent full suspension bike will probably be faster, comfier and offer more control than a hardtail, particularly if you're heading somewhere rocky like the Lake District or Snowdonia. At the opposite end of the spectrum, if you're ploughing through Cotswold gloop in the middle of winter, you might prefer something less likely to clog with mud and which requires less maintenance. A fully rigid singlespeed wouldn't be out of place here.

Despite all that, while some bikes are arguably 'better' than others in certain situations, what's most important is that you're having fun. You can ride pretty much anything on anything. So if all you've got is a basic hardtail, go and enjoy yourself, it'll be fine.

What shall I stick in my bag?

Food and water. Ideally, you want to be drinking around half a litre of water for every hour of exercise. Any less, particularly in hot weather, and you might find you start to suffer. If you're on a long ride, carbohydrate-rich foods, such as bananas and cereal bars, will keep you going for longer.

Pack a **multi-tool** (with a chain splitter), a **spare tube** or two and a **pump**, along with and a few spares (such as chain link, spare mech hanger and a few zip ties). Mechanicals miles from home are no fun.

Water/wind proofs, **spare clothing** and a **hat/buff** could all come in handy if the weather changes suddenly. They're also handy in an emergency – what would happen if you fell off miles from home, in a rainstorm and had to wait hours for help? Could you stay warm? Do you have a **first aid kit** to fix yourself up? A relevant **map** is always worth having, as is a **mobile phone**, although you shouldn't rely on always getting a signal.

Sorted clothing will help you stay comfortable on your bike, especially in bad weather (there's no reason why riding through the winter shouldn't be fun). A 'layering system' is the easiest way to sort this, as you can add/remove layers if conditions change. Wear 'technical' synthetic or wool fabrics next to your skin to move moisture away from the body to keep you warm and dry. (Stay clear of cotton – it absorbs moisture and holds on to it, causing chafing and making you cold.) If it's chilly, an insulating layer over this will keep you warm. On the outside, a wind or waterproof layer will stave off the elements. Thin hats and spare gloves can come in handy when the weather's bad too. A buff can double up as a hat/nose warmer or can be dunked in water and used as a bandana in hot weather – very useful.

Padded shorts are more confortable, but the amount of lycra on display is entirely up to you. Baggy shorts, tights and trousers are all available for the more modest.

Set off a little on the cool side – you'll soon warm up and won't have to stop to change.

And, if it's a hot one, slap on some **sun cream** too!

Riding safely

Guess what – wear a **helmet**. And as 'the best helmet is the one you're wearing', make sure it fits and is comfortable. Do it up correctly (so it doesn't move) and you're good to go.

Gloves might not seem to do much, but they are an easy way to avoid blisters and palms full of gravel. If you've got two pairs, take a spare on wet days – cold hands and sopping gloves don't make bike control easy.

Knee/shin and elbow protectors might make you look like a Stormtrooper on a bike, but they'll help keep you intact. They've improved in comfort and mobility too – all-day rides in them are now perfectly feasible.

The ability to read a **map** and **navigate** in poor visibility could well prove essential on some of these routes. Don't head out in bad weather unless you're confident and capable of doing so.

Some of the routes described in this book point you at tough climbs and steep descents that can potentially be very dangerous. A tiring route into the back of beyond when you're unfit probably isn't the best plan. Too much exuberance on a steep descent in the middle of nowhere could land you in more than a spot of bother, especially if you're alone. Consider your limitations and relative fragility.

Solo rides can be fantastic fun. They can also leave you without help for a very long time. Tell someone where you're going and when you'll be back (and let them know when you are!).

Mountain Rescue

In case of an emergency dial **999** and ask for **Police** and then **Mountain Rescue**. Where possible give a six-figure grid reference of your location or that of the casualty. If you don't have reception where you are, try and attract the help of others around you. The usual distress signal is six short blasts on a whistle every minute. If you don't have a whistle, then shouting may work.

Mountain Rescue by SMS text

Another option in the UK is contacting the emergency services by SMS text – useful if you have a low battery or intermittent signal, but you do need to register your phone first. To register, simply text **'register'** to 999 and then follow the instructions in the reply. Do it now – it could save yours or someone else's life. *www.emergencysms.org.uk*

Rules of the (Off) Road

We're sure you know your countryside code. You've probably seen signs telling you to leave gates as you find them, or how to pass a logging truck at a trail centre. We think it all boils down to a few simple rules:

Respect the countryside – leave no trace, leave gates as you find them, look after the environment.

Look after the trail – avoid fragile trails in the wet, don't cut corners, keep singletrack single!

Enjoy your ride! And make sure everyone else does too – always give way and keep smiling.

A few thoughts

Think about the trails you're riding. If it's wet, maybe don't pick the really soft ones. You won't have much fun and you'll probably just knacker the track. Try and plan a route that stays on tougher surfaces – we've given plenty of pointers on this under each route.

Don't ride off the edges of the trail and don't cut corners. All it does is widens and straightens trails. Who wants that? Keep singletrack single and twisty. If you're scared of puddles or want to ride in straight lines, buy a road bike.

Ever wondered why dog walkers think it's a good idea to hang their little poo bags in trees? They probably wonder the same about bikers who drape inner tubes over bushes. Cut it out. And food wrappers may be sticky, but you wanted to eat from them, so tough – put the wrapper in your pocket. There's absolutely no argument for littering. If you carried it out, you can carry it home.

Acknowledgements

Tom

Much as I'd like to pretend I did all this by myself, I didn't. A lot of people helped with this book: Amy in the Clwyds and with general Welshness, Pete in the Cotswold mud, John in Surrey, Nick on Gower, Richie near his house, Chipps and Kelvin in Calderdale, Stu in his cafe in Reeth, Rich, Hazel, Russ and Clair all over the place, En-cyclo-pedic Andy in the Lakes (as usual), the North Pennines, the Peak, the Howgills and basically all over the place. And pretty much anyone who's ever shown me a trail anywhere!

Andy

More than half a lifetime of riding these trails wouldn't be the same without the people I have met along the way, who have showed me trails or stood in bogs with me when things haven't quite worked out. There are too many to list, but special mention has to go to Andy McKenna of Go-Where, a fellow trail diviner, photo model and bivvy artiste without whom a lot of these trails wouldn't be here.

Area Map

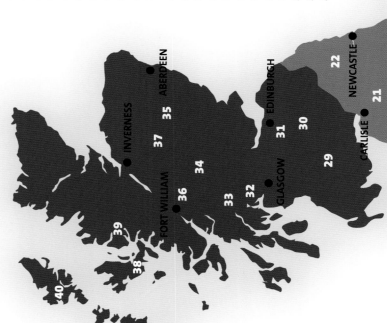

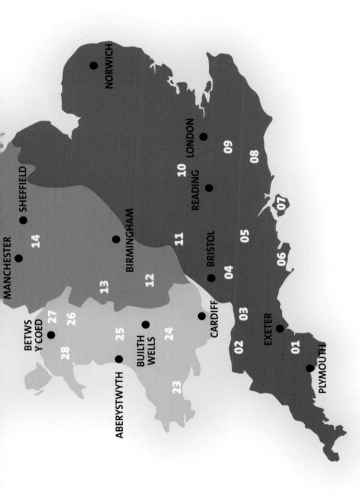

NORWICH

SHEFFIELD

MANCHESTER

BETWS Y COED

ABERYSTWYTH

BUILTH WELLS

CARDIFF

BIRMINGHAM

LONDON

READING

BRISTOL

EXETER

PLYMOUTH

01 02 03 04 05 06 07 08 09 10 11 12 13 14 23 24 25 26 27 28

Southern England

Dartmoor
Exmoor
The Quantock Hills
The Mendips
Salisbury Plain & the Surrounding Areas
Dorset, Swanage & the New Forest
Isle of Wight
The South Downs
The Surrey Hills – North Downs
The Chiltern Hills
The Cotswolds

Hound Tor, Dartmoor. **Photo**: Benjamin Haworth.

01: Dartmoor pony.   **02**: Agricultural trails in the Cotswolds.   **03**: Porlock Weir, Exmoor.   **04**: Broadway Wood, Cotswolds.
05: The Seven Sisters, South Downs Way, Sussex.   **06**: Cotswolds. **Photos 1-4, 6**: John Coefield.

07

08

09

10

07: Sea of bluebells in the South West.   **08**: Trail fodder.   **09**: Exmoor singletrack.   **10**: Cheddar Gorge, Mendip Hills.
Photos 7-9: John Coefield. **Photo 10**: Benjamin Haworth.

Dartmoor

Flick through this book and you'll find plenty of wild, open places.
They're all incredible places to visit and ride, with their own characters
and attractions. But none get under your skin like Dartmoor. A huge expanse of wild moorland dotted
with weathered granite boulders and windswept tors, there are few roads and even fewer houses.

On sunny days, when the heather is high and the big, open skies are a deep blue, it's beautiful
and oh-so peaceful. But, if you're out at dusk, or when the thick mists roll in, enveloping everything
in clammy greyness and cutting visibility to nothing in an instant, Dartmoor takes on a distinctly
spooky air. You begin to feel the strange emptiness and sense of isolation that gives it a unique feel
and suddenly it's all too apparent why so many ghostly myths and legends have sprung from the
endless bogs and soggy mires that surround you. The deserted moors, the damp silence, the ruined
huts and stone crosses ... *The Hound of the Baskervilles* was a story, right?

The Riding

At times, Dartmoor doesn't seem a great place to ride a bike. Large chunks of land are used for military
training. Other areas lack of Rights of Way. Pick the wrong bridleway on the wrong day and you'll find
yourself trudging through bogs and battered by bad weather. Straightforward-looking rock gardens
prove to be anything but, leaving you irritated and convinced of your own inadequacies as
a rider. So why bother? Because when it's good, it's really good. The singletrack is fast and smooth. The
rock gardens are hugely technical, yet enormously attemptable, full of rounded granite boulders that
encourage you to swoop around and jump over them. Somehow, no matter how technical the trail,
tight the corner or number of times you dab a foot (lots!), the riding keeps a playful and swoopy feel
– and it's a seriously addictive one. Throw in a good mixture of trails, from the really tricky stuff in
Lustleigh Cleave to the easy old railway line out of Princeton, and you've got an area that caters for
everyone. And the scenery is magnificent, which always helps.

When to go

There's always something to ride on Dartmoor. On fine days, the popular areas (Lustleigh Cleave) get
busy, but there are plenty of out-of-the-way trails to explore. These can be vague (take a compass)
and are often boggy in bad weather – so try the bridleways that hold up well when wet (Burrator loop)
or those that are sheltered from the wind (Lustleigh again).

Do remember that Dartmoor is associated with bleakness for a reason. The fog and mist can drop
visibility to single figure distances in minutes, it's windswept and it can be a long way home.
Keep an eye on the forecast.

Hound Tor. **Photo**: John Coefield.

01 Grimspound & Nut Crackers

This is a ride that heads uphill for the first seven kilometres, that finishes with one of the steepest road slogs in this book and which contains at least one horrible climb. Yet I get excited every time I think about riding it.

That's only partly due to my roadie-like love of climbing. It's mainly because this route is brilliant from start to finish. Singletrack descent follows singletrack descent – and each one is terrific. There's the blast down Grimspound, multi-lined at the top, flat-out and grassy lower down. There's the twisty run around Headland Warren, mixing fast flowing turns with tighter, blind corners through old mine workings. There's swoopy stuff, flat-out bits and secret woodland plummets. And then, just when it couldn't get any better, there's Nut Crackers. Flowing over granite boulders and around rolling corners for over two kilometres of solid singletrack, it's one of the best trails in the country. The only downside is that it's virtually impossible to clean – and yet even that doesn't seem to matter as the memory of each dab melts away as you sweep through the next perfect section. I'm already planning my next trip.

Note: *Sorry about the odd 'bone' shape of this ride. It started off as a nice loop, but then we realised that we always rode a variation on that loop which doubled back on itself a little and covered less ground, but which included more of our favourite descents. So we figured we'd stick that variation in instead and give you more of the good stuff. If you want the original loop, see page 18.*

Grade: **Black** » Distance: **26km** » Ascent: **790m** » Time: **3.5+**
Start/Finish: **Manaton car park** » Start Grid Ref: **SX 749812** » SatNav: **Manaton**
OS Map: **Explorer OL28 Dartmoor** » Parking: **Donation for parking** » Cafe: **None on route**
Pub: **Warren House Inn, on the B3212 just off west end of route, 01822 880 208**

Directions

S Leaving the car park, turn **R** onto the lane and then **R** again at the crossroads. After 700m, turn sharply **L** onto a narrow lane and drop to a ford and a gate. Go through this and follow the road uphill.

As the gradient eases, go **SA** through another gate and then turn **R** immediately afterwards, through a gate onto a grassy bridleway. Cross the road, passing Jay's Grave and follow the obvious track to a second road. Turn **L**, then quickly **R** through a gate onto a signed bridleway.

Bear **R**, crossing the stream and then follow the obvious grassy track steeply uphill. As the track splits, keep **L**. As you near the top of the climb, keep **SA** over a vague grassy crossroads, heading for the top of the shallow valley you can see on the right. (If you find yourself at the RAF memorial, you're too far to the left.)

The track soon becomes more obvious and considerably more enjoyable. Follow it **SA**, passing between the two Tors and dropping, with bridleway signs, over a fallen wall and onto a paved descent to the road.

2 Turn **R**. At the very top of the climb, turn **L** onto a grassy and often boggy bridleway. Go over the top of the hill and onto a fun singletrack descent towards a car park. Immediately upon reaching the car park, turn **L**, following low bridleway markers and head towards the bottom of the valley floor (don't climb back up the hill), soon picking up singletrack that twists and turns around blind corners and through mine workings.

Continue **SA** as you join a wider track. After a short distance, directly opposite the remains of some old mine buildings on the right, turn **L** onto a grassy bridleway which soon becomes an obvious and technical climb. Go over the top of the hill and drop towards the farm. Bear **L** past the farm and climb to the road.

Turn **R**, drop into the dip and turn **L**, reversing your earlier route as you climb around the ruins, over the top of the hill and drop rapidly to the road. Continue **SA**, still retracing your earlier steps. Pass Jay's Grave, cross the road and climb over the fields beyond. At the road turn **L**.

Go through the gate and turn **R**, leaving the outbound route and climbing the hillside beyond. Aim slightly **L** and climb to the rocks. Go **SA** over the hilltop onto a fast, narrow and technical descent. Drop to a gate, through the trees and to the road. Turn **L** and climb steeply. Go **SA** over the crossroads, pass your car in the car park and continue along the lane. Shortly after leaving the green, turn **L** through a gate onto a signed bridleway. Respect signs asking mountain bikers to keep their speed down.

3 Keep **R** upon joining a wide track. As this ends, turn **L** onto a signed bridleway. A fantastic, always wet and technical descent drops to the river. Cross the bridge and keep **SA**, beginning to climb. Keep **L** as the track forks. You'll almost certainly have to push at some point. Turn **L** at the bridleway junction, signed *Nut Crackers*. (If you want to push further up the hill in order to ride back down before turning, you won't regret it. Just sayin'.) Climb and then descend a short distance, before turning **R** at a bridleway signpost. Superb technical singletrack weaves up and down the hill and over rocks before swooping down towards the river. Ignore all turnings. As the descent ends, bear **R**, slightly uphill, to a gate.

Go through the gate and follow wide tracks **SA** to a bridge. Go over the bridge and then turn **L** onto a signed bridleway. Rejoining the main track, turn **L** and climb steeply to the road. Turn **L** and climb for an eternity back to Manaton – the car park is on the far side of the green.

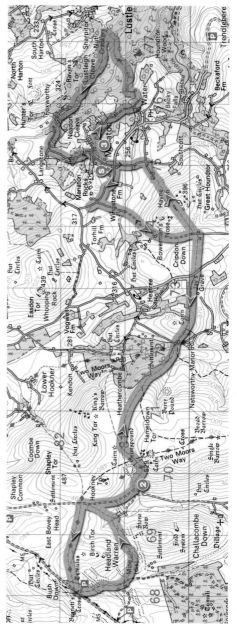

More riding

'The Original Route'

As we said earlier, this was to be our original route – and it's a cracker. It follows the main ride at the beginning and at the end, but then heads off to the north via warp-speed singletrack, a tight hillside traverse and a tree-lined wriggle before an impossible climb carries you high above Lustleigh Cleave – at which point you swoop over rounded rocks and into deep natural berms before rejoining the main route at the top of the fantastic Nut Crackers. Brilliant.

Grade: **Very Black** » Distance: **29km** » Ascent: **910m** » Time: **3hrs+**
Start/Finish: **Manaton car park, SX 749812** » OS Map: **Explorer OL28 Dartmoor**

The Route » Manaton – Wingstone Farm – Bowerman's Nose – Jay's Grave – east via Grimspound to the road at SX 697808 – north on the road to SX 695816 – west, then south and east to loop around Headland Warren and return to SX 695816 – east to SX 709825 – roads east and south to SX 732817 (below Easdon Tor) – bridleways to North Bovey – south-east to Barnecourt – Peck Farm – Sharpitor – Nut Crackers – Foxworthy – Manaton

Hound Tor

Another stunning and technical singletrack ride. Overlapping the main ride, you get to ride Nut Crackers again. You also get the brilliant descent from Hound Tor, the flying singletrack mile of Haytor Down and the tight and technical splashy descent from Water. The bad news – you pay for your fun with a lot of climbing and a dull drag along the bottom of Lustleigh Cleave. Is it worth it? No question.

Grade: **Black** » Distance: **20km** » Ascent: **630m** » Time: **3hrs+**
Start: **Hound Tor car park, SX 739791** » OS Map: **OL28 Dartmoor**

The Route » Hound Tor car park – Leighon via Greator Rocks – Black Hill – SX 769783 – Lower Down – Houndtor Wood – Water – east to Nut Crackers – Neadon Cleave – road to Manaton – Hayne Down – Hound Tor car park

Princetown & Burrator

Head out into the middle of the (Dart)moors, admire the big, open view and enjoy the bleakness. Hop waterbars and pop off rocks, or relax and cruise down to Burrator for a picnic. Good trails mean easy enough year-round riding and the navigation's straightforward – but take care: open moors aren't much fun in wind and rain. A Dartmoor classic.

Grade: **Blue/Red** » Distance: **20km** » Ascent: **330m** » Time: **2hrs+**
Start: **Princetown, SX 590735** » OS Map: **OL28 Dartmoor**

The Route » Princetown – South Hessary Tor – Burrator Reservoir – Yellowmead Down – Sheepstor (village) – Ditsworthy Warren – Nun's Cross – Princetown

Postbridge

Two rides in one. Head out around the first part for easy (relatively speaking – it's still Dartmoor!) but hugely enjoyable riding, or tackle the southern section for some real technical challenges, including the 'Bellever Rock Garden'. Good singletrack, easy cruising and mine workings in the first option, lots and lots (and lots) of rocks in the second. Beautiful central-Dartmoor scenery from both.

Grade: **Red (Loop 1)/Black (Loop 2)** » Distance: **17km/22km** » Ascent: **370m/580m** » Time: **2hrs+/3hrs+**
Start: **Postbridge, SX 648789** » OS Map: **OL28 Dartmoor**

Loop 1 » Postbridge – roads west past Runnage farm to Soussons Down – forest roads to Headland Warren (SX 682809) – Warren House Inn – Bennett's Cross – SX 682809 – west over Headland Warren and around Challacombe Down to Sousson's Farm – Pizwell Farm – Postbridge

Loop 2 » Postbridge – Bellever – Laughter Hole – Dunnabridge Pound – Sherberton – Combestone Tor – Clapper – Babeny – Laughter Hole – re-ride bridleway towards Dunnabridge Pound, turning north to Bellever Tor – east into woods on Bridleway and then forest roads to Postbridge

Headland Warren. **Photo**: John Coefield.

More information

Main Towns

Tavistock and Okehampton are reasonably close and relatively easy to negotiate. Moretonhampstead, Bovey Tracey and Newton Abbot are closer still, and only really good for food and tourist information.

Maps

OS Explorer OL28 Dartmoor
Harvey Maps *Dartmoor for Cyclists* – colour-graded tracks for difficulty

Bike Shops

Dartmoor Cycles, Atlas House, Tavistock, 01822 618 178, www.dartmoorcycles.co.uk
The Bike Shed, Fore Street, Exeter, 01392 426 191, www.bikesheduk.com

Accommodation

No matter what sort of accommodation you're after, you could do worse than look at www.dartmooraccommodation.co.uk (Very useful.)

There's a basic but incredibly well-situated campsite right in the middle of Dartmoor behind the Plume of Feathers pub (01822 890 240, www.theplumeoffeathersdartmoor.co.uk) in Princetown. It also has a bunkhouse, and the pub does good food.

For groups, there's a good, central bunkhouse between Postbridge and Two Bridges – Powdermills Bunkhouse, 01822 880 277, www.spirit-of-adventure.com

The Fox Tor Cafe is a good, bike friendly choice in Princetown, 01822 890 238, www.foxtorcafe.com

Another good option is the YHA-run Great Hound Tor Camping Barn, near Manaton (YHA main no.: 0870 770 8868) and there's a nicely-located YHA in Bellever (0845 371 9622) and a good independent hostel in Moretonhampstead – Sparrowhawk Backpackers, 01647 440 318, www.sparrowhawkbackpackers.co.uk

Food & Drink

There are pubs and cafes in every village on Dartmoor. Particularly good are:
The Fox Tor Cafe, Princetown 01822 890 238, www.foxtorcafe.com
The Hound of the Basketmeals (van, parks in Hound Tor car park, brilliant name)
Warren House Inn, on the B3212 nr Postbridge, 01822 880 208, www.warrenhouseinn.co.uk

Tourist Informaton Centres

Moretonhampstead, 01647 440 043
Okehampton, 01837 530 20
There are also several visitor centres run by the Dartmoor National Park Authority, including:
High Moorland Visitor Centre, near Princetown 01822 890 414
Haytor Visitor Centre, 01364 661 520

Outdoor Shops

There's not a huge amount of shopping on Dartmoor itself. Head for Tavistock.

Useful Websites

www.dartmoor.co.uk » **www.dartmooraccommodation.co.uk** » **www.dartmoor-npa.gov.uk**

Guidebooks

South West Mountain Biking – Quantocks, Exmoor and Dartmoor, written by Nick Cotton & Tom Fenton, published by Vertebrate Publishing

Lustleigh Cleave. **Photo:** Benjamin Haworth.

Exmoor

The South West has a lot of moors – Exmoor, Dartmoor, Bodmin (Moor) –
and they often seem rather similar. They've all got wild ponies. They've all inspired novels.
They've all got 'beasts' (even Exmoor, although despite once being thought a puma or leopard,
the Exmoor beast has now been given 'figment of the imagination' status. Which is a shame.).
So, why visit Exmoor?

Well, for starters, because even a cursory glance over its 700 square kilometres of green and rolling
hills, wooded valleys and rocky coastline gives you a pretty (in both senses of the word) good idea of
the sheer beauty of the place. Because the rugged coastline contains some of the largest sea cliffs in
England and because the villages, with their thatched cottages and covered markets, are some of the
prettiest in the country. Even the wild ponies here aren't just any old ponies – they are Exmoor Ponies,
the oldest native breed of horses in the UK. And, as a former Royal Hunting Forest, the region is home
to hundreds of huge Red Deer – including the largest stag in Britain: the nine-foot tall 'Exmoor
Emperor'. Lots of reasons, then, to visit Exmoor! (Sadly, not everyone comes to Exmoor for the views
or the riding – the Emperor was shot not long before publication by a deer stalker.)

The Riding

The riding on Exmoor is incredibly varied – not only in style, but also in quality. Pluck a route off a map
and there's a pretty good chance that you'll find yourself slogging across a tussocky, soul-destroying
bog on a 'track' that doesn't exist (although it will, at least, be memorable). However, take a little time
to plan and there's some great riding to be found. Singletrack, for example, is scarce on Exmoor – but
when you find it, it makes you grin from ear to ear and possibly burst into song. Some of it is stupidly
steep (Horner Wood), some of it is scenic (Simonsbath) and some of it flows and flows and flows
(Porlock – absolutely one of the best bits of singletrack in existence). Elsewhere, there are moorland
trails to rival anything you'll find anywhere. They're never as technical as, say, the Peak District, but
that just means they're faster and swoopier. And then, if you want a break, there's a whole raft of easy
riding – and you can choose between sea views and hillside cruising. So, to summarise: plan carefully
– head for the wrong place and get stuck on rubbishy trails; get it right and you'll find nothing but
stunning riding.

When to go

Exmoor's pretty good year round. While the more open stuff might get a bit battered in bad weather,
the stuff in the trees stays sheltered. Things do get boggy and muddy in places in the winter though,
and Exmoor is definitely at its best in the (theoretically dry) summer months.

Will Wykes on the South West Coast Path. **Photo**: John Coefield.

02 Porlock Hill

Forest singletrack, moorland blasts and lots of up and down amidst cracking scenery make this an Exmoor classic. The start is tough, heading up Dunkery Hill via steep tarmac (double chevron time!) and forest tracks. Halfway up, at about the point where you're questioning the choice of route, a bridleway swings off east. A real rollercoaster on dusty, rock-littered singletrack, it's enough to re-assure the most climbing-phobic of riders. Sadly for them, the next section completes the climb to Dunkery Beacon (including the height you just lost …). It's actually a good climb – loose and rocky. Atop the Beacon, admire the view and then drop to Horner Wood for the second highlight of the ride, plunging into the trees on narrow singletrack. It's not particularly technical, just stupidly steep – off-the-brakes stuff it is not! A hideous climb follows, before a second brake-burning descent into Porlock.

The extension is a great ride in its own right. The climbing in the first half is a real pig (ever smelt the burning clutches of cars struggling up Porlock Hill?), but the optional drop to Porlock Weir and the descent of Hawk Combe take in some of the best singletrack in the UK, making all the effort totally worthwhile.

Grade: **Red (Black with extension)** » Distance: **20/32km** » Ascent: **710/1200m** » Time: **2.5hrs+**	
Start/Finish: **Porlock** » Start Grid Ref: **SS 887467** » SatNav: **Porlock**	
OS Map: **OL9 Exmoor** » Parking: **Pay & display in Porlock**	
Cafe: **Horner Tea Gardens, Horner, 01643 862 380** » Pub: **The Royal Oak, Porlock, 01643 862 798**	

Directions

⑤ From the main car park in Porlock, turn **R** onto the main road (towards Minehead), then immediately turn **R** up *Doverhay* – the road that runs up the edge of the car park. Go up through the houses, keeping **L** at the junction as you leave Porlock.

Climb steeply in the woods and around sharp bends. As you begin to descend, and just after a road comes in from the right, bear **R** onto a wide dirt track. Follow this downhill and through gates to the road.

Turn **R**, then follow the road around to the left. At the crossroads, fork **R** off tarmac onto a wide dirt track signed as a bridleway to *Brockwell*. Ride into the woods to a track crossroads and turn **R**, uphill, signed as a restricted byway to *Webber's Post*.

Climb steeply out of the woods to a grassy area. Bear **L** across this onto the road. Turn **L** and climb for 200m before turning **L** onto narrow singletrack, signed as a bridleway to *Brockwell*. A superb gradual descent drops across open countryside. Ignore bridleways on the left.

As you near the trees, the track forks. Bear **L** and drop downhill, through the woods. At the road turn **R** and then turn **R** up the second bridleway – a wide track signed as a bridleway to *Dunkery Beacon and Webber's Post*.

② Climb 'with interest', keeping **SA** at junctions. Go **SA** over the road onto a wide track. Follow this to Dunkery Beacon. There are multiple tracks here – the bridleway passes **SA** beneath the Beacon before descending gently on the left hand of the two parallel tracks.

Easy to miss: drop away from the summit. As the gradient flattens, turn **R** onto vague singletrack. Keep **SA** over the next track and descend across the hillside, trending slightly **L**. At the junction, turn **L** on the wide track and follow this up to the road.

Turn **R**, then **L** at the next junction. Drop steeply around hairpins. At the church at Stoke Pero, continue **SA** off the hairpin through a small farmyard onto a bridleway. Go through gates into a field and bear **L**, following a vague, but increasingly obvious track into the woods. A superb and very steep descent drops to the river.

3 Cross the bridge and go **SA** up the steep track opposite. Go **SA** over the wide track (you might have to push here), following signs for *Granny's Ride*. Ignoring turnings, follow singletrack uphill and to the left. Just before leaving the woods, turn **R** onto *Flora's Ride*. Ignoring turnings, ride out of the woods and across grass to join a stony track. Follow this to the road. Turn **R** and begin to descend.

Easy to miss: Keep your speed down and look out for what looks like a small grassy parking area on the left. Turn sharp **L** across this onto singletrack running into the woods. Drop steeply before turning sharp **L** on a wide track. Follow this down to a gate. Immediately after the gate, turn sharp **L** onto more singletrack and drop to the road. Continue **SA**, downhill, into Porlock.

Extension/second ride

Porlock – west to minor (yellow) road at SS 883 467 – permissive (footpath on map) bridleway through woods to SS 867472 – uphill on Byway into Worthy wood to SS 856475 – brilliant singletrack descent to Porlock Weir – road/bridleway south (uphill) to Wescott Brake – Hawkhead Combe – Shillett Wood to SS 863455 – climb north and run east along top edge of Homebush Wood – Porlock via SS 882462

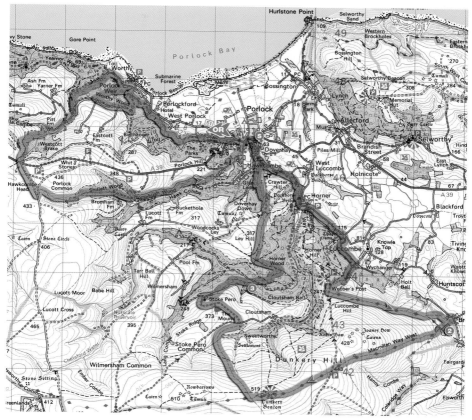

More riding

Withypool & the Simonsbath Singletrack

Leaving Withypool on wide trails, hitting some superb singletrack alongside the River Barle and finishing with a fast moorland descent, this southern Exmoor loop is a great little ride. The singletrack is perfect, not too technical (a couple of sections excepted), but fast and twisty and through a beautiful valley. The remainder of the ride is pleasant cruising, culminating in one of the swoopiest pieces of moorland descending in the South West.

Grade: **Red** » Distance: **27km** » Ascent: **560m** » Time: **3hrs+**
Start: **Withypool, SS 844354** » OS Map: **OL9 Exmoor**

The Route » Withypool – SS 824367 – Pickedstones – Simonsbath – Two Moors Way – Flexbarrow – Great Ferny Ball – Horsen Farm – Sherdon Farm – Withypool Cross – Sportsman's Inn – White Cross – Porchester's Post – Withypool

Selworthy & Dunster

A pleasant ride. From Selworthy to Dunster, there's a fair bit of climbing and a long, easy cruise through the woods. Sandy singletrack leads to Minehead, the sea and ice creams. A big pull onto the South West Coast Path gives a ride with a sea view to Selworthy Beacon, from where a steep descent leads to picturesque villages and the start. NOT one for busy periods unless you're very careful – the coastal path fills with families.

Grade: **Red/Blue** » Distance: **25km** » Ascent: **680m** » Time: **3hrs+**
Start: **Selworthy, SS 919468** » OS Map: **OL9 Exmoor**

The Route » Selworthy – East Lynch – Tivington – Tivington Common – Knowle Hill – Grabbist Hill – Ellicombe via SS 887467 and Penny Hill – Alcombe – seafront through Minehead to Greenaleigh Farm – South West Coast Path to North Hill and Selworthy Beacon – farm park near Bossington –Selworthy

Exford & Winsford

A long road stretch, a field crossing and a fast, stony descent lead from Winsford to Exford. An easy climb runs from here to the top of a bizarre (and tricky) downhill made of stone shelves (to the appropriately-named 'Stone'). Easy valley-bottom riding then runs back to Winsford. If it's quiet, you can extend the route (+16 kilometres and 500 metres of ascent), exchanging the long starting road drag for flying moorland descending and pleasant riverside cruising alongside the River Barle. We say quiet as the section around Tarr Steps is popular with walkers, and it's just not worth it when it's busy.

Grade: **Red** » Distance: **22km** » Ascent: **400m** » Time: **2.5hrs+**
Start: **Winsford, SS 906348** » OS Map: **OL9 Exmoor**

The Route » Winsford – road to Comer's Cross – SS 856360 – North Court – Exford – Hillhead Cross – Stone – Lyncombe – Nethercote – Winsford

Horner Wood. **Photo**: John Coefield

More information

Main Towns

The biggest town in the area is Minehead, so head there for bike shops and supermarkets. Otherwise, Porlock and Lynton are the best for shops in the north, and Dulverton is by far the best in the south. The majority of Exmoor's other villages have village shops and a pub or two.

Maps

OS OL9 Exmoor
OS Landranger 181 Minehead & Brendon Hills

Bike Shops

Pompy's Cycles, Minehead, 01643 704 077, www.pompyscycles.co.uk
If you need anything else, Bridgwater near the M4 has a few shops. See page 36.

Accommodation

There are campsites all over Exmoor and an OS map will reveal numerous options. If you're riding the main route here, try the Sparkhayes Farm site in the centre of Porlock (01643 862 470) or Burrowhayes (01643 862 463, www.burrowhayes.co.uk) in Horner, which is literally on the route.

There are YHA Hostels in the north in Minehead (0845 371 9033) and centrally near Simonsbath (01643 831 437) and Exford (0845 371 9634). There are also independent options: Exmoor Bunkhouse in Countisbury, (01598 741 101) and Base Lodge in Minehead, (01643 703 520).

For B&Bs and hotels, see the websites below. Anywhere central or around the Porlock/Dunster area will be handiest for riding from.

Food & Drink

Horner Tea Gardens, Horner, 01643 862 380
Royal Oak, Withypool, 0161 831 506, www.royaloakwithypool.co.uk (also offers accommodation)
The Ship Inn, Porlock, 01643 862 507, www.shipinnporlock.co.uk (also offers accommodation)
The Royal Oak, Porlock, 01643 862 798
Exmoor Forest Inn, Simonsbath, 01643 831 341, www.exmoorforestinn.co.uk (also offers accommodation)

Tourist Information Centres

Dunster, 01643 821 835 » **Dulverton**, 01398 323 841 » **Porlock**, 01643 863 150, www.porlock.co.uk/visitors
Minehead, 01643 702 624, www.mineheadtic.co.uk » **Combe Martin**, 01271 883 319, www.visitcombemartin.com » **Ilfracombe**, 01271 863 001, www.visitilfracombe.co.uk

Outdoor Shops

Not a huge amount around. You can pick up small items in many camping shops, and in larger villages like Porlock and Dulverton. Otherwise, there are a couple of small shops in Minehead.

Useful Websites

www.visit-exmoor.co.uk » www.exmoor.com » www.exmooraccommodation.co.uk

Guidebooks

South West Mountain Biking – Quantocks Exmoor Dartmoor, written by Nick Cotton & Tom Fenton, published by Vertebrate Publishing

Worth Knowing

Dunster Forest Estate has a few easy waymarked routes. Downhillers should head to Combe Sydenham for the runs there. Alternatively, stop off in the Quantocks (page 31) on the way home for some of the best singletrack in England.

Horner Wood. **Photo**: John Coefield.

The Quantock Hills

Considering their diminutive size, the Quantocks punch way above their weight. It's probably fair to say that they contain more (legal) natural singletrack than any other area in England. They also contain more bridleways per square kilometre than anywhere else in the country. So, if you see a trail, chances are that you can legally ride it and chances are that it will be singletrack. We can't really think of a better recommendation than that.

Then there's the friendly Quantock 'feel'. Perhaps it's their small size, the ever-present ponies, or the perfectly-placed grass banks on which to lie and admire the sea views ... whatever it is, this is a particularly pleasant place in which to spend time. Add this to the fantastic riding and you have one of the best spots in the UK. It's certainly one of our favourites. The only downside is that if you're there for a couple of days, you're likely to end up repeating tracks. Although, thinking about it, that's not really a downside at all.

The Riding

A good way to think of the Quantocks would be as a natural trail centre. There's singletrack every-where, it's relatively easy to ride and is unbelievable amounts of fun when taken at speed. Think 'red grade' and you're close. There are flat out sections, rough, tricky little rock gardens and true roller coasters of turns and stream crossings – all singletrack and all great fun.

Rides here often take on a 'clover leaf' pattern, dropping up and down the hillside and returning to the same point multiple times. This makes it very easy to shorten or lengthen routes – or to re-ride singletrack. However, despite being relatively low (the highpoint is about 350 metres), the Quantocks start close to sea level and are steep-sided, so you pay for each climb, but get full value from every descent. If you're hunting for singletrack, you'll be nipping up and down a fair bit, so even short rides are soon felt in the legs.

At the top of the hills is the Great Ridge, covered in open heathland, low gnarled trees and sandy tracks. This gives pleasant cruisy riding, or a speedy way of connecting the fun bits. And with views stretching into Wales, we'll forgive you for dawdling here. Begin to descend, and you find the singletrack, dropping through heavily wooded and remarkably green combes to tiny villages and superb country pubs. We really can't think of a reason why you shouldn't dash to ride here right now.

When to go

You should be ok year-round in the Quantocks. The bridleways along the top of the ridge are rideable in the wet (even if they do catch the wind), and, for the most part, the tracks up and down the combes hold up well.

Weacombe singletrack. **Photo**: Benjamin Haworth.

03 *Quantocks Classic*

This route demonstrates exactly why the Quantock Hills are so good. It contains three fantastic singletrack runs that, taken alone, would be the highlight of virtually any other ride. Stack them one after the other and you have something really special.

Smith's Combe is rocky madness followed by quite literally rollercoaster singletrack splashing through streams and twisting through shoulder-high bracken. The track down Weacombe is long, with sweeping turns and consistent high speeds. Somerton, meanwhile, races flat out across open ground before twisting into the heather, bouncing over a fallen tree and jerking round a hairpin onto a fun, splashy run along the valley bottom. On paper the route doesn't look too tiring, being relatively short and without much climbing. But with barely a flat metre along the way it's no pushover and the climbs are steep – you're likely to be pushing by the end. Luckily, it's easily shortcut-able with no loss in quality. A brilliant, brilliant ride.

An excellent extension adds the fantastic singletrack beneath Lady's Edge. Unfortunately, this also adds the steep(!) climb/push out of Hodder's Combe. It's worth it though.

Grade: **Red** » Distance: **18km** » Ascent: **700m** » Time: **3hrs+**	
Start/Finish: **Car park by the green in Holford** » Start GR: **ST 154411** » SatNav: **Holford**	
OS Map: **Explorer 140 Quantock Hills** » Parking: **Free car park in Holford/lay-by on A39**	
Cafe: **Snack van in lay-by on A39, Combe House Hotel, Holfords, T: 01278 741 382**	
Pub: **The Plough Inn, Holford, T: 01278 741 232**	

Directions

S Turn **L** on the road beside the green (keep it to your left). As the road bends right, continue **SA** on a wide track. Climb steadily, keeping **R** at the fork, to open ground. Continue in the same direction, ignoring turnings, to a fork. Keep **R** and then keep **R** at the next junctions, crossing the hillside.

Easy to miss: As a track merges from the left, look for a plantation down on the right. When you're directly above it, turn **R** on a grassy track heading aiming straight for the trees.

The track becomes rocky as you pass the plantation. Splash across the stream on superb rollercoaster single-track. Watch the corners – some are totally blind and there may be walkers.

At the bottom, turn **R** across the stream. Climb steeply (give it a shot – you might be surprised). At the top, turn **R** and climb grassy trails to a wide track. Turn **R**, then bear **L** at the fork to the Bicknoller Post (a big wooden post, with 'Bicknoller' written on the side).

2 Go **SA** past the post. Cross the main track and immediately bear **R** to descend an obvious track heading into the combe. Endless singletrack runs downhill, eventually passing through a gate onto a wide track. Go through a second gate and turn **L** on a signed bridleway.

Follow this to the next valley and keep **SA** until a short descent leads to a narrow bridge and T-junction. Turn **L** and climb. As you near the top, keep **SA** over a grassy crossroads.*

At the top, turn **R** and follow the wide track around the head of a wide valley. Climb slightly and then descend towards a track junction at the Halsway Post. Fork **L** then, after about 20m, turn **L** onto singletrack.

* Optional Extension – Yet another fantastic singletrack descent!

At the top, turn **L** on the wide track and ride to the Bicknoller Post. Turn **R**, then immediately **R** again (effectively back on yourself) across a small grassy area onto a steep singletrack descent.

Fantastic singletrack descent. Splash across the stream, then keep **R**, crossing a second stream and go **SA** up the steep and obvious climb up the opposite hillside. (If you've gone wrong, just look for an incredibly obvious steep climb.)

Climb out of the trees to a grassy crossroads. Turn **R** and follow the track over the hilltop. Keep **SA** on the main track, ignoring turnings, to a T-junction with a wide track. Turn **R** and follow this around a valley head.

Easy to miss: As you begin to climb, keep an eye out for singletrack on the hillside to the right – turn **R** onto this, rejoining the directions at **point 3**. (To ensure you're in the right spot, follow the main track to the junction at the Halsway Post and then backtrack 20m.)

❸ Superb singletrack runs across open land, into the bracken and then into the woods. Pop over the tree, keep **R** at the switchback and splash through the stream.

From here, there are multiple tracks and lines flitting about. Keep roughly **SA** and it doesn't matter which you pick – just don't climb too high up the valley sides – and you'll end up at the car park.

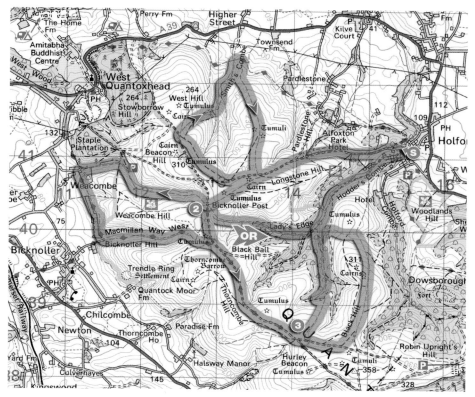

More riding

Quantocks Explorer

Taking in ALL of our favourite Quantocks trails, this is a brilliant ride. As it's essentially a bigger version of the main ride, this route gives you a chance to ride all the good stuff on that again and then try out a few new trails as you head east to investigate the Great Wood. Once in the trees, you can either stick to the bridleways and forest roads, or go singletrack hunting through the bushes. There's some good stuff to be found ...

Grade: **Black** » Distance: **27km** » Ascent: **880m** » Time: **3hrs+**

Start: **Holford Green car park, ST 154411** » OS Map: **Explorer 140 Quantock Hills & Bridgwater**

The Route » Holford – west to Bicknoller Post via Longstone Hill – Smith's Combe – southeast to Bicknoller Post – Weacombe via ST 119405 – Bicknoller Hill – Bicknoller Post – Lady's Edge – west to Holford Combe – ST 155390 – Great Bear – Crowcombe Park Gate – Triscombe Stone – ST 168365 (go exploring!) – Quantock Combe – Ram's Combe – Crowcombe Park Gate – Hurley Beacon – ST 144390 – Holford

Aisholt & the Western Combes

And now for something completely different. The riding the Quantocks is known for is all roughly situated west of the north/south line between Nether Stowey and Crowcombe – and that's where everybody heads. Further east, the riding is rather different – there's less moorland and more sunken-lane riding. This route explores some of these trails. It's rather less technical (through still predictably hilly), but fun nonetheless, allowing you to see a new area and get away from the crowds. In addition (you lucky people) there's a great optional singletrack finish (if it's dry – otherwise the original flat-out descent is much better) and a rather good pub halfway round the route in Bagborough.

Grade: **Blue/Red** » Distance: **16km** » Ascent: **580m** » Time: **1.5hrs+**

Start/Finish: **Hawkridge Reservoir car park, SW of Spaxton, ST 206361** » OS Map: **Explorer 140 Quantock Hills & Bridgwater**

The Route » Hawkridge – Aisholt Wood – Luxborough Farm – ST 182336 – ST 174344 – West Bagborough – Heathfield – Rock Farm – ST 170346 – The Slades – Hawkridge

Optional dry weather finish: from The Slades, head south-east and then east downhill to Durborough Farm and then Aisholt.

More information

Main Towns

Nothing but villages in the Quantocks, and the biggest of these, Nether Stowey, has a couple of small food shops and that's it. There are also small shops in Crowcombe and Kilve. Head east to Bridgwater for everything else.

Maps

OS Explorer 140 Quantock Hills & Bridgwater

Bike Shops

The Bicycle Chain, Salmon Parade, Bridgwater, 01278 423 640, www.bicyclechain.co.uk
St John's Street Cycles, Bridgwater, 01278 441 500, www.sjscycles.co.uk

Accommodation

There are a couple of choices of campsite. To the north is Moorhouse Farm (just north of Holford, has a peacock, well located. 01278 741 295, www.moorhousecampsite.co.uk). To the south is Quantock Orchard Caravan Park, near Crowcombe, (01984 618 618, www.quantock-orchard.co.uk). It's no further from the riding, but the climbs in the morning will be steeper and the evening run home a little less fun.

There aren't any hostels in the Quantocks. The closest is YHA Minehead (0845 371 9033). There is a group bunkhouse a short drive away – Campbell Farm bunkhouse, North Petherton (near Bridgwater) 01278 662 537.

Recommended B&Bs:
The Old Cider House, Nether Stowey, 01278 732 228, www.ochc.co.uk
Chilcombe Stables (B&B)/**The Coachhouse** (sleeps 4–6), Bicknoller, 01984 656 224, www.thecoachhousebicknoller.co.uk
The Hood Arms, Kilve, 01278 741 210, www.thehoodarms.com

Food & Drink

Cafes

Cafes are thin on the ground in the Quantocks. There's the odd village shop, a snack van or two and the up-market Combe House Hotel in Holford (01278 741 382, www.combehouse.co.uk).

Pubs

Pubs, however, aren't thin on the ground, and there are some good 'uns!
The Carew Arms, Crowcombe, 01984 618 631, www.thecarewarms.co.uk (offers accommodation)
The Blue Ball Inn, Triscombe, 01984 618 242, www.blueballinn.info (offers accommodation)
The Hood Arms, Kilve, 01278 741 210, www.thehoodarms.com (offers accommodation)
The Rose & Crown Inn, Nether Stowey, 01278 732 265, www.roseandcrown-netherstowey.co.uk (offers accommodation)
The Rising Sun, Bagborough, 01823 432 575, www.risingsuninn.info (offers accommodation)
The Plough, Holford, 01278 741 232

Tourist Offices
Bridgwater, 01278 427652, www.visitsomerset.co.uk
Quantocks AONB Service, 01823 451 884, www.quantockhills.com

Outdoor Shops
Nothing close, we're afraid. There's a Millets in Bridgwater, and Minehead has a couple of independent shops – try Exmoor Rambler (01643 862 429).

Useful Websites
www.thequantockhills.com

Guidebooks
South West Mountain Biking – Quantocks, Exmoor, Dartmoor, written by Nick Cotton and Tom Fenton, published Vertebrate Publishing

Worth Knowing
Of course, the Quantocks isn't all singletrack. Head for the eastern end of the hills and the character of the area changes. It's very green here and the riding's all about quiet tracks enclosed by hedgerows and earth banks – good for a less technical ride but, if we're honest, most people head to the Quantocks to ride. Try the Aisholt route on page 34 if you fancy a look around.

Lady's Edge. **Photo**: John Coefield.

The Mendips

Within striking distance of the M5, not a million miles from Bristol Airport and virtually within sight of the city, there's a lot of hustle and bustle near the Mendips. To their south lies the spectacular Cheddar Gorge. An amazing sight, and the site of the discovery of the oldest human skeleton in the country, it's justifiably popular and crowded with tourists, so the road up through the gorge can be slow going.

However, stick with it and get up on to the moorland that covers the top of the hills and you find yourself in a sea of heather and bracken – it feels like the middle of the nearby Quantocks. Drop into the pine forest to the west and you could be in Welsh woodland. Pick a sunny day and ride the superb singletrack bridleway that runs along the north side of Beacon Batch, ducking through the dappled treeline and across limestone streams and you could almost be on the continent (although that may just be me …). That's the beauty of the Mendips – they're remarkably close to a lot of busy areas, and yet offer peace, quiet and good riding that you simply weren't expecting.

The Riding

There's something here for everyone. Nothing like a nice cliché to start off with (and that was nothing like a nice cliché). It's not even strictly true: there's not 'something' here for everyone, just a load of bridleways that, no matter who you are, all fit into the 'not too hard, not too easy, just fun' bracket. At the top of the hill, you have Beacon Batch: nice views and great, cruisy moorland trails through the bracken. Dropping down on the north side, there are fast grassy descents, tricky rocky sections and brilliant, swooping singletrack. Riding surfaces are generally sandy or grassy higher up, with some dirt and stone based trails lower down. There are rocky sections, but nothing too technical – just a bit slippery in the wet. Moving east, Rowberrow Warren is exactly what you'd expect from a plantation – stone-based forest roads – although there are a few narrower and rockier sections near the stream to the west. And a fair number of singletrack runs that are well worth exploring (hint hint). To the south is Cheddar Gorge. There's not as much to go at here and it tends to get a bit choked with walkers, but there are some worryingly steep and rooty trails to play on and the Gorge is pretty impressive, so a trip wouldn't be a waste of time.

All in all, it's a small area, but a great one for riding. Combining it with a trip to the Quantocks would make a great weekend away.

When to go

Like the Cotswolds to the north, this isn't the best of places to head for in winter. It all gets a bit sticky. Try the Quantocks instead.

Cheddar Gorge. **Photo:** Benjamin Haworth.

04 Burrington Combe & Beacon Batch

There's a lot of good riding on this route – some challenging climbs, a superb traverse and some great, fast descents. Do a bit of exploring as you pass through the trees in Rowberrow Warren and you might find even more.

From the little car park at the bottom of Burrington Combe, head steeply uphill through the woods and out to open ground. The best bit of the ride is next – a little premature perhaps – but it's easy to re-ride later if you fancy it. It's a fantastic traverse of Beacon Batch, flitting in and out of the treeline. Initially fast and open, with a multitude of different line choices and overtaking opportunities, it soon narrows and ducks into the woods, where it fires along, splashes through a couple of just-tricky-enough stream crossings, and then breaks back out into the open for a long and fast descent towards Rowberrow.

Fun over (for now), the route turns upwards, climbing through the trees to give another good, rough descent. It then takes a spin around the lanes and bridleways of the surrounding villages, finishing with a tough little climb and rapid descent to return to the top of the woods. If you don't fancy this, just stay high after the first climb. Breaking out on to open moorland, a satisfying sandy trail leads across the top of the Mendips before a rattling descent and fast swoop through the woods drop to Burrington and the finish.

The shortcut misses the extended loop away from Beacon Batch, but retains most of highlights of the ride and allows you to spend a little more time exploring the woods.

Grade: **Red** » Distance: **23km (15km with shortcut)** » Ascent: **720m (480m with shortcut)** » Time: **2.5hrs+**
Start/Finish: **Car park at bottom of Burrington Combe** » Start GR: **ST 476587** » SatNav: **BS40 7AT**
OS Map: **Explorer 141 Cheddar Gorge & Mendip Hills West** » Parking: **Free parking in Burrington Combe**
Cafe: **Sandwich time** » Pub: **The New Inn, Blagdon, T: 01761 462 475; The Swan, Rowberrow, T: 01934 852 371**

Directions

S Turn **R** over the cattle grid. Take the next **R** – *Ham Link*. Continue **SA** over the junction, signed *Unsuitable for Vehicles*.

Drop to tarmac and turn **R**. Cross the cattle grid and bear **R** off the wide track. Follow the obvious track uphill through the woods. Reaching open ground, bear **R** on vague tracks (away from the trees on the left). At a wide track, turn **L** and descend.

Go through the car park and turn **L** on the road. Go around the bend and turn **R** on a bridleway. A tricky climb leads to a gate. Go through this and turn **R** at the post. Follow a grassy track along the edge of the trees and onto singletrack.

Break out onto open ground and continue **SA** over two grassy crossroads to the edge of the woods. Turn **L**, soon bearing **R** to run just inside the woods to a gate.

Continue **SA** through the gate onto a fast, slightly downhill, track. Go **SA** over the crossroads and continue for 200m before moving **L** through the fence onto a parallel track. Keep going **SA**, climbing up around a bend to a T-junction. Turn **R**, downhill, then almost immediately **L**, uphill.

At the junction, turn **L** and climb along the edge of open ground At the fork, bear **R**, then keep **SA** 50m later, away from the barn. Keep climbing, ignoring a fork to the right.

Shortcut: Continue **SA**, ignoring all turnings and keeping **SA** at crossroads, until you reach a gate leading out of the woods and on to open ground. Rejoin at **point 3**.

② After 500m, turn **R**, downhill, on a signed bridleway. Follow the bridleway at junctions, keeping downhill to a stream. Cross the stream and immediately turn **R** to follow a track along the left bank. Continue **SA** onto the wide track past the houses. At the junction, follow bridleway signs **SA**, off the main track and towards *Apple Tree Cottage*.

Go **SA** past the house and down through the woods to a T-junction. Turn **L** and ride to a car park.

Continue **SA** onto tarmac and continue to the main road. Cross and go **SA** up a bridleway. At a T-junction with a wide track, turn **L**. Follow this, ignoring turnings, to the road.

Turn **R** and then **L** – *Cheddarcombe Lane*. At the end, keep **SA** for a tricky climb – can you clean the steps?

At the road, turn **L**. Go **SA** over the crossroads (*North Down Lane*) and keep **SA** at the next junction. Follow the road onto a dirt track and keep **SA** into the woods as the track bends right.

A short descent drops to the stream. Immediately before the water, turn **R** and ride uphill, soon crossing the stream to pick up a wide track. Climb steeply and continue **SA** as you join the next track.

At the crossroads, turn **L** and climb steeply. Go past the downhill tracks and bear **R** at the fork. Continue **SA**, ignoring all turnings, to a gate on the edge of the woods. **(Shortcut rejoins here.)**

③ Go through the gate and **SA** onto the obvious track.

Keep **SA**, following tyre tracks and obvious trails, until the main track bears left and up to the trig point – past *'No Bikes'* signs. Keep **SA** here onto grassier and boggier tracks and drop to a gate.

Turn **L** at the gate, and follow singletrack and rocky trails downhill to the post and gate you encountered earlier.

Go through the gate, down over the rocks to the road and turn **L**. At the car park, trend **R** up the obvious track, and then bear **R** off this and onto grass, retracing your earlier tracks. Continue **SA** over the grassy area – don't trend right and retrace your steps any further – and then ignore a turning to the left. As you reach the woods, the track becomes more obvious. Follow it into the trees.

Keep **R** at the junction and descend to a gate and a wide track. Turn **L** and go **SA** onto tarmac and over the road junction, reversing your earlier route. Turn **L** at the main road to return home.

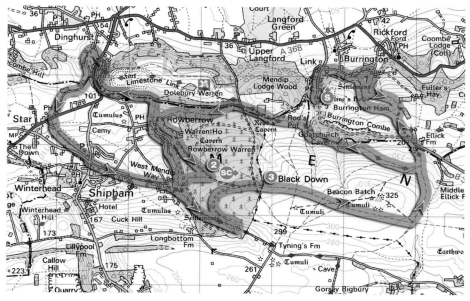

More riding

Big (Cheddar) Cheese

While there's a fair bit of road and easy cycleway on this route, it's a great way to explore the area outside the usual confines of Black Down. There are some good descents (the drop into Cheddar being a fun example), some unexpected singletrack (over Compton Hill) and the usual high-standard Beacon Batch riding to start and finish.

Grade: **Red** » Distance: **37km** » Ascent: **880m** » Time: **4hrs+**

Start/Finish: **Burrington Combe, ST 476587** » OS Map: **Explorer 141 Cheddar Gorge**

The Route » Burrington Combe – Burrington – road near Ellick Farm – ST 490577 – west along bridleway at bottom of Beacon Batch into Rowberrow Warren at ST 465585 – south through woods to ST 467574 – Black Down – south to Ashridge Farm – Cheddar – cycleway west through Axbridge to King's Wood – Wavering Down – Crook Peak – Barton – Winscombe – Shipham – Rowberrow Warren – Black Down – Beacon Batch – west then north to Ellick Farm – Burrington – Burrington Combe

Further Afield

You're in luck – the Quantocks (page 31) are under an hour's drive away. Fast and open singletrack, rocky singletrack, woodland singletrack – they're brilliant. Add some amazing views, a friendly 'feel' and bridleways everywhere and you've got a superb place to ride. We'd happily drive for much longer than an hour to ride there!

Failing that, pop into Bristol. The ever-popular Ashton Court and Leigh Woods trails have recently been revised, while the singletrack through 50-Acre is still as rough, natural and brilliant as ever. You'll find Ashton Court at the south end of the Clifton Suspension Bridge and Leigh Woods a tiny bit further out of town on A369.

Ashton Court Grid Ref: **ST 558727** » SatNav: **BS41 9JN**

Rowberrow Warren. **Photo**: Benjamin Haworth.

More information

Main Towns

Cheddar has some basics, but Bristol, about 30 minutes' drive north (and then longer when you get lost and stuck in traffic) is the place to head for most things.

Maps

OS Explorer 141 Cheddar Gorge & Mendip Hills West
OS Explorer 142 Shepton Mallet & Mendip Hills East

Bike Shops

Bad Ass Bikes, Burrington Combe, 01761 462 011, www.badassbikes.co.uk
There are loads more in Bristol — too many to list.

Accommodation

If you want to camp, there's Cheddar Camp, near Shipham (01934 743 166, www.cheddarcamp.com) or Netherdale near Sidcot (01934 843 007, www.netherdale.net).

Moving indoors, there's a YHA Hostel in Cheddar (0845 371 9730) and an independent bunkhouse run by a cave preservation society — Mendip Bunkhouse (0845 475 0954, www.cerberuspeleo.org.uk)

For everything else, try www.visitsomerset.co.uk or www.mendiphillsaonb.org.uk

Food & Drink

Pubs

The New Inn, Blagdon, 01761 462 475; **The Swan**, Rowberrow, 01934 852 371
The New Inn, Blagdon, 01761 462 475, www.newinnblagdon.co.uk (accommodation)
The Swan, Rowberrow, 01934 852 371, www.swan.butcombe.com

Tourist Offices

National Trust Information, Cheddar, 01643 862 452, cheddar gorge@nationaltrust.org.uk

Outdoor Shops

Head for Bristol for a wide range.

Useful Websites

www.mendiphillsaonb.org.uk
www.badassbikes.co.uk — there's a free trail guide available from Bad Ass Bikes.

Guidebooks

There's a free route guide put together by Bad Ass Bikes. Try their website or pop in to the shop to get it.

Worth Knowing

If you want guiding around the area, try www.bikethemendips.com

Salisbury Plain & the Surrounding Areas

Salisbury Plain stretches for miles across the open countryside of southern England. Add the Marlborough Downs and Cranborne Chase, and you're looking at a seriously large area. It's relatively flat too, giving huge, open skies that stretch for miles from horizon to horizon. You definitely don't feel hemmed in around here! While there are plenty of wooded areas, there's more grassland, which only increases the feeling of space. (The plain is one of the largest areas of chalk grassland in western Europe and is home to a number of different grasses, rare plants and species of wildlife, including several rare butterflies.)

Away from the natural stuff, mankind has had a huge impact on the area. It's full of Stone Age burial barrows, earthworks and stone circles – the most noticeable obviously being Stonehenge and the incredible fields of rocks at Avebury (OK, we're stretching the 'plain' a little here!) There's also the amazing chalk White Horse at Westbury, which you can get right up to on a bike. Nowadays, the plain is notoriously well known as a military training ground. There are tank crossings, warning signs and firing ranges all over the place – including the 'lost' village of Imber. In 1943, the entire population of the village was booted out so that American soldiers could pretend it was part of Germany and practise invading it. It's been shot to pieces on a regular basis since then, and is opened up once a year so that the public can have a look.

The Riding

Wide, open countryside in the heart of southern England – the Salisbury Plain is a beautiful place. Relatively flat, and with stone-based, dirt and grass tracks, the riding isn't that technical. This is the place to visit for a relaxed cruise or to cover some big miles. This is off-road road riding. It's touring country. It's satisfying rather than thrilling. That doesn't mean that that the riding is no fun – blasting around in the big ring is always entertaining and descents are descents wherever you are. Around here they tend to be high-speed, rather than technical, with big sweeping corners and rattly, stone-strewn tracks. And, as ever, there are always cheeky little lines and snippets of singletrack around that'll make anybody smile.

We can't ignore the views, especially around here where they really add to the feel of the riding. In such a wide, open country you can see for miles – just try not to stop and stare if you spot a tank!

When to go

When it isn't muddy! If you think horses, bikes and walkers create boggy messes, you should see what a tank can do.

Cherhill Down. **Photo**: Tom Hutton.

05 The Big Country

This is an ideal choice for a big XC day ride or for a flat out blast in the big ring. This is a fairly long route, almost entirely off road, but it isn't particularly tricky and there's not too much climbing, so it doesn't require too much effort to get around. That said, there aren't many shortcuts once you've started, so it's about as committing as this style of ride gets.

The starting climb from Steeple Langford is the trickiest of the day, a narrow bridleway that picks its way over rocks and roots to gain a pleasant cruise across open ground. A combination of dirt tracks and quiet lanes leads through pleasant surroundings to the first crossing of the A303 – take care, it's fast – before a good forest bridleway leads to a fun descent weaving down a grassy gully. A tough climb and more quiet lanes lead towards Upton Lovell, which is reached via the best downhill of the ride – a fast, loose plummet over rocks and roots. It's wide and open enough that you can relax and really go for it. You'll be forgiven for not staying relaxed for long. The rattle of gunfire and the rumble of heavy machinery mark the approach to Imber and Ministry of Defence land. If it's been muddy and the tanks are out, it can get a touch sticky (!) here. If not, it's pleasant cruising through peaceful countryside. The ride now heads south in a similar manner, crossing a grassy airstrip, a couple of roads and passing a sheep hospital before a fast and rutted run for home.

Grade: **Red** » Distance: **34km** » Ascent: **480m** » Time: **3hrs+**
Start/Finish: **Langford Lakes car park** » Start GR: **SU 037369** » SatNav: **Langford**
OS Map: **Landranger 184 Salisbury & The Plain** » Parking: **Langford Lakes Car Park** » Cafe: **Sandwich time**
Pub: **The Rainbow on the Lake, Steeple Langford, T: 01722 790 251, www.therainbowonthelake.co.uk**

Directions

S Turn **L** from the car park. At the T-junction, turn **R**, then quickly **L** on a signed bridleway between houses. Follow this uphill under the railway bridge.

As the bridleway ends, continue **SA** on a wide track. Keep **R** at the fork and then keep **SA** onto grass as the track kinks right. Continue **SA** into the woods and through a gate. Keeping the fence to your left, continue **SA** across fields to a second gate. Go through this and follow a track to a T-junction. Turn **R** and follow the wide track to the road.

Turn **R**, then **L** onto a track as the road bends right. Follow this through the trees and into the open, where it turns to concrete. Continue **SA**, ignoring turnings, until you reach a crossroads with a minor road. Turn **R**. At the junction, continue **SA** towards Down Farm. As the tarmac swings left into the farm, continue **SA** onto grass, through the woods and across the busy A303.

2 Follow the dirt track through the woods to an open field. Continue **SA** on a grassy track to a road. Go **SA** across the road and through the gate, then immediately bear **R** across a grassy area to a track running along the fence at the edge of the trees. Follow this for a fun descent. Ignore all turnings to a gate.

Turn **L** onto the road, then quickly **R** on a track signed *Public Path*. Follow this uphill, ignoring turnings, until you reach a tarmac farm access track. Continue **SA**. After 1km, just after a track joins from the left, turn **R** onto a dirt track after farm buildings. Follow this into the woods for the trickiest descent of the ride.

At the bottom, go **SA** over the road and up the lane ahead. Follow this through Upton Lovell and across the A36. Climb steeply up the tarmac drive ahead, past the farm at the top, until you reach a signed byway on the **R**.

Cherhill Down. **Photo:** Tom Hutton.

Follow this alongside woods, then continue **SA** along field edges as the track ends. When the track appears to end at a field, turn **L**, then **R** on a bridleway. Drop, following hedges and going through gates, to a wide track. Go **SA** through the gate ahead, into a field, and bear **L** to another gate and a river crossing. Continue in the same direction, across another field, to the road.

3 Turn **L** to Chitterne. Turn **R** along the main road through the village. Turn **L** towards the church, then immediately **R** onto *Back Lane*. Follow this as it bends to the left, then turn **R** on a track signed *Imber Range Path*.

Climb on singletrack, then keep **SA** across fields until Imber comes into view. Go **SA** over a wide track as the buildings disappear again and then, as they reappear, turn **R** onto a second wide track, signed as a byway. Follow this to the road.

Cross the road and follow the track to climb and then drop to trees and a multi-track junction. Keep **SA** and, as you climb again, keep **R** at the fork. Keep **SA** over grassy airstrip, bearing **L** on the obvious track beyond.

Keep **SA** over another multi-track junction and across the A303. Keep heading south on the wide track, ignoring a turning to the right. At a crossroads by a radio mast, turn **R**. Pass the sheep hospital and keep **SA** over the tarmac track to a steep descent. At the bottom, follow tarmac **R** and then **L** through the underpass.

Follow the lane to Steeple Langford. Go **SA** over the main road onto *Duck Lane* and follow this home.

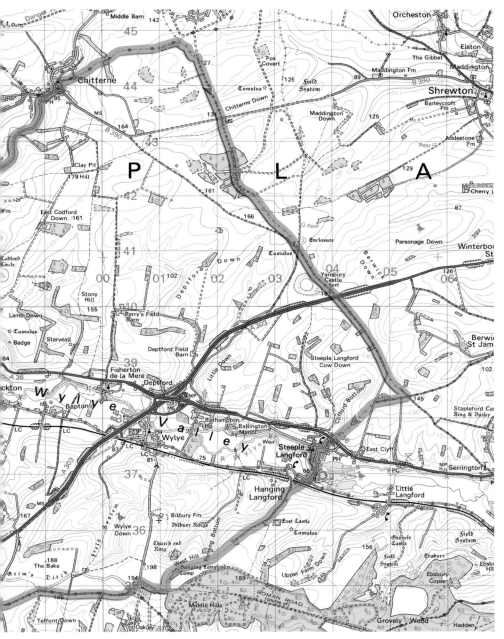

More riding

Beckhampton & the White Horse

A mid-length ride through the north of the area. As is par for the course around here, it's not a technical or particularly hilly ride, although there are a couple of stiff climbs and corresponding entertaining descents. Instead, this is a ride for those who like to get into a nice pedalling rhythm and tap out the miles – although whether that's head-down and flat out or looking up and admiring the big views and open skies is up to you.

Grade: **Red/Blue** » Distance: **28km** » Ascent: **380m** » Time: **2.5hrs+**
Start/Finish: **Beckhampton, SU 076692** » OS Map: **Landranger 173 Swindon & Devizes**

The Route » Car park (SU 076692) – Beckhampton – south across Allington Down towards All Cannings – road to Bishops Cannings – SU 027660 – SU 030674 (Wessex Ridgeway) – SU 047680 – Cherhill Down – Wessex Ridgeway

Cranbourne Chase

Just to give you a chance to explore the whole area, we're heading south now on a well-known local loop. The riding's similar, albeit with bigger hills. Stiff climbs, fast wide descents and some unexpected sections of singletrack carry you through quaint villages, up to potential sea views and past the former home of Guy Ritchie and Madonna. Watch out for the mud in the winter though!

Grade: **Red/Blue** » Distance: **27km** » Ascent: **620m** » Time: **3.5hrs+**
Start/Finish: **Compton Airfield car park, ST 886187** » OS Map: **Landranger 184 Salisbury & The Plain**

The Route » Airfield car park – West Wood – Shepherd's Bottom – Washer's Pit – Stubhampton Bottom – ST 906148 – ST 919160 – Tollard Green – road to Tollard Royal – north towards Monk Down – Win Green – Elliott's Shed – Manor Farm – Spring Farm – Cann Common – road to Melbury Abbas – East Compton – Airfield car park

Barbury Castle & the Marlborough Downs

And a third area to visit ... Starting high up at Barbury Castle, this ride makes extensive use of the ancient Ridgeway to maintain height and admire the view before dropping down and south to follow on easy tracks (albeit with a few sticky climbs and swift descents) past numerous horse gallops before picking up the Ridgeway once more for the return leg.

Grade: **Red/Blue** » Distance: **32km (20km with shortcut)** » Ascent: **590m** » Time: **3hrs+**
Start/Finish: **Barbury Castle, SU 157759** » OS Map: **Landranger 173 Swindon & Devizes; Landranger 174 Newbury & Wantage**

The Route » Barbury Castle – Ridgeway east to SU 191746 – south and east on road and byways to skirt around Ogbourne St George to SU 215750 – Moore's Wood – Whiteshard Bottom – Poulton Downs – Ogbourne Maizey – SU 167731 (SHORTCUT – north to Barbury Castle) – Old Eagle – Manton Down – west to Sarsen Stones – north along Ridgeway to Barbury Castle via Hackpen Hill

More information

Main Towns

This is a huge area. The biggest towns are Devizes and Marlborough in the north, Salisbury and Warminster in the middle and Shaftesbury further south. The large number of other sizeable towns will all have the basics.

Maps

Landranger 173 Swindon & Devizes » Landranger 174 Newbury & Wantage » Landranger 184 Salisbury & The Plain

Bike Shops

Bikes and Boards, Devizes, 01380 729 621, www.bikesnboards.co.uk
Stonehenge Cycles, Fisherton Street, Salisbury, 01722 334 915, www.stonehengecycles.com
Cyclogy, Chippenham, 01249 461 997, www.cycologybikes.co.uk

Accommodation

As you'd expect from a big area, options for accommodation are well spread. If you want to ride from where you're staying, you're best off trying to find a pub that offers beds, (we've tried to list a few below) or googling for a B&B.

www.wiltshiretouristguide.com – reasonable for accommodation.

There is a YHA Hostel in Salisbury (0845 371 9537) and a campsite near Stonehenge and handy for our main ride (Stonehenge Campsite, Berwick St James, 07880 734 732, www.stonehengecampsite.co.uk). Further north, and well-located for the riding there is the Barge Inn, Honeystreet – a little odd but offers camping (01672 851 705, www.the-barge-inn.com).

Food & Drink

The Bear Hotel, Devizes, 01380 722 444, www.thebearhotel.net
The Rainbow on the Lake, Steeple Langford, 01722 790 251, www.therainbowonthelake.co.uk
The Waggon and Horses, Beckhampton, 01672 539 418, www.waggonandhorsesbeckhampton.co.uk (near Beckhampton ride, no accommodation)
Castle and Ball Hotel, Marlborough, 01672 515 201, www.oldenglishinns.co.uk/marlborough
Two Brewers, Shaftesbury, 01747 854 211, www.2brewers.co.uk (no accommodation, but real ale)
Red Lion, Avebury, 01672 539 266, www.red-lion-pub-avebury.co.uk

Tourist Offices

Amesbury, (near Stonehenge), 01980 622 833 » **Avebury,** 01672 539 179, www.visitkennet.co.uk
Devizes, 01380 800 400, www.visitkennet.co.uk » **Marlborough,** 01672 515 190, www.visitkennet.co.uk
Salisbury, 01722 342 860, visitorinfor@wiltshire.gov.uk » **Shaftesbury,** 01747 853 514

Useful Websites

www.spambiking.co.uk – local club, lots of events including the SPAM challenge
www.wiltshiretouristguide.com
www.ukbikepark.com – downhill and 4X riding at the UK Bike Park near Blandford Forum

Dorset, Swanage
& the New Forest

Dorset – a place for sunny days, seaside trips and summer holidays. But perhaps not an obvious choice for mountain biking – more on that later! The Isle of Purbeck, which we've focused on here, is one of the many places claiming to be the sunniest place in Britain and is dotted with quaint villages, narrow country lanes and great pubs. There's a steam railway (which the ride overleaf crosses), a ruined castle (at the start) and a proper Victorian Pier (nowhere near).

There's also some amazing scenery, as Purbeck is sat at the eastern end of the awesomely-named Jurassic Coast – a chain of limestone cliffs, rocky coves and gob-smacking stone arches that stretches for miles along the south coast. Unsurprisingly popular with holiday makers, it's equally attractive for all manner of outdoorsy activities, drawing rock climbers, walkers and watersports enthusiasts – apparently it's one of the UK's top scuba spots. While it's never going to match the Quantocks or Peak District, there's some surprisingly good mountain biking. And where else can you finish a day's riding with a swim in the sea?

For the New Forest, see page 56.

The Riding

The riding on Purbeck is better than you might think, and that's not damning it with faint praise – it's good! It's never overly technical, but the trails are fast and swoopy with a number of great singletrack runs, which means fun riding for pretty much everyone. That said, there are definitely some steep slopes, tough climbs and rapid descents which you underestimate at your peril. As a general rule, the riding is dirt, stone track or grass-based – and so best in the dry, when pedalling feels easy and speeds are high. It's true that there is some field-edge stuff, but the general feel of the area and the views mean they're never dull. On the subject of views, the ridge of hills that separates Purbeck from the mainland is both an unavoidable and unmissable feature. It's always a stiff pull to get up onto it, but once you're there, the views roll inland and stretch out towards France and are pretty impressive.

Riding finished? Obviously, you're going to go for a swim in the sea. But once you're done, try visiting Monkey World near (www.monkeyworld.org) Wareham. An ape rescue centre, they take in animals from around the world – and have a huge number of Chimpanzees and Orangutans. And watching them is almost more fun than riding ...

When to go

The best time to visit is on a fine, sunny day – and your chances of getting one are high. It's not too bad in the wet, although the grassy stretches do become a bit of a slog and the singletrack slower and, to be honest, a lot less fun. It's the wind you really want to watch out for though. A lot of the riding is high and exposed, and not particularly pleasant when there's a cold wind whipping in off the sea.

Old Harry, Isle of Purbeck. **Photo**: Tom Hutton.

06 Purbeck Explorer

Do you like having fun on a bike? Riding fast, playing on singletrack and enjoying the view? Of course you do – although you've probably never thought of the Isle of Purbeck as the place to do so. Well, this route delivers on all counts, taking in a pretty extensive tour of the area at the same time. There's a little cruise to Old Harry – the easternmost point of Purbeck – where the high cliffs and chalky spits make for a pretty spectacular position. Then there's a rapid descent and stiff pull up onto the ridge of the Purbeck Hills. While there's some fast, fun downhilling up here, it's the view over to France that makes this stretch memorable. The eastern stretch of the route is a pleasant amble through attractive surroundings, but it's the final half of the ride that we always look forward to. This kicks off with a rubbly limestone descent that rattles down to the steam railway. A long, beautifully twisting singletrack run beneath Nine Barrow Down keeps the grin factor high and, if that weren't enough, the final leg down from the golf course is a sandy, multi-line blast that definitely adheres to the 'save the best for last' school of thought.

Grade: **Red** » Distance: **40km** » Ascent: **800m** » Time: **5hrs+**
Start/Finish: **Studland post office** » Start GR: **SZ 034824** » SatNav: **Studland**
OS Map: **OL15: Purbeck and South Dorset** » Parking: **Options in Studland**
Cafe: **Loads in Studland** » Pub: **Bankes Arms, Studland, T: 01929 450 225, www.bankesarms.com**

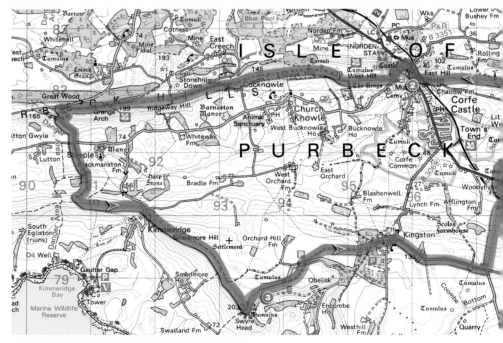

Directions

(S) From the post office, turn **L** onto *School Lane*. Follow this downhill, keeping **SA** around the shelter. As the road bends left, turn **R** onto a bridleway to *Old Harry*.

Ride to Old Harry; admire the view then turn **R**, uphill, on a grassy bridleway. Keep going **SA** through gates, over junctions and past the obelisk before eventually following the obvious track sharply right and downhill.

Turn **L** on the road. Keep **L** at the junction and then turn **R** onto a wide bridleway. Climb steeply, keeping **R** at all junctions. As you reach the top, keep **L** and follow grassy track along the ridge. Ignore turnings dropping off the sides. Go past the TV mast and cross a good track onto a fast descent.

(2) At the road, turn **R**, then **L** at the T-junction. Turn **L** after the castle. Follow the road for 300m, cross a bridge and turn **R** onto a bridleway. At the junction, keep **R**, uphill. At the top, keep **L** along the ridge. Drop to the road and continue **SA** up the obvious track.

As the climbing eases, turn **L** through the gate and then **R** onto grass (past a bizarre road sign). Keep **SA** onto an obvious track and pass Grange Arch. As you approach the road by the shooting ranges, go through the gate and turn **L** onto a grassy track.

Drop to the road and turn **L**. As the road bends left, continue **SA** towards Steeple Leaze Farm. Go **SA** through the buildings onto a track leading into the trees.

Climb to a gate, then kink **R** and **L** to continue climbing, then bear **L** across fields. Turn **L** at the far side, go through a gate and follow field edges to the road. Turn **R** then quickly **L**. After 50m, turn **R** onto a wide track.

Ride uphill and through gates. As the track bends left, continue **SA** through a gate onto grass and follow field edges to Swyre Head. Gaze out to sea, then turn sharp **L** and drop towards the trees.

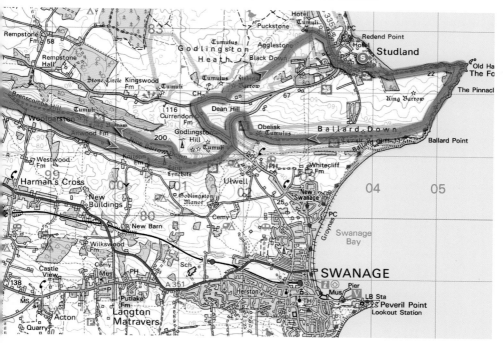

③ Ride along the edge of the woods. After the trees, bear **L** across the field. Go through trees to the road and turn **R** to Kingston. Turn **R** onto the main road. Ride uphill, away from the houses. Immediately opposite the turning to *Worth Matravers*, turn **L** onto grass bridleway. Ride the field edge, continuing **SA** as the track bends into the field.

Great slippery limestone descent! Continue **SA** at the bottom, up the lane to the main road and go **SA** into fields. Follow vague tracks and bridleway markers to a farm and follow farm tracks to tarmac. Ride past houses and turn **R** at the T-junction. Climb uphill a short way, before turning **L** onto a bridleway.

At the T-junction, turn **R**. The bridleway narrows to singletrack. Ignore turnings and keep **SA** as a wide bridleway drops to the right. Keep **SA** again as a second bridleway drops to Ailwood Farm. Eventually, the track widens by a small 'quarry'. Fork **L** uphill on a wide track. As the track 'hairpins' left, keep **SA** onto grass. Keep **SA** again to drop to the road. Turn **L**, keep **L** at the fork and climb to a T-junction.

Turn **R** past the golf course entrance before turning **L** onto a bridleway. As you reach the golf course, turn **R** onto a swoopy bridleway. Keep **L** as a footpath goes right, then follow the bridleway **R** and go **SA** over the multi-track junction (you can usually follow tyre tracks).

Drop to a T-junction with a wide track and turn **L**. Follow this to tarmac and turn **R**. At the road, turn **R** to Studland.

More riding

Lulworth Cove

Ok, the route doesn't actually go down to Lulworth Cove – but it's a fantastic feature and well worth a look/picnic stop. Starting in nearby West Lulworth, the route runs west over the downs and through open countryside towards Osmington, before heading back again just behind the sea cliffs (and within sight of the channel!). It's easy riding, but the countryside is lovely and there are some wonderfully long stretches of off-road riding.

Grade: **Red** » Distance: **22km** » Ascent: **360m** » Time: **2hrs+**
Start/Finish: **West Lulworth, SY 726828** » OS Map: **Landranger 194**

The Route » West Lulworth – west on road to Daggers Gate, north west to Chaldon – road towards Winfrith Newburgh, but turn west on outskirts – bridleway west to Five Marys – Moigns Down – Upton – east to near South Downs Farm – east to road at Daggers Gate – West Lulworth

The New Forest

The New Forest is a beautiful place. Pine forests and sandy surfaces give it a continental feel and the Forest Ponies are always nice to see. A relaxed atmosphere is helped by the proximity to the coast and by frequently sunny weather. If you want a nice, easy day, perhaps pootling with children or pub-riding with non-riding friends, then the miles of easy tracks will serve you well. Unfortunately, if you want anything more than this, you're going to be disappointed, as bikes have to stick to approved (read: wide and easy) tracks. Shame. There's a relaxed atmosphere here – which isn't hurt by the proximity to the coast and frequently-sunny weather. If you want a chilled out day then the miles of easy riding on forest tracks will serve you well.

www.thenewforest.co.uk has a particularly informative section on cycling, including maps, bike shops/hire and various other bits of useful information. It's also got loads of information on the forest, its wildlife and towns. Did you know that the New Forest Ponies, whilst wild, are in fact owned by anybody who owns property which comes with common grazing rights?

When to go: The mainly stone-based tracks and quiet lanes in the New Forest allow riding year round. However, as the surroundings and the wild ponies are the main attractions, we'd go when the weather's good!

More information

Main Towns

The main (only) town here is Swanage. It's a heavily tourist-focused place, so expect crowds on busy days. Otherwise, you're right by Bournemouth. If you're in the New Forest, Southampton isn't too far.

Maps

OS Explorer OL15 Purbeck and South Dorset » *OS Explorer OL22 New Forest*

Bike Shops & Bike Hire

Charlie the Bikemonger, High Street, Swanage, 01929 475 833, www.charliethebikemonger.com
On Yer Bike, Charminster Road, Bournemouth, 01202 315 855, www.onyerbike.co.uk
There are bike hire centres all over the New Forest. An internet search will bring up pages of them.

Accommodation

There are campsites all over the Isle of Purbeck. They range from big family and caravan sites to small, basic fields. Try Herston (01929 422 932, www.herstonleisure.co.uk), Tom's Field in Langton Matravers (01929 427 110, www.tomsfieldcamping.co.uk) or Woodyhyde (near Corfe Castle, 01929 480 274, www.woodyhyde.co.uk).

There's a YHA Hostel in Swanage (0845 371 9346) and an independent hostel that's particularly focussed on the outdoors – the Swanage Auberge (01929 424 368, www.swanageauberge.com).

For everything else, try www.visitswanage.com or www.virtual-swanage.co.uk. Swanage itself can get pretty busy, so, unless that's what you're looking for, we'd be inclined to stay a little way out of town.

For the New Forest, see www.thenewforest.co.uk, which has lists of campsites, B&Bs and cottages. There's also a YHA hostel in a great location at Burley (0845 371 9309).

Food & Drink

Shell Bay Cafe, Studland, 01929 450 363, www.shellbay.net
Square and Compass, Worth Matravers, 01929 439 229, www.squareandcompasspub.co.uk
Bankes Arms, Studland, 01929 450 225, www.bankesarms.com (accommodation)
Red Lion, Swanage, 01929 423 533, www.redlionswanage.co.uk (accommodation)
(New Forest) **The Oak Inn**, Bank (near Lyndhurst), 023 8028 2350

Tourist Offices

Swanage, 01929 422 885, www.visitswanageandpurbeck.com
Lyndhurst, 023 8028 2269, www.thenewforest.co.uk

Outdoor Shops

Jurassic Outdoor, Swanage, 01929 424 366, www.jurassicoutdoor.com » Loads more in Bournemouth

Useful Websites

www.mountainbikedorset.co.uk » **www.visitswanage.com** » **www.thenewforest.co.uk**

Guidebooks

Mountain Bike Guide Dorset, written by Colin Dennis, published by Ernest Press

Isle of Wight

The Isle of Wight is the largest island in England. It's been the scene of Viking raids and English-French medieval battles. It was raced around by a fleet of American and British yachts in 1851 (the first America's Cup race), is one of the best places in the world to search for dinosaur fossils, and hosts the Isle of Wight music festival every year. You can visit The Needles, a row of chalk stacks rising out of the sea in Alum Bay, or travel over in Cowes Week to watch the yacht racing. Failing that, you could just travel over to visit some of the villages, swim in the sea or relax. Perhaps you could even go for a bike ride ... there are a whole lot of reasons to visit the Isle of Wight!

On a totally different note, get hold of an Isle of Wight map and a big magnifying glass (digital/online mapping will make this easier) and have a good look at the cliffs along the south coast. It turns out that there's a bit of a tradition for cartographers and surveyors to work their names into their maps. Sometimes they worked their initials into the tree symbols in forests. In this case, Trevor (SZ 314849 – under Warren Farm) and his mate Bill (SZ 485766 – near Blackgang) worked their names into the cliffs. Sneaky!

The Riding

The Isle of Wight is a little like the South Downs – which is understandable when you think about it. Most (well, all) of the good riding is in the south of the island. To the west, the riding focuses around Brighstone Forest – which hides a lot of very worthwhile singletrack. It's easy to link the singletrack in with the surrounding bridleways to give a number of decent loops and pretty much guaranteed sea views – and that's always a good thing. Elsewhere on the island, a quick glance at a map reveals that the south-eastern corner is laced with bridleways. As a general rule, these aren't particularly technical, there aren't many rocks around and the trails are grass and mud-based. Much of the riding is field-edge stuff and pretty uneventful. Doesn't sound great? Don't worry – the Island has a couple of aces up its sleeve. Firstly, it's hilly, way more so than it appears on a map. Expect tough climbs with big views and fast, often steep descents. Secondly, there's singletrack everywhere. True, it's generally short, but it's fast and flowing with just the right amount of corners – the sort of stuff that everybody enjoys. Particular highlights include the woods at Upper Hyde, Stenbury Down and the drop from St Catherine's Down.

When to go

As mentioned above, the riding here tends to be grass and mud-based. It's not unrideable in winter and in wet months, it's just slippery, prone to erosion and nowhere near as fast and fun as it is in the dry. We'd aim to visit in the summer.

Steph Duits above Freshwater. **Photo**: Tom Hutton.

07 Isle of Wight Figure-of-Eight

We wanted to show off the island in a neat loop, but we kept remembering trails we'd missed. But when we put them all in, we were climbing the descents and descending the climbs. So we went with a big figure-eight that also gives two shorter options. Both short loops have big hills (but great views), rapid descents and sweet stretches of singletrack. They're also surprisingly tough – those hills are steep and often grassy riding. Underestimate the big figure-eight at your peril!

Both start in Godshill and use the same, fun singletrack start before splitting off to explore different areas. On the southern loop, there's a lovely stretch of riding atop St Catherine's Hill, before a steep singletrack descent, some pleasant cruising and a flat-out blast into Chillerton. Passing through some lovely countryside and getting up onto the hilltops, it definitely shows off this corner of the island. The northern loop busts a lung on the way up Stenbury Hill, but rewards your efforts with a rolling singletrack descent that gradually unwinds around the hill. There's more singletrack to come, but it pales compared to the tight and twisty woodland riding through the woods above Upper Hyde. Fast, wide singletrack, it's the sort of stuff you want to ride all day.

So, choose a loop, link them both or ride them on consecutive days and then carry on to explore the rest of the island. There's plenty of good riding to be found!

Grade: **Red** (both loops = black) » Distance: **20km** (North), **27km** (South) » Ascent: **380m** (N), **370m** (S)
Time: **2hrs+** (N) **3hrs +**(S) » Start/Finish: **Godshill car park** » Start GR: **SZ 530816** » SatNav: **Godshill**
OS Map: **OL29 Isle of Wight** » Parking: **Free parking, Godshill**
Cafe: **Old World Tea Rooms, Godshill, T: 01983 840 637** » Pub: **The Taverners, Godshill, T: 01983 840 707**

Directions

S Cross the main road and ride up Hollow Lane. At the T-junction, turn **R**. Just before the houses, turn **L** onto singletrack bridleway (GL21).

Go **SA** over the road. Keep **L** around the pond and **L** at the junction. Follow singletrack behind the house to the road. Turn **L**.

At the T-junction, turn **R**. At the crossroads, turn **L**, downhill. After 1km, just before a post box, turn **R** into Roud Lane.

Southern loop:

S2 Follow Roud Lane through fields. Pass a wide track on the left and then turn **R** up a wide bridleway. Climb **L** of the farm buildings to the road. Turn **L**.

After 1.5km, pass houses and, immediately after left turning, turn **R** onto the narrow Crocker Lane. Climb steeply and go through a gate onto a dirt track. Continue **SA** (trending **R**) as you reach fields. Keep trending **R** on grassy tracks through gates until you gain the ridge.

Keep heading **R** until the tower comes into sight. Just before it, turn **L** through a narrow gate. Keep **R** on singletrack. Join a wide track and, after a short distance, turn **L** through another gate. Descend steeply on field-edge singletrack, then swing into the woods. Follow the trail to a wide track. Turn **R**.

At the road, turn **R**. After 200m, turn **L** onto a wide byway. At the water works, turn **R**, climb a short rise and ride to the road. Turn **R**.

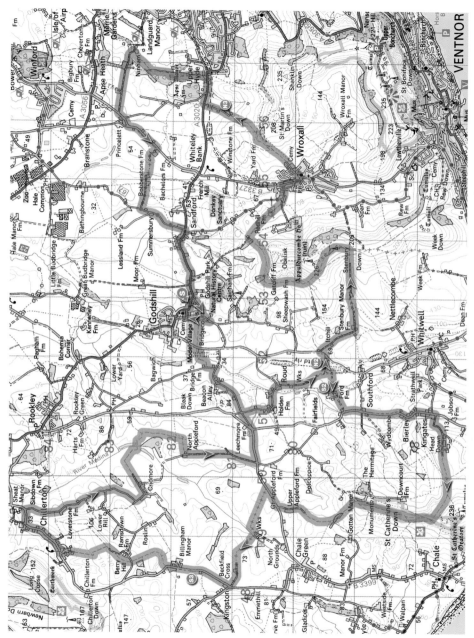

S3 After 1km, pass a farm on the left and then turn **R** onto a grassy bridleway. Climb to the road and go **SA** on a grassy bridleway (G15). Climb to the ridge and turn **R**. Pass a turning on the right and then turn **L** across fields on bridleway G15a. As you near trees, keep **L**, then follow the track **R** into the woods. Descend fast to Chillerton.

Keep **SA** to the main road. Turn **R** and ride out of the village. Take the next road on the **R** and follow it, keeping **L** at junctions, until it ends. Keep **SA** on a wide track. Trend **R** across fields and cross a small bridge to obvious, but short-lived singletrack. As the track turns grassy, follow it **R** around field edges.

After 900m, turn **R** (straight ahead is a footpath). Climb to a farm and turn **L**. At the road, turn **L**. At the junction, bear **R**, (ignore the sharp right). Go **SA** over the crossroads and **L** at the T-junction.

After 400m, turn **R** onto singletrack. Ride to the road and turn **L**. Turn **R** in Godshill to the car park.

Northern loop:

N2 Follow Roud Lane into fields. After 1km, turn **L** up a wide bridleway. At the road, turn **L**, then first **R** up a wide bridleway. Climb this, ignoring turnings, to a grassy bridleway crossroads atop Stenbury Down.

Go **SA** and soon turn **L** on a tarmac track. Pass the radio mast and, as the track splits (a footpath bears right), turn **L** through a gate into fields. Follow the grassy track to obvious singletrack. Drop and go **SA** through the gate. Traverse the hillside, through gates, to a high deer fence. Keep **SA** to a crossroads of wide tracks. Turn **R** through a big gateway.

Bear **L** across the field. At the road, turn **L**. Turn **R** at the main road. Just after the church, turn **L** (Station Road). Climb until this ends and keep **SA** on bridleway V31. Climb to a grassy area, keep **SA** and then bear **R** (in effect **SA**) onto a wide track. Climb, ignoring turnings, to a gate and turn **L**. Descend to a multi-track junction and keep **SA** into fields and bridleway NL30.

N3 Drop to a farm track and go under a bridge to the road. Turn **R**. After 500m the road drops slightly. Turn **L** onto bridleway NC37a, signed *Ninham*. Follow the main track as it twists through the woods. Ignore turnings, drop around hairpins and cross a wooden bridge before turning **R** through a narrow gate on bridleway SS19 (if you reach a stile, you've gone too far).

Cross fields to a wide track. Turn **L**. At the road, turn **L**. Keep **SA** at junctions and, after 900m, turn **R** up byway NC33. Keep **SA** past farms to a lane. Turn **L**. At the main road, turn **R** to Godshill.

More riding

Brighstone Forest

A big, but easily shortened ride, linking the open downland and sea views on Compton Down to the inland trails between Shorwell (good pub) and Newport. As an added bonus, it takes a cruise through Brighstone Forest. This route uses the marked bridleways through the woods, but keep your eyes open and you'll find plenty of twisty singletrack tucked away in there.

Grade: **Red** » Distance: **35km** » Ascent: **710m** » Time: **3–6hrs**
Start/Finish: **Freshwater Bay car park, SZ 350856** » OS Map: **Landranger 196 The Solent & Isle of Wight**

The Route » Freshwater Bay – Compton Down – SZ 401850 – SZ 419845 – Limerstone Down – Shorwell via SZ 454829 – Lorden Copse – Newbarn Down – Garstons – Carisbrook Castle – Carisbrook – Bowcombe Down – Brighstone Down (now explore a bit!) – Westover Down – SZ 401850 – Freshwater Bay

Ryde Link

If you took the ferry over from Portsmouth, this is a great way of linking to the riding in the south of the island. (Obviously, you could do this on tarmac, which would be quicker and less tiring, but off-road is always more fun!) Do bear in mind how hilly the Isle of Wight is though – you're looking at a really big (60 kilometre-plus) day in the saddle. If you're really pushed, this isn't a bad ride in its own right, as it's got some good, fun singletrack in its first half.

Grade: **Red (Black** when linked to main route!) » Distance: **30km** » Ascent: **480m** » Time: **3hrs+**
Start/Finish: **Ryde Ferry, SZ 593 929** » OS Map: **Landranger 196 The Solent & Isle of Wight**

The Route » Ferry/Pier – east along seafront – Nettlestone – Hill Farm – Ashey Manor – Nunwell Farm – Alverston – Queen's Bower – Windford – Cheverton Farm – Apse Heath – (join main route here if desired) – road to Newchurch – Haseley Manor – Arreton Down – Combley Farm – Havenstreet – Haylands – Ryde

The Island Tour

A man goes into the doctor's. The doctor tells him he has onomatopoeia. 'What's that?' the man asks, fearing the worst. 'It's exactly what it sounds like,' replies the doctor ... Pretty much the same as this route – it's a tour of the Island. Cyclists have been riding laps of the island for years, usually taking two or three days to do so, although it's entirely possible to do it in one if you're fit. Most commonly done on road (there's an annual event run by the Wayfarer Cycle Touring Club – see their very useful website for plenty of useful information – www.cycleisland.co.uk), although there is an alternate off road version. Use the routes here to create the basis for a DIY loop or visit local MTB club 'Extremists' for a more detailed suggestion – www.extremists.co.uk

More information

Main Towns

The shortest ferry route from the mainland will deposit you in Ryde, which is fairly touristy, but has a decent selection of shops. For a wider range, head to Newport, which has a wider range of shops, including a good bike shop. In the north is Cowes – a lovely place and good for sailing, but not so handy for the best riding.

Maps

OS OL29 Isle of Wight

Bike Shops

Wight Mountain, Orchard Street, Newport, 01983 533 445, www.wightmountain.com

The Bike Shed, East Lane, Merstone, Nr Newport, 01983 868 786, www.the-bikeshed.com

Tav Cycles, High Street, Ryde, 01983 812 989, www.tavcycles.co.uk

Extreme Cycles, Ventnor, 01983 852 232

Accommodation

There are loads of campsites around. We like Compton Farm Campsite (01983 740 215, www.comptonfarm. co.uk) on the west of the island for its beachside location and proximity to Brighstone Forest, while the splattering of sites in the east near Shanklin are brilliantly located for riding.

There's a youth hostel right at the western tip of the island in Totland Bay (01983 752 165) and a summer-only one in Brighstone (0845 371 9348) – www.yha.org.uk

For everything else, the official Isle of Wight website (www.islandbreaks.co.uk) is useful as is bike hire site www.wightcyclehire.co.uk

Food & Drink

There are loads of places to eat and drink on the island, many of which are superb.

The Island Deli, Ventnor, 01983 853 344

The Garlic Farm, Newchurch, 01983 867 333, www.thegarlicfarm.co.uk

The Crown Inn, Shorwell, 01983 740 293, www.crowninnshorwell.co.uk

The Steamer Inn, Shanklin, 01983 862 641, www.thesteamer.co.uk (offers accommodation)

The Crab and Lobster, Bembridge, 01983 872 244, www.crabandlobsterinn.co.uk, (offers accommodation)

The Buddle, Niton, 01983 730 243, www.buddleinn.co.uk

Tourist Offices

Ryde, 01983 813 818 » **Newport**, 01983 813 818

Outdoor Shops

There are Blacks and Millets in Newport, and independent shop Wight Outdoors in Freshwater.

Useful Websites

www.extremists.co.uk – lots of useful information, including recommended sections of trail and a good route for an off-road lap of the island

www.wightlink.co.uk – you're going to have to get there somehow!

www.islandbreaks.co.uk – the official tourism site

www.wightcyclehire.co.uk – useful for accommodation as well as cycle hire

Above Freshwater. **Photo**: Tom Hutton.

The South Downs

The South Downs is the UK's newest National Park, designated as such in April 2011. As national parks go, it's fairly long and thin, (roughly 70 miles long and, at its narrowest, about seven miles wide) and not particularly high (Butser Hill tops out at around 270 metres). However, as it's essentially one long line of hills, covered with chalk trails, sea views and climbs steep enough to make grown men cry, there's plenty of interest for the mountain biker.

A result of the chalky deposits of the sea which once covered much of northern Europe, the hills that were formed once the sea had retreated are now flat-topped and rounded, and covered in open grassland. The wide ground, rounded hills and wide valleys, combined with long views out to sea and open sky above make the area feel far bigger than it actually is. Visit on a cloudless summer's day, with the sun reflecting painfully off the chalk and the grass dry and comfortable to lie on and not only do they feel big, but also incredibly peaceful. Quite why it's taken so long to designate the area a national park is anybody's guess.

The Riding

Riding on the South Downs is usually associated with wide, chalky trails – mainly because the South Downs Way is the first thing that springs to mind. This 96-mile(ish) long trail runs from Winchester to Eastbourne and is one of the UK's great long-distance rides. If you fancy a challenge, the 'double' (there and back!) has been done in under 24 hours! For everyone else, the steep hills, heavily rutted trails and sharp, puncture-inflicting flint provides difficulty enough. Away from the SDW, the steep slopes, ruts and flints continue, but there are also grassy trails, short sections of singletrack and mile upon mile of open countryside to cruise through. Rides here can be relaxed, sun-soaked affairs, huge days out or tough, hilly rides – if you think the south is flat, try Butser Hill! There's not too much that's technical, but there's plenty of speed on the long, long descents to be had. Combine a ride with a tour around Friston Forest if you want more singletrack, enjoy an ice cream whilst gazing out to sea or lie back in the sun. If you want all three, try the ride overleaf ...

When to go

Being about as far south as it's possible to go, the South Downs are, weather-wise, one of the more amenable areas of the UK. However, the chalky trails become as slick and slippery as ice in the wet. Ride in the summer for the most under-tyre security.

South Downs near Brighton. **Photo**: Tom Hutton.

08 Friston Forest & the South Downs Way

Although perhaps not one of the 'classic' South Downs rides, this loop is a great introduction to the area. You get sea views, a short stretch along the South Downs Way and an optional finish along some of the brilliant singletrack to be found in Friston Forest. The ride warms up along a few forest roads. Dull? Maybe, but better than tarmac. From there, a couple of grassy descents and a stiff little climb lead to Birling Gap and the sea. It's never too early to stop for an ice cream, so pop the bikes down and have a rest before heading up a quiet grassy valley, gradually gaining height and climbing to Warren Hill. Joining the South Downs Way for the first time, a quick undulating stretch of wide track leads to a fast-as-you-dare-while-watching-out-for-walkers descent as the SDW narrows and drops to Jevington (where the Banoffee Pie was invented). There's a shortcut home here, or a series of climbs and descents on sunken trails that wind to Wilmington. Admire the chalk Long Man with his two sticks (he's from 16/1700 AD) and then climb the SDW onto open grassy ground. Once across this, you've got an option: either turn right for fields and forest roads or turn left for a short, fun descent and then a couple of unbroken (s)miles of stunning singletrack that duck and dive through Friston Forest before depositing you, grinning, at the car park. Tough choice.

Grade: **Blue/Red** » Distance: **32km** » Ascent: **670m** » Time: **2.5–5hrs**
Start/Finish: **Seven Sisters Country Park** » Start GR: **TV 519995** » SatNav: **BN25 4AD**
OS Map: **Landrangers 198 & 199** » Parking: **Seven Sisters Country Park**
Cafe: **Seaside cafe at Birling Gap; Tea Rooms in Jevington, Cafe in Seven Sisters Country Park**
Pub: **The Tiger, East Dean, T: 01323 423 209**

Directions

 From the car park, head back towards the road and turn **R** on to a wide dirt track, following signs for several different walks and cycle routes.

Follow track to Westdean. As you reach the houses, turn **L** and then immediately **R** up a tarmac lane. Follow this until it swings left and then continue **SA** onto a stone track. Ignore ALL turnings (even the ones for the cycle routes, unless you fancy exploring!). Eventually, descend fast and straight and continue **SA** onto a slightly narrower track as the main route swings right.

Go **SA** over junctions until you reach tarmac. Turn **L**, then take the first **R**. At the T-junction with the road, turn **R**. At the fork, keep **L** and then go straight over the main road, passing to the right of the church. After 200m, turn **L** through a gate into a field (if you reach the car park, you've gone too far). Head for the left-hand (near) edge of the wall and go through a gate. Cross the next field and turn **R** to descend fast on a grassy track. Go **SA** onto tarmac, and turn **R** at the T-junction.

Follow the road round and then fork **R** just after the green, on to *Went Way*. **Ignore** all turnings until this ends and continue **SA** through a gate and onto singletrack. Bear slightly **L** and climb to a gate. Climb to a field and continue **SA**, passing to the **R** of the barn with the red roof. Continue **SA**, keeping to the **R** of the bushes, and drop across the field to a gate. Go through this onto a good track and follow it around to the **L**. At the road, go **SA**.

Go around the corner and bear **R** (effectively continuing **SA**) onto a grassy bridleway by the bus stop. Keep **R**, climbing into the trees as you reach an open grassy area. Follow the obvious track for a short distance beyond the trees and then turn **L**, dropping to and crossing over the road onto a wide concrete track.

Follow this to farm buildings, ignoring all turnings. Pass just to the left of the barn and follow grassy tracks along the base of a shallow valley. As you near the hut and the circular pond, swing **L** through the left-hand gate and continue to follow vague grassy tracks through fields. Keep the fence just to your left and climb to the road.

2 Go **SA** (slightly **L**) over the road onto a good track. Follow this around to the **L**, climbing slightly towards benches and the trig point.

Continue to follow the track (you're now on the South Downs Way) **SA** over the road and through the golf course. Ignore turnings for a fast, initially swoopy and then rattly descent to Jevington.

Shortcut: Turn **L**, then take the next **R**. Continue **SA** onto a narrow track running between trees as the road ends. Climb this to the woods. Rejoin the directions at **point 3**.

Turn **R** and ride past the The Hungry Monk (now closed, home of the Banoffee pie). Turn **L** onto *Green Lane* – a dirt track signed as a Byway and opposite the Old Post Office. After 200m, turn **R**, following *Byway* signs. A good climb and long descent drop you to Folkington. Keep **L**, on the main track (ignore the road turning to the right) and climb away from the village. Drop speedily down to the road in Wilmington and turn **L**.

At the top of a short rise, turn **L** onto the South Downs Way. Climb steeply around corners and then keep **SA** and traverse open ground on grassy tracks. Go through gates and into trees.

Turn **L** at the junction and drop downhill. Keep **R** at the next junction, and then **R** again, now climbing gently. Cross open ground to the trees. At the track junction, turn **R**, into the trees, then immediately **L** onto the singletrack.

3 **(Shortcut rejoins here)** After 200m or so, turn sharply **R** back on yourself at the singletrack junction. Follow this singletrack as it weaves through the woods, crossing fireroads and grassy tracks but always running roughly downhill.

Eventually, (and we do mean eventually!), you'll go round some sharper, rootier corners and reach a fork. Bear **L** here and continue to follow singletrack and cross forest roads until you cross one wide track and are presented with a trail that drops very steeply off the other side. Either plummet down this to the road (and turn **L** and ride in to West Dean), or turn **L** at the top and then keep **SA** at the fork and then, as the houses of West Dean begin to appear, keep **L** towards them.

Once in West Dean, keep **R** and retrace you tracks to the car park.

More riding

The South Downs Way

Maybe not a 'Sunday Ride' in the strictest sense, unless you're really going for it! While you obviously don't have to ride the whole thing (!), at almost 100 miles in length, the SDW is a massive ride that most people enjoy over a couple of days. It's not too technical, but does cover some tough climbs and fun, fast descents. Inevitably, such a long, obvious bridleway was always going to offer a tempting challenge to a few nutters – with the goal being the sub-24 hour double. The current record is under 18 hours ... (www.southdownsdouble.net). For everyone else, there are plenty of stopping points, water taps and food shops along the way. More information, including a downloadable guide, can be found on www.nationaltrail.co.uk

Grade: **N/A** » Distance: **152km** » Ascent: **Approx. 4,000m** (west–east) » Time: **9hrs(!) + (2 days for mortals)**
Start/Finish: **Winchester or Eastbourne** » Map: **Harvey Maps South Downs Way**

Ditchling Beacon to Harvey's Cross

Classic XC-style South Downs riding. Not too technical, but with some lovely stretches of singletrack and lots of the fast, chalky ridgeline cruising for which the Downs are rightly renowned. It's a long ride, but don't let the distance put you off as it's well worth it. Failing that, it's easy to split this ride into two with a little imagination if you don't fancy the full thing.

Grade: **Red/Black** » Distance: **44km** » Ascent: **920m** » Time: **5hrs+**
Start/Finish: **Kingston Near Lewes, TQ 393083** or **Ditchling Beacon, TQ 333129** » OS Map: **Landranger 198 Brighton & Lewes**

The Route » Kingston near Lewes – Kingston Hollow – Lewes – Lewes Prison – northwest to TQ 377122 – north and west around Blackcap – west on South Downs Way to Ditchling Beacon – west to TQ 316128 – Lower Standean – High Park Farm – Stanmer Down – Balmer Down – Housedean Farm – south to TQ 367078 – Newmarket Hill – Upper Bevendean – Bullock Hill – The Bostle – Swanborough Hill – Swanborough Manor – Kingstone near Lewes

Butser Hill

A fantastically-named hill in a fantastically pretty area (the village of East Meon is rather nice!). The riding's about as technical as it gets around here, and there's plenty of scope to extend the route onto the fantastic Queen Elizabeth Country Park singletrack (see page 73). There's also plenty of height to play around with, including a few steep sections. Open trails and wide easy sections contrast with a couple of deeply eroded and narrow sections – keep-you-on-your-toes stuff – to make for a great ride.

Grade: **Red** » Distance: **20km** » Ascent: **410m** » Time: **2hrs+**
Start/Finish: **Queen Elizabeth Country Park, SU 718185** » OS Map: **Landranger 198 Brighton & Lewes**

The Route » QECP – north-west to Butser Hill – north on the right-hand bridleway to road – west to Frogmore – East Meon – north to SU 718185 – Drayton – south via Henwood Down to Coombe Cross – south to village – east on road then trail east past Tegdown Hill – Butser Hill – retrace tracks to QECP

More information

Main Towns

What with the Downs covering such a massive area, there are several big towns. As a general rule, the biggest towns are to the south, along the coast – Eastbourne in the, err, east, Brighton and Worthing in the middle. At the far west end, away from the routes listed here, is Winchester. Right in the middle of the park, smaller, but still with plenty of shops, are places like Petersfield and Lewes.

Maps

OS Landrangers 185 Winchester & Basingstoke; 197 Chichester & the South Downs;
198 Brighton & Lewes; 199 Eastbourne & Hastings
Harvey Maps South Downs Way

Bike Shops

Quest Adventure, Ardsheal Road, Worthing, 01903 573 700, www.questadventure.co.uk
Evolution Cycles, Cavendish Place, Eastbourne, 01323 737 320, www.evocycles.co.uk
Phoenix Cycles, Seaside, Eastbourne, 01323 729 060, www.phoenixcycles.co.uk
Cuckmere Cycles, Seven Sisters Country Park (Friston Forest), 01323 870 310, www.cuckmere-cycle.co.uk
Lewes Cycleshack, Cliffe High Street, Lewes, 01273 479 688, www.lewescycleshack.co.uk
Evans Cycles, Brighton, 01273 772 357, www.evanscycles.com
Baker Street Bikes, York Place, Brighton, 01273 675 754, www.bakerstbikes.co.uk
Freedom Bikes, George Street, Brighton, 01273 681 698, www.freedombikes.co.uk

Accommodation

The bigger towns on the south coast offer plenty of accommodation and plenty of distractions when you're not riding, but you might need to drive out to ride. Staying further inland can be quieter and better for riding from the door.

There are a number of YHA Hostels in the area:
YHA Alfriston, 0845 371 9101 (nice and quiet, but basic)
YHA Arundel, 0845 371 9002 (camping facilities)
YHA Eastbourne, 0845 371 9316
YHA Telscombe (near Lewes), 0845 371 9663
YHA Truleigh Hill, Shoreham-by-Sea, 0845 371 9047 (camping facilities)

There are campsites all over the place, although we'd particularly recommend Blackberry Wood Campsite, Streat, 01273 890 035, www.blackberrywood.com (as recommended by Cool Camping ...).
There's also Spring Barn Farm, Kinstone near Lewes (01273 488 450, www.springbarnfarm.com).

There aren't any South Downs-specific accommodation sites that we know of, but a quick google should reveal plenty of options. Try www.visiteastbourne.com or www.visitbrighton.com. We've also heard good things about cycle-friendly B&B The Guesthouse East (www.theguesthouseeast.co.uk) in Eastbourne.

Food & Drink

With such a big area, it hard to recommend any cafes in particular. There's virtually always an ice cream van on Ditchling Beacon, and plenty of seaside cafes if your ride takes you that way. Good fish and chip shops abound, and the majority of South Downs villages have a quaint tea shop or two.

Pubs

The Tiger Inn, East Dean, 01323 423 209, www.beachyhead.org.uk

The Giant's Rest, Wilmington, 01323 870 207, www.giantsrest.co.uk

The Snowdrop Inn, Lewes, 02173 471 018, www.thesnowdropinn.com

Harvey's Brewery, Lewes, www.harveys.org.uk (not strictly a pub, but does brewery tours)

Tourist Offices

Brighton, 01233 290 337, www.visitbrighton.com » **Chichester**, 01243 775 888, www.visitchichester.org
Eastbourne, 0871 663 0031, www.visiteastbourne.com » **Lewes**, 01273 483 448, email lewes.tic@lewes.gov.uk

Useful Websites

www.southdowns.gov.uk » **www.nationaltrail.co.uk** » **www.southdownsdouble.net**
www.bikedowns.co.uk » **www.southdownscycling.com**

Guidebooks

South East Mountain Biking North and South Downs, written by Nick Cotton and published by Vertebrate Publishing

Mountain Bike Rides in the South East, written by Max Darkins and published by Rough Ride Guides

Mountain Biking on the South Downs, written by Peter Edwards and published by Cicerone

Worth Knowing

There are a couple of natural-feeling trail centres in the South Downs. Friston Forest (visited by the main route) has a waymarked route that winds through the trees on dirt trails, while Queen Elizabeth Country Park (near Southampton) has a couple of great volunteer-built loops. The red route is the one to head for here – five miles of turns, roots and chalky singletrack. www.qecptrailcollective.co.uk

The Surrey Hills – North Downs

The Surrey Hills sit halfway along the North Downs in a particularly green part of England. Consisting of a few sizeable hills (for the South East) and covered in trees, they're the sort of place that's always going to attract mountain bikers. It gets better too, because they're riddled with singletrack.

The areas most riders head to are Leith, Holmbury and Pitch Hills. The former is the highest point in the South East, so there's plenty of height to play with, while the latter two have a fairly unique and mountain-bike-friendly access arrangement.

Back in the 1920s, the hills were a private estate owned by Reggie Bray, Lord of the Manor of Shere. He took the pioneering step of opening up his land to the public, granting them a right to roam and welcoming them onto the hills. This is still the case today, with a charity named The Hurtwood Control managing and conserving the land. They've been particularly kind to mountain bikers too: we can ride freely upon mile after mile of superb singletrack. In return, they ask that we remember that we're not the only people using the area, we keep speeds down, we stick to existing trails (don't modify them or build new lines) and generally be courteous and responsible. And that all seems pretty reasonable when you consider the great riding we get in return.

The Riding

Summing up the Surrey Hills riding is easy: singletrack. Woodland singletrack.

There's pretty much every sort of tight, twisty tree-lined singletrack you'd ever want here. You won't find rock gardens or open moorland crossings, but you'll get pretty much everything else: swoopy, bermy singletrack, rooty, techy singletrack and easy, cruisy singletrack. It's mainly natural in feel, with a couple of man-made stretches, and all seems to fit together into one seamless whole – especially given that rides here essentially consist of speeding around trying out anything that takes your fancy. The entire place feels like one big playground.

Outside the woods, there's all manner of opportunity for cruising broad, easy tracks through beautiful leafy countryside (and it is leafy). These are spot on for easier riding, great for creating longer loops and seeing the countryside, and ideal for linking the singletrack hotspots.

When to go

As is the case in most of southern England, riding around the Surrey Hills is much, much more fun in the summer. It's the woodland singletrack that defines this region for many. Ride it in the wet and you'll not only damage the trails (a major point of contention in the area), but they'll be slow and sluggish to ride. Better to let them dry out first. It's also worth noting the proximity of the area to London. It can get very busy here on fine days.

Near Holmbury Hill. **Photo:** Tom Hutton.

09 Surrey Hills Singletrack

Instead of marking out a route, we've taken a slightly different approach for the Surrey Hills. There are a couple of reasons for this. Firstly, we figure that you're most likely to head to this area for singletrack. We certainly do! Secondly, it's nigh on impossible to give accurate directions to it and, for various reasons, we're not sure we should try to.

Instead, we want to encourage you to go and explore. Follow tyre tracks, ride things you like the look of – play in the woods.

But of course, this wouldn't be a guidebook if we didn't give you a few pointers!

You want to head for the area around Pitch, Holmbury and Leith Hills. That's where the good stuff is. Holmbury St Mary and Peaslake make good starting points.

Very, very roughly speaking, Pitch Hill has the technical, steep, rooty stuff. Holmbury has some straighter and faster trails, like the fantastic *Telegraph Road*, a few tighter, more interesting runs and the smooth, heavily-bermed *Barry Knows Best* which drops towards Peaslake. Leith Hill is more sprawling, with all sorts of short runs to discover as well as a few great long stretches of trail like *Summer Lightning* and *The Regurgitator*.

For **Holmbury Hill**, park in Holmbury St Mary and make your way up towards the Youth Hostel and then bear left towards the top of the hill. From the viewpoint, turn around and either head left towards the top car park and on to various tight and twisty runs heading towards *Barry Knows Best* or ride straight ahead for *Yoghurt Pots*, *Telegraph Road* and various other options.

Over on **Pitch Hill**, park in Peaslake (the village shop sells tea in mugs and brilliant samosas) and ride straight out of the back of the car park to reach the top of the hill. Again turn around and head back in roughly the same direction, bearing slightly rightwards to pick up the best and rootiest of the singletrack.

For **Leith Hill**, either park in the main car park or near The Plough in Coldharbour. Have a play around near the tower, then head over towards the bowling green and the area between Coldharbour, Broadmoor and Westcott to find some good long runs, including *Summer Lightning* and *The Regurgitator*.

If you want something a little different, try the big, sprawling ride from Ranmore (Big Day Out, opposite) on which links the singletrack honeypots mentioned here with the brilliant cross country riding typical of the North Downs. It's also a very accommodating ride, easily shortened or adapted to suit your riding tastes.

Suggested routes

Big Day Out

A big day out and a ride of two halves. The northern half of this route takes relatively wide and open trails. We'd give it a 'blue' grade as it's relatively straightforward, but, with some tough climbs and a couple of seriously fast descents, it's great fun and definitely worth riding. Meanwhile, south of the car park is a big 'cliff' – take one of the brake-boiling descents down this and you're committed to a real challenge of a climb back up. Don't worry about this though – the good news is that you're now only a short sprint from the singletrack-infested woods on Holmbury and Leith Hills. Follow the route below or just head off into the trees and explore.

So, if you want a short blast, do the northern half of the ride. Or, for a big day out, ride the whole thing, stopping to explore the singletrack as you go.

Grade: **Red** » Distance: **38km** » Ascent: **880** » Time: **3hrs+**
Start/Finish: **Ranmore Common car parks, TQ 127502** » OS Map: **Landranger 187 Dorking & Reigate**

The Route » Car park at TQ 127502 – east on road to Ranmore Common – north to Blagden Farm – north to TQ 148536 – west and then south to the entrance to Polesdean Lacey (TQ 135527) – west then south to TQ 125501 – south to Stockman's Coomb Farm – west through Deerleap Wood to TQ 101473 – south to Sutton Abinger – roads south to YHA at TQ 104449 explore Holmbury Hill (climb to trig point, drop down same side) – Holmbury St Mary – east through Pasture Wood to Ashes Farm – Leith Hill Tower – explore singletrack to join and follow byway running from Coldharbour to Wescott – Stockman's Coomb Farm – White Downs – climb to Ranmore Common and car park

West from Godalming

A decent length ride this, and, despite the best efforts of some tough hills, it's not too arduous an outing. Unless it's wet, when the rooty singletrack gets slow and slippery and the sandy commons grind away at your drivetrain. Although there's not a great deal of singletrack along the route, as is the case with the rest of the North Downs the riding really is rather good. There aren't any particularly long descents or climbs, just good undulating riding through Surrey's typically green and leafy surroundings. Keep an eye on the map though – it's easy to get hideously lost around here ...

Grade: **Red** » Distance: **40km** » Ascent: **670m** » Time: **3.5hrs+**
Start/Finish: **Puttenham Common car park, SU 920460** » OS Map: **Landranger 186 Aldershot & Guildford**

The Route » Car park – north to Lascombe – North Downs Way east and under the A3 – Polsted Manor – Compton Common – Hurtmore – Eashing – Upper Eashing – Godalming Station – wiggle through Godalming via Holloway Hill – Busbridge Lakes – SU 978402 – west to Great Enton – Wheelerstreet – Moushill – SU 915407 – Truxford – Woolford Farm – road to Elstead – Charleshill – Fullbrook Farm – Cutt Mill House – car park

More information

Main Towns
Guildford, Dorking and Godalming will have pretty much everything you'll ever need.

Maps
OS Landranger 186 Aldershot & Guildford
OS Landranger 187 Dorking & Reigate

Bike Shops
Head for the Hills, Dorking, 01306 885 007, www.head-for-the-hills.co.uk
Nirvana Cycles, Westcott, 01306 740 300, www.nirvanacycles.com
Pedal and Spoke, 01306 731 639, www.pedalandspoke.co.uk
Cycleworks, Guildford, 01483 302 210, www.cycleworks.co.uk
Beyond Mountain Bikes, 01483 267 676, www.beyondmountainbikes.com
Mountain Trax, Barkham, 0118 976 1130, www.mountain-trax.com (handy for Swinley Forest)

Accommodation
You can expect to pay a bit more for accommodation around here. It is Surrey after all! A couple of the pubs listed below offer B&B and are very handily located. For posher stuff, www.visitsurrey.com has some upmarket suggestions. Otherwise try:

YHA Holmbury St Mary (0845 371 9323) – halfway up Holmbury Hill with the singletrack run of *Telegraph Road* finishing less than 100m away.

YHA Tanners Hatch (0845 371 9542) – on Ranmore Common near Dorking. Also ideal.

Puttenham Eco Camping Barn (01629 592 700, www.puttenhamcampingbarn.co.uk) – more like a hostel. No parking, but arriving by bike gets you a discount.

If you want to camp, the Holmbury YHA has an area for tents, and Etherley Farm (01306 621 423), on the road south from Holmbury to Okley (grid ref: TQ 139432), is also well-situated.

Food & Drink
Pubs
The Hurtwood Inn, Peaslake, 01306 730 851, www.hurtwoodinnhotel.com (also does accommodation)
King's Head, Holmbury St Mary, 01306 730 282, www.kingsheadholmbury.co.uk
The Abinger Hatch, Abinger Common, 01306 730 737, www.theabingerhatch.com
The Plough Inn, Coldharbour, 01306 711 793, www.ploughinn.com (also does accommodation)
Cafes
Peaslake Village Stores, Peaslake, 01306 730 474, www.peaslakevillagestores.com (not really a cafe, but sells good food (vegetable samosas!) and you can sit outside)
Leith Hill Tower cafe, Leith Hill – handily placed serving hatch.
There are also decent cafes on Reigate and Box Hills. The latter is usually full of road riders – which means it must be good.

Tourist Offices

Guildford, on the High Street, 01483 444 333

Outdoor Shops

There are plenty in the area – Guildford has a Field and Trek, a Cotswolds, a Blacks and several independents.

Useful Websites

www.visitsurrey.com – on the posh side, but information on everything, including accommodation
www.friendsofthehurtwood.co.uk – home of the Hurtwood Control, who manage the Pitch Hill area
www.mtbsurreyhills.com – local mountain bike club, including 'pub' and 'tea shop' sections

Guidebooks

South East Mountain Biking North and South Downs, written by Nick Cotton and published by Vertebrate Publishing
Mountain Bike Rides in the South East, written by Max Darkins and published by Rough Ride Guides
Mountain Biking on the North Downs, written by Peter Edwards and published by Cicerone

Worth Knowing

The Surrey Hills are easily accessed by train from central London. The popular option is to take a train to Dorking (from Waterloo or Victoria) and ride from there (or change to a train to Gomshall if you're feeling lazy!), although Guildford, Godalming and Box Hill are all possible start points.

We know it's not in the Surrey Hills, but we couldn't not mention Swinley Forest. While it's no longer the explore-as-you-please singletrack mecca that it once was, it is a beautiful forest with a fantastic looping trail running through it that's well worth a trip. Head north, towards Reading picking up the A303 and stopping at The Lookout to find it.

The Chiltern Hills

Those who've never visited the Chilterns often feel inclined to dismiss them as a load of farmers' fields in an area that deluded Londoners think of as 'hilly'; as a waste of good riding time and only worth riding if you're unlucky enough to live there – certainly not worth a drive.

That was what I thought and so, despite growing up within 20 miles of them, I'd been riding for a decade before I finally went for a look. What a chump. With something like a fifth of their area covered by trees and woodland, the Chilterns have enough tight and twisty trails to entertain even the hardest-to-please riders. There are country pubs for après-ride food, and a unique chalky landscape to admire while you eat. The deer parks and the recent re-introduction of Red Kites will appeal to wildlife-lovers and the whole area is incredibly easy to access by road and rail. Don't make the mistake I did, the Chilterns are well worth a visit!

The Riding

There's a lot of woodland in the Chilterns – which is always promising. You don't get the mazes of singletrack found in places like the nearby Surrey Hills (page 75); instead, these are faster, more open trails which lead to places, rather than chasing around in circles. Not overly technical (just a few lumps of sharp flint and roots to trip over), they're flat-out-fast in the summer and slower and slidier in the winter – always fun though. Climbs and descents are never over-long, as, whilst the Chilterns are far from flat, the hills aren't exactly gigantic. But they can be steep, and, if the trails are sticky, truly tough. There are, as ever, a few dull field-edge tracks to link the fun bits, but as they usually give good views and are pleasant, leafy cruises, they're far from ride-spoilers. In a nutshell – nothing over technical, just lots of fast, twisty bridleways – the sort of riding that everybody, no matter how good they are, can enjoy.

When to go

The Chilterns aren't known for technical rocky riding because there isn't any. They're full of dirt trails through the trees – and that doesn't always drain particularly well, leaving them a touch gloopy in winter. To experience the singletrack at its fastest and dustiest best, wait for dry weather.

Near Nettlebed. **Photo**: Tom Hutton.

10 Nettlebed

A big ride through leafy countryside, mixing singletrack, woodland blasts and satisfyingly pedally sections into a great XC loop. It's not overly technical, but, with loads of fast runs through the trees, it is a lot of fun. This is typical 'old woodland' riding. One minute, it's fast and open. Speeds are high, banks are jumped and corners taken in foot-out, leaf scattering style. Then it narrows to singletrack, hopping roots, mincing past brambles and flicking through little chicanes. All great fun. The highlight is probably the wide singletrack from Cookley Green – and it's sublime. Well surfaced and pedally, It's easy to reach silly speeds as you lean through corners and sprint down straights. Of course, it's not all fun. There are a few tough climbs to tackle and, like everything here, it can be a slog in winter. But who cares. The riding is good, the woods are green and yes, that pond in Russell's Water is the one from *Chitty Chitty Bang Bang*.

Grade: **Red** » Distance: **38km (numerous shortcuts)** » Ascent: **680m** » Time: **: 4hrs+**
Start/Finish: **Nettlebed** » Start GR: **SU 701868** » SatNav: **Nettlebed**
OS Map: **Explorer 171 Chiltern Hills – West** » Parking: **Plenty in Nettlebed**
Cafe: **The Field Kitchen, Nettlebed, T: 01491 641 831** » Pub: **The White Hart, Nettlebed, T: 01491 641 245**

Directions

S▶ Starting at the road junction in Nettlebed, head off the main road and up the B481 towards *Watlington*. After 400m, on a right hand bend, turn **L** on a singletrack byway.

Follow this past houses, keep **SA** on the wide track through the farm and turn **R** at the road. Keep **L** as the road forks, then turn **L** at the T-junction with the main road.

Shortcut: Keep **SA** on the road, ignoring turnings for 2km to Cookley Green. Ride almost through the village before turning **R** on a wide track, rejoining the directions at **point 3**.

After 200m, turn **L** on a bridleway. Ignoring turnings, follow the bridleway as it twists fast through woodland.

At a wide track near houses, move **L** to continue **SA**. Keep **SA** onto double track along a field edge. As you climb a slight rise, turn **R** through the hedge onto another field edge track.

Follow this, ignoring turnings, to a lane and go **SA**. As the road, turn **R**, and then keep **SA** off the road onto Swan's Way. Go **SA** across three roads. At the fourth (white concrete barriers), turn **R**, signed bridleway and the *Oxfordshire Way*. Climb to the hotel and go **SA**, steeply uphill.

2 At the road, turn **R**. Keep **SA** at the junction (signed *Nettlebed* and *Henley*). As you reach Tree Barn, turn **L** into the farmyard. Keep **R** of the car park, through the yard onto a concrete track. Keep **SA** as this turns to dirt and drop into the woods.

At the junction with the wide track, go **SA** uphill, following white arrows painted on trees, onto singletrack (soon becomes obvious). Follow singletrack and arrows across crossroads until you reach a wide gravel track. Turn **R**, still following arrows, and then go **SA** (more arrows). At the fork with the permissive bridleway, keep **R** and drop through a farm to the road. Turn **R**, uphill.

Shortly after the Cookley Green 30mph signs, turn **L** on a wide track. Follow this past houses and keep **SA** as it narrows.

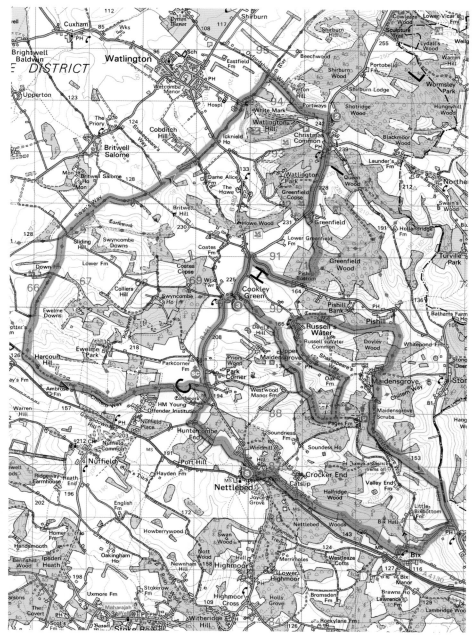

3 Ignoring turnings, descend to a T-junction and bear **R**. At the second T-junction (in the valley bottom), turn **L**. Follow the track to a track crossroads. Turn **L** and climb steeply to the road.

Turn **L** and ride past the pub to Russell's Water. Turn **R** after the pond and follow the track to a gate and farmyard. Go through the yard and onto singletrack. Ignoring turnings, follow this to drop fast along the wood edge to a T-junction with a wide track. Turn **R** onto singletrack along the edge of the field. Go **SA** into the woods and up the climb ahead. Continue onto fun singletrack. At the fork, bear **L**.

Go **SA** over the road, then immediately **R** off the wide track (it's private) onto a bridleway. Ride up through the woods to open land and cross the field. Go through the houses. Turn **R**, then almost immediately **L** on a wide track. Follow this to a fork and bear **L**. Drop fast to the road.

Turn **R**, then take the second **R** – White Lane. Climb steeply and follow the road right around the green. Ignore a turning to the right and continue **SA** onto a bridleway signed *Nettlebed* as the road bends left.

Ignore turnings and follow this through woods. As you reach houses, keep **SA**, (forking **L** as you do). Keep going until you reach a T-junction with a road. Turn **R**, then **L** and ride back to Nettlebed.

More riding

The Ridgeway

Britain's oldest road, and one of its chalkiest. The full thing runs from Avebury (of stone circle fame) to Ivinghoe Beacon. Cyclists can't use it all, but there's a significant chunk running east from Goring that's allowed, letting you cross a chunk of southern England with minimal effort. Think open fields, blue skies and the occasional chalk horse/Iron Age fort. It also makes a great 'spine' from which to create routes (see *Guidebooks* page 87, and the Barbury route in the Salisbury Plain section, page 50).

Grade: **Blue** » Distance: **c.65km** » Ascent: **c.800m** (east–west) » Time: **5hrs+**
Start/Finish: **Wherever you like!** » Map: **OS Landrangers 173–176** » More information: **www.nationaltrail.co.uk**

Near Princes Risborough. **Photo**: Tom Hutton.

Goring and the Thames

I've got great memories of this ride: the Thames steaming smokily on frozen mornings, fast woodland singletrack, friends crashing over walls on nightrides … good times! This isn't a hard ride and there's a fair bit of easy cruising, but it's got some twisty and lumpy sections in the woods. The icing on the cake, however, is the riverside run between Whitchurch and Goring. It's fast, narrow and swoopy with incredible views. Easily rideable from Reading, via Caversham.

Grade: **Blue/Red** » Distance: **22km** » Ascent: **330m** » Time: **2hrs+**
Start/Finish: **Goring Station, SU 602806** » OS Map: **Explorer 171 Chiltern Hills – West**

The Route » Goring – road east to Woodcote – Common Wood – Nuney Green – Cross Lanes – Mill Farm – Lilley Farm – New Farm – Mapledurham – Whitchurch – Goring

Wendover

Right at the top of the Chilterns, this 30-kilometre ride contains almost 25-kilometres of off-road. And it's good stuff too – a classic Chilterns mix of wide woodland trails, fast singletrack and rapid descents. There's a fair bit of up and down and the trails become hard work in the wet, so this route is best ridden in the dry. Figure-of-eight in shape, it's easy to shorten and is right by Aston Hill (see page 87) if you want to spice things up with a downhill run or two.

Grade: **Red** » Distance: **32km** » Ascent: **680m** » Time: **2.5hrs+**
Start/Finish: **Wendover, SP 870079** » OS Map: **Explorer 171 Chiltern Hills – West**

The Route » Wendover – The Hale – Hale Wood – Boswells Farm – Icknield Way past Smalldene Farm – Dunsmore – Little Hampen – Buckmoorend – Brockwell Farm – Longdown Farm – Icknield Way to Whiteleaf – road back up towards Green Hailey – Honor End Farm – Hotley Bottom – Rignall Farm – SP 869036 – Dunsmore – Upper Bacombe – Bacombe Warren – Wendover

Stonor

Similar terrain to the main ride (not that surprising, being so close...), this short loop has some tough grassy/muddy climbs (predictably harder in winter), a good descent from Ibstone and a seriously steep final drop into Stonor.

Grade: **Red** » Distance: **18km** » Ascent: **400m** » Time: **1.5hrs+**
Start/Finish: **Stonor, SU 736886** » OS Map: **Explorer 171 Chiltern Hills – West**

The Route » Stonor – north on road to SU 736896 (near Balhams Farm) – Launder's Farm – Northend – Hale Wood – Ibstone Common – south to SU 750928 – south to road and then east to Turville – Dolesden – Kimble Farm via Great Wood – west to SU 743885 – Stonor

More information

Main Towns

There aren't many towns in the centre of the Chilterns (try Nettlebed or Watlington), but you've got Henley to the east, Wallingford to the west and High Wycombe to the north if you need to get hold of something. Otherwise, head south to Reading.

Maps

OS Explorer 159 Reading
OS Explorer 171 Chilterns Hills – West
OS Explorer 172 Chilterns Hills – East
OS Explorer 181 Chilterns Hills – North

Bike Shops

AW Cycles in Caversham, Reading, 0118 946 3050, www.awcycles.co.uk
Henley Cycles, Henley-on-Thames, 01491 578 984, www.henleycycles.co.uk
Rides on Air, Wallingford, 01491 836 289, www.ridesonair.com
Mountain Mania, Tring, 01442 822 458, www.mountainmaniacycles.co.uk
Buckinghamshire Bikes, Aylesbury, 01296 482 077, www.buckinghambikes.co.uk

Accommodation

www.chilterns-stay.co.uk – good for everything from camping to hotels.

There's YHA in Streatly on Thames (0845 371 9044) – near Goring, and handy for routes. Staying in Reading is also an (livelier) option.

Campsites

White Mark Farm near Watlington (01491 612 295, www.whitemarkfarm.co.uk) is probably the handiest for rides in the central area.

www.chilternsaonb.org has a good list of alternatives.

Food & Drink

The Fox and Hounds, Christmas Common, 01491 612 599, www.foxandhoundschristmascommon.co.uk
The Crown, Pishill, 01491 638 364, www.thecrowninnpishill.co.uk
The Lamb, Satwell, 01491 628 482, www.thelambpub.net
Black Horse, Checkendon, 01491 680 418

Tourist Offices

Wallingford, 01491 826 972 » **Henley-on-Thames**, 01491 578 034

Outdoor Shops

Head to Reading. There are several in the town centre and a big Cotswold Outdoor on the way to J11 of the M4.

Useful Websites

www.chilternsaonb.org – everything you need to know, including links to accommodation
www.bucksmtb.co.uk (routes, local shops, events – all sorts!)
www.rideastonhill.co.uk – the local DH tracks, and a short XC loop

Guidebooks

South East Mountain Biking – Ridgeway & Chilterns, written by Nick Cotton and published by
Vertebrate Publishing
Mountain Bike Rides in the South East, written by Max Darkins, published by Rough Ride Guides

Worth Knowing

If you're in London, there should be a few trains heading out of Paddington or Euston that'll take you right to
the riding. You can ride from Reading for the southern Chilterns, while Wendover and Henley-on-Thames are
also handy starts to rides.

For something totally different – and a lot steeper – try Aston Hill. You need to pay to ride, but there's a
great set of DH runs and a short-but-very-sweet XC loop to play on. www.rideastonhill.co.uk

The Cotswolds

The Cotswolds are quintessentially 'English': rolling farmland, country manors and oak trees. Proper afternoon tea stuff, and a rather nice spot to visit. It's one of those places where you feel relaxed, especially on sunny days when the fields are full, the hedges are green and the birds are out.

Pretty villages, character-filled and built from local yellow Cotswold limestone, break up the open countryside here and there. Some are bustling former centres of silk production, some are sickeningly twee tourist traps and almost all make great cafe and pub stops. They've inspired poets and composers (visit Bibury to see what William Morris called 'the most beautiful village in England') and have also, in utter contrast, provided totally different and much louder entertainment – the famous Castle Combe race circuit was essentially given an ASBO in 2001 for being too loud! And, when they have fantastic names like 'Guiting Power' and 'Birdlip', they're good for keeping guidebook authors entertained too.

The Riding

In keeping with Cotswold MTB tradition, let's start off by talking about the mud. After all, the area is notorious for it. It's not even nice mud. It's thick, sticky, jam-your-wheels-up mud. And it's definitely not fun. But, when the sun comes out, the dirt hardens and the trails transform into fast-rolling speedways – well, that's much better! High speed seems effortless now, the singletrack comes alive and rides are completed in half their winter times. Technical aficionados should head for the hills around Cheltenham and the trails south of the M4. This isn't the Alps, so you shouldn't expect epic descents and huge rock gardens, but you can look forward to steep-sided hills, slippery roots and enough rocks to keep you on your toes. Get into the trees, and there are some great little sections of singletrack too. Meanwhile, over in the eastern Cotswolds, the hills are shallower, and the trails predominantly wider and faster. Great for getting your legs pumping and for covering huge distances at high speed, but equally good for easy days of relaxed cruising through open countryside.

When to go

This was pretty much covered above. If you really must visit in the winter, either pray for frozen trails or bring mud tyres and your best sense of humour. In the summer, bring fast tyres and plenty of sun cream.

Chavenage Green. **Photo:** John Coefield.

11 Winchcombe & Cleeve Hill

From the hustle and bustle of Winchcombe to Cleeve Hill – the highest point in the Cotswolds – and back again via some stiff climbing and a couple of excellent descents, this is a great little blast. Sadly, no bridleways run right to the very top of the mighty Cleeve Hill (a whole 330 metres high!), so you'll have to settle for a high point just below. Never mind, the views still stretch into Wales. The ride is about more than just a pretty view though, cramming in a couple of stiff climbs, a singletrack traverse and descents that range from woodland slithers to high-speed stony motorways. But pick your day carefully: this is a fantastic ride in sunny August, but a right slog in muddy January. The ride's only 20 kilometres long, and quick riders will have it in the bag in a couple of hours. Look overleaf though – the Bredon Hill ride is close enough to roadie over to, and there are some great descents around Snowshill, easily reachable to the north-east.

Grade: **Red** » Distance: **20km** » Ascent: **480m** » Time: **2hrs+**	
Start/Finish: **T-junction in Winchcombe Centre** » Start GR: **SP 025283** » SatNav: **Winchcombe**	
OS Map: **Landranger 163 Cheltenham & Cirencester** » Parking: **Pay and display in Winchcombe**	
Cafe: **Juri's Tea Room, T: 01242 602 469; several more in Winchcombe**	
Pub: **White Hart, Winchcombe, T: 01242 602 359; lots more in Winchcombe**	

Directions

S From the main T-junction in Winchcombe formed by North Street and the High Street, turn **R** (if you're on North Street) and head towards Cheltenham. Take the second **L** onto *Vineyard Street*, following signs for *Sudeley Castle*.

Keep **R** past the castle and follow the lane along the valley. At the end, turn **R** through a gate onto an obvious track. Climb steeply to the road.

Turn **R**, ride into the woods and turn **L**. Keep **L** at the fork and ride **SA** through the farm onto a rough track. Follow this to a small car park. Just before reaching it, turn **R** through a gate into a grassy field.

After 400m, turn **L** through a second gate and ride along field edges (muddy in winter) to join a wide track. Ignoring turnings, follow this to the road.

2 Turn **R** and, after 500m, turn **L** through a gate onto a signed bridleway running into the nature reserve. Admire the view for a minute and then drop around the woods on obvious tracks. Swing to the **R** around a large switch-back and go **SA** through the gate. At the T-junction, turn **L** and continue to descend.

(*Very* easy-to-miss) After about 75m, turn **R** onto singletrack. If you hit a technical, rocky section of track, you've missed the turning, so hang a U-turn and have a more careful look.

Climb singletrack to a multi-track junction. Go **SA**, crossing the gully, and continue climbing, following bridleway signs, to a gate.

Go through the gate and keep **L**, hugging the fence. Bear **L** down the obvious rocky descent and trend **L** across the plateau*. Follow vague tracks to a gate leading into the woods. Fly or squelch – depending on the season – down an entertaining descent to the road.

*OR: Wet Weather Alternative: Keep **R** across the plateau, crest a small rise and turn **R** onto the obvious track behind the houses. Follow this to a small car park by a cattle grid and rejoin the directions at **point 3**.

Take care – the road can be busy. Turn **R** and climb for 1km to the Rising Sun pub. Turn **R** immediately before this onto Rising Sun Lane and cross the cattle grid into a small car park. Turn **L**.

3 Follow good tracks across the grassy common. Keep **R** past the lone building up a short, steep rise and follow the obvious track past the golf course. Keep **SA** through the gate.

At a T-junction after a second gate turn **L**, pass through a third gate and rattle down to join the main road. Turn **R** to return to Winchcombe.

More riding

Crudwell Classic

Dubious name, good ride. This is another route where you get the bike up to speed and pedal happily away as the countryside whizzes past. Almost an 'off-road road-ride', it's not technical, but it is pretty long and is a great choice if you want a straightforward ride through beautiful countryside. Quintessentially Cotswoldian and definitely best on a sunny day.

Grade: **Blue/Red** » Distance: **44km** » Ascent: **400m** » Time: **4hrs+**
Start/Finish: **Crudwell, ST 955929** » OS Map: **Landrangers 162, 163 & 173**

The Route » Crudwell – road to Chedglow – Fosse Gate – Rodmanton – Windmill Tump – Macmillan Way towards Tarlton Down – Lowesmoor – Crackstone – Hampton Fields – off road south to Avening – Avening Ho – Barton End – Tiltups End – Chavenage Green – Chavenage Ho – south past Beverston to Hookshouse – Home Farm – Doughton – south via bridleway and road to Shipton Moyne – Fosse Way north to Chedglow – Crudwell

Bredon Hill

High-speed descents, good singletrack and two big climbs – this route gives a great couple of hours of riding. The highlight is the singletrack blast off the top of the hill and through the woods – sweeping through corners and launching over old badger sets. Sadly, it's over quickly, but that just makes the ride up for the second run easier! The hill itself is pretty interesting. It's got a herd of deer, an Iron Age fort and a tower whose stature boosts the height of the hill past the 1,000 foot mark.

Grade: **Red** » Distance: **20km** » Ascent: **410m** » Time: **2hrs+**
Start/Finish: **Kemerton, SO 945371** » OS Map: **Landranger 163 Cheltenham & Cirencester**

The Route » Kemerton – Bell's Castle – Bredon Hill (east below Lalu Farm to SO 973394) – Netherton Fields – Kersoe – Ashton-under-Hill – Wychavon Way – Bredon Hill Fort – Westmancote – Kemerton

Castle Combe

Slightly away from the Cotswolds 'proper', this ride passes close to Castle Combe race circuit – don't expect peace and quiet! Easy enough to be ridden fast and hard, technical enough to keep you on your toes, it's just about spot on for less-experienced riders to pick their way around while faster riders barrel through with equal enjoyment.

Grade: **Red** » Distance: **23km** » Ascent: **480m** » Time: **2.5hrs+**
Start/Finish: **Biddestone, ST 863734** » OS Map: **Landranger 163 Cheltenham & Cirencester**

The Route » Biddestone – West Yatton – Long Dean – West Yatton Down – Green Barrow Farm – Castle Combe Circuit – Castle Combe – Truckle Hill – North Wraxall – Thickwood – Widdenham Farm – Weavern Farm – Biddestone

Wotton Wanderer

Tracing a big loop through the south-west Cotswolds, this is a great route that makes the most of its hilly surroundings – it's got over 800 metres of descending! With downhills ranging from fast, open trails to steep singletrack and rocky rattles, there's plenty of fun to be had. However, don't forget that you've got to go up to come down, and the climbs here are steep and tricky to ride without dabbing. So make sure you're feeling fit if you want to get the most from this ride!

Grade: Black » Distance: **40km** » Ascent: **960m** » Time: **4hrs+**
Start/Finish: **Wotton-under-Edge, ST 758 933** » OS Map: **Landranger 162 Gloucester & Forest of Dean**

The Route » Wotton – south on road to Alderley – south-east on bridleway to ST 780898 – Tresham – roads east to Boxwell – north to ST 807935 – west on bridleways to Ozleworth Bottom – Ozleworth Park – north to the A4135 – roads north and east to ST 797971 near Becombe – west on bridleways and singletrack (NOTE – it's easy to get lost here – just follow singletrack roughly SA/west and you'll be fine) to ST 747977 above Dursley – golf club – Kingshill – drop north-west to Sandpits (ST 748992) – south on road to ST 735911 – climb back to Stinchcombe Hill – Stancombe Park – North Nibley – south-east through woods to ST 759944 – Coombe – Wotton

Photo: John Coefield.

More information

Main Towns

Cheltenham is easily accessible to the west of the Cotswolds and will have most things you need, as will Cirencester in the centre. Most of the smaller villages, such as Winchcombe, Wotton-under-Edge or Tetbury have small supermarkets and shops containing the basics.

Maps

OS Landranger 150 Worcester & The Malverns
OS Landranger 151 Stratford-upon-Avon
OS Landranger 162 Gloucester & Forest of Dean
OS Landranger 163 Cheltenham & Gloucester
OS Landranger 164 Oxford
OS Landranger 172 Bristol & Bath
OS Landranger 173 Swindon & Devizes

Bike Shops

Noah's Ark, Brimscombe (near Stroud), 01453 884 738, www.noahsark.co.uk
Cheltenham Cycles, Cheltenham, 01242 255 414, www.cheltenhamcycles.co.uk
Leisure Lakes, Cheltenham, 01242 251 505, www.leisurelakesbikes.com
Roylan Cycles, Cheltenham, 01242 235 948, www.roylancycles.co.uk
Williams Cycles, Cheltenham, 01242 512 291, www.williams-cycles.co.uk
Ride 24/7, Cirencester, 01285 642 247, www.ride-247.co.uk

Stinchcombe Hill. **Photo**: John Coefield.

Accommodation

A quick google will reveal several tourist websites to the area, all with decent accommodation sections. Otherwise, try www.cotswoldsaccommodation.com

If you want something cheaper, there's a Youth Hostel at Stow-on-the-Wold, (0845 371 9540), which is reasonably central.

There aren't actually many campsites around the area. Folly Farm Campsite (just of the A436 west of Bourton on the Water, 01451 820 285, www.cotswoldcamping.net) and Far Peak Campsite (just south of Northleach, 01285 720 858, www.farpeakcamping.co.uk) are both nice and central.

Don't forget that both Bristol and Bath are within striking distance should you fancy somewhere livelier.

Food & Drink

The Plough, Ford, 01386 584 215, www.theploughinnatford.co.uk (offers accommodation)
Halfway House Kineton, 01451 850 344, www.thehalfwayhousekineton.co.uk (offers accommodation)
Royal William, Painswick, 01452 813 650, www.royalwilliam.co.uk
The Woolpack, Slad, 01452 813 429, www.thewoolpackinn-slad.com
Butchers Arms, Sheepscombe, 01452 812 113, www.butchers-arms.co.uk
Farmers Arms, Guiting Power, 01451 850 358, www.farmersarmsguitingpower.com

Tourist Offices

Bourton-on-the-Water, 01451 820 211, bourton.vic@cotswold.gov.uk » **Cheltenham**, 01242 522 878, tic@cheltenham.gov.uk » **Chipping Campden**, 01386 841 206, information@visitchippingcampden.com » **Chipping Norton**, 01608 644 379, chippingnortonvic@westoxon.gov.uk » **Cirencester**, 01285 654 180, cirencestervic@cotswold.gov.uk » **Stow-on-the-Wold**, 01451 831 082, stowvic@cotswold.gov.uk » **Stroud**, 01453 760 960, tic@stroud.gov.uk » **Tetbury**, 01666 503 552, tourism@tetbury.com » **Winchcombe**, 01242 602 925, winchcombetic@tewkesburybc.gov.uk

Outdoor Shops

There's a huge Cotswold Outdoor (01285 863 930) in South Cerney in the Cotswold Water Park, and several other options in Cirencester and Cheltenham.

Useful Websites

www.thecorrective.com – information on Leckhampton Hill DH runs (good fun!)
With the Cotswolds being the Cotswolds, there are numerous touristy websites for the area, such as:
www.visitcotswolds.co.uk

Guidebooks

Cotswolds Mountain Biking – 20 Classic Rides, written by Tom Fenton, published by Vertebrate Publishing

Worth Knowing

If you like organised events, the Hell of the North Cotswolds (www.honc.org.uk) is a brilliant 'off road reliability trial' and good tour of the area. Meanwhile, there's a good series of Trailquest events in the area. See www.midlandtrailquests.co.uk for details.

Northern England

2

The Malvern Hills
The Long Mynd
The Peak District
Calderdale & the South Pennines
The North York Moors
The Yorkshire Dales
The Howgills
The Lake District
Isle of Man
High Cup Nick & Cross Fell
The Cheviots & Northumberland

Richard Barson riding the Bowderdale singletrack in the Howgills.
Photo: John Coefield.

01: Sticks Pass, Lake District. **02**: North York Moors nourishment. **03**: Pushing up to Helvellyn Lower Man, Lake District. **04**: Climbing up the back of Garburn Pass, Lake District. **05**: Wise words on the North York Moors. **06**: Howgills puncture scene. **All photos**: John Coefield.

07: John Horscroft up on Hope Brink, Peak District.   **08**: Cranberry Clough, Peak District.   **09**: Lakeland sheep.   **10**: South Pennines riding on Windy Hill.

All photos: John Coefield.

The Malvern Hills

Did you know they've been selling bottled Malvern spring water since the 1600s? That's earlier than almost anywhere else in the world. In fact, Great Malvern was the first place to bottle water on a commercial scale – something they did so well that it permeated all levels of society: Queen Elizabeth I allegedly refused to travel without a bottle of the delicious liquid at her side.

They didn't just bottle the water either. When miraculous healing powers were attributed to the waters here in the 19th century, they were quick to capitalise on the new fad for 'Water Cures'. As the crowds rushed to soak themselves in soothing baths, they booked out every hotel that could be built, transforming the little village of Great Malvern into a decent sized town.

It's the Malvern Hills which brought about this transformation (and the reason mountain bikers visit today). Water trickles down through the hills, which are made from some of the oldest and hardest rock in Britain. It's so hard that, not only does it do a superb job of filtering and removing impurities from the water, it leaves virtually no mineral trace as it does so. Eventually, this clean and pure water spurts out through the numerous springs at the bottom of the hills at an incredible rate of up to 60 litres a minute! Not bad for a bit of rainwater.

The Riding

The Malverns manage to cram an incredibly large amount of riding into a tiny area. Trails cross and re-cross each other with such regularity that you need a special extra-large scale map to unravel them. Once you've done so, however, you can cover a lot of distance and ride a lot of totally different trails without ever going too far from home.

The riding here ranges from wide, hard-packed trails to relatively technical singletrack. If you know where you're headed, you could as easily find a gentle pootle as you could a technical singletrack-fest. Trail surfaces are usually good, although there are a few muddy and grassy patches here and there – especially at the southern end, where the trails are more overgrown. There's a fair bit of rock around, although it usually appears in small outcrops, rather than big, loose rock gardens. The fun stuff is generally singletrack, which varies from the characteristic Malvern trails – arrow straight, fast runs between tight hairpins – to really narrow, twisty stuff. There's also the main run down the ridge – fast and narrow with blind corners and fading rocky drops. It's a great area, although, sadly probably not enough for an entire weekend's riding – try combining a ride here with one on the Long Mynd, or in the Forest of Dean.

When to go

Mid-week, mid-night, mid-rainstorm, whenever everyone else stays at home – the Malverns get REALLY busy. Even on a drizzly mid-week ride you can expect to meet (lots of) people. Not only does this make for a very 'stop/start' ride, it also means you really do need to watch your speed – particularly on the descent off Worcestershire Beacon. Other than that, the Malverns ride well whatever the weather.

Malvern Hills singletrack. **Photo**: Tom Hutton.

12 Malvern Hills Classic

Given the tiny area it covers, this route packs in a lot of riding. It's got big hills, great singletrack and fast descents. Traversing the Malvern Hills from their northern end, it criss-crosses itself, giving a ride that's particularly easy to shorten as you see fit. The first hill doubles as both the start and finish of the ride – a relatively benign lower section, followed by some classic Malvern arrow-straight singletrack that links 180-degree hairpin with 180-degree hairpin. A chance to admire the view follows, as wide, easy tracks contour around North Hill and up toward the route's high point at Worcestershire Beacon. High point is followed by highlight, with a kilometre-long fast and rocky descent that drops and weaves down to the road at Malvern Nick. Watch out for walkers! Crossing the road and heading further south, the scenery and route change as you move into the trees. Pleasant traversing and climbing leads to fast singletrack and a steep climb to Black Hill. Catch your breath and then drop onto more fast singletrack around hairpin bends on the way back to the road. Soon after comes the most technical section of the route – narrow, rocky and exposed singletrack that crosses rocky steps and then tiptoes delicately around the hillside and into the woods. Really superb, natural stuff. A cafe, a tough climb and an easy 'ledge' ride see you back at the top of the opening hill and an easy descent to the car.

Grade: **Red** » Distance: **17km** » Ascent: **970m** » Time: **2hrs+**

Start/Finish: **North Malvern Quarries car park** » Start GR: **SO 771469** » SatNav: **WR14 4LT**

Map: **Harvey Maps 1:10,000 Malvern Hills** » Parking: **Pay and display at start**

Cafe: **St Ann's Well Cafe, T: 01684 560 285, www.stannswell.co.uk**

Pub: **The Nag's Head, Malvern, T: 01684 574 373, www.nagsheadmalvern.co.uk**

Directions

S From the car park at the northern end of the hills, head south (away from the entrance) on the tarmac bridleway climbing to the left of the pay and display machine and past the houses.

Keep **R** after the houses, climbing more steeply. As the gradient eases, turn sharp **R** onto a narrow track (small wall holding up the edge of the track and small rock crag ahead).

Climb around tricky switchbacks until you reach a T-junction with a good track. Turn **R** and, ignoring all turnings, traverse around North Hill and then descend gently around Table Hill, eventually reaching a fork. Bear **L**, uphill.

At the multiple track junction at the top of the hill, go **SA** and drop a short distance to a good track. Turn **R** and, ignoring all junctions, ride to another many-track junction by a low circular stone marker/thing. Bear slightly **L**, staying on the main obvious track. Follow this uphill and then around to the right. Keep **SA** across the hillside at the next many-way junction and then follow the track as it contours around the hillside and then begins to climb back leftwards towards the top of Worcestershire Beacon.

Keep **L** at fork by bench and climb to T-junction with good track at the top of the ridge, just below the summit. Turn **R** and descend **CAREFULLY**, as this track gets very busy in summer. Watch out for the drop halfway down!

② **(Go slow – you don't want to miss this bit!)** After 300m or so, go **SA** across the tarmac track and follow a grassy track to the left of the small grassy knoll. Follow rocky singletrack down the left hand side of the ridge, ignoring all junctions, to another circular stone thing.

Go **SA** over (around!) the stone marker onto a narrow track (tarmac track immediately to the right). Follow this downhill – watch your speed and the final corner – to tarmac. Turn **R**, then quickly **L** into the car park.

Go **SA** through the car park. Turn **L**, then **L** again on to the main road. Ride through Wyche Cutting and, almost immediately, turn **R** onto a signed bridleway (the Wyche Inn is just down the hill if you need a breather).

Follow this downhill until the track splits into three. Take the **RH** track and then immediately turn sharp **R**. Keep **L**, uphill, at the fork and climb around switchbacks towards the ridge. Just beneath the ridge, keep **L** on grassy singletrack and descend. Ignore a turning to the right, swing around a big left-hand bend and then keep **L**, downhill, as the track forks by a bench.

Head back into the trees and keep descending, keeping **SA** at a track junction on a big left-hand bend. Follow the track as it moves onto more open ground and begins to climb.

At the fork, bear **R**, off the main track, onto singletrack. Climb around a right-hand and then a left-hand switch-back and to the ridge. Turn **R**, climbing (pushing!) very steeply up the main ridge track before turning **R** halfway up onto a thankfully flat track. Follow this around the hillside, descending gently.

Keep **SA** as you join your previous track by a bench. Keep **L**, uphill, at the fork and keep **R** just below the ridge, retracing your tyre tracks. This time, however, keep **L** around the second switchback and then keep **L** (not around the corner) at the third. Follow the wide track back up to the road, turn **L** through the cutting and then turn **R** back into the car park.

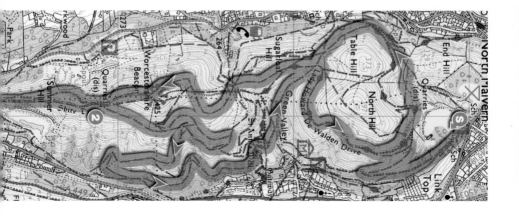

③ Keep **SA** through the car park and follow the tarmac road up through the second parking area. Keep **SA** through this and follow the tarmac track up, past the circular stone waymark and up to the junction by the grassy knoll and just below the steep climb towards the summit.

Go **SA** over the junction, still on the tarmac track, then bear **R** onto singletrack. Go past the lone tree and keep **L**, uphill, at the fork. Descend rapidly on the wide grass track, going around the head of a valley, around the hillside and then down to a junction. Keep sharp **R**, effectively treating the junction as a switchback and drop to a bench.

Turn **R** at the bench onto virtually hidden singletrack. Tackle three tricky rocky steps and then follow single-track through an awesome position. Ignore the first turning on the left and then turn **L** at a grassy area that effectively forms a singletrack crossroads.

At the main track, turn **L** and ride to St Ann's Well. Stop at the cafe or turn **L**, behind the building. Go **SA** at the junction and drop to the road.

Shortcut: Go **SA** across the top of the road and pick up a wide track. Follow this back to the car park.

Turn **L** onto a wide track. Climb over rocks to a junction with a good track and turn **R** to traverse the hillside. Follow the track until you reach the switchback climb you tackled at the beginning of the route (bench just beyond it). Drop onto this, around the corners and retrace your steps to the car park.

More riding

More of the Malverns
We've obviously tried to show you our favourite route around the Malverns, but that doesn't mean there's nothing more to find. Sadly, the close nature of the tracks on the hills here means it's impossible to describe further rides without full directions. Instead, try riding some of the descents off to the west, or exploring the southern end of the ridge. If you want an easy ride, without much climbing, you could park at Wyche Gap and ride straight along the ridge to the Beacon, perhaps with a quick loop on the terrace around North Hill thrown in for good measure.

Further Afield
You're quite close to some of the best riding in the Cotswolds (page 89). A quick run down the M5 to Cheltenham and you've got a choice between several great rides. Stay west of the motorway instead, and it's a similar distance to the Forest of Dean (below), with its rooty singletrack and short downhill runs. Failing that, head over to the Brecon Beacons or across to Mid Wales for a guaranteed good ride.

Forest of Dean
Although the Forest covers a massive area, relatively little of it is legally available to mountain bikers. While we're allowed to ride the wide, surfaced forest roads wherever we like, it's only in the Cannop Valley that we get free reign. But don't worry – with rooty singletrack, short downhill runs and a couple of great man-made loops – there's some brilliant riding tucked away. For your first visit, try the new Verderer's Trail. Graded blue, it's a short loop with a decent surface and a pump-track-esque finish. Next, try the Free Miner (FODCA as was) with its twisty turns and rooty gullies. It's on the short side, but well worth multiple laps. After that, you could either go singletrack hunting or head up the hill from the cafe to find the numerous downhill runs. With tight lines, rooty corners and a really nice dirty/loamy surface, the runs are rough and fast. They might be short, but they are a lot of fun.

More information: **www.fodmtb.com** » Bike Shop: **Pedalabikeaway Cycle Centre**
Start GR: **SO 608118** » SatNav: **GL16 7EH**

More information

Main Towns
Malvern has pretty much everything you need.

Maps
Harvey Maps 1:10,000 Malvern Hills, available from local shops. The extra detail comes in handy given the number of tracks around here (even the OS 1:25,000 on the previous pages isn't quite detailed enough). Just remember you'll be moving around the map a lot faster than usual!

Bike Shops
Back on Track, North Malvern Road, Malvern, 01684 565 777, www.backontrack-bikes.com (just down the hill from the start car park)

Bike Hire
Malvern Bike Hire, Malvern, 01684 572 445, www.malvernbikehire.co.uk

Accommodation
www.malverntrail.co.uk is a cycle-orientated site with plenty of links to accommodation. We'd look there first.

Berrow House (01531 635 845, www.berrowhouse.co.uk) over the hill in Ledbury has camping and bunkhouse facilities, and is worth a look.

Food & Drink
There are loads of places to eat in Malvern, from pubs to pizza restaurants.
The Nag's Head, Malvern, 01684 574 373, www.nagsheadmalvern.co.uk
The Wyche Inn, Malvern, 01684 575 396, www.thewycheinn.co.uk (accommodation)

Tourist Offices
Malvern, 01684 892 289, www.visitthemalverns.org

Outdoor Shops
Time Outdoors, 01684 899 144 in Malvern, and Harpers Bazaar, 01684 568 723 in Malvern Link.

Useful Websites
www.malverntrail.co.uk – lots of links for bike/outdoor shops, accommodation, food and so on
www.backontrack-bikes.com – the local shop has a few routes on their website
www.malvernhills.org.uk

Worth Knowing
You can get the train out to Malvern from Birmingham if you a) live there, and b) don't fancy the drive.

The Long Mynd

**As with most places in this book, the Long Mynd is within an Area of
Outstanding Natural Beauty. It's a seven mile-long ridge running north to
south through the Shropshire countryside, close to the border between England and Wales.**

At the foot of this ridge, you'll find Church Stretton – a busy little town full of tourists and pubs.
It has a long association with the textile industry, the remains and legacy of which can still be seen:
head out of town and up Carding Mill Valley (or ride down it – much more fun!) and you'll pass the
eponymous mill. Once buzzing with industry, it now buzzes with tourists. Climb higher, however,
and you instantly forget the bustle below. The open grass and moorland feel a lot wilder and more
isolated than you might expect. Fittingly, there's even an area called the 'Wild Moor', which doesn't
contain much other than a few wild ponies and a Ring Ouzel or two. Look west into Wales and there's
nothing but beautifully hilly countryside to be seen. Perfect for making a quick escape to some 'real'
countryside without having to travel too far. Did we mention that the riding's pretty good too?

The Riding

If you've heard of the Long Mynd, you've probably heard of Minton Batch – a two kilometre-long,
downhill run consisting almost entirely of singletrack. It's fast, with a smooth-ish dirt surface and
a lot of really nice corners. It's every bit as good as you might have heard and to visit the Long Mynd
without riding it would be like getting fish without chips. Silly.

Of course, that doesn't mean that the rest of the riding isn't any good – there's plenty more worth
seeking out. There's great singletrack at the northern end of the hills; fast and grassy descents drop off
the ridge towards Little Stretton and rocky descents range from the loose and slidey to the hard and
fast. (Carding Mill being a prime example of the latter, although you'll want to ride it mid-week, as it
can get VERY busy with walkers.) Atop the ridge, there are some great views – west is Wales, east is
England (how's that for alliteration?) and broad, dirt/stone based trails across open land from which to
admire them. (These easy top trails also allow quick transfers between descents.) Down at the bottom,
you're going to have to do a bit of road work to link trails – don't worry too much though, you won't
have to touch tarmac anywhere else.

When to go

Many of the trails on the Long Mynd are grass or dirt based, with a few stone tracks thrown in.
The area holds up reasonably well in wet weather – if you use the stone tracks like Carding Mill and
those off to the east of the ridge you'll get a decent ride in. The others, as usual, will be soggy, easily
eroded and nowhere near their best in the wet. Since these are the best trails here (in our opinion
at least), we'd pick a dry day out of choice. Oh, and watch your speed on descents like Carding Mill –
it's seriously popular with walkers.

Minton Batch. **Photo:** Benjamin Haworth.

13 Minton Batch Tour

A real tour of the Long Mynd, this, finishing with one of the best singletrack descents in the UK. What with the area essentially consisting of a high, steep-sided ridge, and this route nipping up and down one side of it, you can expect stiff climbs and steep descents. The start is gentle enough – and a lot of fun – a narrow and fast singletrack that contours north along the side of the ridge. A big climb follows, cresting the ridge for the first time and revealing surprisingly remote-feeling countryside. Admire the views, perhaps try the descent into Carding Mill Valley (fantastic fun unless it's busy, in which case it's rammed with walkers) and then cruise over to the descent we keep banging on about – Minton Batch. It's got just the right surface, the right gradient and the right number of twists. It's just *right*. From there, it's back uphill again via forest roads for a final, grassy descent, this time at warp speed, into Little Stretton.

Grade: **Red** » Distance: **30km** » Ascent: **810m** » Time: **3hrs+**			
Start/Finish: **Carding Mill car park** » Start GR: **SO 445944** » SatNav: **SY6 6JH**			
OS Map: **Explorer 217, The Long Mynd & Wenlock Edge** » Parking: **Free car park**			
Cafe: **Loads in Church Stretton** » Pub: **The Ragleth Inn, Little Stretton, T: 01694 722 711**			

Directions

S▶ Head downhill, back towards Church Stretton. How far you go depends on where you've parked – turn **L** up a singletrack bridleway climbing steeply through the heather.

Push uphill and follow singletrack behind the golf club building. Continue **SA** through a gate to a wider track. Keep **SA** behind the car park to a wide track junction.

Keep **SA** on wide track. Ignore turnings, then keep **SA** onto singletrack. Follow this around the hill to a gate. Turn **R** onto grass and drop to a lane. Go **SA** over this and climb on more singletrack. Stick with this to the road.

Turn **L** up the lane to a sharp right-hand bend. Turn **R** onto singletrack (marked as a footpath – it isn't) and climb steeply. Follow this uphill until you cross a shallow gully and join a wider track. Turn **R**, then trend **L** onto open ground onto a vague grassy track.

Follow this uphill, keeping left at junctions and trending **L**, with the track becoming increasingly obvious. Go **SA** at the track junction by the large cairn, and continue to another junction of big tracks.

Optional Route – Carding Mill descent (quiet days only!) – turn **L** and drop over rocks and slabs to the road. Go through the buildings and turn **R** onto a narrow signposted bridleway climbing the hillside. Turn **R** at the road for a long climb. Keep **R** at the junction, re-joining the route midway through **point 2**.

2 Keep **SA** on a wide, well-surfaced track. Keep **SA** at junctions to the road. Go **SA** across this and continue along the track.

At the crossroads, keep **SA** to the road. Turn **R** (Optional Route rejoins) and ride for 2.5km to the entrance to the gliding club. Immediately before the entrance, turn **L** alongside the fence and then **R** onto a signed grassy bridleway (don't take the track running back parallel to the road).

Drop fast into the valley on superb singletrack. Keep **SA** past the farm at the bottom to the road.

Turn **R** and follow the lane to a crossroads. Turn **R** and keep **SA** as the road enters the forest. Stick to the main track, ignoring turnings, until you reach a long straight. Keep **SA** along this to a crossroads. Turn **R**. At the edge of the woods, go **SA** following bridleway markers to a wide, grassy track.

3 Turn **R**, then soon turn **L** following bridleway markers to skirt the gliding club. Rejoin the main track and keep **SA** to the road. Turn **R** on tarmac for 2km. Immediately opposite a small area of trees and a car park, turn **R** on a signed (permissive) bridleway. Follow the obvious grassy track along the wide ridge and drop steeply. Follow the track to the **R**, around the hillside and drop fast into the valley. Follow the track past the campsite to the road.

At the road junction, turn **L**. Turn **L** again on the main road and ride back to Church Stretton.

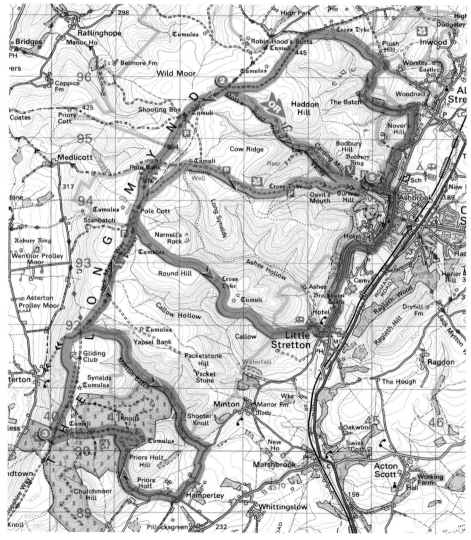

More riding

The Long Mynd & the Stiperstones

Starting and finishing on the Long Mynd, this ride heads over towards Wales on a mixture of rocky, rubbly and grassy trails (with the inevitable bit of tarmac thrown in). It's good riding in an XC kind of way, but skirts Eastridge Woods at the halfway point, allowing a little diversion onto the superb trails there if you fancy a more technical diversion. Heading back in isn't via the usual Minton Batch or Little Stretton descents, but instead follows a couple of great stretches of singletrack beneath Haddon Hill.

Grade: **Red** » Distance: **38km** » Ascent: **1,200m** » Time: **4hrs+**

Start/Finish: **Carding Mill, SO 449942** » OS Map: **Explorer 217 The Long Mynd; Explorer 216 Welshpool**

The Route » Carding Mill – Mott's Road – south at top to SO 420953 – Priory Cottage – Coates – Bridges – west to car park at SO 369976 – Gatten Plantation – SO 373999 – north to The Hollies – SJ 379021 near Snailbeach – east on forest road just inside Eastridge Woods – Vessons – Huglith Farm – Westcott Hill – road south to Stitt Farms – track and roads east to Robin Hood's Butts – east on track marked as footpath SO 451962 – The Batch – east to SO 455955 – unmarked (legal) singletrack south past Nover's Hill back to Carding Mill

Photo: Benjamin Haworth.

Haddon & Hope Bowdler Hills

Starting once again in Church Stretton, this figure-eight loop first heads east, exploring the little-ridden Hope Bowdler Hill via some steep climbs and open singletrack. That done, it heads back through town onto the tough climb up Carding Mill Valley before sweeping back down on fast grassy trails and steep singletrack. A hidden singletrack run lands you, grinning, back in Church Stretton.

Grade: **Red** » Distance: **19km** » Ascent: **670m** » Time: **2.5hrs+**

Start/Finish: **Carding Mill, SO 449942** » OS Map: **Explorer 217 The Long Mynd**

The Route » Carding Mill – east through town, across railway and A49 to Hazler and SO 467932 – north to Willstone Hill – south to Hope Bowdler – road west to SO 462924 (Hazler Hill) – west into Church Stretton – west through town to start – Carding Mill – Mott's Road – Robin Hood's Butts – east on track marked as footpath SO 451962 – The Batch – east to SO 455955 – unmarked (legal) singletrack south past Nover's Hill back to Carding Mill

Further Afield: Local(ish) woods – Hopton and Eastridge

Trail centres of sorts ... but not really. Excellent for natural, twisty, steep and techy riding. Eastridge has a marked red route along superb singletrack, but contains tons more than that: ex-national downhill runs, slippery rocks and awesome little steep bits – but nothing so hard that you shouldn't try it (you really should!). Brilliant fun.

Hopton, meanwhile, has long been a great destination for downhill riding, with loads of fast and rooty trails to go at. It's always had a couple of family and XC routes, but, if we're honest, they were a bit rubbish. Now, however, it's got a new red route, which is far from rubbish. It's nicely technical, with plenty of roots, rocks and lovely corners. Again, nothing too hard –just good fun. When you wipe the grin from your face, get over to Ludlow and thank Pearce Cycles who were behind it!

Eastridge
Start/Finish: **Up a minor road west of Habberley, south of Pontesbury** » Start GR: **SJ 392028** » SatNav: **SY5 0SQ**

Hopton Woods
Start/Finish: **Hidden up a track just west of Hopton Castle, near Craven Arms**

Start GR: **SO 348778** » SatNav: **Hopton Castle**

More information

Main Towns
Your only real option is Church Stretton – which is a decent size, having a supermarket, bike shops and a decent array of pubs and cafes.

Maps
OS Explorer 217 The Long Mynd & Wenlock Edge
OS Explorer 216 Welshpool & Montgomery

Bike Shops
Plush Hill Cycles, The Square, Church Stretton, 01694 720 133, www.plushhillcycles.co.uk
Blazing Bikes, Shropshire Hills MTB Centre, 01694 781 515, www.blazingbikes.co.uk
Pearce Cycles, Fishmore Road, Ludlow, 01584 879 288, www.pearcecycles.co.uk

Accommodation
You could do worse than stay at the Shropshire Hills MTB Centre in Marshbrook (01694 781 515, www.mtb-shropshire.co.uk) which not only offers camping, but also 'camping pods', a bike shop and wash and a cafe.

If you don't fancy that, there are a number of campsites around. There's a rather nice site in Little Stretton – The Small Batch Camp Site (01694 723 358, www.smallbatch-camping.co.uk) – which is right at the bottom of a nice long descent. Handy.

There's a YHA Hostel in All Stretton (01694 722 593), and another over the other side of the ridge in Ratlinghope (01588 650 656).

Otherwise, have a look at www.shropshiretourism.co.uk. They have lists of B&Bs, cottages, hotels and the like for various towns across Shropshire, including Church Stretton.

Food & Drink
There are plenty of cafes and restaurants in Church Stretton.
The Shropshire MTB centre in Marshbrook has a small cafe, 01694 781 515, www.mtb-shropshire.co.uk
The Ragleth Inn, Little Stretton, 01694 722 711, www.theraglethinn.co.uk
Yew Tree, All Stretton, 01694 722 228
Old Copper Malt House, Church Stretton, 01694 720 037 (Chinese restaurant on the side)
The Station Inn, Marshbrook, 01694 781 208, www.stationinnmarshbrook.co.uk

Tourist Offices
Church Stretton, 01694 723 133, www.shropshiretourism.co.uk » **Carding Mill National Trust**, 01694 723 068, cardingmill@nationaltrust.org.uk

Outdoor Shops
The Outdoor Depot, Church Stretton, 01695 724 293, www.theoutdoordepot.co.uk

Useful Websites
www.shropshiretourism.co.uk » **www.shropshirecycling.co.uk**

Guidebooks
Wales Mountain Biking – Beicio Mynydd Cymru, written by Tom Hutton, published by Vertebrate Publishing

Worth Knowing
The two local bike shops, Plush Cycles and Blazing Bikes, along with Saracen, Shropshire Council and various other local organisations, have put together a handy trail map/guide. You can see it online on the shop websites, or buy it for a quid in the shops.

Carding Mill. **Photo:** Benjamin Haworth.

The Peak District

There are two distinct and very different sides to the Peak District – the Dark (north) and the White (south). If we were to create some sort of Dr Jekyll/Mr Hyde analogy here, then the green and overgrown White Peak, with its serene woodlands, pretty limestone valleys and quaint villages would play Dr Jekyll. The Dark Peak, in keeping with its name, would be Mr Hyde; its wild and bleak moors, desolate peat bogs and moody gritstone crags creating about as great a contrast with its southern alter ego as you can get.

The two halves of the Peak are named after the rock types found there. In the north, it's Millstone Grit – a rough, hard sandstone. You can spot it everywhere – bordering fields in dry stone walls, built into houses and in the craggy edges that dot the horizons. Its slow erosion into sand gives the uniquely gritty surface of many of the tracks in the area. This same rock sits under the moors, where its solid nature means that water is unable to drain away, leaving constantly wet areas of peat bog. This dark gritstone creates, defines and names the northern half of the Peak District.

The White Peak is named for its pale limestone – and again, this local rock that gives the area its character. It's affected much more by water than grit, with water corroding and cutting into it, creating deep fissures, valleys and underground caves. As a result, the ground is less waterlogged (not that you'd believe it, churning through the sticky mud in winter!), more useable and habitable – hence the greater proliferation of villages and farms.

The Riding

The Peak is hilly. This is both good news – lots of descents – and bad – just as much climbing. As the hills tend to be steep, but relatively short, most rides go up and down a fair few times – your legs will know you've been for a ride!

Dark Peak locals are lucky. They've got a load of the UK's most sought-after trails on their doorsteps. Almost universally rocky, the riding is definitely on the technical side. Line choice is often paramount – although, as the bridleways around here are often fairly wide and straight, the hang-on-and-hope approach usually proves equally effective. It's suggested that there aren't many corners in the Peak District, and to an extent, that's true – there's not a huge amount of twisty singletrack to be found. However, what there is is sublime and as you don't come to the Peak to ride smooth singletrack, it's hardly a big deal.

White Peak riding couldn't be more different. It's Kent on steroids. The scenery is trees, fields and rolling hills rather than moors and rocky outcrops, and the bridleways are grass or dirt, rather than sand and rock. In general, the riding is less technical, but you can expect twisting woodland singletrack, high-speed rubbly descents and roots and tight corners to make things interesting. And when you do encounter rocks, watch out – they'll be limestone and thus approximately one million times more slippery than glass.

When to go

The rate at which the gritty, sandy muck wears away your drivetrain and brake pads in wet weather is pretty scary, but that's more or less the only reason not to ride in the Dark Peak year round. A few tracks do suffer badly (Cut Gate, Whinstone Lee Tor) in winter or in prolonged spells of bad weather and shouldn't really be ridden, but there's always something stonier and more erosion-resistant to ride. The White Peak is best left for summer. The sticky mud and slippery limestone means you'll struggle in the wet and probably end up on your arse. Also bear in mind just how busy the Peak gets in summer ...

Jon Barton and Tom Fenton riding Cut Gate. **Photo**: John Coefield.

14 *This is Ladybower – Dark Peak*

There are two real hotspots for Dark Peak riding – around the Hope Valley and around Ladybower. It's in these two areas that the majority of the Peak's 'classic' trails lie. Starting from Ladybower, this route tackles the steep slabby climb and swoopy descent of Whinstone Lee Tor, shows off the Peak District in all its finery from the top of Hope Brink and then fires down a choice of fantastic rocky tooth-looseners. Hagg Farm, a great descent in its own right, appears here as a 'just cleanable' climb, while the final rattle from Lockerbrook to Ladybower is one of our favourite in the Peak.

The Beast is one of the most talked about and notorious descents around. Rocky right from the start, it's gritstone boulder followed by gritstone step followed by gritstone boulder followed by ... there's barely a smooth metre on it! If, however, you prefer slightly speedier descents, take *Potato Alley* via Blackley Hey (the climb's easier too). If we're honest, we take this option nine times out of ten, as it's faster and longer, but it's your choice!

Note: *While this route is a brilliant introduction to the Peak, it isn't the most all-weather route around – Whinstone Lee Tor suffers particularly badly in the wet. Best ridden in dry weather.*

Grade: **Red** » Distance: **26km/24km** » Ascent: **720m** » Time: **3hrs+**	
Start/Finish: **Fairholmes, Ladybower Reservoir** » Start GR: **SK 172893** » SatNav: **S33 0AQ**	
OS Map: **OL1 The Peak District Dark Peak Area**	
Parking: **Pay and Display at Fairholmes, or free car parks on the access road**	
Cafe: **Fairholmes Cafe, T: 01433 650 953** » Pub: **Ladybower Inn, T: 01433 651 936**	

Directions

S► From Fairholmes car park, make your way back to the entrance roundabout turn **R** to follow a narrow road through a gate and beneath the dam to the other side of the reservoir. Keep **SA** along the road, riding south.

After 2.25km, at a gate blocking the road, turn **L** through a narrower gate into a field and onto a flagstone bridleway signed *Footpath Derwent Edge*. Climb increasingly steeply(!) to the buildings and follow the bridleway between them. Cross the stream and a technical climb leads through gates to a track T-junction just after a wall. Turn **R**. At the top of climb, bear **L** gently downhill for a fast and peaty descent.

Easy to miss – after almost 2km, shortly after the riding becomes technical and rocky, turn **R** onto a flatter bridleway. (If you reach the road, don't worry – it was fun, wasn't it! Just climb back up about 100m to find the track.) Follow this, through gates, downhill to the road by the pub and turn **R**.

2 At the traffic lights, turn **L**. There's a cyclepath on the right-hand side of the road. Ride to the dam and turn **R** through a gate to cross this. On the far side, turn **L**. After 250m, bear **R** off tarmac and onto a wide permissive bridleway. At the road, turn **R** uphill to Thornhill village.

Turn **R** immediately after the telephone box. Follow the road into the village of Aston and, after two steep dips, turn sharp **R** up a narrow lane signed *Win Hill and Hope Cross*.

Turn **L** onto a bridleway as the road ends. Ignoring turnings, climb steadily to the top of the ridge. Turn **L** along the grassy track at the top and descend along the ridge, bearing **L** at vague junctions, to join a wide track (the Roman Road). If you get lost, chances are you stayed too high – look **L** and downhill for the wide track in question.

3 Climb through gates to the bridleway junction at Hope Cross.*

Go **SA** at the junction. Follow the track around the side of the hill and onto a fast and rocky descent. Turn **R** upon reaching tarmac. At the main road, go **SA**, past a farm and climb to a track after woodland junction. Turn **L**.

*Optional descent – *The Beast*: Turn **R** and descend with 'interest'. Keep **L** round the hairpin at bottom (don't go **SA** through the gate), then bear **R** across the bridge. At the road, go **SA** towards Hagg Farm. Go **SA** through the gate onto a rocky and technical climb. Keep **SA** at the top.

Follow the obvious track first down and then over the top of the hill and into woods for a fast and rocky descent to the road. Turn **R** to return to Fairholmes.

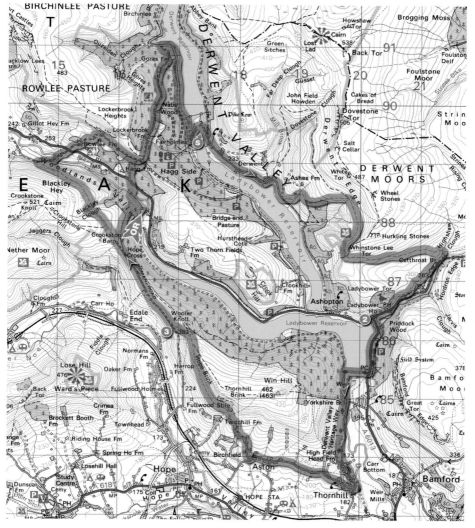

15 Jacob's Ladder

A UK classic that everyone disagrees about. Clockwise or anti-clockwise? Technical climbs or steep descents?

Tom (writing) prefers anti-clockwise. He likes longer descents and tricky climbs. He starts on the most notorious climb around – Jacob's Ladder. True, he usually pushes, but maybe one day … The following descent is a long tooth-rattler, Roych Clough has a two-kilometre, flat-out descent around loose corners and, after a great climb onto Rushup Edge, there's a twisty drop down Greenlands to finish.

John (editing) likes clockwise. He's a fan of steep downs and longer, but more rideable ups. Get up to Rushup Edge easily, enjoy the rock steps and then drop into Roych Clough. It's a gradual, rubbley climb back out, as is the Ladder, while the front is incredibly steep at the top, fast in the middle and boulder-filled at the bottom – a great finale.

At the time of Tom's writing, he's clearly right, so the route goes anti-clockwise. If you're more like John, sorry, you'll need to ignore the directions and use the map to reverse the route, which is pretty easy. You'll be pleased to hear that they both agree the drop to Hayfield is fantastic.

Grade: **Red/Black** » Distance: **24km** » Ascent: **750m** » Time: **3hrs+**			
Start/Finish: **Main Edale car park** » Start GR: **SK 124852** » SatNav: **Edale**			
OS Map: **OL1 The Peak District Dark Peak Area** » Parking: **Pay & Display in Edale**			
Cafe: **Penny Pot Cafe (by the station), T: 01433 670 293** » Pub: **Cheshire Cheese, Hope, T: 01433 620 381**			

Directions

S Turn **R** out of the car park and along the road. After just over 1km, follow the road left, across a bridge and then immediately turn **R** towards *Barber Booth*.

Head up the lane until it ends. Keep **SA** through the buildings and gates and continue in the same direction as the track turns to dirt.

Climb gently through more gates, trying not to look at the steep hillside ahead (you're going straight up it!). Go through a gate, cross the ford (or bridge) and immediately turn **L** through a narrow gate.

Time for the most notorious climb in the country. Keep to the main track and keep climbing for as long as you can – sadly there's a cruel sting in the tail that usually defeats even the most valiant of efforts. Keep **L**, in the narrow gully, just after cresting the top.

Follow the main track over the top of the climb, up a short rise and then past Edale Cross, ignoring all turnings. Rattle downhill for a couple of kilometres, keeping **SA** and continuing to descend when you meet tarmac.

2 At the bottom of the valley, bear **L** through a gate.

Short Cut: Climb steeply, then turn sharp **L** onto a wide track. Climb to a gate and go **SA** through this. Follow obvious singletrack to a wide track. Turn **L**.

Climb steeply, then fork **L** up a rocky track to a gate. Go through this and **SA** onto a fantastic singletrack descent. At the bottom continue **SA** along the lane.

For a cafe/shop break, turn **R** at the T-junction and drop into Hayfield. Otherwise, turn **L** climbing steeply out of the village and take the second bridleway on the **L** – a narrow track, continuing to climb. Keep **SA** as this meets a wide track. Climb uphill, eventually bearing **L** through double gates.

Climb uphill around Mount Famine and then begin the fast and loose descent to Roych Clough. Ford the stream, tackle the steep climb out and keep following the track to a gate by the Rushup Edge road.

DO NOT go though the gate on to the road. Turn **L** through a narrow gate and follow singletrack to another gate and wider track. Keep **SA** up this (away from the road) for a technical (and just cleanable) climb onto Rushup Edge.

3 Go through the gate at the top of the climb. Keep **SA** at the junction after 100m. After a further 700m, turn **R** through a narrow gate in the wall. Go into the field and turn **L**. Follow the track through gates, across fields and onto a better track. Descend to the road.

Turn **L**. Ride over Mam Nick and descend for 50m before turning **R** through a gate by a bus stop. Keep **L** and ride down a wide track to another gate. Go through the gate and onto the swoopy Greenlands descent. As you reach the lane, move onto the tarmac and follow it to a T-junction with the main road. Turn **R** to Edale.

Note: Shortly before going to print, the Chapel Gate descent was resurfaced. It probably did need some attention, but one of the most technical descents in the Peak (and the classic finish to the anti-clockwise loop) vanished in the process.

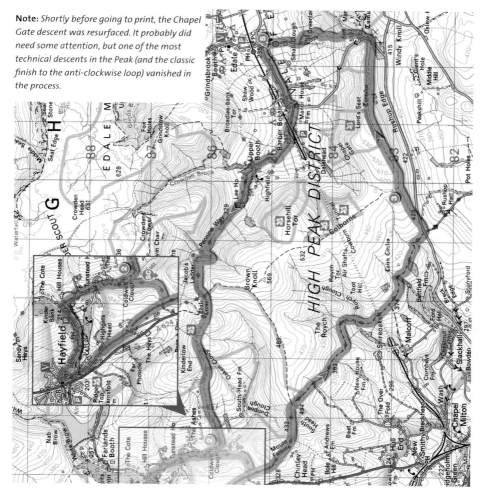

16 *Five Dales – White Peak*

Starting in Bakewell and tracing a big loop through the heart of the White Peak, this is a great introduction to the area. The trails are typical for the White Peak: a tricky limestone descent (to Youlgreave), fast-running singletrack through the woods (Darley Dale, Manners Wood) and a couple of fast, rubbly blasts (from Birchover and down towards Chatsworth).

As is often the case around here, it's a very XC route – not particularly technical (with the exception of the aforementioned descent and a tough climb out of Darley Dale, but lots of fun and with plenty to see. Equally White Peak-esque is the 'filler' – field edge runs through green and pleasant countryside, stretches of old railway line and a couple of short spins along the road – and, in true southern Peak style, it's all best ridden in the dry, as it gets a little squelchy and slow-rolling in the wet. A really satisfying cross country loop and the White Peak in a nutshell.

Grade: **Black** » Distance: **36km** » Ascent: **810m** » Time: **4hrs+**

Start/Finish: **Old Railway Station, Bakewell** » Start GR: **SK 222690** » SatNav: **Bakewell**

OS Map: **OL24 The Peak District White Peak Area** » Parking: **Pay & Display at start, lots more choice**

Cafe: **Lots of good ones in Bakewell!** » Pub: **Queen's Arms, Bakewell, T: 01629 814 586**

Directions

S▶ Turn **R** along the Monsal Trail from Bakewell (accessed from the old station at the top of Station Road). At the road, turn **L**, then immediately **R** along a wide track/bridleway.

Ride until the main track is signed ahead as *Private*, then turn **R** into fields, following bridleway signs. Drop towards the river and turn **L**, following bridleway markers.

Turn **R** at the lane and **L** on the main road. Just before Haddon Hall car park, turn **R** through a gate on a grassy bridleway. Follow this through gates and along field edges to farm buildings. Go **SA** through a narrow gate and bear left to the trees. Go through a narrow gate and follow the obvious track down a technical descent. Cross the bridge and ride to the road. Turn **L**.

At the junction near the church, go **SA** across the main road onto Bradford Road. Drop downhill, keeping **L** at the fork. Just before the road bends right, bear **L** onto a narrow, signed bridleway. Turn **L** at the bottom.

Follow the track uphill to a track junction near a caravan site. Turn **L**. Just after the second house, bear **R** across a field past rickety old caravans. Go through a gate and cross a second field.

Cross the road into another field. Cross this and go through a gate. Drop to the river, clamber to the road and turn **R**. Take the next lane **L**, towards Birchover.

2 Just after the village shop, turn **R**.

Keep **SA** as road turns to track and turn **L** at the farm buildings. Wiggle between the buildings to a fast, rubbly descent. At the end, take the lane downhill, turning **R** at the road to Darley Dale.

Turn **L** at the junction, cross the river and turn **L** 300m after the bridge. Ride to the main road and turn **R**, then quickly **L**. Climb steadily, ignore three turnings to the right and then take the fourth – a narrow lane 100m before the road turns left and begins to descend.

Follow this lane, turning **R** onto a bridleway just before the corner. Climb through the woods and, as you reach their far edge, turn **L**.

Fun singletrack traverse through the woods. Go **SA** through the gates and continue to the road. Turn **L** and descend around hairpins. Just after the house, turn **R** onto a wide track.

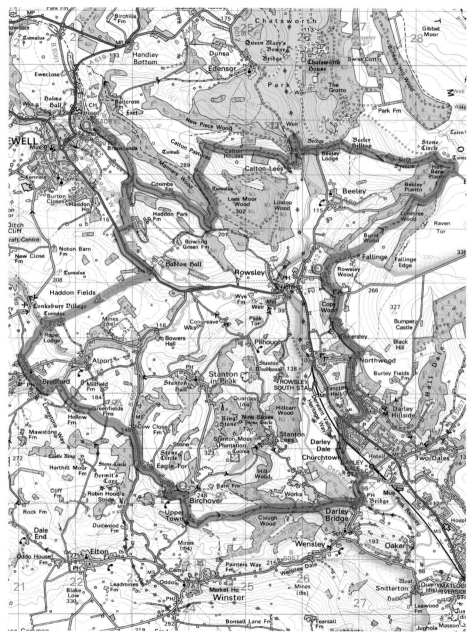

③ Easy to miss: Follow the wide track for about 200m before turning **L** onto a signed singletrack bridleway that drops into the trees. Follow this, crossing a bridge and then turning **R** uphill to a gate.

Go through the gate and uphill to farm buildings. Turn **L** through the 'yard' and follow the track to the road. Turn **R** and climb steeply uphill for 1km.

As the road bends right, turn **L** through a small parking area to a wide track. Follow this downhill to the road and turn **R**. Cross the small bridge and follow the road right before turning sharp **L** to a car park. Ignoring turnings, stay on the track running below the car park and then around to the right. Climb gently and zigzag up through houses to a gate. Turn **L** beyond this and climb singletrack until it ends.

Turn **L** through the gate and into fields. Climb a short distance before bearing **L** off the main track onto vague grassy singletrack. This peters out immediately – continue in the same direction to a gate into the woods.

Go through the gate and follow the track around **L**. Twist and turn through the woods before dropping downhill. Keep **L** at first junction, and then fork **R** at the next on to a fast descent. Turn **R** at the wide track.

Ride through a farm. Just after passing under a railway bridge turn **R** to rejoin the Monsal Trail and return to Bakewell.

More riding

Cut Gate – Dark Peak

Cut Gate is unquestionably one of the UK's best trails. The southern end is steep – almost unrideable in ascent but seriously good fun on the way down while the northern end is something special. Whereas most Dark Peak trails are relatively short rocky tests, this is almost seven kilometres of fast, flowing singletrack. Swoopy and peaty, narrow and rocky, flat out and eye-watering – it's everything you could ever want from a descent. Even the sections that have been repaired and surfaced by the National Park have left narrow and winding singletrack. It's superb.

Note: *Keep clear in the wet. It turns into a boggy mess.*

Grade: **Red** » Distance: **28km there and back (shorten if necessary)** » Ascent: **760m** » Time: **3hrs+**
Start/Finish: **SK 172893** » OS Map: **OL1 The Peak District Dark Peak Area**

The Route » Fairholmes – track north on eastern side of reservoirs – Slippery Stones – Cranberry Clough – Mickleden Edge – Langsett – and back again!

Castleton – Dark Peak

A ride for those who love technical descents (and don't mind a, ahem, 'small' amount of climbing to reach them). Once you've made the initial climb up the old broken road (tarmac drops!), the route shoots out in a series of loops. It's all a bit convoluted and contrived, but it's got several fast, fun and rocky reasons for being so. Greenlands is a fast, twisty and multi-line rut from top to bottom. The drop from Hollins Cross to Castleton starts in grassy ruts, hits some singletrack, negotiates a superb off-camber corner and then drops through a really technical gully between stone walls. Bash back up the broken road for the toothy chaos of Cave Dale (or the faster and more amenable Pindale!). A personal favourite.

Note: *The directions in bold (opposite) are included in the hope that Chapel Gate will one day return to its former rocky glory. Ignore these sections until then. See the note on Jacob's Ladder for more information (page 119).*

Grade: **Black** » Distance: **20km** » Ascent: **560m** » Time: **2.5hrs+**
Start/Finish: **SK 150829** » OS Map: **OL1 The Peak District Dark Peak Area**

The Route » Castleton – Blue John Cavern – SK 124834 (Mam Nick) – **Rushup Edge – Chapel Gate – road to SK 125835 (Mam Nick again)** – Greenlands – Hollins Cross – south-east to Hollowford Road – Castleton – Blue John Cavern (Broken Road again) – Oxlow House – Limestone Way – Cave Dale – Castleton (**Pindale option:** Oxlow House – Dirtlow Rake – Pin Dale)

Bakewell Blast

A fast spin through the heart of the Peak. Leave the puddings and tarts for later and tackle a tough climb and flying singletrack descent out of Bakewell. Spin along the Monsal Trail, follow the road through pretty Great Longstone and then nip along the narrow track from Hassop. Another steep climb leads to a flying descent to Edensor and Chatsworth before a gravel track heaves you up to the top of the final woodland drop home.

Grade: **Red** » Distance: **23km** » Ascent: **550m** » Time: **1.5hrs+**
Start/Finish: **Bakewell Old Railway Station, SK 222690** » Map: **OL24 The Peak District – White Peak Area**

The Route » Bakewell Old Station – roads through village to Holme Hall – north to Monsal Trail – west to Thornbridge Hall – road east to Hassop – bridleway to Pilsley – south on road – west to Edensor – Calton Lees – Calton Pastures – Manners Wood – Bakewell

Ashover – White Peak

One of our favourite White Peak night rides, this is a brilliant little loop. Lots (and lots) of singletrack, fast and narrow descents and two just-about-cleanable-if-you're-lucky climbs – one of which is short enough to allow repeat attempts. Perfect corners, the odd rock to keep things interesting and a tricky little bridge over a river. A couple of hours' worth of fun if you're riding fast.

Grade: **Red** » Distance: **11km** » Ascent: **300m** » Time: **1.5hrs+**
Start/Finish: **Ashover, SK 349633** » OS Map: **OL24 The Peak District White Peak Area**

The Route » Ashover – south-west to SK 346625 – south to SK 352617 – Cocking Tor – Blakelow Hill – road to Amber Hill – road to Vernon Lane Farm – Kelstedge – Ashover

Linacre North – White Peak

With great singletrack descents and tough climbs linked by easy cruises, this is a good fun, but not overly technical ride. Typically White Peak in feel, it's definitely at its best in summer when the leaves are out and the trails dry and fast. That's when the descents from Wigley, down Johnnygate Lane and out of Cartledge are at their best – speedy, twisty and full of fun.

Grade: **Red** » Distance: **23km** » Ascent: **550m** » Time: **2.5hrs+**
Start/Finish: **Linacre Reservoirs car park, SK 334729** » OS Map: **OL24 The Peak District White Peak Area**

The Route » Linacre Reservoirs – Old Brampton – Westwick Farm – Frith Hall – Wigley – Grange Hill – Grange Lamb Farm – Johnnygate Lane – Millthorpe – SK 315774 – Cartledge – Barlow Lees – Barlow – Cutthorpe – Linacre

More information

Getting About

The Dark Peak has a superb train service running through the Hope Valley. Bike-friendly, there are stations in virtually every village between Sheffield and Manchester – making linear routes particularly easy: www.thetrainline.com

Main Towns

In the Dark Peak, the main towns are Hathersage, Hope and Castleton (and in roughly that order). All have the usual tourist shops, and virtually every village has a half-decent pub. For outdoor shops, head to Hathersage. For bike shops, Hope. For anything else, it's time to brave Sheffield's totally uncoordinated traffic light system or the traffic jams through Glossop.

In the White Peak, Bakewell is the most central town, with good food, puddings and outdoor shops. Buxton and Matlock are bigger if you need anything else.

Maps

OS OL1 The Peak District Dark Peak Area
OS OL24 The Peak District White Peak Area

Bike Shops

18 Bikes, off the main road in Hope, 01433 621 111, www.18bikes.co.uk
Bike Garage, High Peak Garden Centre, Bamford, 01433 659 345, www.bikegarage.co.uk
Sett Valley Cycles, Union Road, New Mills, 01633 742 629, www.settvalleycycles.co.uk
High Peak Cycles, Glossop, 01457 861 535, www.highpeakcycles.co.uk
The Bike Factory, Beech Road, Whaley Bridge, 01663 735 020, www.ukbikefactory.com
Stanley Fearns, Bakewell Road, Matlock, 01629 582 089, www.stanleyfearns.co.uk
Mark Anthony, Spring Gardens, Buxton, 01298 22 002, www.activesport.co.uk
The Bike Tree, Abbeydale Road, Sheffield, 0114 236 5858, www.thebiketree.co.uk
JE James, Bramall Lane, Sheffield, 0114 292 3102, www.jejamescycles.co.uk (also a branch in Chesterfield)
Langsett Cycles, Infirmary Road, Sheffield, 0114 234 8191, www.langsettcycles.co.uk
Over Ride Cycleworks, Shalesmoor, Sheffield, 0114 272 8518, www.over-ride.co.uk

Bike Hire

Derwent Cycle Hire, Fairholmes, Ladybower, 01433 651 261
Alive Bike Hire, Castleton Road, Hope, 07538 892 065, www.alivebikehire.co.uk
Bike Garage, High Peak Garden Centre, Bamford, 01433 659 345, www.bikegarage.co.uk

Accommodation

You're spoilt for choice when looking for somewhere to stay in the Peak. Not only is there accommodation everywhere, but there are at least two comprehensive sites for finding it: www.peakdistrictonline.co.uk and www.visitpeakdistrict.com.

Camping first. In the Dark Peak there's a great little campsite at North Lees (01433 650 838) under Stanage Edge. If you want to ride from your tent, there are good two sites in Edale – Fieldhead (01433 670 386, www.fieldhead-campsite.co.uk) and Upper Booth Farm (01433 670 250, www.upperboothcamping.co.uk). Failing that, join the masses with their caravans on one of them.

There are several sites in the in the centre of the White Peak, near Bakewell – try Lathkill Dale (01629 813 521, www.lathkilldalecampsite.co.uk) or Greenhills Holiday Park (01629 813 052, www.greenhillsholidaypark.co.uk). There's also Park Head Campsite near Monsal Head, 01629 640 463.

There are Youth Hostels throughout the Hope Valley in the Dark Peak (Castleton, Hathersage, Edale) and several in the White Peak (of which Eyam, Bretton and Youlgreave are probably best positioned for riding). See www.yha.org.uk for more info. There are plenty of bunkhouses around for groups – there's a YHA one in Edale, and Thorpe Farm Bunkhouses near Hathersage are good (01433 650 659, www.thorpe-bunk.co.uk).

If you want something more upmarket, there are B&B's everywhere. You're best off looking for places in the Hope Valley/Bakewell if you want to ride from the door in the Dark/White Peak respectively. Alternatively, although set away from the main Peak, Millbrook B&B near Holmfirth is very bike-friendly (01226 766 267, www.millbrook-bb.co.uk). More centrally, there's the Woodbine Cafe and B&B in Hope (07778 113 882, www.woodbine-hope.co.uk). See the general websites suggested above for more options.

Stanage Plantation. **Photo**: John Coefield.

Food & Drink

Woodbine Cafe, Hope, 07778 113 882, www.woodbine-hope.co.uk (accommodation)

Outside Cafe, Hathersage, 01433 651 936, www.outside.co.uk

Bakewell – try one of the many, many 'original' Bakewell pudding/tart shops

The Old Nag's Head, Edale, 01433 670 291, www.the-old-nags-head.co.uk

The Cheshire Cheese Inn, Hope, 01433 620 381, www.thecheshirecheeseinn.co.uk (accommodation)

The Yorkshire Bridge, Ladybower Reservoir, 01433 651 361, www.yorkshire-bridge.co.uk (accommodation)

The Ladybower Inn, Ladybower, 01433 651 241, www.ladybower-inn.co.uk (accommodation)

Old Poet's Corner, Ashover, 01246 590 888, www.oldpoets.co.uk (real ale, good for the Ashover loop)

The Barrel Inn, Bretton, 01433 630 856, www.thebarrelinn.co.uk (accommodation)

Crispin, Great Longstone, 01629 640 237, www.thecrispingreatlongstone.co.uk

Monsal Head Hotel, Monsal Head, 01629 640 250, www.monsalhead.com (amazing location, accommodation)

The Grouse Inn, Froggatt, 01433 630 423 (nice no fuss food)

Tourist Offices

Shared website: www.peakdistrict.gov.uk

Edale, 01433 670 207, edale@peakdistrict.gov.uk » **Castleton**, 01629 816 572, castleton@peakdistrict.gov.uk
Bakewell, 01629 816 558, bakewell@peakdistrict.gov.uk » **Fairholmes (Derwent)**, 01433 650 953,
derwentinfo@hotmail.co.uk

Outdoor Shops

Hathersage is your best bet in the Dark Peak – try Outside (01433 651 936) although there are also lots of smaller shops in Hope and Castleton, or between the two – Hitch and Hike (01433 651 013) in the High Peak Garden Centre. In the White Peak, Bakewell has a range of shops, including Cotswold Outdoor (01629 812 231). Matlock and Buxton both have plenty of choices.

Useful Websites

www.peakdistrictonline.co.uk – good for accommodation
www.peakdistrict.gov.uk – official website of the Peak District National Park Authority
www.visitpeakdistrict.com – official tourism website for the Peak District and Derbyshire
www.ridesheffield.org.uk – MTB trail advocacy group for Sheffield/eastern Peak

Guidebooks

Peak District Mountain Biking Dark Peak Trails, written by Jon Barton, published by Vertebrate Publishing
White Peak Mountain Biking The Pure Trails, written by Jon Barton, published by Vertebrate Publishing

Worth Knowing

While the Dark Peak is rideable in any weather, try and stay away from peaty trails like Cut Gate and Whinstone Lee Tor if it's wet. They'll thank you for it.

Cut Gate. **Photo**: John Coefield.

Calderdale & the South Pennines

They weren't kidding about those Dark Satanic Mills. The South Pennines (we're going to focus on Calderdale) are a bit of an in-your-face reminder of the UK's industrial heritage – a deep and steep valley with a canal cutting the length of it.

There are brick mill buildings and chimneys on the valley bottom (but not a whole lot of sunlight) and rows of terraced houses crammed onto the sides above – everywhere you look, signs of the area's textile-producing past loom large. And then, right in the middle, is the hippy town of Hebden Bridge. Art shops, poetry readings and wholemeal bread … not really sure what it's doing in the middle of Calderdale, but everyone seems happy enough. Alongside the jazz-playing didgeridooists are increasingly large numbers of mountain bikers, making the most of the stone-slabbed packhorse trails across the moors and the steep, technical descents into the valleys. And when two bike companies, a couple of MTB skills coaches and one major magazine (*Singletrack*, who helped us with this section of the book – thanks!) have chosen to base themselves here, you know something's right.

The Riding

Calderdale's great in that it's got a little bit of everything. (Or nearly everything – if you want forest singletrack, you're out of luck.) There are big, broad moorland tracks. There's fast peaty singletrack (when it's dry). There are stone-slabbed packhorse trails which, when taken at speed, are guaranteed to rattle your teeth loose. And, if you've been keeping up to date with your Internet riding videos, you'll know that there is an abundance of steep, rocky and incredibly technical drops and climbs to play on. You can stay 'local', sticking roughly to the confines of one valley – racking up any number of incredibly steep metres of ascent and playing on descents. Or you can get out over the hills, racking up miles and exploring the hilltops and moorsides before dropping into new and unexplored vales. Whatever you choose, it's all good, rocky fun.

When to go

You can ride in Calderdale all year round – if you're careful. Stay on the stonier tracks (i.e. not High Brown Knoll or the Permissive Bridleway to Cant Clough) unless it's frozen out. Obviously, there's nothing stopping you tackling the sloppy bits – just consider your impact on the trails and marvel at what the gritty gloop does to your drivetrain.

Pennine Bridleway near Gorple. **Photo:** John Coefield.

17 Widdop & Rodwell End

Virtually everybody you speak to will have ridden this route – or a variant of it – on their first visit to Calderdale. It's the classic 'intro to the area' and is, as you might expect, a bit of a corker. There's a pleasant cruise along the canal towpath to get you warmed up. There's a steady, but enjoyable climb out of the valley – a rare beast around here. There are a few sweet little sections of singletrack, sadly marred by an over-abundance of gates, and there's a flat-out rocky highway down to Gorple Reservoir. And that's not even halfway! Things get much more interesting on the climb from Widdop. It's a classic: steady to begin with, but steepening and loosening just where you don't want it to. Then there's a nice fast cruise and, if it's dry, a superb permissive singletrack – sweeping across the moor and tracking a stream down to Cant Clough Reservoir, it's fast, technical and great fun. A quick spin through nice scenery and a stretch on the road leads to the return leg above Todmorden. This starts fast, narrows a bit, speeds up again and then dives down a flagstone packhorse trail. Once your eyeballs have stopped rattling around, there's more narrow and straight-ahead fast singletrack and then ... a choice. Keep left for singletrack and an oh-so-steep (and correspondingly fast) plummet to the road (which is brilliant) or go right for the classic rocky, hairpinned and cliff-edge zigzags down to the car park (even more brilliant). A great ride.

Grade: **Red** » Distance: **33km** » Ascent: **800m** » Time: **: 3.5hrs+**
Start/Finish: **Rodwell End picnic area just east of Todmorden** » Start GR: **SD 956247**
SatNav: **Eastwood (or Todmorden)** » OS Map: **OL21 South Pennines** » Parking: **Rodwell End free car park**
Cafe: **Loads in Hebden Bridge** » Pub: **Stubbing Wharf, on the A646, 01422 844 107, www.stubbingwharf.com**

Directions

S Turn **L** on the main road, then **R** on a lane signed *Mankinholes* and *Lumbutts*. Follow the road right, then nip **L** onto the canal towpath just before the bridge.

Follow this, crossing the canal as necessary, for 2km, to the Stubbing Wharf. Turn **L** off the towpath, and then **R** on the main road.

After 200m, turn **L** up *Church Lane*. Climb steeply and, as the road bends left, keep **SA** on a wide bridleway signed *Jack Bridge*. Keep **L** (uphill) at the fork. At the road turn **L**, then keep **SA** on a wide bridleway as the road bends left.

Immediately upon reaching buildings, turn **R** on to a grassy bridleway. Follow this through fields, following *Pennine Bridleway* signs. Continue **SA** onto, and then off, a short stretch of tarmac and drop through woods to a lane. Turn **R**.

At the T-junction, turn **L**, following the Pennine Bridleway. Continue onto a track as the lane ends and drop to Gorple Reservoir. Turn **L** after the gate and follow the track around the reservoir. Keep **SA** on the other side and ride to the road.

2 Turn **L**. At Widdop Reservoir dam, turn **L** across the dam, still on the Pennine BW, and follow the track around the reservoir and up a tough climb. Stick with the track as it gradually descends across the moor. *

* Optional wet weather route: Keep **SA** on the wide track. Descend for 1.5km and turn **L** onto a wide track, following Pennine BW markers. Ride alongside the reservoir and keep **L**, uphill, at the end of the water. Climb over to Cant Clough Reservoir and turn **R** through a gate as you reach a track T-junction.

Easy to miss: Pass through a gate and continue to descend. The track bends sharply left and makes a short climb to a right hand bend. Turn **L** here onto vague grassy singletrack opposite a stile. Follow this down the side of a small valley, cross the moor to the river and follow this to the reservoir.

Go through a gate and follow a wide track **R** around the reservoir, keeping **SA** through a gate (wet weather route rejoins here).

Turn **L** across the dam, following Pennine BW signs. Once across the dam, follow the track **R** and continue to the road.

③ Turn **L** for 3km before turning **R** on a lane dropping to Shore. Descend a short way and then turn **L** on a wide, signed bridleway. Keep **L** on singletrack past the house.

Follow the bridleway **SA** across the hillside, ignoring turnings, eventually descending flagstones to tarmac. Turn **R**, descend a short way and go **SA** up a narrow bridleway climb. Ignore a bridleway descending to the right and continue **SA** to the golf club.

Follow the access lane to the road and turn **R**. Shortly afterwards, turn **L** past the church. Ride out of the houses and then turn **R** on singletrack immediately after a house (the amazingly-named Bean Hole Head). Follow this to a lane and turn **R**.

At the houses, you have a choice:

a) SA past the church-like building and descend fast and steep. (Great fun.) Turn **R** under the bridge and then **R** on the main road.

b) Turn **R**. As you enter the buildings, turn sharp **L** onto an unlikely and unsigned bridleway. Drop via rock steps, switchbacks and cliff edges (techy fun!) to the car park.

Rodwell End. **Photo**: John Coefield.

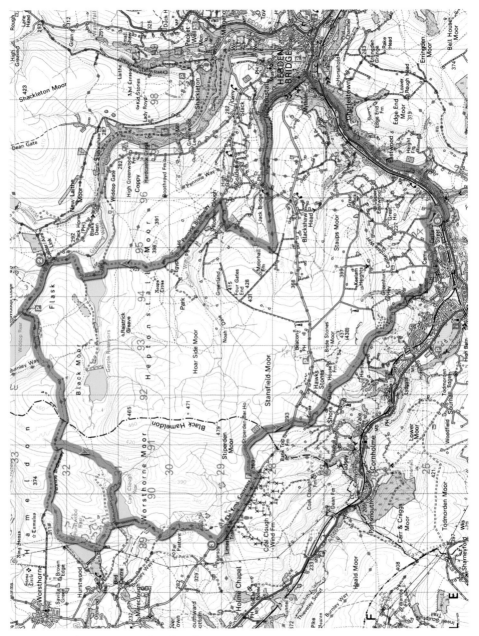

More riding

High Brown Pecket Well

An easy start leads to a choice – fast, fun and rideable, or techy down and even worse up? Swoopy peaty singletrack over High Brown Knoll and a steep, technical and improbably-long plunge from Pecket Well to finish. A nice little run.

Grade: **Red** » Distance: **18km** » Ascent: **440m** » Time: **2.5hrs+**

Start/Finish: **National Trust car park, SD 988292** » OS Map: **OL21 South Pennines**

The Route » Car park at SD 988292 – N and then W to Walshaw – E to SD 989313 – (OPTION: down and up via waterfall [Lumb Falls]) – SD 995324 – Small Shaw – High Brown Knoll – SE 019289 – Dimmin Dale – SE 004298 – Pecket Well – car park (via either descent – we prefer the northern one)

Ogden & Oxen

A lot of permissive stuff on this one – always a good thing in more ways than one. A moorland start, a pleasant road cruise and then a bit of grassy singletrack. Good start. A steep descent onto fast and often splashy singletrack, more moorland weaving and then a tough climb to the finale – a fast, sandy and multi-lined flyer back to the reservoir. Another great ride.

Grade: **Red** » Distance: **18km** » Ascent: **: 440m** » Time: **2.5hrs+**

Start/Finish: **Ogden Reservoir, SE 066309** » OS Map: **OL21 South Pennines**

The Route » Ogden Reservoir – east on permissive BW to SE 045306 – road N to SE 030329 – west on unmarked trail around Sunny Bank – road S to Cock Hill – Roms Greave – Lane Head – Bodkin – unmarked track to Low Fold and then Upper Town – Oxenhope – Upwood Farm – Black Moor – Lane Bottom – Thornton Moor Reservoir – Ogden Reservoir

Whirlow Common. **Photo**: John Coefield.

The Trail Centre

Lee Quarry & Cragg Quarry

A trail centre oddity, Lee and Cragg Quarries don't go near any trees. Rather obviously, they're set in a couple of quarries linked by a two-kilometre stretch of trail. Both feature red routes (Cragg's is a little easier and more flowing), with an emphasis on skill development. Being quarries, you can expect predominantly rocky trails, slabs and obstacles, with black graded sections here and there. There's also a pump track, a few downhill style sections and a load of trials and easier obstacles. Good fun.

Trail Count: **Lee Quarry: Red, 6km; Black, 2km** » **Cragg Quarry: Red, 4.5km**
Start: **Near Bacup, SD 866211**

Cragg Quarry. **Photo:** John Coefield.

More information

Main Towns

Todmorden and Hebden Bridge, the latter being the better, in terms of shops.

Maps

OS OL21 South Pennines Burnley, Hebden Bridge, Keighley & Todmorden

Bike Shops

Blazing Saddles, on the main road in Hebden Bridge, 01422 844 435, www.blazingsaddles.co.uk

Ride-On, Bacup Rd, Rawtenstall, 01706 831 101, www.rideon.co.uk

Accommodation

There are YHA hostels in Mankinholes (above Todmorden) and over the hill in Haworth. www.yha.org.uk www.visitcalderdale.com and www.hebdenbridge.co.uk both have sections on accommodation and are as good a place to start a search as any.

There's not a great deal in the way of camping that we know of, sorry.

Food & Drink

Stubbing Wharf, on the A646, 01422 844 107, www.stubbingwharf.com

The Staff of Life Inn, Todmorden, 01706 819 033, www.staffoflifeinn.org.uk, offers accommodation

The Packhorse, Widdop, 01422 842 803, www.thepackhorse.org, offers accommodation

Tourist Offices

Hebden Bridge, 01422 843 831, hebdenbridge@ytbtic.co.uk

Todmorden, 01706 818 181, todmorden@ytbtic.co.uk

Outdoor Shops

You should be able to pick up the basics in Hebden Bridge.

Useful Websites

www.visitcalderdale.com – tourist information, including accommodation

www.hebdenbridge.co.uk – local news and information

www.singletrackworld.com – *Singletrack* Magazine

Guidebooks

West Yorkshire Mountain Biking – South Pennine Trails, written by Benjamin Haworth, published by Vertebrate Publishing

Worth Knowing

Todmorden and Hebden are both on the train line between Manchester and Leeds (although they're a little far from the latter). Perfect for a car-less day's riding.

The North York Moors

Drive east across the north of England and the North York Moors rise out of the surrounding countryside like a wall, before stretching across to the North Sea in one giant, peaty plateau. There aren't any particularly notable peaks or hills, but the plateau is cut through with deep valleys, so there are plenty of steep hillsides and features to keep things interesting.

And interesting it most certainly is – that peat, when dry, creates lovely smooth, dry and hollow-sounding trails. These ride fast, with beautifully swoopy turns and multiple line choices. The local sandstone litters the area with rounded, gritty boulders and rocks, which add character to the trails. In some cases, they dominate, leaving hard, rubbly riding. In others, they simply add easily swooped-around or hopped obstacles. Of course, we should remember that all this has formed as the bogs dry out – it doesn't take much rain to re-soak the ground.

The Riding

I have a love/hate relationship with riding in the North York Moors. The singletrack here is possibly the finest moorland singletrack in the country. Fast running, rumbling peaty trails that swoop around smooth corners and over peaty hummocks between rounded boulders. Fast, free and easy – singletrack rarely gets better. And that's a problem, because once you've ridden even the smallest stretch of it, it's all you want to ride. You want more, but you can't have it – because the (legal) singletrack here is almost invariably spread out and it's hard to fit more than a handful of sections into an average ride. Instead, you're stuck with 'linking' trails. That's not to say that these are bad: wide, stone-based tracks that are rideable in all weathers, they are actually rather good. They offer easy riding on which to relax and enjoy the superb scenery. But I'm greedy and as a product of today's trail centre world of instant gratification, all I want is more of that fantastic singletrack. Now.

When to go

The Moors don't fare well in wet weather. At all. The entire area acts like a giant sponge, soaking up and holding on to any water that comes its way. That's not to say you can't ride in the wet – there are plenty of predominantly stone-based trails, it's just that the bridleways are less fun and more easily eroded than in summer. Luckily, the trails dry relatively quickly, so you don't have to wait too long after rain to get the best from the area, and you can always go to Dalby if it tips it down.

Glaisdale Moor. **Photo:** John Coefield.

18 Danby Fryup

Is Fryup the most technical descent in the North York Moors? You'll find out soon enough. It's certainly the best named. Out of Danby, the route starts with a warm up – a bit of field-edge riding and a lot of (windswept) road. Great views though. When you reach Danby High Moor, things really pick up. A couple of great, peaty stretches of singletrack carry you up towards the brilliant old railway line around Rosedale Head. To begin with, this isn't particularly promising, but soon narrows into tight, sweeping singletrack on a nice hard, speed-conducive surface. A few rocky steps and a grassy slither finish things off nicely. A good tough climb leads back up to the moors and moor (boom, boom, tish) singletrack. Narrow flagstones pave the way (photo previous page), interspersed with stretches of rumbling peat here and there. And then … Fryup. One of the best views and hardest descents here. Tight turns and rocky steps are mixed with a really scary gradient – saddles down and brakes on! Things soon ease, and it's fast riding on grassy trails all the way out of the valley. Last and definitely not least is Danby Rigg. Push up the steep climb and stretching in front of you is a one of the best trails in the UK. Fast rolling, smooth and sweeping with just the right amount of rocks and gullys to pump, hop and dodge, it's a great finale.

Grade: **Red/Black** » Distance: **33km** » Ascent: **720m** » Time: **3hrs+**
Start/Finish: **Danby** » Start GR: **NZ 708084** » SatNav: **Danby**
OS Map: **OL26 NYM Western Area; OL27 NYM Eastern Area** » Parking: **Lots in Danby**
Cafe: **Farmhouse Fodder Tea Garden, en route at Dale Head Farm, T: 01751 417 353**
Pub: **Lion Inn, en route at Blakey Ridge, T: 01751 417 320**

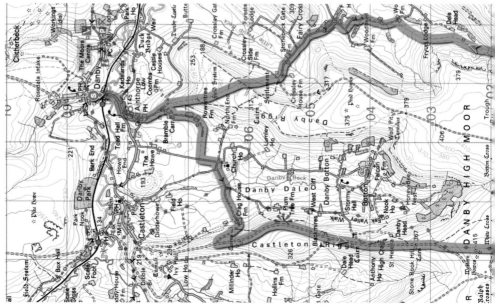

Directions

⑤▶ From the centre of Danby, head south towards the railway station and Castleton. Follow the main road away from the houses and into the village of Ainthorpe. Take the second **L** (Brook Lane) and follow this uphill.

Turn **R** onto a wide tarmac track by tennis courts and follow the track away from the buildings. Turn **R** through the farm and go through fields to the road.

Turn **L** and then take the first **R** down a narrow lane. Ignoring turnings, climb steeply uphill through a gate to the main road. Turn **L**.

Four kilometres of tarmac follow. Sorry. After 3km, pass a lane on the left. 1km after this, continue **SA** onto a signed (low metal sign) singletrack bridleway as the road bends right.

Follow uphill singletrack until it flattens and reaches the road. Go **SA** onto more peaty singletrack, which descends and then climbs to the road. Turn **L**.

② 700 metres after the Lion Inn, turn **L** onto a wide gravel track. Drop downhill a short way to a crossroads and turn **L** onto the old railway line. Follow this as it gradually narrows, eventually becoming a superb section of singletrack as it rounds the head of the valley.

As you round a sweeping left hand bend (trees ahead and to the right of you), turn **R** as a bridleway crosses the track. Slip and slide down to the farm, turn **L** onto the access track immediately after the buildings and then keep **SA** along the lane.

After 2km, turn **L** up a wide bridleway just as you reach terraced houses. Climb past the farm buildings and turn **R** onto a grassy track immediately after a gate. The track becomes vague in places, but essentially just keep **SA** and climbing and you'll reach the road.

③ Turn **L**. Stick to the road for 1.5km, ignoring a wide turning on the right, until you reach a 'crossroads' formed with a narrow singletrack bridleway.

Turn **R** onto a narrow signed bridleway which switches between singletrack and packhorse flagstones. Keep **SA** over a crossroads and continue to a T-junction. Go **R** for a few metres and then **L** onto a vague trail. Drop your saddle(!) and plunge on to the most technical descent on the moors.

At the bottom, follow the grassy trail out of the valley. Keep **L** and cross the stream at a grassy clearing and then continue **SA** to the road.

Turn **L**, and then **L** again at the T-junction. Climb steeply and then descend gently to a second junction and go **SA** (slightly **R**) onto an obvious track. Climb steeply uphill (the last few metres are a carry) and then cross Danby Rigg on one of the finest and swoopiest trails anywhere. Keep **SA** onto grass through the gate and drop to the road.

Turn **L** and follow the road downhill into Danby.

More riding

Goathland & Fylingdales

This was almost our main North York Moors route. A relaxing cruise for much of the way, it allows you to check out the views, revel in the beautiful surroundings and generally chill out. A couple of faster bits and short singletrack sections keep the technical interest up, with the 'drop off the edge of the world' towards Levisham Station being particularly memorable. But it's the final section of this ride that makes it great. The final four or so kilometres across Two Howes Rigg are along some of the finest, swoopiest and best pieces of moorland singletrack you'll find anywhere. Superb. **Note**: *This definitely isn't one for wet weather – it gets really boggy!*

Grade: **Red** » Distance: **36km** » Ascent: **600m** » Time: **3.5hrs+**
Start/Finish: **Goathland, NZ 832012** » OS Map: **OL27 NYM Eastern Area**

The Route » Goathland – Mill Moor – NZ 852028 – east to Stony Leas – South around Worm Sike Rigg to Whinny Nab (SE 866949) – Hole of Horcum – Levisham Moor – Levisham Station via SE 821918 – north through the woods via Wardle Rigg to SE 824962 – Simon Howe Rigg – Two Howes Rigg, taking west fork – Goathland

Urra Moor

A good, fun figure-eight route in the middle of nowhere. There's classic fast, peaty and swoopy North York Moors singletrack and there are long, easy cruises – perfect for admiring the views and for reliving the singletrack sections with your mates. There's a fast and foot-out loose descent on a hair-pinned shooter's track, a superbly tight-turned moorland singletrack and, on the start and finish 'straight', a narrow, stone-slab singletrack. The latter may well prove slightly out of reach on the way up, but it's a guaranteed tooth-loosener on the way down.

Grade: **Red/Black** » Distance: **33km** » Ascent: **760m** » Time: **3hrs+**
Start/Finish: **Clay Bank viewpoint, NZ 572035** » OS Map: **OL26 NYM Western Area**

The Route » Clay Bank – road south to NZ 572033 – Urra Moor – Bloworth Crossing – Ouse Gill Head – West Gill Head – West Gill – road near Low Mill – north to Monket House – Ouse Gill Head – Cockayne – SE 609963 – Slape Wrath Moor – East Bank Plantation – Bridleway north around Urra Moor via NZ 581021 – Clay Bank

The Trail Centre

Dalby Forest

As England's largest trail centre, Dalby Forest has riding for pretty much everybody. The red route is one of the longest of the grade anywhere. With no real hills to speak of, major climbs and descents are limited, but the incredibly varied singletrack more than makes up for this. There are tight sections, twisty sections, fast sections and flowing sections. The old black trail is great fun, mixing great man-made sections with more natural feeling riding. And then there's the World Cup course with its smattering of black-graded obstacles and drops. All are worth riding.

Trail Count: **Ellerburn Trail, 4km, Green** » **Adderstone, 12.4km, Green** » **Blue Route, 13km, Blue** » **Red Route, 35km, Red** » **Black Route, 10km, Black** » **World Cup Course, 6km, Black** » **Skills/jump area**
Start: **Dalby Forest Drive, near Pickering, SE 857873** » SatNav: **YO18 7LT**

Fryup Edge. **Photo**: Tony Harker/John Coefield Collection.

More information

Main Towns
Pickering (south), Guisborough (north), Whitby and Scarborough (east coast). If you're really stuck, try Middlesbrough, but expect to get lost and stuck in traffic.

Maps
OS OL26 North York Moors Western Area
OS OL27 North York Moors Eastern Area

Bike Shops
Bike Scene, Park Lane, Guisborough, 01287 610 735, www.bikescene.co.uk
Bike Traks, High Street, Great Ayton, 01642 724 444, www.biketraks.com
Big Bear Bikes, on the main road in Pickering, 01751 474 220, www.bigbearbikes.co.uk
Purple Mountain, Dalby Forest Visitor Centre, 01751 460 011, www.purplemountain.co.uk

Bike Hire
Purple Mountain, Dalby Forest Visitor Centre, 01751 460 011, www.purplemountain.co.uk

Accommodation
There are YHA hostels in Osmotherley (west), Helmsley and near Pickering (south). See www.yha.org.uk for details. There's an independent hostel near Pickering that's great for groups (High Mill, 01751 477 113, www.highmillpickering.co.uk) and a very well located hostel right in the centre of things in Glaisdale (Bank House Farm Hostel, 01947 897 297, www.bankhousefarmhostel.co.uk).

Surprisingly, there aren't too many campsites (lots for caravans though). There's a very basic but nice site in Glaisdale – Hollins Farm, 01947 897 516

Try www.yorkshire.com for everything else!

Food & Drink
Cafes
There are cafes in every village. These are a few of our favourites:
Molly's Tearoom and Store, Rosedale Abbey, 01751 417 468
Forge Tea Shop, Hutton-le-Hole, 01751 417 444
Stonehouse Bakery, Danby, 01287 660 006
Goathland Tearooms, Goathland, 01947 896 446
Pubs
Duke of Wellington, Danby, 01287 660 351, www.dukeofwellingtondanby.co.uk, offers accommodation
Blacksmith's Arms, Lastingham, 01751 417 247, www.blacksmithslastingham.co.uk
Horseshoe Inn, Levisham, 01751 460 240, www.horseshoelevisham.co.uk, offers accommodation
The New Inn, Cropton, 01751 417 330, www.newinncropton.co.uk, offers accommodation

Tourist Offices
The NYM National Park Centre in Danby, 01439 772 737, www.northyorkmoors.org.uk » **Sutton Bank National Park Centre**, 01845 597 426, www.northyorkmoors.org.uk » **Pickering, 01751 473 791**

Useful Websites
www.northyorkmoors.org.uk
www.muddybums.org.uk – great local site

Guidebooks
North York Moors Mountain Biking – Moorland Trails, written by Tony Harker, published by Vertebrate
Publishing

Rosedale Head. **Photo**: John Coefield.

The Yorkshire Dales

The various Yorkshire Dales are impressive places to visit no matter what your preferred activity. They are, to put in simply, one of the most beautiful areas of the country. The landscape is stunning, predominantly consisting of huge rounded and open hillsides which arc from valley to valley, but vary subtly from dale to dale.

Yet it's the features and eccentricities that really mark the place in your memory. Dry-stone walls cling to the hillsides at impossible angles, crazy pavements of jagged limestone coat the hilltops and waterfalls plunge into chasmic limestone gorges and down smooth-slabbed streambeds. When you're done gawping, award-winning breweries and cheese factories await in twee, character-filled villages. 'More cheese, Grommit?'

The Riding

The Yorkshire Dales cover a massive area, so there's a lot of riding around. If you'll forgive the huge generalisations, here's a (very) simple breakdown: in the south, around Malham, you can expect a lot of broad, straightforward trails bounded by dry-stone walls. The trails are relatively fast and the miles slip by easily. In the west, it's a little more technical, with plenty of slippery limestone sections and good riding on interesting trails. More centrally, you can expect grassy trails, hillside crossings and a fair few broad, but rather rocky, trails. It's good stuff and, with villages spaced out, rather wild. Moving east towards Nidderdale and gritstone country, you'll find sandier trails, moorland crossings and some looser, rockier riding. Up north, towards Swaledale, the riding is more technical. There are still plenty of well-surfaced tracks and trails, a fair bit of fast grassy riding and some superb rocky descents and climbs – we like Swaledale a lot.

When to go

With plenty of stone-based tracks, you'll always find something rideable in the Dales. Watch out though – there's a lot of limestone up here, so it's going to get slick. That said, you do need to pick your route carefully, as rides often cross boggy or exposed ground. Equally, don't forget where you are – there may be plenty of villages about, but you can still find yourself in the wrong valley with a lot of high ground between you and home.

Fremington Edge. **Photo**: John Coefield.

19 Swaledale – Fremington Edge

This is a good ride. How could it not be? It's the best ride in the best dale in the Dales. There's a big, tantalisingly-close-to-being-doable climb (Fremington), a stunning grassy and rocky descent through old quarry workings (Fremington again) and a long downhill singletrack over grassy moorland (off Reeth High Moor). Then there's the usual breathtaking Dales scenery (everywhere) and a superb cafe at the finish (the Dales Bike Centre) – there's not much more you could really want from a ride! Or is there?

Maybe it wasn't long enough. Maybe you fancied crossing a desolate moonscape, tackling one of the most technical and rocky descents in Yorkshire and then enjoying a fast cruise across the hilltops. Well, by happy coincidence, the extension contains all of these things. (Although you do sacrifice a fantastic singletrack descent ... Tough call.)

Note: *the ride starts from the Dales Bike Centre, where, apart from the superb cafe and accommodation, there are showers, a bike wash and a bike shop. They also offer guided rides. And if all that seems like a bit of a plug, it is, because they've always been very friendly and helpful when we've visited.*

Grade: **Red/Black** » Distance: **31km/40km** » Ascent: **800/1,200m** » Time: **3hrs+ / 5hrs+**	
Start/Finish: **Dales Bike Centre, Fremington** » Start GR: **SE 046988** » SatNav: **DL11 6AW**	
OS Map: **OL30 Yorkshire Dales: Northern & Central Areas** » Parking: **Dales Bike Centre**	
Cafe: **Dales Bike Centre, T: 01748 884 908** » Pub: **Buck Hotel, Reeth, T: 01748 884 210, www.buckhotel.co.uk**	

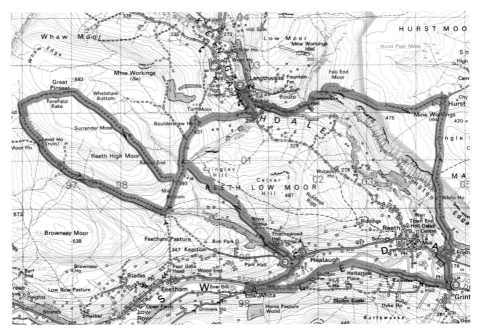

Directions

S Turn **L** out of the Dales Bike Centre and follow the road around the corner before turning **R** up a narrow lane signed *High Fremington*. At the T-junction, turn **L** and keep climbing.

Keep **SA** through the gate as road turns to track and attempt to clean the rocky climb beyond. Go through the gate at the top and follow the wide track down to Hurst.

Turn **L** at the houses, go through the gate and climb the wide track. At the top, keep **SA** onto a narrow trail as the main track swings right.

Drop to a gate in the stone wall and then follow a grassy track, which becomes more and more obvious before swinging sharply back on itself and dropping through the old quarry on a stunning descent.

At the bottom turn **R** in front of the house on a wide track. Ignoring turnings, follow this around the hillside to Langthwaite.

2 At the road, turn **L**. Turn **L** again on the main road. After 600m turn **R** on to a gravel track opposite a house (just after antique petrol pumps).

Follow the track past houses and keep **SA** across the fields when the track swings left through the wall. Climb grass and bog to the farm and the road.

At the road, turn **L**. Ignore a bridleway on the right, cross a ford and then turn **R** up a wide track. Follow this to the top of Great Pinseat and then, bearing slightly **L**, stick with the now vague track as it drops to the river.*

Keep **SA** through gates and ignoring turnings to ride fast out along the valley past old mine workings. Keep **R** at the fork.

At the road turn **L**. Splash through the ford again and, immediately after the steep climb beyond, turn **R** through a gate onto a stony track. After 100m, turn **R** onto singletrack.

Keep **SA** as a grassy track joins from the right (stone wall now on your left) and drop to a house. Go **SA** over the house access track and continue to descend, (a wall now on your right). Stick to the track, hugging the wall as it bends **R** around a grassy area and then go through a gate into the woods. Keep **L**, join a track and ride to a lane.

3 Turn **L**. At the main road, turn **R**. After a kilometre, turn **L** over a bridge, then immediately **L** again. Climb uphill for further than you think you should, passing a building and a footpath on the left, before turning **L** onto a signed bridleway. Drop through gates and fields towards the river and some nice stretches of singletrack.

Upon entering a field, bear **R** (finger post sign) and join a good track. As the track swings left to a bridge, keep **SA** through gates, to eventually join the road. Turn **L** and then keep **SA** at the main road to return to the Dales Bike Centre.

*Optional Extension via Gunnerside Gill – see introduction: Sadly, we've not got room for full directions.

The Route » Head west over Melbecks Moor to NY 946014 – drop steeply due west into Gunnerside Gill (NY 940012) – Winterings – Barf End – footpath (WALK!) south east to SD 963983 – west to Gunnerside – Hag Wood – east along river to Low Houses – climb to SD 990975 – road south to SD 982964 – north and east around Gibbon Hill to Harkerside Moor – descend Grinton Gill to Grinton – road to Dales Bike Centre

20 *Tour of Pen-y-ghent*

A great tour around Pen-y-ghent in the centre of the Dales. Impressive views all around, nicely varied riding and the impressive Hull Pot (a big hole in the ground to look at just off route) make this one of our favourites. Starting in Horton in Ribblesdale, the route climbs away from the houses in typical Yorkshire Dales style – on a wide, stone-based track hemmed in by high dry-stone walls. It's a decent climb, which soon gives way to grassy trails as the gradient eases. After a quick stop to admire Hull Pot and a touch of tricky route finding, the ride gets going again across open moorland. The track here has been resurfaced, creating a wide, fast singletrack across what would otherwise be deep and tussocky bog. More grassy singletrack and a slippery descent drop into Littondale. A quick spin along the valley bottom and the return leg begins with another good climb up a stone track. Once up, it's time for the final descent to Horton. Still on stone tracks, this is an eye-watering, flat-out descent on wide and straight trails. All good fun!

Grade: **Red** » Distance: **27km** » Ascent: **600m** » Time: **2.5hrs+**
Start/Finish: **Horton in Ribblesdale** » Start GR: **SD 809720** » SatNav: **Horton in Ribblesdale**
OS Map: **OL2 Yorkshire Dales: Southern & Western Areas; OL30 Yorkshire Dales: Northern & Central Areas**
Parking: **Car park in Horton** » Cafe: **Pen-y-ghent Cafe, Horton, T: 01729 860 333**
Pub: **The Game Cock, Austwick, T: 01524 251 226, www.gamecockinn.co.uk**

Directions

S With your back to the church, head **R** along the main road through Horton in Ribblesdale (away from the sharp bend in the road). Follow this for around 300m, passing a car park on the left and then turn **R** up a wide signposted bridleway between the houses.

Follow this uphill away from the houses and out onto open moorland. As the good track ends at a stone wall, ignore the Pennine Way on the right (footpath) and continue **SA/L** on a vague grassy track.

Don't keep too literally straight ahead, or you'll fall into the massive and very impressive Hull Pot! Instead, after 200m, bear **R** onto a narrower and fainter grass track. (If you do reach Hull Pot, don't worry; it's well worth a look. Just turn around, bear **L** [now you're facing the other way!] and backtrack slightly to pick up faint singletrack and follow this through the stone wall.)

2 Stick to the track as it becomes more vague. Continue **SA** to reach a dry-stone wall with a good track in front of it. Go **SA** over the track to the top corner of the wall and continue **SA** on a vague grassy track (keeping the wall on your right). The track soon becomes much more obvious (it's been surfaced). Keep going through gates until the track turns back to grass. Keep **SA**, go through several stone walls and eventually merge with a better track. Keep going in the same direction, until at a stone wall, the track swings **L**, downhill. Follow it down through gates and fields to the farm. Ride through the farm and follow the track out to the road.

3 Continue along the road, ignoring a turning to the right just after some houses and then turn **R** over the SECOND of two stone-based tracks crossing the river (just under 3km after the houses).

After crossing the river, turn **R** on a wide track and climb to the road. Turn **L**. After 2km, as the road begins to drop, turn **R** past a house onto a wide track – signed as the *Pennine Way*. Follow the track past the house and then around to the left as the Pennine Way branches off rightwards. Stick with the track, descending fast and ignoring turnings. Keep **R** at the junction near the bottom and drop to the road.

Turn **R** and follow the road back to Horton in Ribblesdale.

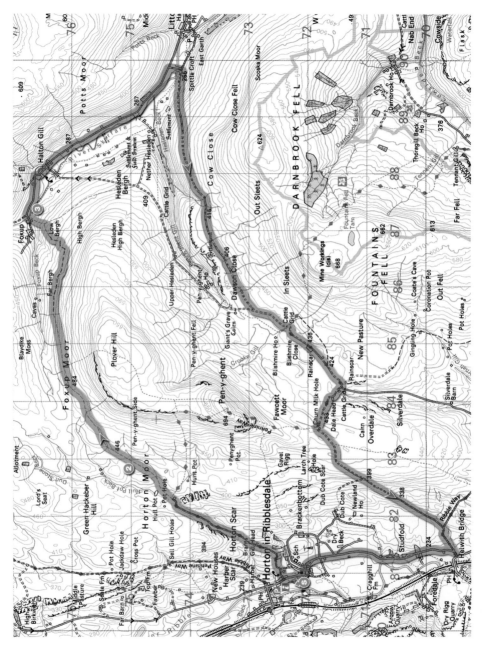

More riding

Malhamdale

This ride's for you if you just want to relax, pootle around and admire the view. It's not technically hard, and there's not too much climbing, but the surroundings are very pleasant indeed and the riding's nice and steady. The route heads out of Kilnsey on Mastiles Lane – a wide, well-surfaced track that we've seen described as one of the best in the Dales – and makes its way over towards Malham Tarn. The return leg is a little more technical. Grassy trails lead away from the tarn, splash through a couple of streams and then steepen as they swoop down alongside the impressive chasm of Cote Gill.

Grade: **Blue/Red** » Distance: **19km** » Ascent: **450m** » Time: **1.5hrs+**

Start/Finish: **Tennant Arms, Kilnsey, SD 974678** » OS Map: **OL2 Yorkshire Dales Southern & Western Areas**

The Route » Tennant Arms, Kilnsey – Mastiles Lane west over Kilnsey moor to the road near Malham Tarn – bridleway north-east to Cote Gill – Hawkswick Cote – Kilnsey

Ribblesdale

Lots of limestone, lots of crazy rock formations, a few pretty villages, bridge/ford choices and some fast descending. Starting in Settle, this ride explores the very western edge of the Dales, away from some of the more usual areas. It's a long route, but there's not too much climbing and tracing it out on a map should reveal a road splitting it through the middle if you can't hack the full thing.

Grade: **Red** » Distance: **37km** » Ascent: **800m** » Time: **4hrs+**

Start/Finish: **Settle, SD 820636** » OS Map: **OL2 Yorkshire Dales Southern & Western Areas**

The Route » Settle – NE to SD 838664 – Stainforth – NE to SD 833685 – Helwith Bridge – Horton in Ribblesdale – B6479 to SD 787746 – Long Scar – Trow Gill – Thwaite Plantation (SD 750694) – east to SD 769692 – north to SD 771706 – Wharfe – south to SD 779692 – Wood Ho – Feizor – Giggleswick Scar – Settle

Pen-y-ghent. **Photo**: John Coefield.

Wensleydale – Hawes & the Roman Road

Boasting a cheese factory and some cracking riding right in the middle of the Dales, there's no good reason not to visit Wensleydale. This route is a big, one up, one down affair and covers a fair distance. The ascent isn't particularly taxing, as there's not a huge height gain and the climb is (in true Dales style) mainly on well-surfaced tracks. The descent is similar, although the loose stone tracks now allow for a lot of high speed and sketchy fun!

Grade: **Red** » Distance: **30km** » Ascent: **520m** » Time: **2.5hrs+**

Start/Finish: **Hawes, SD 874898** » OS Map: **OL30 Yorkshire Dales: Northern & Central Areas; OL2 Yorkshire Dales Southern & Western Areas**

The Route » Hawes – minor roads north and then east to Bainbridge – SW onto the Roman Road over Wether Fell – Green Side – Kidhow – Dodd Fell – Ten End – Hawes

Nidderdale – Pateley Bridge to Appletreewick (and back)

Not overly technical, but covering a fair amount of ground via some fun descents and tough climbs, this is a great way to explore the south-east Dales. Highlights include the grassy gully descent to Appletreewick, the Craven Arms there and the old mine remains just west of Pateley Bridge – which give a lot of lines to play around and have fun on.

Note: *The Bike Livery behind the Craven Arms in Appletreewick makes a great spot from which to start rides. www.thebikelivery.com*

Grade: **Red** » Distance: **36km** » Ascent: **800m** » Time: **4hrs+**

Start/Finish: **Pateley Bridge, SE 159656** » OS Map: **OL2 Yorkshire Dales Southern & Western Areas; Explorer 298 Nidderdale**

The Route » Pateley Bridge – west to SE 156654 – north to Corn Close – west to Ashfold Side – Greenhow – road west over Craven Moor to SE 069630 – SW to SE 062621 – Kail Hill – Woodhouse – Appletreewick – Skyreholme – Eller Edge Nook – SE 128592 (near Bramley Head) – east to SE 141602 – north to SE 136611 – Benny Bent – Bewerley – Pateley Bridge

Mastiles Lane. **Photo**: John Coefield.

Fremington. **Photo**: John Coefield.

More information

Main Towns

Once you're in the Dales, there are villages everywhere. The large(r) places are all around the edge – Leyburn, Pateley Bridge, Skipton, Settle, Sedbergh.

Maps

OS OL2 Yorkshire Dales Southern & Western Areas
OS OL30 Yorkshire Dales Northern & Central Areas
OS Explorer 298 Nidderdale

Bike Shops

Dales Bike Centre, Fremington, 01748 884 908, www.dalesbikecentre.co.uk
3Peaks Cycles, Market Place, Settle, 01729 824 232, www.3peakscycles.com
Leyburn Bikes, Moor Road, Leyburn, 01969 623 565, www.leyburnbikes.co.uk
Dales Bike Doctor – mobile shop/repair service, 015242 73195, www.dalesbikedoctor.co.uk
There are several more in Skipton.

Bike Hire

Dales Bike Centre, Fremington, 01748 884 908, www.dalesbikecentre.co.uk

Accommodation

The ever-friendly and perfectly-located Dales Bike Centre in Fremington is always worth a visit.
Great accommodation, a 24-hour cafe (amazing cakes), bike shop and lots of helpful advice. 01748 884 908, www.dalesbikecentre.co.uk

www.mtbthedales.org.uk has a very good list of cycle-friendly accommodation of all types and is worth a look.

Also of note is the New Inn in Appletreewick (01756 720 252) – a decent pub offering accommodation, with the unique Bike Livery behind it offering workshop, bike storage and cleaning facilities.
See www.the-new-inn-appletreewick.com and www.thebikelivery.com

There are youth hostels in Ingleton, Malham, Kettlewell and Hawes if you want somewhere cheap and basic – www.yha.org.uk

There are a number of campsites in the Dales. Even a brief glance at an OS map should reveal several.

Food & Drink

Cafes

There are cafes around every corner. These are some particularly good ones:

Dales Bike Centre, Fremington, 01748 884 908, www.dalesbikecentre.co.uk

The Dalesman Cafe (roadie favourite – it's got to be good!), Gargrave, 01756 749 250

Pen-y-ghent Cafe, Horton-in-Ribblesdale, 01729 860 333

Pubs

New Inn, Appletreewick, 01756 720 252, www.the-new-inn-appletreewick.com offers accommodation

Station Inn, Ribblehead, 01524 241 274, www.thestationinn.net offers accommodation, camping, bunk barn

The Green Dragon, Hardraw, 01969 667 392, www.greendragonhardraw.com, offers accommodation

The King's Arms, Askrigg, 01969 650113, www.kingsarmsaskrigg.co.uk

Tan Hill Inn – the highest pub in Britain! Tan Hill near Reeth, 01833 628 246, www.tanhillinn.com, offers accommodation

Tourist Offices

There are National Park Centres (www.yorkshiredales.org.uk) at:

Aysgarth Falls, 01969 662 910, aysgarth@yorkshiredales.org.uk » **Grassington**, 01756 751 690, grassington@yorkshiredales.org.uk » **Hawes**, 01969 666 210, hawes@yorkshiredales.org.uk » **Malham**, 01729 833 200, malham@yorkshiredales.org.uk » **Reeth**, 01748 884 059, reeth@yorkshiredales.org.uk

Outdoor Shops

Lots dotted around. Try Inglesport in Ingleton, or head into Skipton for multiple options.

Useful Websites

www.mtbthedales.org.uk » **www.dalesbikecentre.co.uk** » **www.thebikelivery.com** – good for routes **www.cyclethedales.org.uk**

Guidebooks

Yorkshire Dales Mountain Biking – The North Dales, and *Yorkshire Dales Mountain Biking – The South Dales*, both written by Nick Cotton, published by Vertebrate Publishing

Mountain Biking in the Yorkshire Dales, written by Ian Boydon, published by Cicerone

Worth Knowing

The Bike Livery, 01756 720 319, www.thebikelivery.com

We didn't know where to put this – it's not a shop, or accommodation or even a cafe. But you can store, clean and wash bikes there. John Pitchers, the very friendly owner, also offers guided rides and general advice on the area.

The Howgills

Legendary walking guide writer Alfred Wainwright thought the Howgills
looked like a herd of sleeping elephants. With their bare, rounded foreheads
and smooth flanks, it's a good description. Although not overly high – Bram Rigg Top,
the highest point, rises to 672 metres – or expansive, the Howgills feel big and wild.

The hills seem to rise vertically and precipitously. There's no shelter other than prickly gorse bushes, and wind and rain frequently batter the area. It's the perfect spot for a wild day out. From the tops, you can see into both the Lake District and the Yorkshire Dales. (The Howgills are technically in Cumbria, but, lying east of the M6, feel more like Yorkshire – indeed, prior to 1974 they were part of the latter county.) Pick a fine day and the views, the riding and the scenery will come together to show why the Howgills are so highly regarded by mountain bikers. Pick a bad day and the steep hills, howling wind and lack of shelter will give you a day to 'build character'!

The Riding

The Howgills ride as they lie – halfway between the Dales and the Lakes. They look like the Dales – open and grassy – but don't have the wide, relatively easy trails often found in that area. Instead, there's plenty of singletrack and tricky rocky trails, just like the Lakes – but then they are less technical than anything there and don't really 'feel' like Lakeland riding. The defining feature of the area (and the trail everyone comes to ride) is undoubtedly the long singletrack run along the entire length of Bowderdale. Best ridden south to north, this seven-kilometre bridleway begins at the very top of the Howgills and then dives down over rocks and grass to swoop along above the river, stalling occasionally as it tackles tricky stream crossings and little rock gardens. Elsewhere, Howgill riding is generally pretty demanding. It's often tricky and the hills are big and steep. In addition, starting out along many of the bridleways means committing to a long ride. All this means that the area isn't particularly beginner-friendly. But, if you're fit and technically adept, it's up there with the best.

When to go

The Howgills have some lengthy bridleways (often with grassy and relatively soft surfaces), which run over high, open ground and deliver you to the middle of nowhere. Make of that what you will, and don't even think about tackling our main ride in high winds. It's no fun at all.

Bowderdale. **Photo**: John Coefield.

21 Howgills – Bowderdale Singletrack

Not only is this route long and technical, it's got a lot of steep climbing and, once you've dropped off the back of Bram Top Rigg and onto the Bowderdale singletrack (which is fantastic), you're in the middle of nowhere and pretty much committed to finishing the loop. But, don't worry about that — this is one of the UK's great rides and well worth the effort. From Sedbergh, the ride launches vertically upward at a particularly unpleasant angle on energy-sapping grass ... it might be best to give in early and save some energy. At the top, you'll want both a breather and a chance to admire the view, unless you picked a wild and windy day, in which case you'll want to scuttle off the tops as fast as possible! The highlight of the ride follows as rocky and technical singletrack (slippery when wet!), taking a steep line down into the valley below. It then drops, weaves and clambers along the hillside above the river, alternating fast-running and flowy sections with technical stream crossings. Brilliant fun. From there, road work, a possible pub stop and a long, drawn-out climb give way to a fun descent through some hobbit-sized trees and a great stretch of fast, gorse-lined singletrack that leads virtually all the way back to Sedbergh. Top notch.

Grade: **Black** » Distance: **38km** » Ascent: **980m** » Time: **5hrs+** » Start/Finish: **Sedbergh**
Start GR: **SD 657921** » SatNav: **Sedbergh** » OS Map: **OL19 Howgill Fells & Upper Eden Valley**
Parking: **Pay and display or on street in Sedbergh** » Cafe: **Fish and chips, tea rooms and others in Sedbergh**
Pub: **Black Swan, Ravenstonedale, T: 01539 623204; lots in Sedbergh**

Bowderdale. **Photo**: John Coefield.

Directions

S From the main Sedbergh car park, turn **L** and follow the one-way system round the town centre (**R** at the T-junction, then **R** again). Follow the main road around a sharp left-hand bend and turn **R** immediately after the *Dalesman*.

Follow the road for 600m, uphill and to the left. At a crossroads, turn **R** up a narrow lane signed *Permissive Path to the Fell*. Follow this to the farm, and go **SA** through a gate. Climb to a second gate and turn **L** immediately beyond.

Easy to miss: A short distance after the gate, bear **R** onto a narrow track running uphill.

Climb the increasingly obvious track to a grassy area and keep **R**. Follow the track trending **R**, uphill. Keep **SA** over a small rise and then **SA** over a grassy crossroads by a cairn.

Keep going as the gradient eases and traverse the side of the valley before climbing to a ridge. Turn **R** on the ridge (in effect **SA**). Bear **R** at two forks, following bridleway signs and passing close to the summit of Arant Haw. Drop rapidly, then climb to a gate and turn sharp **L** in front of it to climb steeply past the summit of Bram Rigg Top onto an obvious track to the summit of The Calf.

2 Bear **R** at the trig point, cross a grassy area, passing ponds to the right and left and pick up a rocky track dropping into Bowderdale.

Ride singletrack the length of the valley. Climb out and follow the wide track **R** and downhill to farm buildings. Turn **R** on the road, keep **L** at the junction and then turn **R** immediately in front of the underpass. Turn **R** after 200m.

As the road ends, turn **L** (looks like someone's drive). Go through the yard and the gate beyond, then ride across fields aiming for a barn and the river. Pass the barn, cross the river and keep **SA** on the road out of the nursery. Bear **L** at the farmhouse.

After 1km, keep **R** and follow the lane downhill. Take the next **R**, through a gate and keep **L** into a field. Pass **L** of the barn and climb steeply between walls to a gate. Go through this and follow grassy tracks to the road. Turn **L**, then **R** at the T-junction.

Turn **R** at The King's Head pub and then keep **SA** at the junction, into Ravenstonedale. Keep **R** after the Black Swan and ride out of the village, turning **R** up a lane signed *Artlegarth* and *Adamthwaite*. Turn **L** at the T-junction.

3 Follow the lane south, keeping **R** (uphill) at the fork. After a bridge, climb steeply and then, as you begin to descend, turn **L** onto a signed bridleway.

Go around the hillside and down a rocky descent to a good track. Keep **SA**. At the farm, go through the gate and then – **easy to miss** – immediately **R** through two more gates onto open (boggy) ground (don't go through the farm). Follow vague singletrack **SA**, downhill and into woods. Drop to the river and go through the **LH** gate into a field.

Climb to the opposite corner of the field and go through a gate to a track. Turn **R** and climb to a farm. Go into the yard and turn **L** through a gate. Keep **L** through a second gate and descend a rocky track.

Ford the river and follow the track up and left. Drop towards the next river and a good track. Turn **R** (ignore the bridge to the left) and follow the track alongside the river to a second bridge on the left (Cautley Spout waterfall ahead). Cross this and follow grassy trails and singletrack through gorse bushes and across streams to the farm at Fawcett Bank. Go **SA** onto a wide track and follow this to tarmac.

Drop to the main road and turn **R** to Sedbergh.

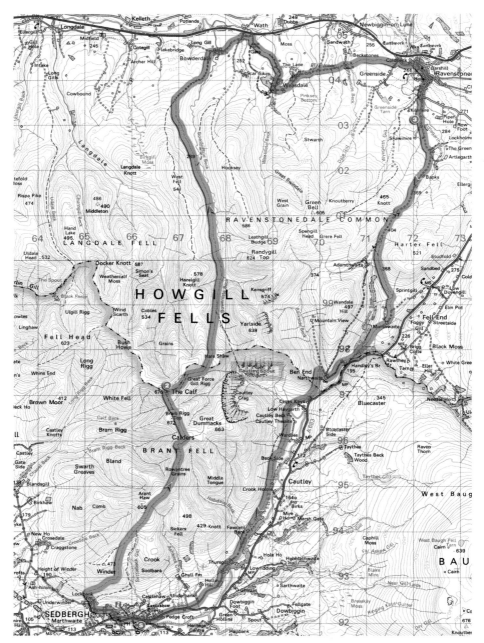

More riding

Sedbergh Sprint(gill)

A short-ish, flat-ish ride that starts on tarmac, swings off-road for a stretch and then crosses the valley to enjoy the final sections of the classic Howgill route – the tumbling descent from Sprintgill and the fantastic undulating singletrack under Brant Fell. If you've just ridden that route, you might fancy something different, but if you're short on time, energy or the weather's bad, this is a great option.

Grade: **Red** » Distance: **23km** » Ascent: **450m** » Time: **3hrs+**
Start/Finish: **Sedbergh, SD 657921** » OS Map: **OL19 Howgill Fells & Upper Eden Valley**

The Route » Sedbergh – east on the A683 to Cautley – minor road then track under Bluecaster – Fell End – Low Dovengill – Sprintgill – Murthwaite – Ben End – Cross Keys – Fawcett Bank – Sedbergh

The Calf

Another short ride out of Sedbergh – but don't think this one's easy – it feels as far vertically as it does horizontally! Sharing the same grassy slog uphill as the main route, this ride swings off just prior to the summit of the Calf for a descent that's grassy and incredibly fast. It's even better/more terrifying in the wet as things get slippery. It rides well in either direction.

Grade: **Red** » Distance: **14km** » Ascent: **590m** » Time: **1.5hrs+**
Start/Finish: **Sedbergh, SD 657921** » OS Map: **OL19 Howgill Fells & Upper Eden Valley**

The Route » Sedbergh – NW briefly on minor roads – Lockbank Farm – Calders – Bram Rigg Top – Bram Rigg – Birkhaw – Sedbergh

Sedbergh & Dent

South from Sedbergh towards Dentdale is this cracking little route. There's a fair amount of road riding, but as it is either through very picturesque scenery or makes a hideous climb easier, it's forgivable. There's an easy fast descent into the valley, a good, wide traverse above it (finishing with a hard and rocky descent) and a good moorland crossing to finish.

Grade: **Red** » Distance: **26km** » Ascent: **600m** » Time: **3hrs+**
Start/Finish: **Sedbergh, SD 657921** » OS Map: **OL19 Howgill Fells & Upper Eden Valley**

The Route » Sedbergh – Millthrop – Gate Manor – Rottenbutts Wood – road SE to Gawthrop, then W to SD 679861 – Wold End Moss – SD 710845 – High Nun Ho – Dent – cross the river and follow a minor road north on the east bank – Hold Ho – Rawridding – Long Moor – Fostrow – Lane Ends – Millthrop – Sedbergh

More information

Main Towns

Sedbergh, Sedbergh and Sedbergh. Great if you like book shops, not so good for everything else. For bigger shops and supermarkets, Kendal is ten miles or so to the west.

Maps

OL19 Howgill Fells & Upper Eden Valley

Bike Shops

Evans, Stricklandgate, Kendal, 01539 740 087, www.evanscycles.com

Accommodation

Try www.sedbergh.org.uk – it has listings for every kind of accommodation you could need. As all the rides we've listed start in Sedbergh itself, it might be convenient to find somewhere as close as possible! There are B&Bs, several campsites and self-catering options in town. That said, the other villages in the area (such as Dent) are all very pleasant.

If you need somewhere for a group to stay, try the Howgills Bunk Barn (01539 621 990, www.howgillsbunkbarn.co.uk).

Food & Drink

The Sedbergh Cafe, Sedbergh, 01539 621 389, www.thesedberghcafe.com
hOwGiLLs Bakery and Tea Room, Sedbergh, 01539 621 058
Duo Cafe, Bar and Bistro, Sedbergh, 01539 620 552, www.duo-sedbergh.co.uk
The Black Swan, Ravenstonedale, 01539 623 204, www.blackswanhotel.com (accommodation)
The King's Head, Ravenstonedale, 01539 623 050, www.kings-head.com (posh, red squirrel in the beer garden)
The Bull Hotel, Sedbergh, 01539 620 264, www.bullhotelsedbergh.co.uk (accommodation)
George & Dragon Hotel, Dent, 01539 625 256, www.thegeorgeanddragondent.co.uk, (accommodation, real ale!)

Tourist Offices

Sedbergh, 01539 620 125, www.sedbergh.org.uk

Outdoor Shops

Your best bet is to head to Kendal and its wide array of outdoor shops if you need anything.

Guidebooks

Yorkshire Dales Mountain Biking – The North Dales, written by Nick Cotton, published by Vertebrate Publishing

Worth Knowing

Lucky you – if you're in the Howgills, then you're right between the Lakes and the Yorkshire Dales. A short drive to the west is the Garburn Pass and Kentmere area, home to some of our favourite Lake District rides (overleaf). Meanwhile, the Yorkshire Dales (page 145) are even handier, with the excellent riding around Hawes and Swaledale close at hand (pages 151, 146).

Bowderdale again! **Photo**: John Coefield.

The Lake District

The only place in England with real mountains, the Lake District contains the country's ten highest peaks. It also has its deepest and longest lakes and is home to England's only Golden Eagle. But – and here's one for pub quiz fans – it's only got one actual 'lake': Bassenthwaite. The rest are mere 'waters'. Luckily for us mountain bikers, there's more than one bridleway. In fact, there's possibly more choice and variety of bridleway here than anywhere else in the country, and there's some fantastic, proper mountain biking on them.

The northern Lakes consists of the area around the A66. In riding terms, it's a much smaller area than the southern Lakes as there simply aren't as many bridleways. You've essentially got two areas: around Keswick (Skiddaw, Borrowdale) and around Ullswater (Helvellyn, High Street). There's a dual carriageway running between the two so moving around is quick and easy.

The southern Lakes is everything south of Ambleside and Langdale. It's a big area and it could well be argued that the southern Lake District is the better half for riding. There are more bridleways, there's more variety in the trails and, with more towns and villages about, more cafes.

Virtually every Lake District valley contains at least one UK classic route – routes like the Borrowdale Bash, Garburn Pass and Helvellyn. When you take into account the green and pleasant scenery, the excellent pubs and cafes, the friendly feel, the wide range of accommodation and bike shops, it becomes obvious why this is pretty much the best place in the country to ride.

The Riding

As there aren't many bridleways in the northern Lakes options are limited. There's little 'easy' riding: rides are either rocky and technical, climb huge hills or head into the sticks. Sometimes, they do all three.

Happily, most of the rides are UK classics. You could tick a summit by climbing Helvellyn or Skiddaw – two of the highest mountains in England. Helvellyn's definitely the more technical, but Skiddaw is brake-boiling fun. Or try the ultimate valley ride, the Borrowdale Bash. It might involve a lot of road, but there's also fantastic technical descending and singletrack riding through beautiful scenery. Prefer a big day out? Head out behind Skiddaw or up High Street – epic routes with great riding and incredible views.

The southern Lakes is also packed with must-do rides – and there are more of them. The riding is often rocky, with slabby rock gardens and loose, boulder-strewn trails appearing in equal measure. There are jagged descents, technical climbs and fantastic singletrack – but also easy lakeside trails and gentle forest roads. There are mountain passes – Walna Scar, Nan Bield and Garburn Pass spring instantly to mind – big, memorable rides with a real mountain feel. If the weather's bad, there are lower-level options around Loughrigg and Little Langdale. Easily accessible, they give great riding but avoid the committing nature of higher rides. Or you can mix and match trail centre singletrack with fantastic natural riding in Grizedale Forest. To be honest, you have to try quite hard to find a bad route around here.

When to go

You can ride in the Lake District all year long – particularly in the south, as there's plenty of sheltered and low-level riding. There are enough stone-based trails in the north that you'll find something to ride at any time of the year – try Borrowdale. However, a significant number of the rides in the north head on to high ground on long, committing bridleways. So, when the weather's bad, stay low. When it's good, steer away from popular areas in order to avoid the flocks of walkers. There's always something to ride.

Dave Balshaw dropping towards Grange on the Borrowdale Bash. **Photo**: John Coefield.

22 Borrowdale Bash

The Borrowdale Bash is a UK Classic. The cynical might suggest that the only way a fifty-per-cent-tarmac route attains this status is by starting in Keswick and by being the only route in Borrowdale. They're right, but they're wrong. True, there's a lot of tarmac, but that gives you time to admire the surroundings and gets you get between the fun bits with the minimum of fuss. And what fun bits! If you like tricky climbs, you'll appreciate the steep and rocky scramble from the pretty village of Watendlath. If technical descending's your thing, you'll love being tumble-dried through the rocks as you batter down the first descent. Dropping over 200 metres in 1500 metres, it swaps sweeping corners and fast straights for a precipitous jumble of rocks and steps (and there's a big run-out area from which to watch your friends' efforts). For singletrack enthusiasts, the traverse from the back of the valley is a treat. Beautifully tricky, it's an enjoyable run over rocky steps and tiny streams – although it's made harder than it should be by the constantly-distracting views. Finally, for those who appreciate the simple pleasures of speed, there is the rocky blast down to Grange, where speed is only limited by your tolerance to tooth and eyeball-rattling.

> Grade: **Black** » Distance: **27km** » Ascent: **760m** » Time: **3hrs+**
> Start/Finish: **Keswick** » Start GR: **NY 265235** » SatNav: **Keswick**
> OS Map: **OL4 The English Lakes North-western Area** » Parking: **Numerous pay and display in Keswick**
> Cafe: **The Lakeland Pedlar, Keswick, T: 01768 774 492** » Pub: **In virtually every village along the route**

Directions

S Sorry, there's a tiny bit of road riding to start. From almost anywhere in Keswick, follow signs for *Borrowdale* and take the B5289 running south down the valley.

Follow the road for 3km before turning **L** up a narrow dead-end road, signed to *Watendlath*. Climb steeply and go along the road until it ends. Bear **R** where the road splits at the houses. Cross the river, go through the gate and keep **R**, heading for the steep and obvious climb, signed *Bridleway to Rosthwaite*.

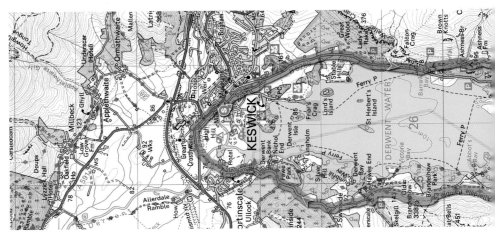

Attempt to clean the climb and then follow the track **SA** over the top of the hill onto a steep, rocky and technical descent. Ignore turnings until the track swings left alongside a wall. Turn **R** through a narrow gate (signed *Bridleway Rosthwaite*) and continue to descend.

At the road, turn **R**. Go over the bridge to the main road and turn **L**. Ride through the village of Seatoller and climb very steeply up the Honister Pass. About 300m after the cattle grid at the top of the steep section, turn **R** onto an obvious track signed *Bridleway*.

2 **Easy to miss:** Drop back into the valley. After approximately 1km, turn **L** onto a narrow singletrack climbing off the main track opposite a low and easy-to-miss wooden signed marked *Bridleway: Grange*. If you miss the turning, you'll reach a group of trees and a gate. Turn around and try again.

Follow obvious and often technical singletrack through a gate and across bridges, ignoring any turnings. Keep going as the track widens and descends fast and rocky into the woods.

Stick to the main track, crossing a bridge and riding through the woods to the river. Turn **L** and pick up a good track through the campsite. Turn **R** upon meeting tarmac and ride into the village of Grange. Turn **L** at the road.

3 Ride out of Grange. Just over 1km from the village, pass houses on the left and then turn **L** onto the **RH** of two signed footpaths (take the one with the large rock in the middle of the track). At the time of writing, there is a move to upgrade this footpath to bridleway status. As it stands, you'll have to push along it for a couple of hundred metres to a gate and a bridleway.

Go through the gate and climb steeply to a fork by a small cairn. Bear **R**, heading for and along the uphill edge of the woods on technical singletrack. Keep **SA** onto a wider and faster track. Look out for walkers and admire the view. Follow the track as it drops to the road at a parking bay. Keep **L** in the parking bay for 10m before picking up the bridleway once more.

At the road, turn **L** (**SA** in effect), dropping around two hairpins. Bear **R** at the next junction, following signs for *Keswick*.

Ride into the village of Portinscale and turn **R** as the road bends left. Ride to the end of the road and cross the footbridge. Turn **R** at the T-junction with the main road and ride into Keswick.

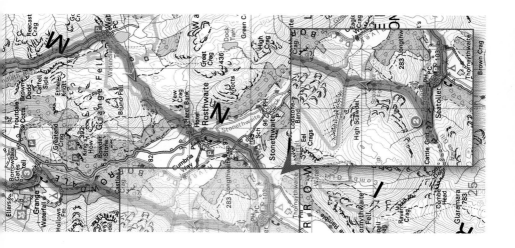

23 Loughrigg & Little Langdale

Head out of Ambleside and straight up the nearest hill. Straight up. Luckily, most of the height is gained on tarmac, so it's not too tough. The climb eases to reveal a wide, stony trail running across Loughrigg Fell. There's a nice desolate feel to the area, which the track crosses swiftly, picking up speed as it drops into a fast and easyish descent (watch the last corner!). Hit the road for a short way before a steep, technical climb lands you on rolling singletrack across Iron Keld. A rocky track leads downhill from here to the main road, and more fun riding takes you through Hodge Close. Then the ride gets really good. The great descents, each preceded by a tough climb, lead home. Reached first is a tooth-rattler over football-sized boulders into Little Langdale, with the preceding climb being a daunting, but sort of doable rock-slab challenge. Next up is an equally rocky, but considerably faster, mossier and 'pingier' descent to Elterwater. It's great fun, with an alternative singletrack route just the north, if you'd prefer something narrower. The final hurdle is a steep and hairpinned road slog that leads to the final superbly-positioned blast across Loughrigg Terrace to home.

Short Option (see map)

A much shorter route takes in the tough climb up Loughrigg, then swings around the tarn and back via a fast single-track descent. It's only about an hour or so in length, but worth doing if you're in a hurry or want an easy ride.

Grade: **Red** » Distance: **31km/10km** » Ascent: **1,120m/350m** » Time: **3hrs+/1.5hrs+**	
Start/Finish: **Ambleside waterfront** » Start GR: **NY 376032** » SatNav: **Ambleside**	
OS Map: **OL7 The English Lakes South-eastern Area** » Parking: **Pay & Display in Ambleside**	
Cafe: **Loads in Ambleside** » Pub: **Lots in Ambleside**	

Directions

S With your back to the waterfront, turn **L** along the road. Take the first **L**, signed *Langdale*. Turn **L** across the bridge and then immediately **R** onto a narrow lane, signed *Under Loughrigg*.

Shortly after the cattle grid, turn **L** up a tarmac lane/bridleway. Climb steeply past buildings and onto open ground. Keep **L** after a short climb and follow the obvious track, ignoring turnings, up and over Loughrigg to a fast descent.

Go **SA** on the wide track. At the road, turn **L** and then immediately **R**. Drop to the junction and go **SA**, following signs for *Coniston*. Cross the bridge, climb for just over 1km until the road starts to descend and then turn **L** onto a signed bridleway just before a house.

2 Climb steeply, following bridleway signs up and round to the right. Ignore a wide footpath dropping off right. Turn **L** immediately after the wall, following bridleway markers. Ignore the obvious turning just before the gate and drop to a second gate. Go through this to a T-junction with a wide track and turn **R**.

Follow the track to the road and turn **L**, downhill. Go **SA** over the main road and onto the lane opposite.

Go through the farmyard and through the gate onto the track. At the T-junction at Hodge Close, turn **L** onto tarmac and drop around bends. As you near the last house, turn **R** through a gate into a field. Ride into the woods and then take the middle track – a low, rocky and slightly sunken track – to drop to a stream. Climb to a T-junction with a wide dirt track and turn **L**.

Keep **SA** until you reach the farm at High Tilberthwaite. Go into the farmyard and turn sharp **R**. Climb steeply to a fast and rocky descent. As you move out onto open ground, turn **R** at the obvious track junction. Ride down through a gate and descend for around a kilometre to an obvious junction. Turn **L** across the river. Ride uphill to the road and turn **L**.

3 After a short way, turn **R** onto a narrow lane. Continue **SA** as tarmac gives way to dirt and descend, ignoring turnings, through the woods to Elterwater.

At the road T-junction, turn **L** into the village. Continue **SA** as the road bends right in the centre of the village. At the main road, turn **L**, then quickly **R** past a car park. Keep **R** at the junction and climb via hairpin bends.

At the T-junction, turn **L**, then **R** onto a signed bridleway. Follow this through the woods and out into the open. Take care – this can get busy with walkers. Follow the fun descent downhill and into the lake.

Emerging from the depths, continue **SA** along the obvious high track towards the woods and keep going to the road. Either turn **L** and then **R** along the main road into Ambleside, or turn **R** and follow the lane for a quieter, but longer, return journey.

24 Grizedale & Parkamoor

A big ride. Some of the best views in the south Lakes, a couple of fantastic rocky descents and one of the best stretches of natural singletrack in the country. It is quite tiring though! Beginning with a forest road climb from the Grizedale Visitor Centre (you could always use the man-made North Face Trail), a rolling bridleway breaks out of the trees and onto the hillside above Coniston Water. It really is lovely up here, with views stretching down to the lake far below and across to the Old Man of Coniston and beyond. Tearing yourself away might be a wrench, but the fast, slabby run to High Nibthwaite should ease the blow. A tough climb gives way to a fun cruise across the top and back towards the trees. Dodge the bottomless puddles, enjoy the rocks and let the brakes off for a fast road blast. A quick forest road climb/technical uphill challenge – your choice – and a plummet down steep singletrack and over rocks drop you into Satterthwaite. Then comes the highlight: a narrow singletrack cuts away from Breasty Haw, rolling downhill on a hard, fast surface and pumping through dips and sweeping around corners and over rocks. Back in the trees, the track steepens, becomes more technical, culminating in a series of steep, rocky hairpins. Another steep climb follows, although you'll be so gobsmacked at how unbelievably good the singletrack was that you'll skip up it in a haze, only waking up for the final rocky (and we do mean rocky) rattle to the centre.

Grade: **Red** » Distance: **27km** » Ascent: **760m** » Time: **3.5hrs+**
Start/Finish: **Grizedale visitor centre** » Start GR: **SD 335 943/SD 342 964** » SatNav: **Hawkshead/ LA22 OQJ**
OS Map: **OL7 The English Lakes South-eastern Area; OL6 The English Lakes South-western Area**
Parking: **Pay & Display at the centre/car park north of centre** » Cafe: **At the visitor centre**
Pub: **Eagle's Head, Satterthwaite, T: 01229 860 237**

Optional Start from High Car Park

Head through the car park, bearing **L** at the fork and following markers for the North Face Trail. Keep following these markers on to the man-made singletrack trail and continue to do so until you reach the visitor centre.

Directions

S From the bike shop, push through the arch in the wall and keep **SA/R** through the grassy picnic area in the visitor centre. Go through the gate on the far side and turn **R** along the forest road.

Upon leaving the buildings, turn **L** through a gate and begin to climb uphill on more forest road. Turn **L** at the T-junction and follow forest road along the edge of the forest. Keep **R** at the fork. Climb up, around a left-hand hairpin and then turn **R**, still on forest roads.

Continue to climb. As the track levels at the top, turn **L** onto a singletrack bridleway signed to *Parkamoor*. Follow singletrack out of the trees and then follow the obvious stone track across the tops.

Drop down and pass buildings before climbing steeply to a T-junction. Turn **R** and follow the trail – which is technical in places – to the road. Drop a short distance to a T-junction and turn **L**.

2 Pass an open field on the right and then, after about 1.5km, turn sharp **L** up a narrow lane. Climb steeply into the woods until the road turns to dirt. Continue **SA** through the gate and, ignoring all turnings, follow the main track through the deep puddles to a farm. Turn **L** on the road and descend to Force Mills.

Keep **SA** through the village. About 200m after the church, turn **L** onto a forest road.

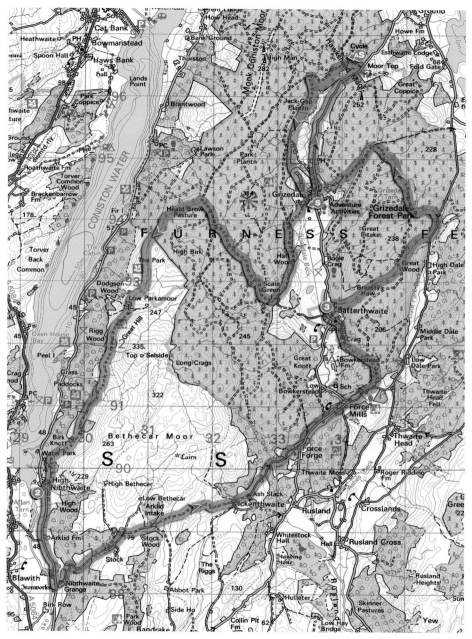

Easy option: Turn **L** at the T-junction, then follow the forest road uphill around wide hairpins. As the climbing begins to ease, turn **R** onto another forest road. Turn **L** at the junction, and then **L** at the next, onto a more open forest road. Follow this for about 150m and then turn **R** onto singletrack, re-joining the main route as it drops into Satterthwaite.

Go into the woods and then turn **L** onto a signed singletrack bridleway. Follow bridleway signs **SA** over forest roads to the top.

Go **SA** over the forest road at the top and onto a narrow singletrack descent. Drop steeply into Satterthwaite.

❸ Drop to the main road and then take the first **R**. At the end of the lane, take the **RH** trail and climb the obvious track.

At the forest road, go **SA** onto a superb section of singletrack. Follow this **SA** across a second forest road and drop to the road. Turn **L**.

Just after a steep rise, bear **L** off the road into a dirt clearing and then bear **R** onto a narrow stony bridleway climbing steeply. Follow this to a forest road and turn **R**. Turn **R** at the junction and then continue onto singletrack as the forest road ends at some boulders. Follow this singletrack to another forest road and turn **R**.

At the fox, follow the forest road around to the left. Keep **R** on forest road at the junction and then, as the forest road bends right, continue **SA** onto a slightly narrower track. Descend over rocks to the visitor centre.

Turn **R** and follow the road to the car park. Or, if you took the optional start, turn **R** and follow the road uphill to the car park.

Grizedale singletrack. **Photo**: John Coefield.

More riding

Helvellyn

How many rides take you to the top of a mountain? How many give a proper summit tick, climb the highest legally-rideable peak in England and sit you nearly 1,000 metres up in the air above a choice of stunning descents? Obviously, this isn't easy. A huge climb on energy-sapping grass and the ridiculous pull up Great Dodd ensure you'll be knackered as you flop onto the summit. But it's worth it. Admire the view and pick a descent. They're all fantastic. The main track is easiest – flat-out around loose turns; it's fun, but full of walkers. Try Sticks Pass instead. Technical singletrack and a plunge down a scree slope – it's awesome, if a little worrying. Or take Grisedale Tarn: initially fast and open, all hell breaks loose above the lake as steps, corners and drainage ditches all hit you at once. Survive that and fast singletrack and numerous rock gardens await.

Note: *If it's wet, climb via the main track from Glenridding. The Dodds get too boggy.*

Grade: **Black** » Distance: **29km (Grisedale route, shortcuts possible)** » Ascent: **1,100m** » Time: **3hrs+**
Start/Finish: **Main car park, Glenridding, NY 385168** » OS Map: **OL5 The Lake District North-eastern Area**

The climb
In the wet » Glenridding – west up main track via Keppel Cove to Helvellyn summit
In the dry » Glenridding – north on road to A5091 – Dockray – High Row – Great Dodd – south along ridge to Helvellyn Summit

The descents
Route 1 » Sticks Pass: Helvellyn Summit – north over Raise to NY 341982 – east via disused mine to Glenridding
Route 2 » Main Track: Helvellyn Summit – north to White Side – Keppel Cove – Glenridding
Route 3 » Grisedale Tarn: Helvellyn Summit – south over Nethermost Pike and Dollywagon Pike – Grisedale Tarn – Grisedale – Patterdale – Glenridding

Back o'Skiddaw

A long ride through a relatively quiet area of the Lake District. The start/finish along Lonscale Fell is technical in places and scenic throughout, with a nice drop to one side. The run into Mosedale is fantastic – fast grassy singletrack all the way down. Roads and stone tracks lead via fast descents to a huge sting-in-the-tail up past Whitewater Dash, a splashy drop to Skiddaw House and a second go at Lonscale Fell.

Grade: **Red/Black** » Distance: **44km** » Ascent: **950m** » Time: **4hrs+**
Start/Finish: **Car pack above Latrigg, NY 280253** » OS Map: **OL4 The Lake District North-western Area**

The Route » Latrigg car park – Lonscale Fell – Skiddaw House – northeast on the Cumbria Way to Mosedale – road north to Calebreck – west to Fell Side via NY 319366 – Branthwaite – Longlands – Orthwaite – NY 249323 – east to Skiddaw House – Latrigg car park

Nan Bield

A bit of a classic, but a tough classic. Steep and technical, you will, without a shadow of a doubt, be putting bike to shoulder for the climbs on this route. Gatescarth is long and loose, while Nan Bield is narrow, steep and technical. The descents mirror the climbs. Dropping to Haweswater is a barrelling descent on a wide trail of loose rocks. Proper rattling and sliding stuff. Nan Bield, meanwhile, is tight singletrack all the way. Highly technical, it's rocky and twisty. One for technical aficionados who don't mind a bit of portage!

Grade: **Black** » Distance: **18km** » Ascent: **840m** » Time: **3hrs+**
Start/Finish: **Kentmere, NY 456040** » OS Map: **OL7 The English Lakes South-eastern Area**

The Route » Kentmere – northwest on road to Stile End – Sadgill – north over the Gatescarth Pass to Haweswater – Small Water – Nan Bield Pass – Kentmere

Walna Scar Variant

Oh, this one's good ... Tight, steep and fun singletrack through Broughton Moor, then a great open-ground crossing on narrow hardpack, interrupted by rocks and puddles. The following descent to Seathwaite starts fast but ends in a jumbled confusion of boulders while the climb up Walna Scar, tantalisingly do-able, always ends within the first hundred metres. The final descent is a grassy challenge, steadily eroding into ever more technical ruts and drops but finishing with a fast and smooth run high above the River 'Lickle'.

   Note: *The classic Walna Scar ride has recently suffered the loss of its final stunning descent, thanks to re-surfacing works. It's still worth doing, and will hopefully one day return to its former rocky glory. Start in Coniston, ride to the start, and finish over Walna Scar and via Spoon Hall.*

Grade: **Red** » Distance: **19km** » Ascent: **680m** » Time: **3hrs+**
Start/Finish: **Broughton Moor, SD 256931** » OS Map: **OL6 The English Lakes South-western area**

The Route » SD 256931 – singletrack bridleway to Stephenson Ground – Carter Ground – Brock Barrow – Seathwaite – Walna Scar to SD 250962 – Jackson Ground – forest roads through Broughton Moor to start

Pass Storming in the Central Lakes

Not 'riding' in the conventional sense and very much an acquired taste for the fit and technically able, there's a lot of (great) fun to be had in and around the central Great Gable area of the Lakes. Start at the end of Langdale, Borrowdale or near Wast Water or Buttermere and look for the high bridleways running up and over Sty Head, Black Sail Pass or via Blea Crag. Expect tougher than tough climbs (with absolutely no chance you'll be riding), but stunning views, a real 'mountain' feel and the most technical descents you'll find anywhere in England and Wales. The startled looks you'll get from walkers are always fun too. Either pick a pass to do as a 'there and back' or create a huge 'valley-hopping' day out.

Grade: **Very black!** » Distance: **Up to you** » Ascent: **Lots ...** » Time: **N/A**
Start/Finish: **N/A** » OS Map: **OL6 The English Lakes South-western area; OL4 The English Lakes North-western area**

Garburn, Green Quarter & Troutbeck

Some of the best riding in the Lakes is between Ambleside and Staveley. Heading out from Ambleside towards Kentmere, the route tackles the legendary Garburn Pass (long, rocky and equally good in either direction), and then climbs to open grassy moorland from which – when it's dry – fantastic singletrack swoops and twists into a tricky little descent to the valley floor. The return leg finishes on a high, dropping fast through the fantastic woods from Jenkin Crag. The views over Windermere are incredible, yet pass unnoticed on the slippery and technical descent.

Don't bother going up onto Green Quarter in soggy weather. It won't be much fun, and the singletrack gets a right battering from tyres every winter – it's getting wider and wider. The alternative descent below gives a great descent into Kentmere – FAST and grassy in places, twisty in others and with a great little rock garden halfway down – hardly a bad choice.

Grade: **Red** » Distance: **37km/32km (winter/short route)** » Ascent: **1,120/960m** » Time: **3.5hrs+**
Start/Finish: **Ambleside lakefront, NY 377031** » OS Map: **OL7 The English Lakes South-eastern Area**

The Route » Ambleside – south on A591 to Brockhole – east on bridleway to NY 400017 – bridleway across river at NY 409019 – Latrigg – NY 416026 – east over Garburn Pass to Kentmere – then either:
Dry weather option » Kentmere – Green Quarter – north-east via Stile End to NY 481050 – Cocklaw Fell – Birk Rigg – Staveley Head Fell – Millrigg Knott – Browfoot
Wet weather option » Kentmere – south-west to NY 443027 – Croft Head – Browfoot – Browfoot – High Ho – Mislet – Dubbs Reservoir – The Howe – Town End – Jenkin Crag – Ambleside

Garburn Pass. **Photo**: John Coefield.
Kentmere. **Photo**: John Coefield.

More information

Main Towns

There are two main gateways to the Lake District, each guarded by a large-ish town – Penrith at the top and Kendal at the bottom. Both have a couple of bike shops, supermarkets and so forth, although Kendal is probably the more useful. Once you're in the Lakes, Ambleside and Keswick are the two main stops for bike parts, tent pegs and food, with the busy Windermere close behind. Places like Coniston and Grasmere are smaller, but still have the basics, and Staveley on the way in handily has a village shop, Wheelbase bike shop and Wilf's Cafe.

Maps

Ordnance Survey
OS OL4 The English Lakes North-western Area
OS OL5 The English Lakes North-eastern Area
OS OL6 The English Lakes South-western Area
OS OL7 The English Lakes South-eastern Area
British Mountain Maps
Lake District 1:40,000 Harvey mapping of the central Lakes

Bike Shops

Askew Cycles, Wildman Street, Kendal, 01539 728 057, www.askewcycles.co.uk
Arragons, Brunswick Road, Penrith, 01768 890 344, www.arragons.com
Wheelbase, Staveley, 01539 821 443, www.wheelbase.co.uk
Bike-Treks, Rydal Road, Ambleside, 01539 431 245, www.bike-treks.co.uk
Ghyllside Cycles, The Slack, Ambleside, 01539 433 592, www.ghyllside.co.uk
Grizedale, Grizedale Visitor Centre, 01229 860 335, www.grizedalemountainbikes.co.uk
Gill Cycles, The Gill, Ulverston, 01229 581 116, www.gillcycles.co.uk
Keswick Mountain Bikes, Main Street, Keswick, 01768 775 202, www.keswickbikes.co.uk
The Lakeland Pedlar, Bell Close, Keswick, 01768 774 492, www.lakelandpedlar.co.uk
Whinlatter Bikes, Main Street, Keswick, 01768 773 940, www.whinlatterbikes.com
Cyclewise, Whinlatter Visitor Centre, 01768 778 711, www.cyclewise.co.uk
Evans, Stricklandgate, Kendal, 01539 740 087, www.evanscycles.com

Bike Hire

Grizedale, Grizedale Visitor Centre, 01229 860 369, www.grizedalemountainbikes.co.uk
Cyclewise, Whinlatter Visitor Centre, 01768 778 711, www.cyclewise.co.uk
Keswick Mountain Bikes, Main Street, Keswick, 01768 775 202, www.keswickbikes.co.uk
Wheelbase, Staveley Mill Yard, Staveley, 01539 821 443, www.wheelbase.co.uk
Whinlatter Bikes, Main Street, Keswick, 01768 773 940, www.whinlatterbikes.com

Approaching Helvellyn. **Photo**: John Coefield.

Accommodation

The Lake District has accommodation coming out of its ears, and there's way too much to list here. An internet search will reveal tourist information sites, accommodation lists and every other bit of information you could possibly need.

There are campsites everywhere – many marked on maps, or searchable on www.lakedistrictcamping.co.uk. Simply driving around usually finds a few. In the north, there are nice but basic sites in Grange (01778 777 298, www.hollowsfarm.co.uk) and Seatoller (01768 777 232, www.seatollerfarm.co.uk) in the Borrowdale Valley and on the route of the Borrowdale Bash. There are dozens of sites around Ullswater – handy for Helvellyn and High Street. More centrally, there's a good National Trust site at the end of Langdale (01539 463 862), although it is a little out of the way. Further south, there are again several sites around Coniston and Grizedale, great for Walna Scar and the riding in the forest.

Predictably, there are also hostels everywhere. See www.yha.org.uk for a full list, but those in Patterdale, Keswick, Ambleside, Coniston, Grasmere and around Keswick are all well-located for mountain bikers.

We couldn't possibly recommend any specific B&Bs, cottages or hotels – there are that many. Try www.staylakedistrict.co.uk and www.golakes.co.uk – two of the main available listings sites. Anywhere near the main towns, or in the central Lakes will do you well.

Food & Drink

Cafes

The Lakeland Pedlar, Bell Close, Keswick, 01768 774 492, www.lakelandpedlar.co.uk (half bike shop, half cafe)

Wilf's, Staveley Mill Yard, Staveley, 01529 822 329, www.wilfs-cafe.co.uk (veggie event caterers, good for Kentmere/Garburn rides)

Bluebird Cafe, Lake Road, Coniston, 01539 441 649, www.thebluebirdcafe.co.uk (handy for Walna Scar)

More? Artisan Bakery, Staveley Mill Yard, Staveley, 01539 822 297, www.moreartisan.co.uk

Pubs

The Mill Inn, Mungrisdale, 01768 779 632, www.the-millinn.co.uk (good food and accommodation)

George Hotel, Keswick, 01768 772 076, www.georgehotelkeswick.co.uk

Watermill Inn, Ings, 01539 821 309, www.watermillinn.co.uk (accommodation)

The Black Bull Hotel, Coniston, 01539 441 335, www.blackbullconiston.co.uk (accommodation + The Coniston Brewery)

Old Dungeon Ghyll, end of the Langdale Valley, 01539 437 272, www.odg.co.uk

Eagle's Head, Satterthwaite, 01229 860 237, www.eagleshead.co.uk (good for Grizedale)

Tourist Offices

www.golakes.co.uk » **Ambleside** 01539 432 582 » **Coniston** 01539 441 533, www.conistontic.org
Keswick 01768 772 645, www.keswick.org » **Kendal** 01539 735 891, www.southlakeland.gov.uk

Outdoor Shops

Everywhere. Virtually every village has one. Head to the towns for bigger shops. Kendal, Ambleside and Kendal have about a gazillion each.

Useful Websites

www.golakes.co.uk – official tourism website
www.lakedistrict.gov.uk – particularly good for learning about the Lakes
www.visitcumbria.com
www.mountain-bike-cumbria.co.uk – good site with lots of information
www.lakedistrictcamping.co.uk

Guidebooks

Lake District Mountain Biking – Essential Trails, written by Chris Gore and Richard Staton, published by Vertebrate Publishing
Mountain Biking in the Lake District, written by Ian Boydon, published by Cicerone
Lake District Mountain Bike Routes, written by Tom Hutton, published by Out There Guides

Worth Knowing

There are two trail centres in the Lakes. Conveniently, one's in the north, at Whinlatter, and one's in the south, in Grizedale Forest. Whinlatter has two fantastic red loops, both of which begin with big singletrack climbs and end with big singletrack descents. Fast, swoopy fun, it's great for a swift blast, bad weather or easy riding in the Keswick area. The blue route at Whinlatter is a hoot too! Grizedale's a bit more involved, with more ups, more downs and slightly trickier riding. We normally combine it with Grizedale's fantastic natural riding, but it's a decent trail in its own right.

Dollywaggon Pike to Grisedale Tarn. **Photo**: John Coefield.

Isle of Man

The Isle of Man is a fast place. Each year, the TT sees racers push harder and harder into the limits of motorcycle performance. World-beating roadie Mark Cavendish honed his ridiculous sprint on the roads around Douglas. Outside the towns, there's no speed limit on the roads – a fact exploited by many a visiting driver. But travel around at that sort of pace and you might find the rest of the island passes by in a bit of a blur – and that would be a shame, as there's a lot to see.

Take a trip on the island's steam, electric or mountain railways. See the sights, which include the world's largest water wheel or the port town of Peel, or try locally-caught and cooked seafood in one of the many restaurants. At 32 miles long, with a high point at 621 metres, the Isle of Man is pretty small, but remarkably hilly. This isn't surprising when you consider that the island is about 70 miles off the coast of Cumbria, in the Irish Sea. Despite its proximity to our shores, it's not actually part of the UK (although it is in Britain), having its own government and currency. However, as everybody speaks English (although Manx is still spoken by some) and uses pounds Sterling (the locally-issued Manx pound), it's an easy place to visit.

The Riding

There's a lot of riding on the Isle of Man. In the north, the bridleways cross high ground, so big climbs and fast descents are guaranteed. The trails are generally stone-based (although there are a few grass and dirt stretches), with the technical difficulty varying from wide, gravelled tracks, through loose rubble to some relatively technical rock gardens. It's never too technical, so most competent riders will be able to have a crack at everything. The views from the hills help to make the effort well worthwhile. Further south, much of the riding moves into plantations – there's even a short man-made loop in the Barrule plantation. The riding is generally lower at this end of the island, although the views are still impressive. You don't get the long off road runs you do in the north, but what's there is great fun. If you want more hints on the stuff in the woods, ask in one of the island's bike shops or check the websites on page 185.

If you prefer going downhill fast, try the Isle of Man DH Facebook page, or www.manxuplift.com for details on the thriving DH scene on the island.

When to go

Whenever the TT isn't on! The racing closes virtually all of the riding in the northern half of the island, fills the accommodation and makes simply getting around tricky. Otherwise, much of the riding on the island is stone-based, so it's pretty rideable in all weather. Things do get higher and more exposed than you might expect, so check the forecast before setting out.

Photo: Andy McCandlish.

25 The TT & the Millenium Way

You've arrived on the Isle of Man, jumped off the Douglas ferry with your bike, and you're keen to ride. You've left the car behind to save on ferry charges so you can't travel far. Naturally, being interested in things that go fast on two wheels, you fancy a look at the TT track too. What you really want is a ride that starts in Douglas, perhaps from the TT Grandstand. A ride that warms up along the road and which then heads up a gentle climb in order to drop down a fast, wide trail and some hidden singletrack. Then you might like to gain some height, preferably up a nice open trail that lets you get good views of the island. Maybe you'd like a couple of little techy sections thrown in too? Ideally, there'd be a breather at the top of the climb, possibly on one of the TT course's more famous corners, from where you could watch the motorbikes race by before taking to the hallowed tarmac itself for a few metres. Psyched up by the screaming engines, and perhaps a little giddy from the exhaust fumes, you want to let rip on a descent now. Obviously, it would be ideal if that descent dropped from the top of the island, maybe along three kilometres of high-speed, technical and rocky track. It goes without saying that it needs to be a corker. Wonder where you could find such a ride ...

Grade: **Red** » Distance: **32km** » Ascent: **530m** » Time: **3hrs+**	
Start/Finish: **TT Grandstand, Douglas** » Start GR: **SC 382774** » SatNav: **IM2 6BN**	
OS Map: **Landranger 95 Isle of Man** » Parking: **Lots in Douglas**	
Cafe: **Lots in Douglas** » Pub: **Lots in Douglas**	

Directions

S▶ Find your way uphill through Douglas to the Grandstand (on Glencutchery Road, SC 382774). With your back to it, turn **R**. Ignoring turnings, go **SA** over the roundabout and climb away from town. As you reach the top, turn **L** onto a narrow lane. Follow this uphill. Bend sharply right and then, on the next right-hand bend, bear **L** onto a good stone track. Follow this steeply uphill, ignoring turnings. At the road, turn **R**. After 700m, turn **R** onto a good byway. Drop fast to the road and turn **L**. As the road bends sharply left, turn **R**. At the next bend, continue **SA** onto singletrack. Upon meeting tarmac, continue **SA** for a tiny distance and then turn **L**. Follow this to a road and go **SA** onto a narrow lane and into Baldrine. Drop to the main road and turn **L**.

Follow the road for 600m, going around a big right hand bend and climbing out of the houses. Take the next left, signed to *Creg na Baa*, crossing the electric railway line as you do. Ride gently uphill for just over 1km and take the third **R**, a narrow lane. Follow this past houses and then continue **SA** through a gate to the road.

2 Turn **L** and then, after a short way, turn **R** onto a narrow lane. Drop downhill and then climb around hairpins. As the road bends right, continue **SA** onto a byway. Go **SA** through gates as the lane bends left to the farm. A loose rocky section soon gives way to pleasant climbing with great views behind you.

At the road, turn **R**. (**Watch Out!** You've just joined the TT course at Windy Corner and there's likely to be some **VERY** fast traffic, so, take care!)

Climb uphill and take the next road on the **L**. Follow this for around 2km before turning **L** onto a signed byway as the climbing eases. This byway climbs slightly before beginning a varied and technical 3km descent.

3 Continue **SA** onto tarmac, and then **SA** at the road junction before taking the next road on the **L**. Drop steeply to a T-junction and turn **R**. Follow this road, ignoring turnings, to another T-junction and turn **L**.

Drop and then climb to a crossroads and turn **R**. Keep **SA** back towards Douglas. Go **SA** over the first major crossroads and then turn **L** at the second to return to the Grandstand. (Alternatively, keep **SA** to the seafront.)

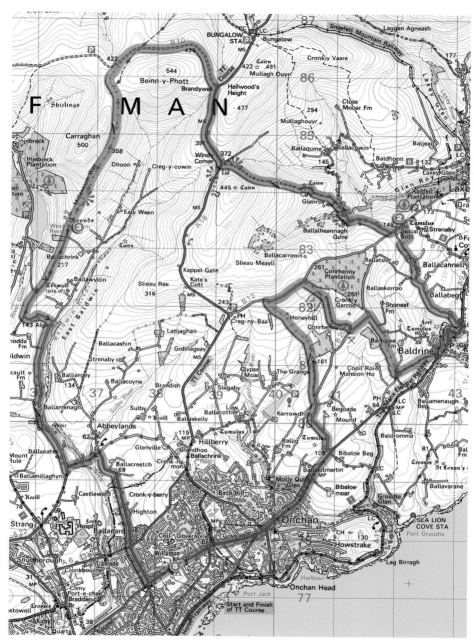

More riding

Isle of Man Tourist Board Routes

Top marks to the IoM Tourist Board – they've put together a decent set of routes, complete with useable maps. We'd recommend the 'Grand Day Out' if you want a good way to explore the north of the island, the 'Hells-8' for a tiring, albeit technically reasonable way to get up high and the 'Southern Comfort' for a great ride in the south with a couple of sections of fantastic singletrack. www.gov.im

The South Barrule Trail & IoM Downhill

If you like your routes waymarked or heading downhill steeply, head into the forests. There's a short singletrack loop in South Barrule Plantation. It's been built by Manx Cycling, so full credit to them. There's not enough to make a decent ride alone (in distance stakes – it's fine fun-wise!), but you could add it to the Tourist Board's 'Southern Comfort' route or any of the other trails in the area. If you prefer going downhill fast, try the Isle of Man DH Facebook page for details on the DH scene on the island.

Grade: **Red** » Distance: **5km** » Ascent: **100m** » Time: **30mins+**
Start/Finish: **Forestry car park, SC 275766** » OS Map: **Landranger 95 The Isle of Man**

The End to End

Exactly what it says on the tin. Either ride it yourself or enter the organised ride – which, although we've not participated in ourselves, has been praised by everyone we've spoken to. A mixture of tarmac, stony, grassy and singletrack trails, the route starts at the most northerly point of the island before heading south. Cruelly, the starting kilometres are flat, so you can see the hills rising ahead of you from a long way off. Relatively easy tracks lead over the tops before forest roads, good descents and very scenic singletrack lead down (literally) to the finish. www.manxe2e.org

   Note: *The 'official' event route uses tracks and trails only open for that occasion.*

Grade: **Black** » Distance: **about 65km** » Ascent: **Lots!** » Time: **Under 6hrs and you're doing well**
Start/Finish: **Point of Ayre, NX 466048** » OS Map: **Landranger 95 The Isle of Man**

More information

Main Towns

The main island town is Douglas. The ferries dock here and there are bike shops, food shops, restaurants, cinemas – the lot. Otherwise, Peel in the west, Ramsay to the north and the cluster of towns to the south will do you well. The smaller places like Laxey (good campsite) are generally good for a food shop and maybe a pub or two.

Maps

OS Landranger 95 The Isle of Man

Bike Shops

Eurocycles, Victoria Road, Douglas 01624 624 909, www.eurocycles.co.im
Bikestyle, Buck's Road, Douglas, 01624 673 576, www.bikestyle.im

Accommodation

What with the TT and various other attractions, it's not hard to find accommodation on the island, except during race week.

The official Isle of Man website should be your first stop: www.visitisleofman.com

For youth hostels, B&Bs and hotels, you really can't go far wrong with this site. Bear in mind how you've travelled over – if you're on bike and carless, stay around Douglas (riding available from the door) and the immediate east coast (the railway will allow bikes most of the time).

There are campsites dotted around the place. We particularly like the one in Laxey (01624 861 866, www.laxey.org) – it's a small, quiet site, very friendly and close to the riding, on the electric train line and just about in riding distance of Douglas.

Food & Drink

www.allmenus.im is rather good for finding places to eat. Otherwise:
La Mona Lisa, Laxey (friendly Italian Restaurant), 01624 862 488
The Bay Hotel, Port Erin, 01624 832 084
The Trafalgar Hotel, Ramsey, 01624 814 601
The White House, Peel, 01624 842 252, www.thewhitehousepeel.com
Woodbourne, Douglas, 01624 676 754
Obviously, there's a lot more to choose from!

Tourist Offices

All of the tourist offices on the IoM share a website: www.visitisleofman.com
The Welcome Centre, Douglas 01624 686 766, tourism@gov.im (very handily located in the ferry buildings.)
Peel, 01624 842 341 » **Castletown**, 01624 825 005 » **Port Erin**, 01624 832 298 » **Ramsey**, 01624 812 228

Outdoor Shops

Outdoors Ramsey, Ramsey, 01624 811 550, www.outdoorsramsey.co.uk
Newson Trading, Douglas, 01624 676 362

Useful Websites

www.visitisleofman.com
www.steam-packet.com – the ferry company
www.manxmtb.com – obvious really
www.manxe2e.org – the End to End official website

Guidebooks

This one! And the tourist website.

Worth Knowing

It's not at all cheap to get a car over on the ferry. Bikes are much more reasonable, although your movements on the island will be more limited. You can sometimes get bikes on the trains, but not always – check first. If you prefer going downhill fast, try the IoM DH Facebook page, or www.manxuplift.com

Photo: Andy McCandlish.

High Cup Nick
& Cross Fell
(aka The North Pennines)

Cross Fell is one of the only places in the UK where the wind has a name. Strong and usually chilly, the 'Helm Wind' blows straight out of Tolkien's middle earth and across the open fells with what feels like, at times, an evil intent.

These open hillsides are frequently described as 'England's last wilderness' – which is a pretty apt description. There's virtually nothing up here (apart from a huge golf ball of a radar station, but who's counting?). There are few trees, just boggy grassland and a few rocks, with the huge views of nothingness stretching out to the horizon in every direction. Even the valleys seem empty – the villages are tiny and spaced right out. I'm sure the appeal of the place doesn't need spelling out. It's beautiful.

Yet it's far from featureless. The massive water-cut chasm of High Cup Nick can be spotted from miles away. Up close, it's sheer size and breathtakingly steep sides are dizzying. Turn away, follow the river over the hill and you'll hear the roar from Cauldron Snout long before you see it. One of our favourite waterfalls in the country, its peat-tinted water drops 60 metres in 180 metres, making it one of the longest waterfalls in the country. Unbelievably, it's been run in a kayak, which makes mountain biking look like a piece of cake!

The Riding

Rides here are big – you don't want to head out without checking the forecast and contents of your Camelbak. Endless bridleways cross wide expanses of moorland; technical singletracks collapse into rivers and long bridleways tackle triple-figure climbs before dropping to valleys beyond – from where the only way home is to clamber back up and over again. This is about as wild and committing as riding gets in England. But – lucky you – there are several great trails to be wild and committed on, including the highly regarded singletrack flyer off Cross Fell.

Wide, stony tracks give (relatively) easy access to the tops. Grassy trails, squelchy when wet, are blisteringly fast when dry. Vague singletrack merges with surrounding grassland, hiding the way ahead for a truly remote feel. Sketchy rock gardens, hidden drops and random holes add technical interest – not always welcome when you're knackered! Even the road sections run along some of the quietest and most picturesque tarmac around. Throw in some stunning scenery, take out all traces of civilisation and you have an amazing place to ride.

When to go

As you might have gathered, this is a pretty wild spot. There's a sinister wind, plenty of potential to get lost, not much shelter and there aren't (m)any houses around. You have been warned. Oh, and the whole place turns into a bog when it rains.

High Cup Nick.

26 *Big Nick*

We struggled to choose our favourite route. They've all got something to recommend them. They all share incredible views, remarkable surroundings and an adventurous feel. In the end, this one won (obviously, or it wouldn't be here, it would be over the page with the others). It won because of the superb, wild and occasionally non-existent bit of singletrack along Trout Beck. A proper bonanza of line-finding, thrutchy moves and stunning surroundings, it's a gem of a trail. And it won because of the final section – a real slog of a climb leads up from Cauldron Snout and over Dufton Fell to where High Cup Nick opens out in all its gigantic glory. From there, it's downhill all the way home. Downhill via technical rocky sections, bumpy grass and eye-wateringly fast and pumpy dirt tracks. No matter how tired your legs were, you'll be wide-awake and grinning by the bottom.

Just in case this sounds too much like fun, please remember that it's a big and serious ride. It's long, technical and committing and there's a fair bit of tarmac (although even that is surprisingly enjoyable). It's a brilliant ride, but be ready for it!

Grade: **Black** » Distance: **50km** » Ascent: **1,100m** » Time: **6hrs+**	
Start/Finish: **Dufton** » Start GR: **NY 689250** » SatNav: **Dufton**	
OS Map: **OL19 Howgill Fells and Upper Eden Valley; OL31 North Pennines** » Parking: **Free car park in village**	
Cafe: **None** » Pub: George and Dragon, Garrigill, T: 01434 382 014, www.garrigillpub.co.uk;	
The Stag, Dufton, T: 01768 351 608, www.thestagdufton.co.uk	

Directions

S» Turn **L** from the car park and follow the road out of town. Ignore all turnings for 3km, zigzagging through the village of Knock, before turning **R** up a lane signed *Christian Centre*.

Ride uphill, passing through gates. Near the top, as the road swings left and the gradient finally eases, turn **R** at a small parking area onto a track signed *Public Bridleway*.

Follow the initially obvious and stony track fast downhill. Now you're going to have to follow your nose a little. Superb singletrack runs along Trout Beck, sometimes fast and obvious, sometimes boggy and thrutchy and sometimes very vague. It crosses and re-crosses the river, but is always there – keep going, you'll find it!

Eventually, join a wide track and keep **SA**. Ignore turnings to the right and follow the track through gates and round to the left. Keep **SA** onto tarmac and descend fast – past the source of the River Tyne.

2 Easy to miss: Don't get carried away – it's easy to speed past the turning. The road opens out a little, passes farm buildings and then runs alongside a stone wall. When the wall swings abruptly away, continue for 100m and turn sharp **R** on a wide track. If you reach a big farm on the left, you've gone too far.

Drop to the river and climb past the house. Follow the track up and around to the **R**. Keep going until you (eventually) meet the road. Turn **R**.

Wet Weather (or the 'your directions are rubbish and I can't find the turning' option): You're welcome to follow the 'dry' route, but it'll be a slippery push. Instead, follow the lane into Garrigill. Keep **R**, crossing the river, and then take the next **R**. Climb to the main road and turn **R**.

③ Follow the road for 2.6km. Ignore the first track on the right then, when the road bends left, turn **R** down a wide track. Keep **SA** at the bottom and ride past houses. As the lane begins to climb steeply to the main road, turn **R** onto a lane. Follow this up to a T-junction. Turn **R**.

As the road splits just before the reservoir, bear **L**. Ride alongside the reservoir and drop to ford the river (leave the bikes and scramble off left to see Cauldron Snout).

Ride from the river and, sticking to the obvious track, climb steeply. When the track becomes grass, continue **SA**, following low marker-posts and occasional sections of stone slab. Keep going, following your nose and soon drop towards the river.

Continue alongside the river, scrabbling over limestone lumps, to an obvious bridge. Cross this and turn **R** along an obvious track.

As you reach a wide, open area, turn **L** and ride to the edge. Admire the view and then turn **R** along the edge, aiming for an obvious track on the far side. Climb this with difficulty.

A brilliant descent over rock and grass. Upon arriving at stone walls and gates, keep **R**, ignoring the obvious track to the left. The descent becomes wider and easier, but much, much faster and no less fun. Drop to the road in Dufton.

Turn **R** to return to the car park.

Threlkeld Side. **Photo**: Steve Elsworth.

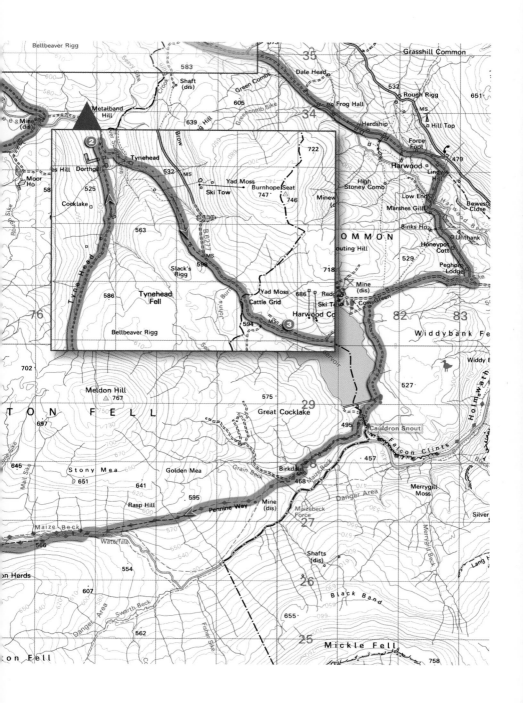

More riding

Bigger Nick

A huge ride through the middle of nowhere – sort of the reverse of the main ride with a slippery grassy descent to finish. A 20-kilometre up-and-over track across moorland, followed by ... another 20-kilometre up-and-over. Incredible views (everyone should see High Cup Nick at some point) and fast descents. The numbers don't lie – this isn't easy – and you don't really want to be up here in bad weather. But you should really go and ride this ...

Grade: **Black** » Distance: **60km** » Ascent: **1,380m** » Time: **All day! (6hrs+)**
Start/Finish: **NY 689250** » OS Map: **Landranger 91 Appleby; Landranger 86 Halthwhistle**

The Route » Dufton – High Cup Nick – Cow Green Reservoir – Harwood – Harwood Common – Garrigill – Skirwith Fell – Kirkland – Blencarn – Knock – Dufton

Not Nick (Cross Fell)

The Kirkland Fell descent has been hailed as one of the best in the country. Grassy, bumpy, rocky and pumpy – it's easy to see why. It also goes past 'Grumply Hill', which makes it a winner even if you don't like the riding. The climb onto Cross Fell is huge and grassy. The views from the top are stunning. Sadly, the section from Rake End to Tees Head is a walk across a trackless bog – a lot of riders PUSH the short footpath section over Cross Fell instead. The descent is well worth it.

Grade: **Red** » Distance: **19km** » Ascent: **640m** » Time: **3hrs+**
Start/Finish: **Kirkland NY 650325** » OS Map: **Landranger 91 Appleby-in-Westmorland**

The Route » Kirkland – Cross Fell – Greg's Hut – Rake End – Tees Head – Wildboard Scar – Grumply Hill – Kirkland

Edmundbyers & Blanchland

A little distance from the other routes here, this is a great little route with a bit of everything. Sweeping doubletrack and fantastic views, fast grassy descents, rocky rumbles – and a few perfect stretches of moorland singletrack. It's wild too, flitting through tiny villages and crossing three big expanses of moorland along the way. Edmundbyers Common is fast, wide singletrack – a decent start but a fantastic finale. Blanchland Moor is crossed first on a big open track, but second time around via a tight and twisty singletrack traverse. And, if it's dry (and only if it's dry – it's not worth the road climb otherwise!), there's another brilliant stretch of singletrack over Bolt's Law. Climbing gently from the road, it drops steeply off the top, arcing through deep gullies before letting off the brakes and screaming off the moor.

Grade: **Red** » Distance: **29/37km** » Ascent: **480/690m** » Time: **3hrs+**
Start/Finish: **Edmundbyers, NZ 014501** » OS Map: **Landranger 87 Hexham & Halthwhistle**

The Route » Edmundbyers – BW west over Edmundbyers Common – BW north to Blanchland – Pennypie House – Aton Fell – Slaley Forest – BW south over Bulbeck Common – Baybridge – road due south to NY 963478 – BW east to Edmundbyers
    Extension from Baybridge – Hunstanworth – road SW to Cuthbert's Hill – BW east over Bolt's Law – BW east to Edmundbyers

More information

Main Towns
There's not a huge amount around here. Try Appleby-in-Westmorland or head west to Penrith.

Maps
OS OL31 North Pennines
OS OL19 Howgill Fells & Upper Eden Valley
OS Landranger 91 Appleby-in-Westmorland
OS Landranger 86 Haltwhistle & Brampton
OS Landranger 87 Hexham & Haltwhistle

Bike Shops
Arragons, Brunswick Road, Penrith, 01768 890 344, www.arragons.com

Accommodation
There's a handily-placed hostel in Dufton (0845 371 9734, www.yha.org.uk). Groups could try the Ormside Mill activity centre near Appleby (01768 351 131, www.ormsidemill.org.uk).

If you're camping, the closest site we know of is the summer-only Westgate Camping Site (07775 933 210) – it's a little way to the north, but still handy for Garrigill.

B&B-wise, try Brow Farm in Dufton (01768 352 865, www.browfarm.com).

Food & Drink
George and Dragon, Garrigill, 01434 382 014, www.garrigillpub.co.uk
The Stag Inn, Dufton, 01768 351 608, www.thestagdufton.co.uk, (also offers accommodation)
The Royal Oak, Appleby-in-Westmorland, 01768 351 463, www.royaloakappleby.co.uk

Tourist Offices
Appleby Council offer TIC service in the Moot Hall in the centre of town, 01768 351 177, tic@applebytown.org.uk

Outdoor Shops
Head for Penrith.

Guidebooks
Just this one!

The Cheviots & Northumberland

What do you expect from a remote national park that lies on the border between England and Scotland? Hopefully, big, empty hills – 'cos that's what you're getting. The Cheviots sit literally on the border between the two countries.

You can climb up onto the hills, (to, say Windy Gyle or Butt Roads – snigger snigger), admire the views north and south and then drop over the border into another country. Literally 'up and over'. And what an up and over! Big, rolling, grassy hills cut by steep-sided valleys and dotted with thick forests. The accompanying views are something else and are made all the better by the conspicuous lack of civilisation (although there are a couple of seriously large army firing ranges that break the quiet). Moving south from the border and off the Cheviots, the countryside is equally impressive. Bleakly beautiful, it's dotted with spectacular sandstone outcrops, weathered into unlikely shapes and formations. The hills are lower, making the big views less frequent, but the closer surroundings more than make up for it, with vibrant heather and bracken splashing colour across the moors.

The Riding

Being very general, the riding in the Cheviots isn't overly technical. It's often steep and you can easily reach eye-watering speeds on the grassy descents – a combination which can get pretty sketchy in the wet – but you don't really get the tight corners or rocky gardens of other areas. (Except on Wooler Common – see page 198) That's not to say it's not fun – trying to make tight corners at high speeds on slippery surfaces will certainly test your commitment and opposite-locking skills! Away from the grassy trails, you get plenty of multi-line rutted descents and a decent smattering of rocky/pebbly/high speed affairs – the type where you've got to hang on and trust your tyres. You also get mile-munching trails across big rolling hills with views that go on and on. Not being overly well-known with other riders, it's likely to be quiet – we've never seen more than a couple of other tyre tracks when we've been. It's a very under-ridden area, which you may find makes riding here very appealing.

When to go

Northumberland is big and open and there aren't many villages or places to hide. Make of that what you will. That said, while a lot of the riding is on grassy surfaces which become hard work in the wet, there are also a fair number of hard tracks and forest roads (i.e. near Rothbury), so you should always be able to find something to ride.

Cheviot Hills. **Photo**: Benjamin Haworth.

27 Alwinton & the Cheviots

A lot of Northumberland 'first rides' take place around Kidland Forest and Coquetdale. Predictably, that's because it gives you a very good (in both senses) glimpse of what Northumberland has to offer, and because it finishes along a great stretch of singletrack. It's not a technical ride, but you need to be good at climbing and descending on grass — because there's a lot of the green stuff. This means that, if it's wet, you need to have big legs for the ups and a love of out-of-control slithering for the downs. (It's more fun than that makes it sound!) The big legs are needed straight away on this ride: the route heads north from Alwinton along Clennel Street (an ancient drove road) — a big and grassy climb that offers even bigger and grassier views across the Cheviots. The reward — other than the views — is a very steep and very fast (grassy) descent to the stream near Uswayford and a rather nice spot for lunch. Push on, and a pleasant forest road traverse leads to more grassy trails and another screamingly fast descent. Some tight turns provide a few foot-out cornering opportunities before depositing you at another (recommended) food stop at the cafe in Barrowburn. Don't eat too much though — the steepest climb of the day follows. A few quick bends through the trees lead to Usway Burn and a beautiful piece of riverside singletrack. Pine trees, rocks, perfect dirt ... awesome.

Grade: **Red** » Distance: **27km** » Ascent: **740m** » Time: **4hrs+**	
Start/Finish: **Alwinton car park** » Start GR: **NT 919063** » SatNav: **Alwinton**	
OS Map: **OL16 The Cheviot Hills** » Parking: **Pay and Display**	
Cafe: **Barrowburn Cafe, Barrowburn, T: 01669 621 176, www.barrowburn.com**	
Pub: **Rose and Thistle, Alwinton, T: 01669 650 226, www.roseandthistlealwinton.com**	

Directions

🄢 Turn **L** out of the car park and follow the road around to the right. Just as you leave Alwinton, turn **L** up a lane, heading for Clennell Street. Ride up to the farm and keep **R** onto a wide track, following purple byway arrows.

Follow the wide grassy track steeply uphill. Ignore a bridleway running off through a gate to the right and stick to the grassy track, ignoring all turnings, until you climb to join a better track in forestry land. Turn **L** (in effect **SA**) onto this track. Keep **L** when the track forks after 2km and drop fast into the trees.

After another 1.5km, keep **SA** onto a narrower trail when the main track bends left. Follow this out of the woods, through a gate, and descend fast around the hillside on grassy tracks. Cross the bridge and climb steeply to a track on the other side.

② Turn **R** and ride 100m to a better track. Turn **L** and, ignoring turnings, ride around the head of the valley. (Technically, the bridleway drops across the valley to the left, but the descent is non-existent and it's a slog back out, so stick to the main track.)

As you pass woodlands on the left, keep **SA** (along the fence) as the track bends right. Climb to rejoin the track and then turn sharp **L** on a marked bridleway as the trees end. Go through the gate and follow the grassy track around to the **R** and across open ground, eventually descending fast to Barrowburn (watch out for the corners!).

Keep **SA** past the buildings for the cafe, or turn **L** across the ford and climb past the bunkhouse, through a gate, and onto a wide track. Descend to the river, tackle the hideously steep climb and drop fast through woodlands.

As the track bends left, continue **SA** to cross a narrow bridge and follow a singletrack bridleway behind the house. Follow this (great riding) alongside the river, through woods and across fields, eventually following bridleway signs uphill and along the fence edge as you reach the farm. Cross the bridge, keep **R** and then go through a gate onto a wide track.

③ Upon reaching buildings at the end of the valley, turn **L**. Pass in front of the buildings and go through a gate onto a wide track. Follow this uphill, bearing **R** onto a grassy track after a short distance. This soon turns to singletrack. Climb uphill, go **SA** over a wider track and cross the river before tackling a very steep grassy climb.

Go over the top of the hill. Ignore a track dropping right and go through the right-hand (smaller) of the two gates. Continue around the hillside and drop fast across the fields to the road. Turn **L** for Alwinton.

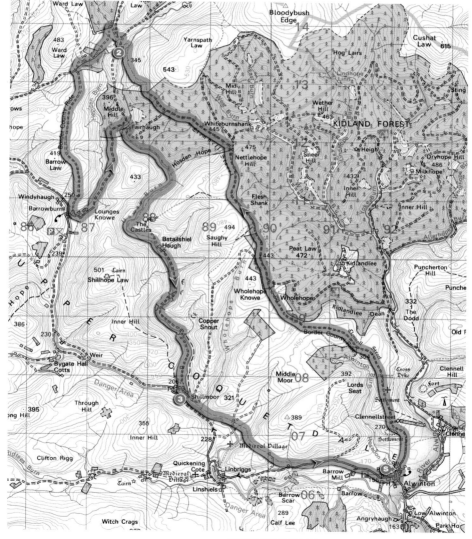

More riding

Wooler Common

This ride is listed as a loop, but, to be totally honest, we'd probably ride the off-road section – right down to the river – as a there-and-back, getting the best of the singletrack in both directions. And what singletrack! From the top of the Common back towards Wooler, it flows down through the valley bowl in long sweeping sections. Dropping from the same point north to the river is a tight, steep plummet. Ride it and see why this is one of our favourite rides in the North East.

Grade: **Red** » Distance: **17km** » Ascent: **500m** » Time: **2hrs+**
Start/Finish: **Wooler, NT 991280** » OS Map: **Landranger 75 Berwick-upon-Tweed**

The Route » Wooler – road south to Earle – road west to Hawsen Burn – Broadstruther – Wooler Common – through the woods – Wooler

Rothbury Round

Nothing technical here, just a big ride with a lot of good scenery and fast riding. An easy, forest-filled start past some of the best views in Northumberland leads to a moorland crossing and fast doubletrack descent. Finishing off is a good climb, a speedy scenic traverse and a fast, twisting descent – with a sting in the tail. If you want to shorten the route, it's easily splittable at Thropton – the first half becoming an XC-style ride with stunning views, the second containing more climbing and opportunities for playing around.

Grade: **Blue** » Distance: **37km (easily shortened)** » Ascent: **580m** » Time: **3.5hrs+**
Start/Finish: **Rothbury, NU 057015** » OS Map: **Landranger 81 Alnwick & Morpeth**

The Route » Rothbury – Whitton – Whitton Hillhead – Simonside Forest – Weather Head – Chartners – Whitefield – Bickerton – Ryehill – Summerville – Thropton – South Cartington – NU 054038 – west and then south to Addycombe – Rothbury

There & Back Again

Start at the Barrowburn 'front room' cafe, climb into the middle of nowhere and go through the gate into Scotland. A flat out descent and a big grassy climb up an ancient smuggling route later and you're back at the border, ready for more rapid grassy descending through stunning countryside. It's definitely worth detouring west, along the border at the top, as the flagstone singletrack up there makes a fantastic and brilliantly-situated piece of riding. A bit of an adventure and an awesome ride.

Grade: **Red** » Distance: **30km** » Ascent: **750m** » Time: **3.5hrs+**
Start/Finish: **Barrowburn, NT 866106** » OS Map: **Landranger 80 Cheviot Hills & Kielder Water; Landranger 74 Kelso & Coldstream**

The Route » Barrowburn – Middle Hill – Hazely Law – over the border to Cocklawfoot – minor road to Belford – west to Windy Law – south along The Street – divert west on flagstone border singletrack to Lamb Hill and back – Barrowburn

More information

Main Towns

Rothbury is the main town in the area we've focused on here. Wooler, Alnwick and Morpeth are all relatively close if you need bike shops and the like.

Maps

OS OL16 *The Cheviot Hills*
OS Landranger 74 *Kelso & Coldstream*
OS Landranger 75 *Berwick-upon-Tweed*
OS Landranger 80 *Cheviot Hills & Kielder Water*
OS Landranger 81 *Alnwick & Morpeth*
OS Landranger 87 *Hexham & Haltwhistle*

Bike Shops

The Bike Place, Bellingham, 01434 220 210, www.thebikeplace.co.uk
Cyclelife, Oak Drive, Alnwick, 01665 602 925, www.cyclelife-alnwick.co.uk
Purple Mountain, Kielder Forest visitor centre, 01434 250 532, www.purplemountain.co.uk

Accommodation

If you want to camp, Clennell Hall is right by Alwinton: 01669 650, www.clennellhall.co.uk

Right in the heart of the Cheviots, the friendly Barrowburn Cafe also runs a bunkhouse – 01669 621 176, www.barrowburn.com

A little further south, in the centre of Rothbury, is Tomlinson's Bunkhouse: 01669 621 979, www.tomlinsonsrothbury.co.uk

Blue Bell Farm, a little out of the way for riding but in a beautiful spot, offers bunkhouse accommodation and camping: 01668 213 362, www.bluebellfarmbelford.co.uk

If you want a B&B, try www.northumberlandbikebreaks.com in Rothbury: 01669 621 167.

Food & Drink

Cafes
On our main route: Barrowburn Cafe, Barrowburn, 01669 621 176, www.barrowburn.com
In Rothbury: Tomlinson's Bunkhouse: 01669 621 979, www.tomlinsonsrothbury.co.uk
Pubs
Rose and Thistle, Alwinton, 01669 650 226, www.roseandthistlealwinton.com

Tourist Offices

Rothbury National Park Centre, Church Street, 01669 620 887, www.northumberlandnationalpark.org.uk
Otterburn, 01830 520 093, tic@otterburnmill.co.uk

Useful Websites

www.visitnorthumberland.com – accommodation, visitor information and so forth
www.visit-rothbury.co.uk – tourist information on Rothbury and Cocquetdale

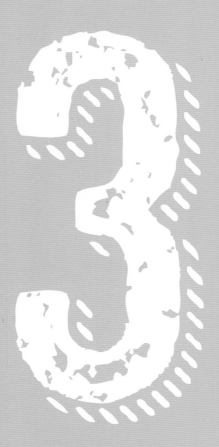

Wales

Snowdon Ranger's Path Photo: Benjamin Haworth

01: Clwyds singletrack.   02: Snowdon summit, the highest point in England and Wales.   03: Signing the book at the top of the Wayfarer pass, Berwyns.

04: Singletrack beneath Moel Famau, Clwyds.   05: Portage back up Rhyd Ddu, Snowdon.   06: Crug Mawr, Black Mountains.

07

08

09

10

07: The Hand pub at Llanarmon.   **08**: Heading up Snowdon.   **09**: Brecon Beacons singletrack.   **10**: Snowdon.   **All photos**: John Coefield.

The Gower Peninsula & Pembroke

Sun! Sea! Sandcastles! Wondering where to go for your summer holiday? You could do worse than South West Wales.

Gower, poking out into the Bristol Channel, is a pretty little peninsula, with an attractive coastline of bays, beaches and cliffs bordering a much quieter, greener interior. Pembroke, in contrast, has a much bigger and wilder feel to it. There are more beaches, more towns and everything's more spread out. It too has a green centre – which this time has a sizeable ridge of hills running through it. Sadly, neither is a premier-league mountain bike destination, as the riding in both is rather limited. That doesn't mean it isn't worthwhile. There's seaside singletrack on Gower and big, fast descending in Pembroke's Preseli Hills. You could make a riding weekend of the two or use either the usual Brecons/ Afan riding. And if you're in the area for a beach holiday, it's definitely worth bringing your bike.

The Riding

There's not a huge amount of riding here, but luckily, what there is will definitely entertain you for a day or two. Gower first: there's nothing particularly technical bar a couple of rocky challenges in the north and some incredibly steep bits on Rhossili Down. Trails tend to be grassy and wide, with fun coming from easily-attained speed and undulations, which, taken with the aforementioned rapidity, become brilliantly pumpy and jumpy. The riding vibe here is one of chilling in the sun, taking climbs easy and admiring the surroundings before heading to the beach for a barbecue and a swim. Pembroke is very different. The main riding area is the Preseli Hills, a seven-kilometre-long wild-feeling ridge well away from the sea. This is big enough to give sizeable descents and climbs – including a great downhill-trending run along the entire length of the ridge. Predominantly grassy, but with a smattering of rocky outcrops and entertaining sections of moorland singletrack, the riding is faster and more open than Gower – and closer in feel to the rest of Wales.

When to go

The Preseli Hills are a boggy no-no in wet weather. And the grassy Gower trails become hard work after rain. And as you're unlikely to have much fun on the beach in such conditions, and you drive past some of the best trail centres in the UK to get to either area, we'd save a trip for a sunny day.

Llangennith, Gower. **Photo**: Tom Hutton.

28 The Gower Route

The classic Gower route with a bit of everything: views, singletrack and grassy runs. The ridge out of Penmaen gets going quickly, with great views on both sides and a wide open and flat out descent off the end. This is followed by the most technical trail on Gower – a narrow, rocky and technical singletrack that drops and climbs into Cheriton. Add plenty of vegetation and a smattering of dampness and you've got a real challenge. Leaving Cheriton, there's a tough road/track climb before a beautiful descent. It's fast, grassy and bounces across an open hillside where there's plenty of time to see your lines and really let go. Take to the road through Llangennith to reach Rhossili down, where an easy singletrack traverse runs alongside the wide beach at Rhossili Bay. The riding's good, the seaside ambience is even better. From here, wide tracks and fields lead back to the Cefn Bryn ridge and home, via the excellent King Arthur Pub at Reynoldston.

Grade: **Blue/Red** » Distance: **33km** » Ascent: **620m** » Time: **2.5hrs+**	
Start/Finish: **Penmaen** » Start GR: **SS 530887** » SatNav: **Penmaen**	
OS Map: **Explorer 164 Gower** » Parking: **Car park at start**	
Cafe: **Lots of small shops along the way**	
Pub: **The King Arthur, Reynoldston, 01792 390 775; The King's Head, Llangennith, 01792 386 212**	

Directions

S From the car park, turn **L** and then immediately **R** onto a wide track. Climb to join another track and turn **L**. Follow this track along the top of the ridge, ignoring turnings, to a road.

Continue **SA** over the road onto a grassy track. Go through a small car park and continue in the same direction along another wide grassy track. Keep **L** at the fork (don't go to the trig point) and begin to descend. Keep **R** at the next obvious fork and descend steeply to a tarmac lane. Turn **L** to the road.

Turn **R**, then sharply **L** after 750m. Climb for 100m and then turn **R** onto a signed bridleway. Follow this uphill and out onto open ground. Continue along this through gates and onto a rocky descent. Cross the stream and attempt to clean the singletrack climb beyond. Continue **SA** along the drive to the road.

Turn **L** and ride towards Cheriton. After a short road descent and climb, turn **L** onto a narrow singletrack bridleway. Follow this to the road and turn **L**.

2 Climb steeply uphill, taking the second signed bridleway on the **R** – a wide stone track. Follow this uphill around corners.

Stick with the track as it runs alongside the hillside and past two houses. Upon reaching open ground, turn **R**, uphill on a grassy track. At the top, turn **L** and begin to descend a fast grassy trail. Keep **L** at the fork and fly downhill to the road at a car park.

Turn **R** onto the road and ride through Llangennith to a mini-roundabout. Turn **L** and follow the road to the pay booth for the campsite. Turn **L** through a gate onto a signed bridleway and then bear **R** to follow a grassy bridleway along the bottom of the hill. Follow this via grassy tracks and singletrack to climb slightly to Rhossili. Turn **L** onto the road and then take the next **L** (after 700m).

3 Follow the road, ignoring turnings, **SA** past the activity centre and onto a dirt track. Now follow bridleway markers around to the **R** and through fields to a farm and the road. Turn **R**.

At the main road, turn **L**. Follow this for 1.5km, past the petrol station, and take the second lane on the **L**, towards Reynoldston. Follow the road through the village and past the King Arthur pub. Keep **SA** over the crossroads and climb to the top of the hill. Turn **R** and retrace your tyre tracks along the ridge to Penmaen.

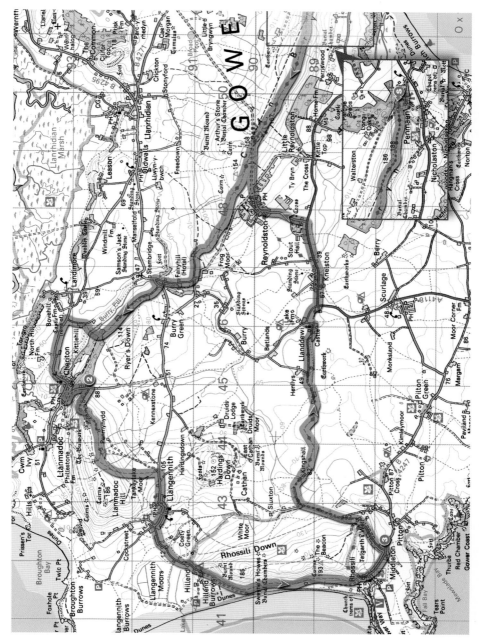

29 The Pembroke Route

You could ride this as a there-and-back along the ridge, or use country lanes to form a loop as we've done here. If looping, expect a fair bit of road to start – not exactly exciting, but giving plenty of warming up and chatting time, and passing some surprisingly interesting fields(!). A big climb – with some tricky little sections – gains the ridge. Once up, vague grassy tracks, rocky sections and fast, wide singletrack (the moorland sort with loads of line choices, a fast surface and lots of things to bounce off and over) carries you more or less downhill along the entire length of the ridge! It's not too difficult, which means you can relax and really enjoy it. There are a couple of bits where navigation can get tricky in bad weather (it's boggy then anyway, so stay away), and a couple of climbs, but otherwise this is a solid seven kilometres of good fun off-road descending.

Grade: **Blue/Red** » Distance: **24km** » Ascent: **400m** » Time: **2.5hrs+**
Start/Finish: **Lay-by near Crymych** » Start GR: **SN 165330** » SatNav: **Crymych**
OS Map: **Explorer OL35 North Pembrokeshire** » Parking: **Lay-by**
Cafe: **None** » Pub: **Tafarn Sinc, Rosebush, 01437 532 214**

Directions

S Head south from the lay-by (as if passing it on the left) towards Mynachlog-ddu. Go through the village and turn **R** just as you leave the houses – following signs for Sustrans Cycle Route No. 47. Ignore all turnings until you reach a T-junction with a main road.

Turn **R**, and then take the next **R** towards Rosebush. Keep **SA** as the junction and then keep **SA** once more onto a dirt track as the road ends.

2 Ride past the quarry and into the woods. Turn **R** after the low gate and then, as the track bends slightly to the right, turn **L** onto a narrower, signed bridleway leading out of the woods.

Go uphill and then back into the trees. At the junction, bear **L**, and then follow the forest road uphill. Ignore turnings to the left and right until you reach the top of the hill, and then, as the track swings right, go **SA** out of the forest.

3 Go through the gate and turn **R** – the track is very vague here and if it's been wet you'll be wading through a bog … Follow the fence line initially and then continue roughly **SA** along the ridge, following vague grassy tracks and sections of singletrack. Ignore all turnings dropping off the ridge.

Drop downhill and then **R** to cross a boggy area. The track vanishes, but wooden posts mark the way. Follow these uphill until the track becomes apparent once more and then continue **SA** once more. Go past rocky outcrops and pick up an obvious track alongside a small forest. Drop fast over grass to a sunken track and turn **R**, through a gate. Follow the track to the road and the parking area.

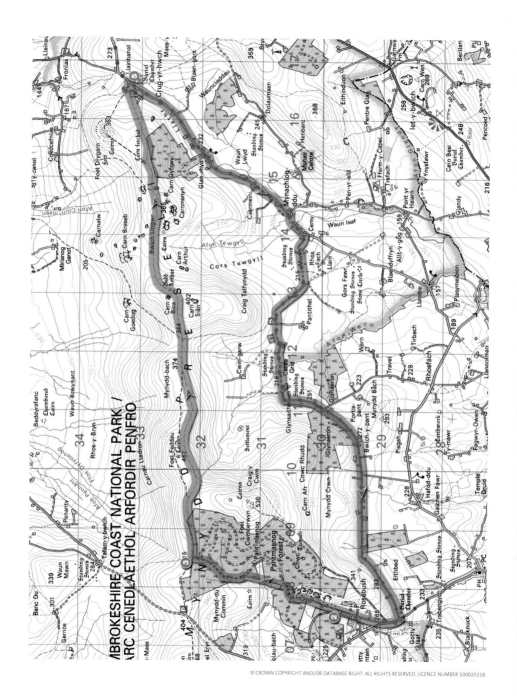

The Trail Centres

Afan Argoed/Glyncorrwg

The dual centre of Afan and Glyncorrwg is top notch – rough, flowing singletrack. Quick riders will love the twists and turns, technical aficionados the rocks, and beginners the sheer amount of singletrack. Highlights are the long descent off the *The Wall* and the entire, completely-singletrack *White's Level* (the W^2 combines these two trails). The *Penhydd* was undergoing a facelift at the time of writing, but will hopefully keep its worryingly narrow, rooty sections. We're not fans of the amount of forest road on the *Skyline*, preferring the *July Trail*, a shortened version which manages to include the best of the singletrack.

Trail Count: **Afan Argoed** » **Penhydd, Red, 17km** » **The Wall, Red, 23km**

Glyncorrwg » **White's Level, Red, 15km** » **July (shortened and better version of Skyline), Red, 22km** » **W² (The Wall and White's), Black, 44km** » **Skyline, Red, 46km**

Start: **Afan Argoed Visitor Centre on the A4107 north of Port Talbot, SS 821951, SA13 3HG**

Glyncorrwg Vistor Centre, Glyncorrwg, SS 872984, SA13 3EA

More info: **Afan, 01639 850 564** » **Glyncorrwg, 01639 851 900** » **www.afanforestpark.co.uk** » **www.mbwales.com**

Brechfa

A really good collection of trails. The green Derwen Trail (and its blue-grade extension) is possibly the best of its grade in the country – a loop of wide, smooth singletrack, sweeping corners and rolling undulations. The Gorlech Trail is a big BMX trail, with descents of big berms, pumping compressions and lofting jumps. The Raven Trail earns its black grade by combining natural-feeling singletrack and even bigger and faster descents than the Gorlech (although the former is our preferred route). It's possible to link the trails for a mammoth ride.

Trail Count: **Derwen Trail, Green, 9km** » **Derwen Extension, Blue, +5km** » **Gorlech Trail, Red, 19km** » **Raven Trail, Black, 18.5km**

Start: **Two car parks – upper for Gorlech trail, lower for everything else** » SatNav: **Brechfa**

Lower: In Brechfa, on the B4310, SN 545315 » **Upper: 2km east of Brechfa on the B4130, SN 587337**

More info: **www.mbwales.com (no centre, no phone)**

Good bike hire: **Bike Brechfa, 01558 685811, www.bikebrechfa.co.uk**

Rhossili Down, Gower. **Photo**: Benjamin Haworth.

More information

Main Towns

There aren't really any towns as such on Gower – you've got small shops here and there, but Swansea's the place for anything more. In Pembroke, the Preseli Hills are a little away from things. Head for Fishguard or Haverfordwest.

Maps

OS Explorer 164 Gower
OS Explorer OL35 North Pembrokeshire
OS Landranger 159 Swansea & Gower
OS Landranger 145 Cardigan & Mynydd Preseli

Bike Shops

Tredz, Swansea Enterprise Park, Swansea, 01792 799 508, www.tredz.co.uk
Wheelies, Uplands Crescent, Swansea, 01792 472 612, www.wheeliesuplands.co.uk
Skyline Cycles, Glyncorrwg and Afan trail centres, 01639 850 011 (Glyncorrwg)/ 01639 851 100 (Afan), www.skylinecycles.tumblr.com
Pembrokeshire Bikes, Rushacre Enterprise Park, Narberth, 01834 862 755, www.pembrokeshirebikes.co.uk
Mike's Bikes, Prendergast, Haverfordwest, 01437 760 068, www.mikes-bikes.co.uk

Accommodation

These are two of the most popular holiday destinations in Wales. If you can't find accommodation here, you're doing something wrong. There are campsites all over Gower, some near the beach, some in the centre. Any will do fine, although we like Hillend Camping Park, (01792 386 204, www.hillendcamping.com).

It's a similar situation in Pembrokeshire, campsites everywhere – but if you're there solely to ride, look at places near the Preseli Hills such as Rhydhowell Farm (tiny – 01239 841 267, www.rhydhowellfarm.co.uk) or the caravan sites at Rosebush (01437 532 206) or Trefach (01994 419 225).

Useful websites for Gower and Pembrokeshire are www.stayinwales.co.uk and www.staysouthwestwales.co.uk. For Gower, www.the-gower.com is basic, but has sorted us out before, while www.pembrokeshireholidays.co.uk does a similar job for Pembrokeshire.

Hostel-wise, there's a big YHA group hut near Rhossili on Gower, with Swansea being the next option, although there is an independent hostel at Llangennith (01792 386 222). In Pembroke, the YHA has several places on the coast, near Haverfordwest, in Cardigan and in Newport, but nothing close to the riding.

Food & Drink

Gower
The King Arthur Hotel, Reynoldston, 01792 390 775, www.kingarthurhotel.co.uk (also does accommodation)
The Worm's Head Hotel, Rhossili, 01792 390 512, www.thewormshead.co.uk
Pembrokeshire
Tafarn Sinc, Rosebush, 01437 532 214, www.tafarnsinc.co.uk (highly recommended for food)

Tourist Offices
Gower » Swansea, 01792 468 321, www.visitswanseabay.com/tic
Pembrokeshire » Fishguard, 01437 776 636, www.pembrokeshire.gov.uk

Outdoor Shops
There aren't many around. Try Swansea, or the bigger towns around the Pembrokeshire coast.

Useful Websites
www.enjoygower.com » www.visitpembrokeshire.com

Guidebooks
Wales Mountain Biking – Beicio Mynydd Cymru, written by Tom Hutton, published by Vertebrate Publishing

Rhossili Down, Gower. **Photo:** Benjamin Haworth.

The Brecon Beacons & the Black Mountains

In 2000 BC, Stone Age man (and woman) arrived in the Brecons and began raising the standing stones that litter the park. Bronze Age man joined in, somehow erecting a massive 12-foot tall monolith underneath Fan Nedd (SN 921193, if you're interested). The Iron Age came, built a few hill forts, and went, later followed by the Romans. In their usual style, they drove a road (Sarn Helen) through the middle of everything and then dug a couple of gold(!) mines. It got a little wild when they left, prompting King Offa to build his Dyke to contain things.

Later, the French, having invaded England, carried on into Wales, bringing a little civilisation and building Brecon Castle. Nothing much happened for a while, until the industrious Victorians crept in, adding a reservoir here, a plantation there and a mine or two in the middle. They even took to manufacturing gunpowder at Pontneddfechan. Luckily, they didn't blow up too much and the stunning Brecon landscape remains.

The Riding

There's a lot of different riding criss-crossing the Brecon Beacons. While a few of the lesser-used bridleways are tussocky, grassy and vague, the remainder give a good spread of great riding. There are broad, stone-based trails, which are perfect for covering distance and admiring the impressive surroundings. Every now and then these 'deteriorate' into technical rocky gardens which, around here, tend to be blocky, sharp-edged and often loose. In other areas, there's superb singletrack. Ranging from sandy moorland to dirt-based trails that fly through the bracken, it's real standout stuff and great fun to ride. And that about sums up the Brecons: memorable and great fun – it's some of the best riding in the UK. Although, for some reason, most rides around here either don't seem to encounter villages, or the villages don't have shops, so take food with you!

When to go

The obvious mountainous/remote rules apply here – the weather can be bad, the snow can be deep, and so on, but generally you'll find something to ride all year round. If it's wet and muddy, our main route can get slimy, but something stonier like The Gap (page 218) will hold up well.

The Gap. **Photo:** Benjamin Haworth.

30 Mynydd Llangorse

A brilliant ride, featuring a of superb and virtually unbroken singletrack run along Mynydd Llangorse. To reach it, you need to haul yourself out of Llangors and up the steep road to Mynydd Troed. Don't worry, it's worth it, as the aforementioned singletrack really is *that* good. Over five kilometres of narrow, non-stop, gently downhill, swoopy and semi-technical riding. With nice views. It's definitely best in summer, but slitherable in winter if you really must. From there, a stiff climb (which we've never cleaned – can you?) leads back up high, ready for a fast grass descent to the vowel-less village of Bwlch. Watch out, there's a definite sting in the tail. Out of Bwlch, a final climb sets you up for the last singletrack blast. It's not long, but it is great fun in a steep and twisty kind of way.

Grade: **Red** » Distance: **26km** » Ascent: **650m** » Time: **3hrs+**	
Start/Finish: **Llangors** » Start GR: **SO 128273** » SatNav: **Llangors**	
OS Map: **OL12 Brecon Beacons National Park (Western Area)** » Parking: **By Llangors Lake**	
Cafe: **Sandwich time** » Pub: **The Castle Inn, Llangors, 01874 658819**	

Directions

S From the lake, follow the access road back into Llangors. Turn **R** at the T-junction and **R** again at the second. Follow the road through Llangors. Shortly after passing The Castle Inn on your left, turn **L** at a grassy area (tree with funky bench around it).

Follow the road out of the village, forking **L** at the junction. Ignore turnings for 2km and then turn **L** at the T-junction. Keep **SA** at the next junction and, on a left hand bend, continue **SA** through a gate onto a signed bridleway through a field. Follow this vague trail slightly uphill (essentially **SA**) to a gate by a farm. Go through this gate and turn **R** through another gate just before the first barn on the left.

Climb easily uphill between trees. Upon reaching open ground, continue **SA** on grassy trails and traverse the field (don't climb the hill on the left!). The track soon becomes more obvious and sections of singletrack appear. Take whichever line appeals, just keep roughly **SA**.

2 Go **SA** over the road. Climb for about 30m before bearing **R** onto a narrow grassy trail. This rapidly turns into superb singletrack. Swoop along this, through gates and into the woods. Go **SA** at the crossroads and climb steeply through gates to fields.

Continue **SA** on vague tracks across the fields, passing buildings on you right. Go through the gate, ford the stream and continue **SA**, climbing steeply up the obvious track ahead.

As the gradient eases, keep following grassy tracks to a wall corner and bridleway junction. Continue **SA**, keeping the wall to your right until your reach a junction marked with a cairn.

Turn **R** and follow the wide track, ignoring all turnings, downhill. Meeting the wall, keep this immediately to your right, riding along the top of the blunt grassy ridge and continue to avoid turnings until the wall ends and the grassy bridleway drops off the end of the ridge.

Descend rapidly and watch out for the steepening at the end. Go through gates to the lane and turn **R**. Keep **L** at the junction and drop to the main road. Turn **R** and follow the road out of Bwlch. Shortly after leaving the village, keep **SA** onto a lane as the main road swings left.

3 As the lane bends right, continue **SA** through a narrow gate onto a signed bridleway (Brecon Venison farm entrance to the right) and climb singletrack.

After the gate, bear slightly **L** (effectively **SA**) across the field. The trail soon becomes more defined. Follow it through more gates to the top of the hill. Undulating singletrack leads over the top and onto the descent.

Drop to a junction with a wider track and turn **L**. Turn **L** on a sharp right hand bend.

At the road, turn **L** and ride into Pennorth. Take the next **R**, keep **L** at the fork and then turn **R** at the T-junction, following signs to *Llangors*. Follow the road around through the next village and back into Llangors. Turn **R**, following signs for the lake and campsites.

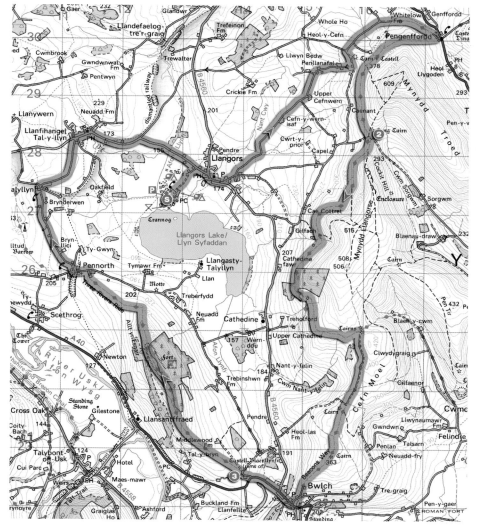

More riding

The Gap

The Gap is *the* ride of the Brecons – the one everyone's heard of. It's a big loop running north under Pen y Fan and back via Talybont reservoir. Although long, the climbs are gentle and well-surfaced, so it's not too tiring (and is definitely worth the effort). The descents are crackers. Mainly fast and wide, there's a big rock garden to tackle at the top and a couple of flat-out runs to finish. And the whole thing runs through spectacular surroundings. A Welsh Classic for good reason.

Grade: **Red/Black** » Distance: **35km** » Ascent: **900m** » Time: **4hrs+**
Start/Finish: **Top of Pontsticill Reservoir, SO 054143** » OS Map: **OL13 Brecon Beacons National Park (Eastern Area)**

The Route » Pontsticill Reservoir top car park – north on road – SO 041163 – SO 048167 – SO 035173 – north over the Gap to road at SO 037237 – SO 045242 – lanes to Tynllwyn (SO 062246) – Llanfrynach – roads east to Talybont-on-Usk – Taff Trail south to SO 109212 – SO 102177 – SO 090161 – SO 073154 – Pontsticill

The Blorenge

The Blorenge is a small and fantastically-named hill on the southern edge of the Brecons. And this route is a great way to explore it. There's some tough climbing, but the reward is superb hillside singletrack and rocky descending. It's one of our favourite Brecon rides and just the thing if you're after a quick blast. We've started high, although it's often ridden from a lower point to give a bigger climb and descent.

Grade: **Red** » Distance: **11km** » Ascent: **450m** » Time: **1hr+**
Start/Finish: **Pond car park, SO 254107** » OS Map: **OL13 Brecon Beacons National Park (Eastern Area)**

The Route » Pond car park – NE around The Blorenge to the Punchbowl – west to SO 278111 – White House Farm – SO 277 101 – SO 270109 – car park

The Best of the Brecons & Black Mountains

There are an endless number of good rides in the Brecons and the Black Mountains and this route mixes two of the best for guaranteed fun. It begins with a pleasant cruise up a valley, followed by a brilliant descent that chops and changes fast between grass and rock. That done, it joins the long singletrack run from the Llangorse ride. Over five kilometres of fast, swoopy fun, this is among the best natural singletracks anywhere!

Grade: **Red/Black** » Distance: **38km** » Ascent: **1,000m** » Time: **4hrs+**
Start/Finish: **Crickhowell, SO 219184** » OS Map: **OL13 Brecon Beacons National Park (Eastern Area)**

The Route » Crickhowell – NE on minor roads past Llanbedr to Cwm Farm (SO 235238) – north on bridleway to SO 204286 – west down Rhiw Trumau and then roads to Pengenffordd – Whitelow Farm – south to SO 161283 – south along west side of Mynydd Llangorse to SO 148257 – SO 159250 – Bwlch – south on roads to Llangynidr – roads east to Crickhowell

Taff Trail. **Photo:** Benjamin Haworth

More information

Main Towns

In the north, Brecon has pretty much everything you could want and is easy to navigate. There are a host of larger places (like Merthyr Tydfil) along the southern edge of the Brecons.

Maps

OS OL12 Brecon Beacons National Park (Western Area)
OS OL13 Brecon Beacons National Park (Eastern Area)

Bike Shops

Biped Cycles, Ship Street, Brecon, 01874 622296, www.bipedcycles.co.uk
Bikes and Hikes, Lion Yard, Brecon, 01874 610071, www.bikesandhikes.co.uk
Gateway Cycles, Brecon Road, Abergavenny, 01873 858519, www.gatewaycycles.co.uk

Accommodation

As per usual for National Parks, there's a wide choice of accommodation in the Brecon Beacons. Broadly speaking, anywhere near Brecon itself will offer relatively easy access to most riding, although staying somewhere more central will probably be more picturesque.

www.mbwales.com is a useful MTB site with a links to accommodation search engines.

www.brecon-beacons.com is a very basic, but useful site for campsites, bunkhouses and hostels.

There are several independent hostels in the area, including a bunkhouse for groups near Ystradfellte and usefully-situated hostels in Bwlch and Llangattock in the central Brecons. See www.independenthostelguide.com for details. Otherwise, there are YHA hostels in Brecon, Abergavenny, Talybont and Llwyn y Celyn – just off the A470: www.yha.org.uk

There are campsites everywhere. Of particular use to bikers (for location), are the Llangorse Lake site (01874 658226, www.llangorselake.co.uk) and Gilestone site near Talybont (01874 676236, www.gilestonecaravanpark.co.uk).

For cottages and B&Bs, try www.breconcottages.com or www.stayinwales.co.uk

Of particular all-round use is The Castle Inn (01874 711353, www.thecastleinn.co.uk), high above Talgarth, which offers B&B, bunkhouse rooms and camping, all beside a decent pub.

Food & Drink

The Castle Inn, Pengenffordd, south of Talgarth, 01874 711353 www.thecastleinn.co.uk (accommodation)
The George Hotel, Brecon, 01874 623421, www.george-hotel.com (accommodation)
Tipple 'n' Tiffin, Brecon, 01874 611866 (decent restaurant)
Nantyffin Cider Mill, Brecon Rd, just west of Crickhowell, 01873 810775 www.cidermill.co.uk (good food and drink)
The Bear, Crickhowell, 01873 810408, www.bearhotel.co.uk (accommodation)

Tourist Offices

National Park Visitor Centre, Libanus 01874 623366, visitor.centre@breconbeacons.org
Abergavenny, 01873 853254, www.visitabergavenny.co.uk
Brecon, 01874 622485, brectic@powys.gov.uk
Crickhowell, 01874 811970, www.crickhowellinfo.org.uk
Talgarth, 01874 712226 www.talgarthcentre.org.uk

Outdoor Shops

Take your pick in Brecon. The biggest is Cotswold Outdoor (01874 622551), but there are also numerous good smaller shops, including Gibb Outdoors (01874 622949).

Useful Websites

www.mbwales.com » **www.mtbbreconbeacons.co.uk** » **www.breconbeacons.org** » **www.travelbreconbeacons.info**

Guidebooks

Wales Mountain Biking – Beicio Mynydd Cymru, written by Tom Hutton, published by Vertebrate Publishing

Worth Knowing

There's a bike bus which runs on Sundays and Bank Holidays from the end of May to the end of September. It runs between Cardiff and Brecon. See www.travelbreconbeacons.info/beacons-bus for details.

Too wet for the Brecons? Need a quick hit? Lucky you – Cwmcarn is just down the road. Mixing 'natural' feeling singletrack complete with rocks, roots and flat corners and flat out berms and bumps, it's one of the best singletrack loops around. www.mbwales.com

You've also got the recently opened Bike Park Wales down the road too: www.bikeparkwales.com

The Gap. **Photo**: Benjamin Haworth.

Mid Wales

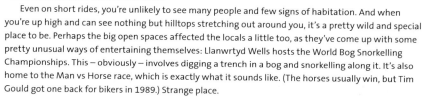

'Mid Wales' might not be a particularly imaginative name, but it does describe the area. Covering Rhayader, Radnorshire and Builth Wells and Llanwrtyd Wells, this is a big place, and it feels it. With few villages and even fewer towns, there's not much around.

Even on short rides, you're unlikely to see many people and few signs of habitation. And when you're up high and can see nothing but hilltops stretching out around you, it's a pretty wild and special place to be. Perhaps the big open spaces affected the locals a little too, as they've come up with some pretty unusual ways of entertaining themselves: Llanwrtyd Wells hosts the World Bog Snorkelling Championships. This – obviously – involves digging a trench in a bog and snorkelling along it. It's also home to the Man vs Horse race, which is exactly what it sounds like. (The horses usually win, but Tim Gould got one back for bikers in 1989.) Strange place.

The Riding

With such a huge region, there's a lot of riding and a lot of variety. Broadly speaking, the further west you go, the more technical it gets, while east means grassier and faster. But that's a massive generalisation and you'll find a real mix wherever you go. There are loose pebbly sections, smooth rock slabs and flat-out fast grassy descents. There are huge uphill slogs and brakes-full-on-and-still-accelerating downhills. Best of all, there are a few of the finest and most memorable stretches of singletrack in the whole country. Some are short and swoopy, others are technical blasts. Some seem never-ending and some are spectacularly situated. But the best ones, the ones that will stick in your mind, give you everything – like the Doethie Valley: a continuous, seven-kilometre run down the entire length of a valley in the middle of nowhere. It's swoopy, it's fast, it's technical and it goes on and on and on. Like many around here, it's a route you can never ride too many times.

When to go

This is a big, remote area with few towns, so be prepared when heading out in bad weather. It also gets a lot of rain – you will encounter soggy sections at the best of times, and these can become virtually impassable after prolonged rain. Despite that, there's plenty of stuff to be done when it's bad – the Doethie Valley route holds up well, as does much of the stuff around Rhayader.

Doethie Valley. **Photo**: Benjamin Haworth.

31 Rhayader & the Elan Valley

Solid climbs, great singletrack and fast descents; open, wild-feeling hilltops and views reaching out over Wales. It's easy to see why this is a Welsh classic. The ride begins with a road/dirt climb out of Rhayader (the oldest town in Mid Wales). Faint singletrack then wriggles across the hilltops before swinging south, weaving between boggy ponds and dropping to the road. Road work and tricky-ish route finding lead to a singletrack drop to the reservoirs. It's not technical, but it is steep, plunging down the hillside in a test of nerves and brakes. A waterside cruise and gentle climb regain lost height, and fast, swoopy singletrack leads back over the hill. The finale is brilliant. Wide straights run over smooth rocks slabs and into big, loose corners. It's fast, it's fun and it keeps going virtually all the way into town!

Grade: **Red** » Distance: **31km** » Ascent: **880m** » Time: **4hrs+**
Start/Finish: **Rhayader clock tower** » Start GR: **SN 971679** » SatNav: **Rhayader**
OS Map: **Explorer 200 Llandrindod Wells & Elan Valley** » Parking: **Lots in Rhayader**
Cafe: **Clive Powell Mountain Bikes, T: 01597 811 343**
Pub: **The Crown Inn, Rhayader, 01597 811 099, www.thecrownrhayader.co.uk**

Directions

S From the clock tower in the centre of Rhayader, head west, towards the reservoirs. Follow the road out through the village, turning **R** up a road signed *Mountain Road to Aberystwyth* just as you leave the houses.

After 500m, turn **L**. Go round a sharp right-hand bend and follow this, ignoring all turnings, until the road swings left. Go **SA** onto a dirt farm drive. Turn **R** through the farmyard and through gates, before following a wide dirt track uphill towards a waterfall.

Splash through the river just before the falls and climb to the road. Turn **L**. As the climbing eases, turn **L** onto a marked bridleway, cross a boggy area and climb onto open land. Follow vague grassy tracks and singletrack around to the **R** at the top of the climb.

Pass through an area of hollows and pieces of rock and begin to descend.

2 Easy to miss: Turn **L** onto a vague track as the valley begins to appear on your right. Take this, crossing the head of the valley and splashing through a stream. Climb steeply on grass to a better trail. Turn **R**, then keep **L** almost immediately to pick up more obvious singletrack. Wade through a couple of boggy sections and pick up the obvious trail once more.

Ignore turnings to the left and continue to follow the trail downhill towards woodland, picking up a good track near the woods and turning **R** onto it to pass to the right-hand side of the trees. At the road, turn **R**.

Follow the road, ignoring turnings, out of the trees. Just before the road drops slightly and swings around a left-hand bend, turn **R** through a gate onto a wide signed bridleway. Follow this over rock slabs to a gate and a stream. Ignore the trail off the left, but continue to follow the course of the stream uphill (the track becomes obvious singletrack as you climb higher). Follow singletrack over the top of the hill and down to a small flat area.

Bear **L** (**don't** climb the obvious track up the slope ahead!) across the flat ground and then swing **R** on grassy tracks. Pick up obvious singletrack, cross the stream and then climb slightly before descending very steeply to the road. If you get stuck in ruts here, stop and go back – there's always an easier line!

3 At the road, turn **R**. As you reach the bridge across the dam, bear slightly **L** onto the Elan Valley Way cycle way (or, if it's full of families, ignore me and stay on the road!). As the cycleway ends, cross the road and go between rocks to stay on the Elan Valley Way. Follow this, climbing all the way, past the next dam, through a rock cutting and on to the road.

Go **SA** on tarmac for a short distance and then **SA** onto a grassy track. Follow this as it swings **R** and uphill. Climb steadily on to moorland and continue to follow the vague track roughly east. As you begin to descend, the track turns into sweeping and fast singletrack which drops to the road.

Turn **L** on the road, uphill. At the top of the hill, turn **R** onto a wide and obvious track. Follow this, ignoring any and all turnings for some distance until it begins to descend. Stick to this track and swoop downhill over rock slabs and around corners.

At the road, turn **R**, then **L** at the main road and descend to Rhayader.

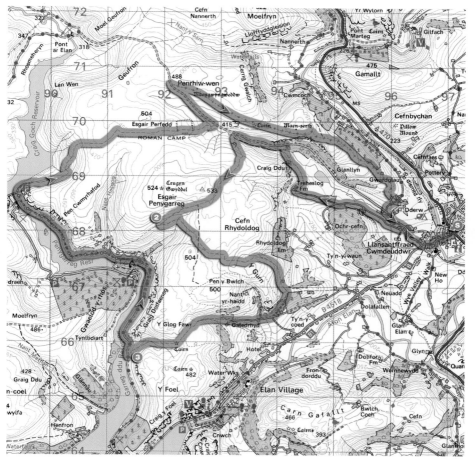

32 *Doethie Valley Singletrack*

Finishing along one of the longest and finest pieces of natural singletrack in the UK, this is an unforgettable ride. Even the car park, sitting beside a huge dam with an incredible water jet sprouting from its base, is memorable. Sadly, the initial forest road kilometres don't live up to the hype and might leave you wondering what the fuss is about. If you like climbing, the next steep, rocky pull will help. It'll have most walking, so top marks if you make it. If climbing's not your thing, the views from the top are superb and the descent is eye-wateringly fast and loose. Do keep your eyes open though, as you really don't want to miss the left turn halfway down. This leads through a gate into the Doethie Valley and onto grassy singletrack, which is where the ride comes alive. And after a couple of narrow and undulating kilometres, that singletrack is still going strong. All thoughts of the forest road start have gone. Then the surface firms up, the speed increases and the fun really starts – and before you know it, you've covered nearly seven unbroken kilometres of sweeping corners, rapid straights and fiddly rock sections on one of the best sections of singletrack anywhere. Superb.

Grade: **Red** » Distance: **24km** » Ascent: **800m** » Time: **3hrs+**
Start/Finish: **Llyn Brianne Dam car park** » Start GR: **SN 793484** » SatNav: **N/A**
OS Map: **Explorer 187 Llandovery** » Parking: **Free parking at start**
Cafe: **Nope** » Pub: **The Royal Oak, Rhandir-mwyn, T: 01550 760 201, www.theroyaloakinn.co.uk**

Doethie Valley. **Photo**: Benjamin Haworth.

Directions

S From the car park, go through the gate, across the dam and follow the road round to the woods.

Continue **SA** over a cattle grid and follow the forest road around the edge of the lake and past a house. Ignoring turnings, keep to the main track, climbing gradually uphill and away from the lake as you do. At the big junction, turn **R**, downhill. Shortly after reaching the top of the climb, ignore a turning to the left and keep following the main track to the edge of the woods. Keep **R** at the junction and go through a gate and out onto open ground.

2 Follow the main track as it swoops fast and easily around to Soar y Mynydd. Upon reaching the buildings, turn **L** to climb steeply uphill over technical ground.

Follow the track over the top of the hill, expansive views open up ahead. Splash through the ever-present puddles before continuing along the track, descending rapidly but easily over loose rock.

3 **Easy to miss:** As you near the bottom of the descent, turn **L** through a gate onto a signed bridleway as the main track makes a steep left-hand turn.

Follow obvious singletrack, passing through several gates. It's technical in places, but gets better and better the further you go. After climbing a short rise to a grassy plateau keep **L**, away from the ruined building, soon picking up singletrack once more.

Eventually the singletrack ends, as all good things must. Cross the field and descend to the lane. Continue **SA** through the farm, turning **L** up a wide track immediately after the farmyard.

A climb and short descent lead back to the woods. Either continue along forest road to the junction and turn **R**, or keep an eye out for a very short section of singletrack that cuts the corner (you'll be able to see the next track through the trees as you do).

Follow the track back around to the reservoir.

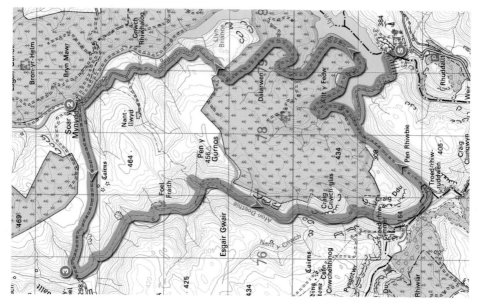

More riding

Radnor Forest & Harley Dingle

Short, easy and brilliant fun – particularly the descent off Great Rhos. Sadly, 'easy' doesn't mean 'effortless'. Grassy slopes and big hills make the climbing a right slog. But it's worth it. The aforementioned descent, right from the route's highpoint, is stunning. It's grassy, bouncy and FAST. Do it in the wet, spray flying, and it's exhilarating. At the bottom, there's a choice: stick to the main track, admire the views and whizz home at high speed, or cling to narrow singletrack across a steep hillside – better, but nerve-wracking!

This ride ought to be awful after rain. But the climb stays rideable, the forest atmospheric and the descents awesome in a splashy, 'argh I can't see' kind of way.

Grade: **Blue/Red** » Distance: **16km/19km** » Ascent: **570m** » Time: **1.5hrs+**
Start/Finish: **New Radnor, SO 212609** » OS Map: **Explorer 201 Knighton & Presteigne**

The Route » New Radnor – north via road and then bridleway past to Whimble – Radnor Forest – north and then west on forest roads to Shepherd's Well – SO 183645 – bridleway descent west to Cowlod then: **Easy** » Byway south to Water-break-its-neck and SO 175601 – bridleways and road east to New Radnor. **Harder** » Bridleway south-east past Three Riggles and Danger Area to SO 200610 – bridleways east to New Radnor

Hergest Ridge & Castle Hill

Starting from either Kington or New Radnor, you can either ride this as one big route or two shorter loops. There's a big climb onto Hergest Ridge (in England), but the views and fast descents make it well worthwhile. The western end of the ride is tougher, with some technical climbs and tricky descents – not to mention a fair splattering of mud in the winter. Link to the Radnor Forest route for a huge day out.

Grade: **Red** » Distance: **30km (full ride)** » Ascent: **800m** » Time: **3.5hrs+**
Start/Finish: **Kington, SO 292567** » OS Map: **Explorer 201 Knighton & Presteigne**

The Route » Kington – west onto Hergest Ridge to top – south to SO 257554 – Gladestry – then: **Option A** » Return via Hergest Ridge, or **Option B** » Gladestry – north to Trewern – north west past Burl Hill to SO 196580 – east to Castle Hill – Stockenny Farm – Yardro – Kitchen Farm – Sunnybank – Gilwern Dingle – Gladestry – Kington via Hergest Ridge

Caban Coch

You're going to get wet feet on this ride. It's the last section that's the wet one – a wide rocky track that splashes through huge puddles and in places seems to be toying with the idea of becoming a river. Great fun on hot days! The remainder is a mix of fast forest riding and open grassy tracks. If you want a huge ride, combine this with the Rhayader route (page 224), and make sure you're feeling fit.

Grade: **Blue/Red** » Distance: **20km** » Ascent: **540m** » Time: **2.5hrs+** » Start/Finish: **Car park at western end of Elan Valley, SN 870633** » OS Map: **Explorer 200 Llandrindod Wells & Elan Valley**

The Route » Car park at SN 870633 – east on bridleway over Rhos y Gelynnen – road to Elan Village – south to SN 937638 – west past Gro Hill to Rhiwnant – west on byway to car park

Irfon Forest

Another area classic that pops up all over the place – and deservedly so. Conveniently starting and finishing in Llanwrtyd Wells, it heads north from town to explore the Irfon Forest. There's a fair bit of forest road along the way, but it's more than made up for by the more exciting sections. There's a stunning rocky descent towards the river, secret singletrack in the forest and a grin-inducing blast to finish.

Grade: **Red** » Distance: **22km** » Ascent: **810m** » Time: **2.5hrs+**
Start/Finish: **Llanwrtyd Wells, SN 879467** » OS Map: **Explorer 187 Llandovery**

The Route » Llanwrtyd Wells – northeast for 1km to SN 883474 – north on road to forest edge – west to bridleway at SN 872500 – Craig Dinas Fach – road north to SN 856507 – forest roads north to Cefn Crug – unmarked singletrack at SN 863516 to SN 866 515 – forest road east to bridleway at SN 877521 – east to Nant yr Amnell – south to Bwlchmawr – south to Llanwrtyd Wells

The Trans Cambrian Way

Fancy a few days' riding? Good views, nice pubs? Try the Trans Cambrian Way – a monster of a route set up by IMBA UK. Starting in Knighton, it runs for 175 kilometres to Machynlleth, climbing around 3,500 metres along the way, which isn't actually much, considering the distance. Expect tired legs and rain, but also incredible views, solitude and fast descents. Usually done over a few days, occasional Vertebrate Publishing photographer John Houlihan has somehow ridden it in 12 hours and 20 minutes (and that's since been bettered by Jason Miles and Dave Powell)!

Grade: **Very Black** » Distance: **175km** » Ascent: **Lots!** » Time: **Days!**
Start: **Knighton** » Finish: **Knighton** » Map: **IMBA Trans Cambrian Trail Guide**

The Route » No directions, we're afraid. IMBA did all the leg work here, so head to www.imba.org.uk where you can find maps and every bit of information you could possibly need. Companies such as www.muckyweekends.co.uk can provide luggage transfers if you'd rather not lug all your own gear.

Other BIG routes

There's huge potential for big, epic riding in Mid Wales. It's not for nothing that several MTB marathons, long distance routes and multi-day tours run through the area. 'Big wilderness' rides head west over towards Strata Florida and over the Monk's trod. They are best left for dry weather, and these are big all-day rides. Not too many options on the way back from Strata Florida, even though there would appear to be on the map. We've also heard good things about riding south from there to the Doethie Valley and Llanwrtyd Wells. Good luck!

More information

Main Towns

Obviously, in such a big area, everything's spread out. In the southern area, Builth Wells is the most central, and the biggest, followed by Llanwrtyd Wells. Further north is Llandrindod Wells, probably the biggest town in the area, and further north again is Rhayader, although there's not a great deal there. If you're in Radnorshire, Kington is closest but Knighton is bigger.

Maps

OS Landranger 147: Elan Valley & Builth Wells
OS Landranger 148: Presteigne & Hay-on-Wye
OS Explorer 187: Llandovery
OS Explorer 188: Builth Wells
OS Explorer 200: Llandrindod Wells & Elan Valley
OS Explorer 201: Knighton & Presteigne

Bike Shops

Clive Powell Mountain Bikes, West Street, Rhayader, 01597 811343, www.clivepowell-mtb.co.uk (shop, guiding, 'dirty weekends', cafe)

Builth Wells Cycles, Smithfield Road, Builth Wells, 01982 552923

Cycle-tec, Builth Wells, 01982 554682, www.cycle-tec.co.uk (not a shop but a repair service)

Cycles Irfon, Ffos Road, Llanwrtyd Wells, 01591 610668, www.cyclesirfon.co.uk

Heart of Wales Bikes, High Street, Llandrindod Wells, 01597 825533

Accommodation

With such a huge area, it's hard to recommend anywhere specific. www.mbwales.com has links to accommodation, and www.visitmidwales.co.uk and www.stayinwales.co.uk are also worth a look. Anywhere near Llanwrtyd Wells or Rhayader would have riding from the door, while Builth Wells and Llandrindod Wells both have good road links to the various different areas.

There are campsites dotted around – there's a basic but good one just outside Rhayader which is linked to a Red Kite feed and conservation centre – Gigrin Farm: 01597 810243, www.gigrin.co.uk

There are no YHA hostels in the area, although they do have a couple of bunkhouses – Dolgoch, at the top of Llyn Brianne, is particularly useful (01782 253274). There are independent hostels in Llanwrtyd Wells (Stonecroft Lodge, 01591 610327), Rhayader (Beili Neuadd Bunkhouse, 01597 810211) and Llandrindod Wells (New Inn Bunkhouse, 01597 860211).

If you want a cottage, try www.forestcottages.co.uk – they are in the woods at the Coed Trallwm trail centre, near Beulah, giving you a choice of three short trails on your door step, and pretty easy access to the riding in the Doethie Valley and around Llanwrtyd Wells.

Food & Drink

There are plenty of restaurants in the main towns – Rhayader, Builth Wells, Llandrindod Wells and Llanwrtyd Wells – and all give plenty of choice.

Rhayader Area

Clive Powell Mountain Bikes, West Street, Rhayader, 01597 811343, www.clivepowell-mtb.co.uk (shop, cafe, evening meals if booked in advance)

Cornhill Inn, Rhayader, 01597 810029

Radnorshire area

The Harp Inn, Old Radnor, 01544 350655, www.harpinnradnor.co.uk (accommodation)

The Stagg Inn, Kington, 01544 230221, www.thestagg.co.uk (accommodation)

Southern area

Stonecroft Inn, Llanwrtyd Wells, 01591 610332, www.stonecroft.co.uk (accommodation)

The Drovers Rest, Llanwrtyd Wells, 01591 610264, www.food-food-food.co.uk (posh restaurant, tea rooms, accommodation)

Tourist Offices

Builth Wells, 01982 553307 » **Knighton**, 01547 529424 » **Llandrindod Wells**, 01597 822600 » **Llanwrtyd Wells**, 01591 610666

Outdoor Shops

Surprisingly for such a wild area, we've always struggled to find outdoor shops around here. There's Elan Leisure in Rhayader, (01686 811007, www.llanileisure.co.uk), but otherwise, the closest place with a range of shops is Brecon.

Useful Websites

www.mbwales.com » www.tourism.powys.gov.uk

Guidebooks

Wales Mountain Biking – Beicio Mynydd Cymru, written by Tom Hutton, published by Vertebrate Publishing

Worth Knowing

The National Cycle Museum in Llandrindod Wells (www.cyclemuseum.org.uk). Everything from Bone Shakers and big-wheeled Penny Farthings up to Grifters, BMXs and the 1996 National MTB Championship-winning Raleigh M-Trax. Got to be worth a look.

It's also easy to mix a weekend here with the excellent riding just south in the Brecon Beacons. See page 215.

The Berwyn Hills & Llangollen

On 23 January 1974, lights shone in the skies above the Berwyn Mountains. Seconds later, a huge jolt shook the ground – a jolt measuring 3.5 on the Richter scale and felt in Liverpool. An earthquake? A plane crash?

Then men in black (suits) arrived in local villages and cordoned off a large area of land. Could it be aliens? UFO fanatics certainly thought so. The Berwyns couldn't be a more perfect setting for their theories. Big, bleak and sparsely populated, they stretch across a sizeable chunk of northeast Wales. The hills and mountains are high, rocky and bare, with a deep covering of heather in the summer. Nearly 25 of the peaks in the area top 600 metres, including Cadair Berwyn, the highest point in Wales outside the national parks. It's a beautiful, wild place, with fantastic scenery and a whole range of wildlife – from peregrine falcons to polecats and, well, who knows what else.

The Riding

Think big. Big hills and big landscape. Big climbs, big descents and big distance. There's not a great deal in the way of singletrack (although what there is, is great), with the best riding being fast, loose descents and steep hillside plummets. You need to tackle a fair bit of easy riding and road work in order to link the good sections, but it's worth it – the rewards are some of the best long and wild loops in Wales. One of these is The Wayfarer – the most famous track around here and the one everyone comes to ride. It's a high, eight-kilometre pass crossing a large chunk of landscape and linking the villages of Llandrillo and Llanarmon via a big climb and a long, fast and rocky descent. The downside is that, as with many routes around here, there is a definite lack of shortcut/retreat options, meaning that rides are committing and best saved for the 'right' day.

When to go

Although there are a few spots that get claggy in wet weather, a lot of the riding in the area is stone based and passable year round. That said, this is a big area with a lot of riding in the middle of nowhere – something to think about in bad weather.

The Wayfarer (and John Horscroft). **Photo:** John Coefield.

33 The Berwyn Hills & the Wayfarer

One of the UK's classic big loops. There's a fair bit of road work in the first half, while the second contains three stunning descents, an equal number of challenging climbs and some incredible countryside. You can start at several points, but we recommend Llanarmon. Starting here gets most of the road and uninspiring off-road sections done early on, ensuring the aforementioned series of climbs and descents are what sticks in your memory. The good stuff begins above Llangynog, where a boggy climb leads to a brake-burning plummet down a grassy hillside and onto a superb stretch of singletrack through an old quarry. From there, a huge climb leads to a high speed rattle into Llandrillo. It's pinch puncture central, so watch out! The return leg is the biggie: The Wayfarer. A long but straightforward climb carries you high into the middle of nowhere, ready for four kilometres of continuous rocky, loose and high-speed descending to the car.

Grade: **Black** » Distance: **51km** » Ascent: **1,440m** » Time: **5hrs+**	
Start/Finish: **The Hand, Llanarmon** » Start GR: **SJ 156328** » SatNav: **LL20 7LD**	
OS Map: **Explorer 255 Llangollen & Berwyn** » Parking: **Considerately on street**	
Cafe: **Small shops in villages en route**	
Pub: **The West Arms Hotel, Llanarmon, T: 01691 600 665; The Hand at Llanarmon, T: 01691 600 666**	

Directions

S From the crossroads in Llanarmon, head south towards Llanrhaeadr-ym-Mochnant, passing The Hand pub on your left. At the top of the hill, keep **SA** (signed to *Maengwynedd*). Drop fast downhill, taking the first lane on the **L** after 2.4km.

After 800m, on a sharp right-hand bend, turn **L** through a gate onto a wide stony track. Follow this through gates, ignoring turnings to the left and right, until you rejoin tarmac. Continue to a T-junction and turn **R**.

Go **R** at the crossroads and then **SA** at the next junction to follow the road into Llanrhaeadr. Keep **SA** through the village, ignoring turnings, and climb steeply away. As you reach the top of the climb, turn **R** up a narrow lane after a couple of houses.

Keep **L** at the first fork, **R** at the second and then follow the lane until it ends. Continue **SA** through gates onto a stony track and follow this uphill, bearing **R** across the field. Stick to the track as it climbs, contouring around the hillside and into a bog. Wade **SA** through this (sorry) and through two gates. At the second, turn **L** and follow grassy singletrack across a flatter area of ground, past a waymarker and onto a steep, grassy descent. Plummet down the hillside, around sharp corners and, after dropping down a particularly steep section, keep **R** towards a hidden gate. If you end up in the bottom corner of the field near the stream, follow the wall right and uphill to the gate.

Go through the gate and turn **L** alongside the wall. Keep **R** at the gate, then turn **R** to drop across the field to a gate. Go through this, through the stream and up to a wide track. Turn **L** and ride to a gate.

Go through the gate and then continue **SA**/bear slightly **R** onto obvious singletrack as the track goes left. Follow this **SA** and downhill into woodland and then through an old quarry for a great, fast descent.

2 At the road, turn **R**. Turn **L** at the T-junction, go over the river and then turn **R** as the road bends. Almost immediately, turn **R** again, behind the church, and follow the lane up the valley. Go through gates and then follow bridleway signs to the **R** as you reach the farm. A good track takes you steeply uphill. At the top, turn **R** on obvious tracks and ride to the road.

Turn **L**, then, after 100m, turn **R** onto a wide track. After a short way, keep **L** at the fork and descend with interest over rocks into the woods. Keep **SA**, ignoring all junctions and watching out for pinch punctures. Cross the river and go through the farmyard onto tarmac. Follow the lane down the valley to Llandrillo.

3 Turn **R** at the T-junction and ride through the village. About 1.25km after leaving the houses, turn **R** onto a narrow lane opposite the turning to the campsite. Keep **SA** until the tarmac ends and you reach a crossroads.

Turn **L** onto a wide stone track and follow this, climbing gradually, to the Wayfarer's memorial at the top of the track. Sign the book, drop your saddle a touch and rattle down over rocks for 4km to the road. Continue **SA**, ignoring turnings, to Llanarmon.

The Wayfarer. **Photo**: John Coefield.

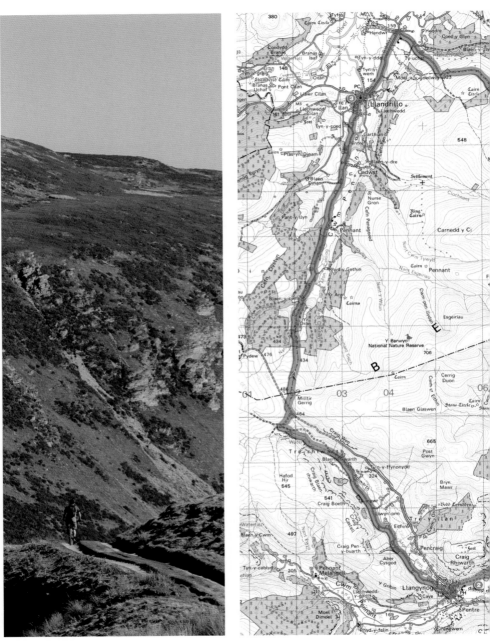

Photo: John Coefield.

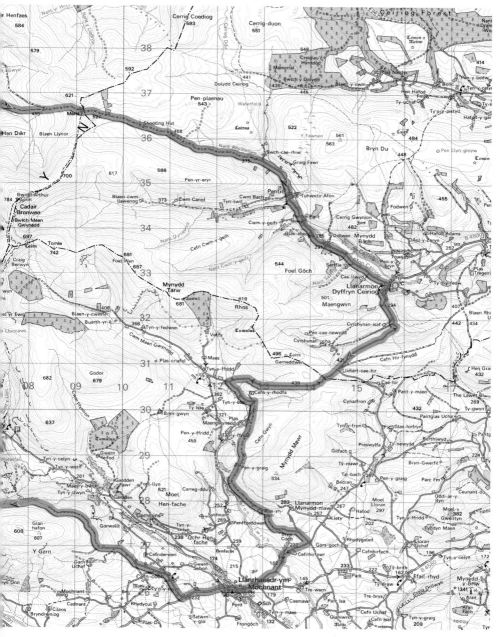

More riding

The Wayfarer

Good riding, fine scenery and a bit of history. 'The Wayfarer' was an early pioneer of off-road cycling – a 'rough stuff enthusiast' – and this pass was one of his favourite rides. There's a small memorial to him at the high point of the route, which is a simple there-and-back up a wide, rocky trail. The eastern side is the more technical, giving a tough climb and a descent, while the western end is much smoother and faster.

Grade: **Red** » Distance: **25km** » Ascent: **860m** » Time: **3hrs+**
Start/Finish: **Llanarmon, SJ 156328** » OS Map: **Explorer 255 Llangollen & Berwyn**

The Route » Llanarmon – west to Pentre – NW to the memorial at SJ 091365 – west again (keep on the southernmost RoW to SJ 051375 – B4401 – Rhydyglafes – Rhos-y-maerdy – return via outward route

Llanarmon & The Lawnt

A shorter ride (with an optional extension), although no worse for it. It's technical and it's hard work. A steep road climb, a bit of a slog and then a fantastic slabby, off camber and often wet descent to the Lawnt. A bit of meandering, a tough climb (made tougher by the 4x4 ruts) and then a fast descent to finish. The extension adds an extra fast and rattly descent, a road climb and 5 kilometres/170 metres of climbing.

Grade: **Red** » Distance: **14km** » Ascent: **400m** » Time: : **1.5hrs+**
Start/Finish: **Llanarmon, SJ 156328** » OS Map: **Explorer 255: Llangollen & Berwyn**

The Route » Llanarmon – east to SJ 171326 – **(Extension** » Tregeiriog – SJ 189335 – Pensarn – SJ 171326 (Rejoin route)) – south to The Lawnt – SJ 178299 – Pant-y-maen – Llidiart-cae-hir – SJ 169320 – west to Llanarmon

The Ceiriog Valley & the Pheasant Trail

This biggish loop, with a fair bit of climbing and some incredible views, explores the area between Llangollen and the Berwyns proper. The highlight is undoubtedly the 'Pheasant Track' over Bryn Du (you'll find out why!). The views from the top are stunning, and the descent, a fast, rocky doubletrack over stone slabs and off-camber slate, is even better.

Grade: **Red/Black** » Distance: **30km** » Ascent: **800m** » Time: **3hrs+**
Start/Finish: **Glen Ceiriog, SJ 205380** » OS Map: **Explorer 255 Llangollen & Berwyn**

The Route » Glyn Ceiriog – east on minor roads (just north of the B4500) to Pontfadog – south via Graig and SJ 234369 to SJ 243354 – west past Caemor Wood – south to Llechrydau – Pen y Gwely – Tregeiriog – SJ 168334 – SJ 157335 – north over Bryn Du to Tyn-y-celyn – Ceigio Forest – north east to SJ 189381 – Glyn Ceiriog

More information

Main Towns

Llangollen, off to the north, is your best local bet. Otherwise, head west to Oswestry for a much bigger choice of facilities. It's a bit of a drive, though!

Maps

OS Explorer 255 Llangollen & Berwyn
OS Landranger 125 Bala & Lake Vyrnwy
OS Landranger 126 Shrewsbury & Oswestry

Bike Shops

One Planet Adventure, Llandegla Trail Centre, 01978 751 656, www.oneplanetadventure.com
Proadventure, Parade Street, Llangollen, 01978 861 912 (not a bike shop, but carry some spares)
Bikeworks, Salop Road, Oswestry, 01691 654 407

Accommodation

The Berwyns don't have anywhere near the same level of tourist accommodation as Snowdonia. There are no YHA hostels in the area, although there is a handy independent option in Llangollen (www.llangollenhostel.co.uk, 01978 861 773), which has plenty of facilities, including bike and canoe (!) storage.

There are a few campsites dotted around the area. The nearest to the riding here is the basic, but picturesque site under the Pistyll Rhaeder waterfall (Tan-y-Pistyll – www.pistyllrhaeadr.co.uk – find the site on a map!).

Failing that, there are plenty of pubs in the area which offer accommodation. We've listed a few below.

Food & Drink

The West Arms Hotel, Llanarmon, 01691, 600 665, www.thewestarms.com (accommodation)
The Hand at Llanarmon, 01691 600 666, www.thehandhotel.co.uk (accommodation)
The Corn Mill, Llangollen, 01978 869 555, www.cornmill-llangollen.co.uk

Tourist Offices

Llangollen, 01978 860 828

Outdoor Shops

Basics are available in Llangollen. Otherwise, it's Oswestry, Wrexham or Betws-y-Coed further into Wales.

Guidebooks

Wales Mountain Biking – Beicio Mynydd Cymru, written by Tom Hutton, published by Vertebrate Publishing
The Best Mountain Bike Trails in North East Wales, written by Sue Savege and Tom Griffiths, published by Bikefax

Worth Knowing

See page 244 for info on the trail centre at Llandegla.

The Clwydian Hills

The Clwyds are in the bit of Wales that adds an irritating extra hour to the
journey between Snowdonia and England. This works to their advantage:
most people hurry past on the A55, cooped up in cars, being jabbed by the
handlebars of badly-packed bikes. You, meanwhile, have saved yourself an hour's worth
of fuel and are now speeding along empty trails, grinning like a loon and admiring the view.

The Clywds are a tiny north/south ridge of hills, only eight kilometres wide and 35 kilometres long,
with a highpoint – Moel Famau – at 555 metres. In other words, minute compared with the mountains
further west. Despite this, the heather-clad hillsides and open grassy trails are well worth a visit.
The riding's good, the views are great and, although it can get busy with walkers, you'll see few bikers,
giving things a nice exploratory air.

The Riding

The Clwyds are small and steep-sided. Climbs and descents are frequently steep, so make sure you're
feeling fit and that your brakes are working well. As in so many areas, there's a nice spread of trails,
making for varied riding. There are wide grassy trails, which tend to be relatively open. They're a
bit of a slog on the way up, but the surroundings are pleasant and they are lightning fast on the
way down. Relatively untechnical, they give flat-out speed that builds and builds as you descend,
and grassy compressions and hummocks to bounce around on. In the middle of the hills, above the
reservoir, are a couple of permissive bridleways that link to tricky bridleway descents. These are great
– narrow, peaty singletrack littered with rocks. Away from these, there are some fast, rocky trails,
which are as entertaining as ever. Finally, further north, the hills mellow a little, offering easy trails
which provide good, gentle riding for beginners.

When to go

If it's wet, all the grassy riding is going to suck the life from your legs. By the time you get to the
fun stuff, you'll be knackered and when you're done, you'll feel guilty about ripping apart the fragile
singletrack. We'd keep driving to the trail centres.

Beneath Moel Famau. **Photo**: John Coefield.

34 Cilcain & Moel Famau

This route might be short, the hills pretty and the singletrack fun, but the steep climbs and tricky descents ensure that it's surprisingly tough. Thankfully, the start is easy – a wide trail and flat singletrack – as you'll want a warm up before the energy-sapping climb that follows. Once up, the reward is singletrack. Technical compared to what's come before, it tackles a couple of mini rock gardens and narrow squeezes before a short and easy-looking climb, which feels neither. A warp speed grassy descent then screams down towards Llangynhafal and a pub. Any over indulgence in the pub may be seriously regretted, as the next kilometre and a half contains 200 metres of altitude gain. Again, there's a singletrack reward. An entertainingly technical trail winds across the hillside before dropping fast over rocks and through heather to the reservoir below. Either finish here or head back up for a fast, slabby descent, a quick whizz along lanes and a superb rocky finale.

Grade: **Red** » Distance: **20km** » Ascent: **650m** » Time: **2hrs+**	
Start/Finish: **Lay-by outside Cilcain** » Start GR: **SJ 171647** » SatNav: **Cilcain**	
OS Map: **Explorer 265 Clwydian Range** » Parking: **Lay-by outside Cilcain** » Cafe: **Village shop in Cilcain**	
Pub: **The White Horse Inn, Cilcain, T: 01352 740 142; The Golden Lion, Llangynhafal, T: 01824 790 451**	

Directions

🅂 Head up the wide track running away from the lay-by (ignoring the turning immediately to the left). After 400m, turn **L** onto a second wide track.

Follow this through gates into fields and then keep **L**, alongside the fence and onto singletrack. Go through a gate beside a white house and onto a wider track. Shortly after the house, turn **R** onto a signed bridleway (signed *Moel Famau*) just before a gate and climb steeply uphill on track and then grass.

Ignore all turnings and pass forest on your left. As the forest ends, keep **SA** onto a fun piece of singletrack. Follow this around to the left and then continue **SA** (**ignoring** a permissive bridleway to the right) up a short technical climb. Go **SA** over the crossroads at the top (*No Bikes* signs to the left and right) and then keep **R**, following permissive bridleway signs, on to a fast and open grassy descent.

Moel Famau singletrack. **Photo**: John Coefield.

2 Follow markers downhill, trending to the **R** and eventually cross a stream. Traverse the bottom of the hillside on grassy tracks to the road and turn **R**, uphill. (Or left, downhill, for a pub stop.)

Keep **SA** through a gate onto a stony track as the tarmac ends and climb steeply(!) to a gate at the top.

Go through the gate and turn **R**, then **R** again onto a permissive singletrack bridleway. Follow this across the hillside. Just before reaching a singletrack T-junction at a broken down wall, turn sharp **L** onto a faint singletrack descent. Drop steeply over rocks towards the reservoir.

3 At the T-junction*, turn **L** and push up singletrack to rejoin the main track (this is a great descent). Turn **R** and speed down the wide track. Join tarmac and, ignoring turnings, continue to a crossroads. Turn **L**.

Follow the road for 600m, passing an obvious farm access track on the right, and then turn **R** through a gate onto a signed byway. Drop down an increasingly steep and technical descent, keeping **R** at the fork after 1km. Descend to the road.

At the road, turn **R**. Turn **R** after 400m up a narrow lane and climb gradually back to Cilcain. Turn **R** at the crossroads in the centre and **L** after the church to finish back at the car park.

****Shortcut:** At the T-junction, bear **R**. Keep **SA** upon joining a wider track and follow this downhill to Cilcain.

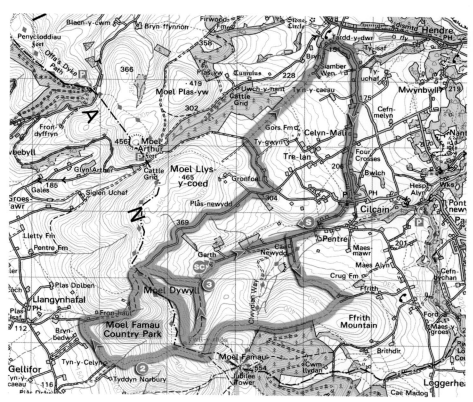

More riding

The Southern Clwyds

Taking in a few of the best trails from the main ride (and with the option to be extended to take in more), this loop explores the whole Clwydian Range. Forest tracks and quiet lanes make up some of the distance, and give a little down time, while steep climbs, fast grassy descents and good open-ground riding make up the rest. Potential extensions include the whole of the loop above (big!), the concessionary singletrack on the main route (tech) or a figure-of-eight involving the rocky descent northwest of Moel Llys-y-coed (fast!).

Grade: **Red** » Distance: **24km** » Ascent: **720m** » Time: **3hrs+**
Start/Finish: **Moel Famau South forest car park, SJ 171610** » OS Map: **Explorer 265 Clwydian Range**

The Route » Car park – NE into woods on forest roads to junction at SJ 178616 – contour north through woods to SJ 168633 (appears to be a dead end on some maps) – W around Moel Famau to Offa's Dyke Path – SJ 151629 – Tyn-y-Celyn – Llangynhafal – south on minor roads to Llanbedr-Dyffryn-Clwyd – Bathafarn Hall – Gryn Motel – Moel Eithinen – Fron Hen – car park

Conquering Hero

Just west of Llangollen is this great, wild XC route. It's not technical, with the majority of the riding taking place on wide tracks, farm lanes and grassy doubletrack. At 13 kilometres it's not particularly long either, although with 650 metres climbing, it's no pushover. But it is good, steady riding in a relatively quiet spot with great views in every direction. There's a short section of footpath you'll need to push along, although as long as you're polite, it shouldn't be a problem.

Grade: **Red** » Distance: **13km** » Ascent: **520m** » Time: **1.5hrs+**
Start/Finish: **Rhewl, SJ 182449** » OS Map: **Explorer 256 Wrexham & Llangollen**

The Route » Rhewl – Cymmo – Wern ddu – SJ 152443 – Bwlch y Groes – Tan-y-foel – Pen-bedw – Moel y Gamelin – Maen-y-goron – Rhewl

The Trail Centre

Coed Llandegla

Bringing a completely new style of riding to North Wales, you'll either love or hate Llandegla. There are several fun trails available, but it's the black route that's the best. With a smooth surface, berms around every corner and jumps on every straight, it cries out to be ridden fast.

Trail Count: **Green 5km** » **Blue 12km** » **Red 18km** » **Black 21km**
Start: **Visitor centre at Coed Llandegla just off the A525, SJ 227520**
More info: **01978 751656, www.coedllandegla.com**

More information

Main Towns

There's not a huge amount in Cilcain. Your nearest big towns are Mold and then Ruthin, a short drive away.

Maps

OS Explorer 265 Vale of Clwyd
OS Explorer 256 Wrexham & Llangollen

Bike Shops

One Planet Adventure, Llandegla Trail Centre, 01978 751 656, www.oneplanetadventure.com

Bike Hire

One Planet Adventure, Llandegla Trail Centre, 01978 751 656, www.oneplanetadventure.com

Accommodation

Mountain bike site www.ridetheclwyds.com is worth a look, as it has lists of accommodation of all sorts.
Minffordd Campsite (01824 707 169) is a nice summer-only site near Llanbedr-Dyffryn-Clwyd, while Fron Farm (01352 741 482, www.fronfarmcaravanpark.co.uk) is a bigger option near Mold.
There are no hostels that we know of in the area.

Food & Drink

The Druid, Llanferres, 01352 810 225, www.thedruidinn.com (accommodation)
The White Horse Inn, Cilcain, 01352 740 142

Tourist Offices

Mold Tourist Information Centre, 01352 759 331, mold@nwtic.com

Outdoor Shops

Either head to Wrexham where, among others, there's a Yeomans Outdoors (01978 263 555), or keep going to Snowdonia.

Useful Websites

www.ridetheclwyds.com (a very useful site – rides, accommodation, food – everything you need!)
www.ridehiraethog.com (similar, covering the area just west)
www.foeldh.com (lots of downhilling in this area. Just one site on it ...)

Guidebooks

Wales Mountain Biking – Beicio Mynydd Cymru, written by Tom Hutton, published by Vertebrate Publishing
The Best Mountain Bike Trails in North East Wales, written by Sue Savege and Tom Griffiths, published by Bikefax

Snowdonia

Where do you head for mountains, rocks and views? When Scotland's full of midges and the Alps are too far? How about the Lake District or Snowdonia? Both are stunningly beautiful, both are filled with rocky trails and pretty villages. Both have cafes, gear shops and nuclear power stations. So, which one?

While the Lakes are pretty and green, Snowdonia is jagged and imposing. The steep-sided valleys are dark and rimmed with splintered crags. There are pretty villages, but the old slate-mining industry looms overhead in slag heaps and abandoned quarries. And that's the appeal of Snowdonia. It's daunting and unsettling, and that sets it apart from other national parks. It's dramatic, wild and scary, full of myths and with a mountainous landscape and atmosphere that's unique in this country.

Interestingly, the Park has a hole in it – the mining town of Blaenau Ffestiniog was left out. Was this a far-sighted plan to avoid planning laws and aid regeneration? Or was it to leave an old quarry out of the Park?

The Riding

Build it and they will come and all that. Well, in the mid 1990s they did and so did we, en masse, to Coed y Brenin. Most bikers visit Snowdonia to ride trail centres, and for good reason. You see, sadly, this beautiful area, with so much for climbers and walkers, lacks bridleways. And the few it has don't form convenient loops. To top it off, the riding is hard and uncompromising. Some trails are steep, craggy and rocky. Others are unrideably technical or boggy. Descents are hard, climbs harder still. But, if you've got the legs, ability to ride rocks (or lots of suspension) and are prepared to carry when necessary, there are fantastic days to be had. Climbs become tests of fitness and ability. Cleaning descents and rock gardens off the brakes and on the edge of control is an unmatchable feeling that leaves you chattering with excitement. And with several true UK classics on offer, including proper summit days on Snowdon and Cadair Idris, there's every reason to explore.

When to go

Apart from the endless bog between the Ogwen valley and Llyn Cowlyd, Snowdonia's bridleways are mainly stone-based and rideable in the wet (as are the many trail centres). But Snowdonia is very much a mountainous region and bad weather is going to be felt. Make sure you know how to get home if things don't go to plan.

Snowdon. **Photo**: Benjamin Haworth.

35 Snowdon

The big tick – a superb ride to the top of Wales. Granny ring out of Llanberis, legs burning before you're even off-road, onto the Tourist Track. Tantalisingly rideable, it's still right on the limit of endurance and ability. Progress is hard, but reasonable and satisfyingly won – until the second bridge ... we're seriously impressed if you can ride that! At the top, you've two choices. Dropping back down the main track is excellent: technical, fast and fun. Alternatively, the Ranger Path is much trickier, and is a descent you're sure to remember for a long time (hopefully not due to scars). Fast, loose and rocky at the start, it soon narrows, dropping into a gully and around a series of bends in a superb position high above the lake. Then it gets really hard, tumbling through 100 metres or so of rocks and drops. Still alive? The riding now eases substantially, with a final heave over a grassy hummock giving access to the last motorway section to Llanberis.

The Ban

There's a voluntary restriction on riding Snowdon between 10am and 5pm from 1st May to 30th September. Outside these times is fine – meaning *really* early starts or winter rides.

Grade: **Black** » Distance: **18km** » Ascent: **1,060m** » Time: **2.5hrs+**			
Start/Finish: **Llanberis** » Start GR: **SH 581599** » SatNav: **Llanberis**			
OS Map: **OL17 Snowdon** » Parking: **Pay & Display by the lake**			
Cafe: **Pete's Eats, Llanberis, 01286 870 117** » Pub: **A few to choose from in Llanberis**			

Tom Hutton and Steph Duits riding Telegraph Road on the Snowdon loop. **Photo**: John Coefield.

Directions

(S) Head south out of Llanberis towards Pen y Pass. At the mini-roundabout turn **R** onto Victoria Terrace.

Keep **SA** over the cattle grid and climb steeply past the cafe. Go through the gate and then, after a short distance, turn **L** onto a bridleway signed *Snowdon*. Climb to the summit!

(2) Retrace your steps over rocky and technical terrain. As the technicality and gradient ease, look out for a large upright rock on the right. Turn **L** at this and bear diagonally down towards the railway line. Cross this at the warning signs and pick up the obvious track on the far side.

Follow this, easily enough at first, but soon becoming loose, swinging around a series of switchbacks and entering some seriously technical sections (it's all rideable, you just might need a few goes!).

Easy to miss: The trail eventually levels and crosses a wide grassy area. Cross this and go through a gate. Continue to follow the track, beginning to descend once more. After a short distance, look out for a series of closely-spaced rain bars crossing the track and a low wooden bridleway marker pointing up the grassy slope to the right.

(3) Get off and push straight up this, gradually veering to the **R** on a vague track. This becomes much more obvious as you reach the top and the track flattens. Follow it to a gate. Just beyond the gate, bear **R** onto obvious singletrack and rocket downhill – watching out for the drainage channels!

Upon joining a wider track, continue **SA** through gates and on to tarmac. As the track ends by a farm, turn **R** through a gate and drop steeply down lanes, ignoring all turnings, to Llanberis high street. Turn **L**, and then **R** by Pete's Eats to return to the car park.

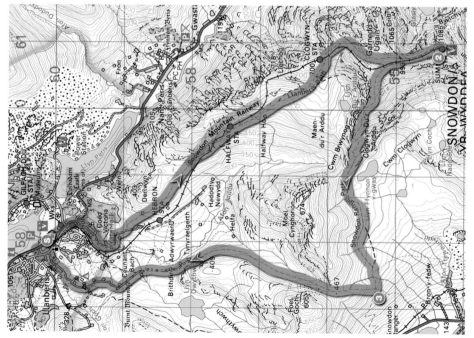

36 Pont Scethin

Battling through gridlocked Barmouth is never a good start to a day. And the stiff climb out of Tal-y-bont won't ease caravan-induced rage. What it will do is get you into the hills in double quick time. And what hills! These are the Rhinogs – smooth, rounded slopes unlike anywhere else in Snowdonia. A short, sweet singletrack drop to Pont Scethin marks the start of the ride proper. Tough climbing follows: innocent-looking, the pull onto Llawlech is anything but, clambering up slabs and steppy singletrack. At the top, holiday traffic will be the last thing on your mind. Stretching ahead is an incredible valley with pristine singletrack cutting across its head. The descent is a corker, a grassy plummet into flowing singletrack which twists and turns down a wide gully, eventually stopping at a rickety old gate. The next couple of kilometres consist of short climbs, descents, gorse bushes and a huge grass snake (at least three feet), before the route turns skywards once more, hauling itself over Bwlch y Rhiwgyr to another cracking descent. This has a rocky opener, a fast, grassy interlude and a woodland finale – a fitting finish to a fantastic ride.

Grade: **Red/Black** » Distance: **20km** » Ascent: **850m** » Time: **2.5hrs+**	
Start/Finish: **Tal-y-bont** » Start Grid Ref: **SH 589218** » SatNav: **Tal-y-bont**	
OS Map: **OL18 Harlech, Porthmadog & Y Bala** » Parking: **Free car park at start**	
Cafe: **Barmouth** » Pub: **None**	

Directions

S Turn **R** out of the car park onto the main road, then take the next **R** up a very straight lane signed as a bridleway.

Climb to the campsite and continue **SA** past it through a narrow gate into the woods. Bear **L** in the trees, up the obvious wide track and follow this uphill and around to the left and a gate. Go through this to the lane and turn **R**.

Bear **R** just before the stone gateposts and follow the lane around the farm until it ends at a gate. Go through this onto a wide track.

Follow the track uphill. Just after climbing a short, steep section, bear **R** off the main track onto a vague grassy singletrack signed as the *Taith Ardudny Way.*

A short but fun descent leads down to Pont Scethin – a nice spot for a sandwich. Go over the bridge and follow flagstones towards the hillside. The flags soon give way to rocky singletrack and technical climbing leads uphill.

2 Go through the gate at the top and continue **SA** over grass and onto singletrack. Take a second to admire the view and then follow the singletrack across the head of the valley. As this ends, descend fast on grass, but watch out for the **L** turn through a gate just after a steeper section.

Go through the gate and turn **R** to continue descending gently on grass. Continue **SA** as the trail eventually turns to singletrack and follow it downhill to a rather out-of-place metal gate.

Turn **R** shortly after the gate, up a short climb. Follow the track as it undulates through pleasant surroundings and continue **SA** as it widens and the going eases.

Continue **SA** through gates with the woods to your left. As the track leaves the woods, pass through two more gates and then turn **R** and then almost immediately **L** onto an obvious stone singletrack trail climbing steeply up the hillside.

3 Follow this steeply around switchbacks and then on to the top. Go **SA** over the hill and drop off the other side on singletrack. This soon becomes technical – stick with the obvious trail as the gradient eases and then follow it, alongside a fence and onto open ground. Continue **SA** across the grassy field to join a concrete track and a gate.

Go through the gate and drop down the road, turning **R** after a few hundred metres.

Go over the bridge and begin to climb uphill before turning **L** onto a signed bridleway just before the houses. Follow this through the woods. Ignore all turnings until you pass a bench and reach an obvious wide fork. Bear **R** here, uphill, and then almost immediately turn **L** onto a wide track to continue descending.

At the road, continue **SA**, downhill to the car park.

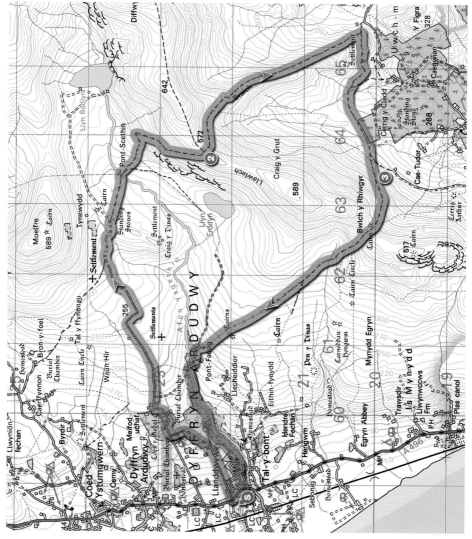

More riding

Capel Curig & Llyn Crafnant

A widely-publicised route, but one for dry weather, and still an acquired taste ... The riding's physically and technically hard. There's also a two-kilometre unrideable bog out of the Ogwen Valley which, if you have a sense of humour and don't mind wet knees, gives access to great, technical lakeside singletrack. So, if you're fit, like technical riding and enjoy soggy feet, this is a good route with some great views.

Note: *You can split the route halfway, using the Marin Trail through Gwydyr Forest as a return leg. This avoids the bog, but also the best singletrack – although you do get the best bits of the Marin.*

Grade: **Black** » Distance: **21km (A) or 30km (B)** » Ascent: **790/900m** » Time: **3.5hrs+**
Start/Finish: **Trefriw, SH 779632** » OS Map: **OL 17 Snowdon**

The Route » Trefriw – Llyn Crafnant – Capel Curig. **Wet option** » Capel Curig – Gwern Gof Uchaf – Helyg – Llyn Cowlyd – Trefriw. **Dry option** (significantly better in wet weather!) » Capel Curig – Ty-hyll – SH 769579 – Marin Trail to car park at SH 790610 – Trefriw

Sarn Helen

A fun ride, starting and finishing in Betws-y-Coed. Head out along minor roads until you reach the Ugly House and then turn south for a big climb, huge puddles and a technical descent. A tough climb and faster descent lead home. Try the route both ways – it has two potentially awesome descents. Unfortunately, both run north-south, meaning you're always going to have to pick one over the other!

Grade: **Red** » Distance: **20km** » Ascent: **620m** » Time: **3hrs+**
Start/Finish: **Betws-y-Coed, SH 791566** » Map: **OS OL17 Snowdon**

The Route » Betws – west on minor road north of/parallel to the A5 to SH 769579 – forest road to Ty-hyll/Ugly House – minor road SW to SH 736567 – south to Dolwyddelan – minor roads NE to Pont-y-pant – Sarn Helen track NE to A5/Betws

Cadair Idris

Summit day number two. Unlike Snowdon, there's only one legal way up and down Cadair, so it's a there and back ride. The lower slopes offer a wide, stone track: easy up, fast down. The middle is grassy (equally fast, but more slippery) and features good singletrack and fast, tight corners. Up top, the riding is rocky and technical. Unrideable in ascent, it's a real challenge to ride down. A proper 'Alpine' feel and stunning views complete a great day out.

Grade: **Black** » Distance: **16km** » Ascent: **880m** » Time: **3.5hrs+**
Start/Finish: **Church at Llanfihangel y-pennant SH 671088** » OS Map: **OL23 Cadair Idris & Bala Lake**

The Route » SH 671088 – north and then west to Cadair Idris summit – turn round and come back down ... !

The Trail Centres

Coed y Brenin

The daddy. The first trail centre in the country, and still one of the best. Trails range from easy to technical XC and all are great fun, although they can get extremely busy. We usually pick *The Beast* as it uses most of the singletrack sections on offer, mixing rocks and roots with berms and jumps. Great fun. For something shorter, the *MBR* trail always gives a good ride.

Trail Count: **Yr Afon, Green 11km** » **MinorTaur, Blue 10km (under construction)** » **Temtiwr, Red 9km** » **Cyflym Coch, Red 11km** » **MBR, Black 18.5km** » **Tarw Trail, Black 20km** » **Dragon's Back, Red 31km** » **The Beast of Brenin, Black 38km**
Start: **Visitor centre on the A470 in Coed y Brenin, SH 720270**
More info: **01341 440747, www.mbwales.com**

Penmachno

Short on facilities and hard to find, but one of the best XC-style loops in the country. The volunteer-built Penmachno is virtually all singletrack, with long sections flowing seamlessly. There's nothing too extreme, just some of the best narrow, fast and flowing singletrack of any trail centre. There are two loops, imaginatively named Loop 1 and – you guessed it – Loop 2. Loop 1 is the first, and best, with Loop 2 being a worthwhile extension if you want a longer ride.

Trail Count: **Loop 1, Red 20km** » **Loop 2, Red 10km**
Start: **Just south of Penmachno village, SH 786498 (No visitor centre)**
More info: **www.mbwales.com**

Gwydyr Forest

Right by Betws-y-Coed, the Marin Trail through Gwydyr Forest has one of the best locations of any trail centre in the country. There's only one trail here, which, being built early on in the development of trail centres, has an old-school feel to it, with forest road climbs and singletrack descents. It's definitely worth riding though, as those descents are stunning.

Trail Count: **Marin Trail, Red, 25km**
Start: **North of Betws, near Llanwrust. SH 790610** (No visitor centre)
More info: **www.mbwales.com**

Cli-machx

A one-trail wonder just north of Machynlleth. Lots of nice, rough singletrack, with some good long descents and – a rarity on man-made trails – some tough technical climbs. But this trail's all about the final descent, which is one of the (if not *the*) longest (and best) singletrack descents in Wales. It's dark, fast and rocky – just watch out for that left-hander!

Trail Count: **Cli-machx, Red, 15km**
Start: **Car park near Ceinws, north of Machynlleth, SH 759063**
More info: **www.dyfimountainbiking.org.uk**

More Information

Main Towns

In the north, Llanberis and Betws-y-Coed have the basics, with Llanrwst, Llandudno, Caernarfon and Bangor a short distance away for bigger shops. Further south, Dolgellau and Machynlleth are the biggest towns.

Maps

OS Explorer OL17 Snowdon (north Snowdonia)
OS Explorer OL18 Harlech, Porthmadog & Y Bala (south Snowdonia)
OS Explorer OL23 Cadair Idris & Bala Lake

Bike Shops

The Holey Trail, Maengwyn Street, Machynlleth, 01654 700 411, www.theholeytrail.co.uk
Beics Brenin, Coed y Brenin Visitor Centre, 01341 440 728, www.beicsbrenin.co.uk
Planetfear, on the main road, Betws-y-Coed, 01690 710 888, www.planetfear.com
1868 Racing, Denbigh Street, Llanrwst, 01492 641 028, www.1868racing.co.uk
Evolution Bikes, High Street, Bangor, 01248 355 770, www.evolution-bikes.co.uk
Dolgellau Cycles, Smithfield Street, Dolgellau, 01341 423 332, www.dolgellaucycles.co.uk
Summit Cycles, North Parade, Aberystwyth, 01970 626 061, www.summitcycles.co.uk

Bike Hire

Beics Brenin, Coed y Brenin Visitor Centre, 01341 440 728, www.beicsbrenin.co.uk
Beics Betws, Betws-y-Coed, 01690 710 766, www.bikewales.co.uk
Beddgelert Bikes, Beddgelert, 01766 890 434, www.beddgelertbikes.co.uk

Accommodation

There are campsites everywhere. The sites around Betws-y-Coed and Capel Curig are handy for the trail centres in that area, as well as Snowdon. Those in the Ogwen Valley are more picturesque, but basic and remote. Further south, there are loads of sites near Dolgellau (try the very friendly Cefn Maelan site above town: 01341 423 338) and loads again near Machynlleth.

There are several YHA Hostels. Try Dolgellau (0845 371 9327), Llanberis (0845 371 9645) and Betws-y-Coed (01690 710 796), or those at Pen-y-Pass (0845 371 9534) and in the Idwal Valley (0845 371 9744). See www.yha.org.uk for more options.

There are a load of independent hostels around too. Our favourite is Reditreks (01654 702 184, www.reditreks.com) in Machynlleth – great for groups. It's run by the bike shop and is tucked away right by the centre of town.

For everything else, try www.snowdon.com, www.staysnowdonia.co.uk or www.visitsnowdonia.info. Anywhere near Betws-y-Coed is nicely central for the north, while Llanberis and Capel Curig are handy for Snowdon. In the south, Machynlleth is always nice to stay in, while Dolgellau is useful for Coed y Brenin.

Food & Drink

Pete's Eats, Llanberis, 01286 870 117, www.petes-eats.co.uk (classic cafe in Llanberis)

The Wynnstay Hotel, Machynlleth, 01654 702 941, www.wynnstay-hotel.com (restaurant, hotel and awesome pizzeria)

Gallt y Glyn, Llanberis, 01286 870 370, www.gallt-y-glyn.co.uk (pizza and pint nights + accommodation)

Caban Cyf, Brynrefail, nr Llanberis, 01286 685 500, www.caban-cfy.org (great cafe, closes early though!)

The Vaynol Arms, Nant Peris, 01286 872 672, (good food, campsite opposite)

Pont-y-Pair Inn, Betws-y-Coed, 01690 710 377, www.hotelbetwsycoed.co.uk (accommodation, food and bar)

Betws Bistro, Betws-y-Coed, 01690 710 328, www. betws-y-coed.co.uk, (posher, but nice)

The Bryn Tyrch Inn, Capel Curig, 01690 720 223 www.bryntyrchinn.co.uk (accommodation)

George III, Penmaenpool, 01341 422 525, www.georgethethird.co.uk, (on the Mawddach Estuary near Dolgellau – lovely spot)

Skinners Arms Hotel, Machynlleth, 01654 702 354

Tourist Offices

Betws-y-Coed, 01690 710 426 » **Barmouth**, 01341 280 787 » **Dolegllau**, 01341 422 888 **Llanberis**, 01286 870 765, www.visitsnowdonia.info » **Machynlleth**, 01654 702 401

Outdoor Shops

Literally everywhere, so don't worry if you've forgotten your tent pegs. In Betws there's Ultimate Outdoors (01690 710 555) and two Cotswold Outdoors (01690 710 710/710 234). Capel Curig and Llanberis both sport Joe Browns (01690 720 205/01286 870 327) with Llanberis also boasting V12 Outdoor (01286 871 534).

Useful Websites

www.mbwales.com » www.dyfimountainbiking.org.uk » www.forestry.gov.uk/mtbwales

Guidebooks

Wales Mountain Biking – Beicio Mynydd Cymru, written by Tom Hutton, published by Vertebrate Publishing

Worth Knowing

As detailed on the Snowdon ride, there's a voluntary ban for bikes on the mountain's bridleways, so please don't ride them between 10am and 5pm from 1 May to 30 September. Thanks!

Scotland

Andy McKenna from Go-Where leads riders out onto the Boreraig Loop on the
Isle of Skye, with Loch Slapin below and Bla Bheinn towering in the background.
Photo: Andy McCandlish.

01: Lunch stop on the Sligachan Loop on the Isle of Skye, enjoying the sun by Loch an Athain.   **02**: Andy McKenna riding with Rik Allsop from Drumlanrig, approaching Glenim on the Lowther Hills route.   **03**: The view down the River Dee from Cnoc Dubh, Deeside. Part of the Ballater routes.   **04**: Andy Stanford and Mike Forrest in the hills above Aberfoyle, early on an autumn morning.   **05**: Descending from the Coire Lair to Achnashellach Station in Torridon, tricky work on the steep bedrock trail.   **06**: Sgurr nan Gillean from the Sligachan trail on Skye, Andy McKenna taking a break from the tough riding.

07

08   **09**   **10**

07: Climbing the Easan Dorcha river, ascending to the foot of the Coire Lair in Torridon.   **08**: Climbing into the crags below the summit of Ben Nevis, via the North Face trail by Fort William.   **09**: You just can't beat the seafood on the Scottish west coast. Mussells in an unknown restaurant.   **10**: Returning to base near the end of the Boreraig route, Skye, with the appropriately named Black Cuillin in the background. **All photos**: Andy McCandlish.

Drumlanrig & the Lowther Hills

At the centre of this area is the impressive pink sandstone castle of Drumlanrig. Built in the late 17th century by the first Duke of Queensberry, it is now the family home of the Duke and Duchess of Buccleuch (spoken 'Bukloo') and Queensberry. The castle is open to the public for tours, giving you the opportunity to see the incredible art collection after a ride.

In the grounds of the castle is a museum to the bicycle, particularly relevant to the area as Kirkpatrick Macmillan, a Scottish blacksmith thought to be the original inventor of the bicycle, is from the nearby village of Keir. So if you visit the area, your bike is coming home ...

Our main ride passes through Wanlockhead, the highest village in Scotland at 461 metres (1,531 feet). Built around lead and other mineral mining first exploited by the Romans, the area is still extensively scarred and shaped by its mining history. There is a museum in the village where you can go below ground and see the conditions miners used to endure. Lead isn't all that was discovered here, and you can hire gold panning equipment in the museum to try your luck in the local rivers after a training session with a local expert.

The Riding

While the natural trails round Drumlanrig don't spike your ride with lots of technical challenges, what they do is take you right out there. Estate tracks over the tops of the hills, cutting into remote glens and taking you over trackless contours are the area's speciality, testing your navigation skills to the max. There are of course some cracking technical spots, like the Enterkin Burn nano-width singletrack where one mistake will see you on a sharp tumble down to the river below.

When to go

With the summer growth hiding some of the less well trodden trails, spring and autumn – when the bracken and grasses die back slightly – would be the best time to visit. The high exposed hilltops where the rides frequent aren't very hospitable in bad weather.

Photo: Andy McCandlish.

37 Wanlockhead & the Lowther Hills

If you are of a certain age, you will understand what is meant by a truly 'old school' ride. Those very words should be conjuring up images of adventures gone by, splashing waist deep through rivers, pressing on into unknown country on non-existent trails and generally taking on a decent adventure with your bike as the vehicle. Well, if you are looking for that, you have come to the right place. Expect to finish this ride with wet feet, tired out, scratched from a tumble and bitten by mysterious insects as you shouldered your bike through a bog. But of course you will have a big smile on your face too. Route finding can be a challenge at any time of year, with faint and non-existent paths in places, open hillsides that require carrying the bike on occasion and plenty of hilltop views to soak up. It isn't all hard going of course, and the singletrack gems it throws back are more than ample payback for any hardships you might suffer. The Dempster Road and Enterkin Burn descents are some of the best singletrack trails in the country.

Grade: **Red** » Distance: **28km** » Ascent: **1,104m** » Time: **4hrs+**
Start/Finish: **Lay-by on A76** » Start GR: **NS 857042** » SatNav: **DG3 4AN (general area)**
OS Map: **Landranger 78 Nithsdale & Annandale** » Parking: **Lay-by on A76**
Cafe: **Halfway round the ride in Wanlockhead is the Hidden Treasures Lead Mining Museum, with excellent cafe (01659 743 87)** » Pub: **The Wanlockhead Inn (01659 745 35) – closed on Mondays**

Directions

S▶ From the lay-by, cross the road onto the single track road under the railway line heading for Coshogle. After around 1km look for a track cutting back on yourself on the **L**. Take this, climbing to Kirkbride farmhouse.

Turn **L** just before the farm on a track and skirt the farm buildings up a grassy track. Go through a gate and the track climbs dead straight in front of you BUT go only a few metres, before going through the gate on your **R**.

The navigation is tricky here, but if the sheep track is visible under the grass, follow this as it contours round the hillside above the ruined church and cemetery on your right. Keep contouring, aiming for the gate on the opposite side of the field. Pass through this and continue on the same line, dropping down through the small burn and climbing steeply up to the wall corner above. Follow the increasingly distinct path up the left of the wall here. It is marked on the OS map, but there isn't much on the ground. Climb over the hillside and descend down the east flank of Knockconey Dod until you pass through another gate and get onto a good grassy track.

Follow the grassy track as it skirts round the north side of the abandoned steading. The singletrack path then drops down into a small glen, splashes through a burn then climbs steeply up through the bracken. Follow this up the hill to meet the well-surfaced estate track. Turn **R** on this and climb.

When the track stops you need to bear **R** over open hillside for a short time, passing through a large washed out burn cutting. At the other side of this the trail gets very distinct and becomes very good singletrack. This is the Dempster Road, descend on it until you reach the Mennock Water, splash through and climb up the banking to the road.

2 Turn **R** on the road and follow it to Wanlockhead. In the village fork left for the mining museum and cafe, or continue straight on to continue the ride. Just as you are leaving the village take the private tarmac road on the **R** that climbs up to the radar station – it is signposted. Climb to the summit of Lowther Hill and the radar 'golf ball.'

Retrace your steps down to the sharp corner with the radio mast and signpost for the footpath. Descend off the steep estate track here, down to the saddle. Go over the gate here and descend on very narrow singletrack – the Enterkin Burn – along the line of the telegraph poles.

3 After descending the Enterkin Burn, meet the track and turn **L** up the climb to the first sharp bend left. Carry straight on here to the west of the ridgeline. Cross the ridge, pass through a gate and into an open field. Follow the line of the track again, down the ridgeline to meet the track for Chapel. Keep descending southwest, staying **R** at the next junction. At the minor road turn sharp **R** and follow it all the way down to the A76 and the lay-by.

Not Long Enough? To add a bit of distance and extend the epic feel start the ride at Drumlanrig Castle where you can use the red route to its most northerly point on the riverside. Leave the red there and keep heading north up the riverside trails to Eliock Wood and the bridge there. Turn right on the main road and rejoin the route at its start point. Nearing the end, instead of turning down to the A76 carry on, use your map to join up tracks and finish back at Drumlanrig Castle.

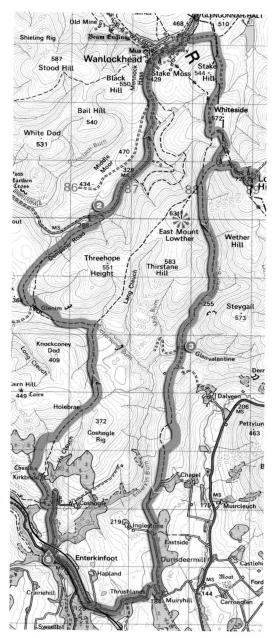

More riding

Durisdeer

Not a technical ride in any singletrack sense, instead this loop will endear itself to you because of the location and terrain it takes you through. Fire roads climb right into the heart of the hills, passing a bothy and opening up tremendous views in all directions once you top out. The climbing soon mounts up as you continue the ride, with the route climbing and descending the hills three times over before the finish. Be careful on the fast and loose fire road descents as more than a few riders have not given them the proper respect and slid off the corners.

Worth noting is the Durisdeer Church Teas which happen every Sunday over the summer. Come the end of the ride you too will be daydreaming of the spread of cakes, sandwiches, scones and more that is laid out, and for a few pounds for church funds, anyone can go in and have a slap up tea. Time your ride right and you won't regret it!

Grade: **Red** » Distance: **24km** » Ascent: **994m** » Time: **2hrs+**

Start/Finish: **Durisdeer Village centre, NS 894037** » OS Map: **Landranger 78 Nithsdale & Annandale**

The Route » Durisdeer – Glenaggart – Par Hill – The Shaw (farm) – south to road at NX 904981 – Fellend – NX 942976 – northwest up Garroch Water and around western flank of Garroch Fell – cross Tansley Burn to NS 921011 – Tansley Rig – Wedder Law – track west over Blackgrain Shoulder – Durisdeer

Photo: Andy McCandlish.

The Trail Centre

Drumlanrig

It would be wrong to be in the area and not partake in the Drumlanrig Castle trails. There are several options, from blue right through to a lengthy red/black trail which will take a few hours to complete. All the trails have a natural feel unlike most trail centres and incorporate roots, rocks and other 'real' trail features. There are family friendly options and the start/finish at the castle has more than a few activities if you are travelling with the kids.

Trail Count: **Various green routes, 3–13km** » **Copy Cat, Blue, 9km** » **The Old School, 20km, Red** » **Magic Eight, Black, 8km**

Start: **Drumlanrig Castle, NX 851994 (well signposted)**

More info: **01848 331 555, www.drumlanrig.com**

More information

Getting About

Although it isn't too far off the motorway, it can take a while to get to Drumlanrig from the M74. Coming up from the south, leave the motorway at Gretna, following the A75 to Dumfries. Once there head north on the A76 to Thornhill, with Drumlanrig a few miles beyond. From the north come off the M74 at junction 14, signposted the A702 to Thornhill.

The Glasgow–Newcastle train stops at Sanquhar, about 15km north of Drumlanrig Castle so is a feasible option.

Main Towns

Thornhill is only a few miles south of Drumlanrig Castle and has everything you could want from a small town – a decent Co-op, accommodation galore, good pubs and other interesting shops. The wide open main street gives a bright and breezy, almost small town America feel.

Maps

OS Landranger 78 Nithsdale & Annandale

Bike Shops

Rik's Bike Shed in the workshops of Drumlanrig Castle is an excellent option. He carries plenty of spares, as well as bikes for sale and hire, and is brimming with local information – look no further. 01848 330 080, www.drumlanrig.com

Bike Hire

Rik's Bike Shed, Drumlanrig Castle, 01848 330 080

Accommodation

There are numerous options for staying in the area, from good campsites right through to posh hotels. The locals recommend a few, such as the cosy Penpont Campsite (01848 330 470, www.penpontfloors.co.uk) or even cosier Glenmidge Smithy Campsite (01387 740 328) with self catering cottages also on site.

The Thornhill Inn (01848 330 326, www.thornhillinn.co.uk) is an excellent choice as is Trigony House Hotel (01848 331 211, www.trigonyhotel.co.uk) near Thornhill.

Food & Drink

The Penpont Tea Rooms just outside Thornhill have the best venison pastries in the world and are well worth nosing into (07765 073 913), as is the Drumlanrig Cafe in Thornhill who do a mean sit-in pizza (01848 330 317). The Thornhill Inn (01848 330 326) and Trigony House Hotel (01848 331 211) also do great after-ride meals and we have heard the Blackaddie Hotel in Sanquhar (01659 502 70) is rated very highly as a gourmet eatery.

Tourist Offices

Moffat, 01683 220 620

Outdoor Shops

The nearest outdoor shops are in Dumfries. Patties of Dumfries (01387 252 891, www.pattiesofdumfries.co.uk) carry a good selection of all outdoor gear. There is also a branch of Mountain Warehouse (01387 274 071, www.mountainwarehouse.com).

Useful Websites

www.dumfries-and-galloway.co.uk – good for all round

www.visitscotland.com – good for accommodation and other attractions

www.drumlanrig.com – more about Drumlanrig Castle and the surrounds

Guidebooks

Scotland Mountain Biking – The Wild Trails, written by Phil McKane, published by Vertebrate Publishing

Scotland Mountain Biking – Wild Trails Vol.2, written by Phil McKane, published by Vertebrate Publishing

Photo: Andy McCandlish.

Tweed Valley: Peebles & Innerleithen

While the Tweed Valley is best known for its groundbreaking trail centres, Glentress and Innerleithen, there is plenty more out there of the more natural persuasion. Long before the 7Stanes project was even a twinkle in the Forestry Commission's eye, riders were covering the hills around Peebles and Innerleithen on hand-made paths, hill walkers footpaths and the likes of the Southern Upland Way.

By all means turn your wheels through the excellent green, blue, red and black trails at the centres, but there is a wealth of riding up just about every hill and glen you can see, so get exploring!

The Riding

The hills are alive with excellent grassy singletrack, gritty hilltop paths and loamy forest trails bashed out by the enduro riders who populate the nearby towns. You can choose from leisurely riverside pootles, fast and furious trail centres or long distance pathways like the Southern Upland Way which link the area across the hilltops with endless other glens and hill ranges. There really is a bit of everything to be had in the Tweed Valley.

When to go

Although the hills and glens down here suffer as much as anywhere in Scotland with the weather, there are plenty of sheltered low-lying options to pursue if the rain and wind close in. You also have the option of taking a day at one of the excellent trail centres where the grit trail surface and forest locations make them pretty much weatherproof. This all adds up to an all year-round destination for good riding.

Photo: Andy McCandlish.

38 St Mary's Loch

This route has a bit of everything. It covers exposed hilltop singletrack, fast downhills, fire road climbs and the odd bit of bike shouldering over boggy ground. On a good day the views can't be beaten, but with poor visibility navigation will become more of a challenge, with short sections on rather ill-defined sections of trail.

Grade: **Red** » Distance: **37km** » Ascent: **921m** » Time: **3hrs+**
Start/Finish: **Car park at Loch of the Lowes, across from the Glen Cafe** » Start GR: **NT 238205**
SatNav: **TD7 5LH** » OS Map: **Landranger 73 Peebles, Galashiels & Selkirk; Landranger 79 Hawick & Eskdale**
Parking: **Large car park at Loch of the Lowes** » Cafe: **The Glen Cafe, T: 01750 422 41 (at start point)**
Pub: **The Tibbie Shiels Inn, T: 01750 422 31, www.tibbieshiels.com (rooms, caravan and campsite available)**

Directions

S Start at the picturesque car park by the Glen Cafe. Cross the bridge on the road to the Tibbie Shiels Inn, passing the hotel on your left as you go through the gate and onto the track climbing the hill east. Follow this track for just short of 3km, looking right for the Southern Upland Way signpost off to your **R** and over a small footbridge. The trail is singletrack from here. Keep following the SUW thistle marker posts over Pikestone Rig, and eventually down Scabcleuch Burn to the road.

2 Turn **L** on the road and follow it through the village of Ettrick, staying **L** at the junction. Continue along the B709 to Hopehouse, where a sign points you **L** up the Captain's Road. Follow these signs up towards Thirlestanehope Farm.

A few hundred metres before the farm the footpath is signposted to the **L** through a gate – follow this. The Captain's Road is marked on the map as continuing straight up the glen from here, but the route is virtually non-existent and boggy. There are new tracks in the glen though, so when you get to a tall deer fence after having passed the farm on your right take the opportunity to cut right across the burn and join the track that climbs up the glen, but on the opposite side to the Captain's Road. Follow this, passing the turn off for Shepherdscleuch on your left, and climb **R** up to the head of the glen on this large scarred track.

3 Where the track turns at the head of the glen, the Captain's Road continues climbing on a poorly defined trail up to the forestry you can see on the skyline – aim for the lowest point where there is a gate marked as the Captain's Road. Go through this and (probably) push along this boggy trail for 600m to get to the linking fire road at the other end. That is the hard bit done!

Join the track, follow it down the Berryknowe Burn, staying **L** at the first junction, then **R** at the next to reach the B709. Turn **L** and descend down to the crossing over the road junction at the Yarrow Water. Turn **L** here, ride for almost 4km before turning **L** onto the Southern Upland Way. Follow the thistle marker posts along the shores of St Mary's Loch to return to your start point.

Not Long Enough? There is always the option of sticking to the Southern Upland Way as it heads towards Moffat. The first section after the excellent descent off the Scabcleuch Burn is single track road, but follow it to the end and the trail turns to track then ultimately superb singletrack over the tops of the hills before descending off to Moffat. Your choice then would be to retrace your steps, or return via the more direct A708.

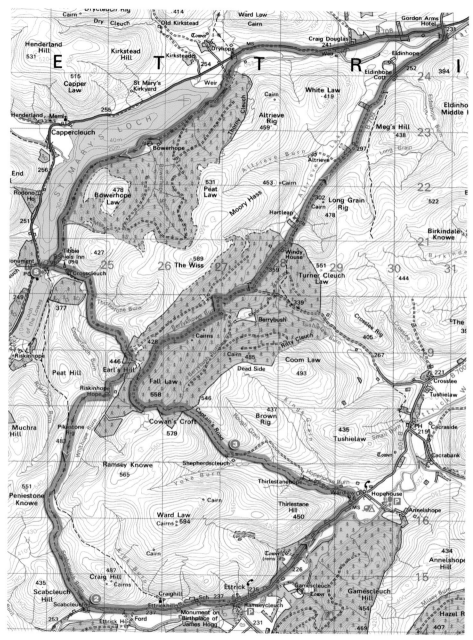

39 Lee Pen and the Black Route

This short and sharp ride is perfect for a sunny summer evening or if you don't have time to take in a more rambling route. After an initial road section to warm up the ride takes a fairly brutal climb on fire road, taking you up to the heights of the Glentress black route. A cheeky hop onto the black route continues the ride over to Lee Pen where the views down over the Tweed Valley are nothing short of superb. A long pause is in order here if the weather is on your side, before the tricky descent down the face of the hill can be tackled. Finish by rolling into one of the excellent pubs on the High Street should you see fit!

Grade: **Black** » Distance: **21km** » Ascent: **765m** » Time: **2hrs+**

Start/Finish: **Innerleithen High Street** » Start GR: **NT 330366** » SatNav: **PH1 4AB**

OS Map: **Landranger Map 73 Peebles, Galashiels & Selkirk** » Parking: **Parking on street, otherwise free car park 200m up B709** » Cafe: **Whistlestop Cafe, Innerleithen, T: 01896 830 374**

Pub: **Corner House Hotel, Innerleithen, T: 01896 831 181 or the Traquair Arms Hotel, Innerleithen, T: 01896 830 229**

Directions

S From Innerleithen High Street head north up the B709 through Innerleithen Golf Course (keep your helmet on!). This road undulates and twists its way up the banks of Leithen Water until the **L** fork for Leithen Lodge. Take this, passing the lodge on your right and carry on up the track until just short of the house marked as Williamslee on the OS map.

2 Fork **L** here, cross the bridge and begin to climb heading southwest up the glen. The track switchbacks right and contours the hillside as it continues to climb up Dunslair Heights. Ascend to a point nearest the boundary wall directly south above you, and you will spot a grassy trail heading across to a break in the wall.

Just the other side of the wall is the Glentress black route. Turn **L** on this and enjoy the twists and turns of the descent ahead. Just as you drop to a low point, watch for trail marker number 80, where you peel off again and follow the boundary wall up a steep climb – you will probably have to shoulder the bike.

3 Follow the heathery trail along the hilltops, passing the trig point at Black Law then on up the tree line to Black Knowe, Mill Rig and Lee Burn Head. The path undulates over these peaks and saddles before the final climb up to Lee Pen.

At the summit of Lee Pen cross the stile and begin the descent, tricky and steep in places as it crosses some rocky and grassy sections – caution is required here. Pass through several gates on your descent, mostly on grassy paths, down to the mast above Innerleithen town below. Just north of the mast take a **L** on a descending trail round the back of the mast hill, dropping back into town either via the mast track, or via one of the many singletracks forking off this, and return to your start point on High Street.

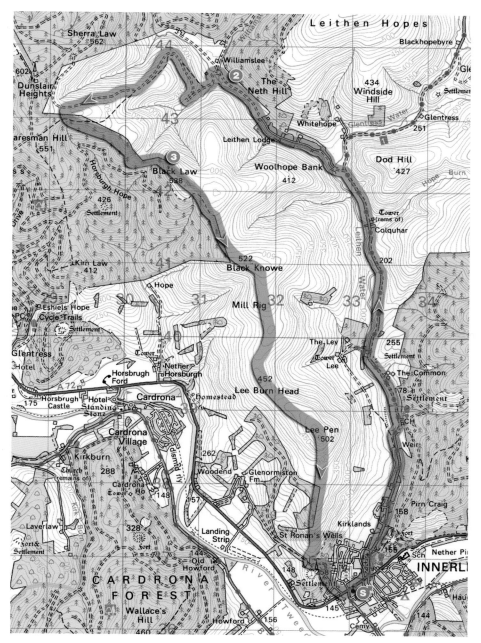

More riding

The Gypsy Glen

The Gypsy Glen is one of the classic rides in the area, the name referring to the trail heading south from Peebles to St Mary's Loch. This ride takes you onto the hilltops from Innerleithen and Traquair, returning to Peebles via the Gypsy, dropping down to the town before climbing steeply up Janet's Brae into the heart of the Glentress trails. You have the choice here of following some of the waymarked trails, or follow the fire road as it contours the hillside to pick up the black descent known as Deliverance. After dropping down this, a faint trail cuts off the waymarked route and descends to Horsburgh Farm where a return via the back road gives a peaceful finish to a great day on the hill.

Grade: **Red** » Distance: **40km** » Ascent: **1,068m** » Time: **4hrs+**
Start/Finish: **Innerleithen, NT 330366** » Map: **Landranger Map 73 Peebles, Galashiels & Selkirk**

The Route » Innerleithen High Street – Traquair – Orchard Rig – Kirkhope Law – Peebles – Glentress – Cardrona – Innerleithen

The Trail Centres

Glentress

Glentress is a trail centre for mountain bikers. The trails are all about enjoying the technical interest of the ride. The green route is gentle singletrack. The blue adds swooping corners and easy, fun jumps. The red rough and ready in places, and fast and jumpy in others. Meanwhile, the long black is technical 'XC-style' singletrack, big climbs and flat-out descents. One ride and it's clear why Glentress is among the most popular centres in the UK.

Trail Count: **Skills Area, 1.5km, Green, Blue, Red** » **Green Route, 3.5km–4.5km, Green** »
Blue Route, 8/16km, Blue » **Red Route, 18km, Red** » **Black Route, 29km, Black** » **Freeride Park, Orange**
Start: **Just off the A72, east of Peebles, NT 284397** » SatNav: **EH45 8NB**
More info: **7stanesmountainbiking.com**

Innerleithen

There are no blue or green routes at 'Inners', just the tricky Traquair XC. A big climb and a big descent, it's a hoot to ride. Particular highlights are the flat-but-flat-out bends and rocky steps of Plora Rigg and the final descent of Caddon Bank, with its warp-speed jumps and diving berms. Elsewhere, the off-piste is rather special. Innerleithen is massively popular for downhill, with an increasing number of 'enduro' trails springing up through its damp and rooty woodland.

Trail Count: **Innerleithen XC, 19km, Red** » **Innerleithen Downhill, various runs, various difficulties, uplift available (booking required)**
Start: **1.5km from Innerleithen, just off the B709 Traquair Road, NT 336358** » SatNav: **EH44 6PW**
More info: **7stanesmountainbiking.com**

More information

Getting About

Being only 30–45 minutes drive south of Scotland's capital, Edinburgh, Peebles and Innerleithen are easily accessed by car. Until recently trains have not been an option, but plans are afoot to resurrect the Borders Railway which will link Edinburgh to the Tweed Valley for the first time since 1969. This is planned for December 2014, so keep an eye on it if train is your favoured mode of transport.

Main Towns

Peebles and Innerleithen, being right on the doorstep of the Tweed Valley trails of Glentress and Innerleithen, have become the first Scottish towns to be properly geared up for mountain biking. It's not surprising when you consider the sheer number of riders that have descended on the area since they were launched – up to 300,000 riders a year. That means you are never far from a bike shop, bike friendly cafe or MTB friendly bunkhouse. Being tourist towns of old, there is also a great selection of cafes, pubs and quirky shops still surviving on their main streets.

Maps

OS Landranger Map 73 Peebles, Galashiels & Selkirk
OS Landranger Map 79 Hawick & Eskdale

Bike Shops

In Innerleithen there is a choice of Alpine Bikes (01896 830 880, www.alpinebikes.com) or I Cycles (01896 833 848, www.i-cycles.co.uk), but Peebles also has BSpoke (01721 723 423, www.bspokepeebles.co.uk) and Glentress Bike Hire (www.glentressbikehire.co.uk). There is also a branch of Alpine Bikes at the Glentress Peel Centre (01721 724 522, www.alpinebikes.com).

Photo: Andy McCandlish.

Bike Hire

Alpine Bikes in Innerleithen and at Glentress Peel Centre (www.alpinebikes.com) both hire good quality mountain bikes, as do Glentress Bike Hire on Peebles main street (www.glentressbikehire.co.uk).

Accommodation

As a popular bike destination, the Tweed Valley is awash with top notch, bike friendly accommodation. Innerleithen in particular has a number of bike specific bunkhouses like the Bike House (07736 321 795, www.thebikehouse.co.uk) or The Bike Lodge (01896 833 836, www.thebikelodge.co.uk), or for a bit more space Innerhaven (01896 888 096, www.innerhaven.co.uk) is a spacious self-catering fully geared up for mountain biking, even down to the friendly owners who are always good for some trail advice. Alternatively head for Caddon View guesthouse (01896 830 208, www.caddonview.co.uk) where the food is out of this world. For something right on the Glentress trails, you could even try one of their comfortable 'wigwams' right at the trailhead (01721 721 007, www.glentressforestlodges.co.uk).

Food & Drink

Sitting on a corner of Innerleithen main street is the Whistlestop Cafe (01896 830 374, www.whistlestopcafeinnerleithen.co.uk), one of our favourites for a relaxing coffee before a ride. Alternatively rides can often be made to take in the super Caberston Cafe in Walkerburn (01896 870 529) where the all day breakfasts are a must. The new Peel Centre in Glentress, not far from one of our rides here, is also good for a lunch or coffee, and you can always browse around Alpine Bikes while you are there.

Tourist Offices

Peebles Visitor Information Centre, 01721 723 159

Outdoor Shops

Awash with bike shops, Innerleithen doesn't have a specific outdoor shop. Peebles has It's Great Outdoors (01721 724 263) on the high street.

Useful Websites

www.7stanesmountainbiking.com – good for trail conditions in Glentress and Innerleithen, but also points to accommodation and other facilities
www.innerleithen.org.uk – good for local information, things going on and news
www.peebles.info – good for tourist information

Guidebooks

Scotland Mountain Biking – The Wild Trails, and *Wild Trails Vol.2*, both written by Phil McKane, published by Vertebrate Publishing
Bike Scotland Trails Guide, 40 of the Best Mountain Bike Routes in Scotland, written by Richard Moore and Andy McCandlish, published by Pocket Mountains

The Pentland Hills

Edinburgh, the ancient capital of Scotland, is positively awash in history. Stand on the castle walls to survey the town and there is classical architecture and cultural gems as far as the eye can see – so much so the town centre has been named as a UNESCO World Heritage Site and has long been known as the 'Athens of the North.'

The Pentland Hills rise just eight kilometres to the south of the town centre and have plenty of history of their own. With forts on the hilltops and other remains of ancient civilisation in the glens there are a total of 12 scheduled ancient monuments in the area.

To protect this fragile area, the Pentlands were designated a Regional Park in 1984, in which the management is committed to a number of aims: to retain the character of the hills, care for them, encourage responsible access and co-ordinate with farming and other land uses. A very active ranger service implements these ideals and so far they are working, even with the tremendous pressure of being so close to a major city.

The Riding

While the Pentlands give the impression of being in the middle of nowhere when you are fully immersed in them, they are actually very handy for the city of Edinburgh and plenty of other towns. As a place to disappear into for a quick escape, some superb singletrack and plentiful short summer evening blast options, they are hard to beat for locals and visitors alike. For more extended rides those short blasts can easily be patched together in a bewildering number of combinations, so there is something there for everyone no matter how long a ride they fancy.

The riding tends not to be too rocky or technical, although there are exceptions, with most of it being on constructed walkers paths or grassy singletrack. If you dig into some of the lower trails above Currie and Balerno however, you better brush up on your root riding!

When to go

Being so close to Edinburgh city, the trails can get quite busy (by Scottish standards) on weekends or bank holidays when the populace decide they want a day out. Summer evenings and midweek at any time of year are preferable for quieter trails, but they never really get that bad so just go for it!

40 Pentlands Tour

This tour of the northern Pentlands takes in just about every type of mountain biking this hill range has to offer. With great views over the city of Edinburgh never far away, you will be climbing the height of the hills no less than three times. Of course this means you have three great descents too, mostly on grassy singletrack, but the final descent down to the car is on cracking trails through the woods where local riders come to polish their downhill skills. Choose a sunny day, take a sandwich and make sure you stop plenty to soak up those views as you travel through some classic Scottish lowland scenery.

Grade: **Red** » Distance: **33km** » Ascent: **985m** » Time: **4hrs+**
Start/Finish: **Bonaly Country Park car park, NT 212675** » Start GR: **NT 212675** » SatNav: **EH13 0PB**
OS Map: **Landranger 66 Edinburgh, Penicuik & North Berwick** » Parking: **Bonaly Country Park car park**
Cafe: **Get a good panini in Riccarton Garden Centre cafe, T: 0131 449 4004**
Pub: **The Juniper Green Inn, Juniper Green, T: 0131 458 5395**

Directions

S» Starting in the Bonaly Country Park car park, head directly up the hill through the car park and through the wooden gate. Bear immediately **R** and follow the singletrack up and over to Torduff Reservoir. Drop down the steps and over the dam, turning **L** round the reservoir itself on tarmac road.

As you reach Clubbiedean Reservoir turn **L** through a small gate just below the dam, following singletrack up the hill alongside a water stream. Follow the trail through the woods before popping out on the track and following this before turning hard **L** in Easter Kinleith Farm. Follow this single track road past the road junction at Harlaw Farm.

Approximately 500m past the junction, where the road takes a hard right, turn **L** up more singletrack up the wall line. Turn **R** just after the ranger centre and follow the track on the west side of the reservoir – an alternative being the singletrack round the far side, making sure you meet up at the far end of the water.

Just 200m after the left for Easter Bavelaw, stay **L** on the trail. Follow this singletrack for approximately 400m. When you reach the road turn **L** and climb up Exponential Hill. It is notorious among locals for being a nasty climb, steepening sharply towards the end. Alternatively jump off onto the side of the road where a singletrack path (only metres off the road) can help to take your mind off the gradient!

2 Turn **R** at the top of the hill, then almost immediately **L** onto a track through a gate. Climb on this variously grassy and gravelly trail to the top of a pass where there is a stile.

Cross the stile and take the grassy singletrack climbing up to your **R**. This goes over the shoulder of Cap Law, before dropping to Nine Mile Burn. Enjoy the fast and furious grassy descent. Turn **L** at the bottom onto the single track road, then **L** again on the A702. It is a busy road, so be careful here.

Around 1km after Silverburn village take the grassy (and boggy on occasions) trail to the **L** of the road. This climbs up and over the steep pass between Scald Law and Carnethy Hill. Drop down into the glen at the far side and turn **R** on the trail at the bottom. Follow the potholed tarmac down past Glencorse Reservoir by around 500m.

3 Turn **L** here, up the steep climb to the Army shooting range centre. Turn **R** at the top, skirting round the buildings to a car park where you can see the steep fire road climbing up Castlelaw Hill. It is only marked on the OS map as a single dotted line, but it is a full width red blaze track. Climb this up and over the shoulder, then descend through a drystone wall.

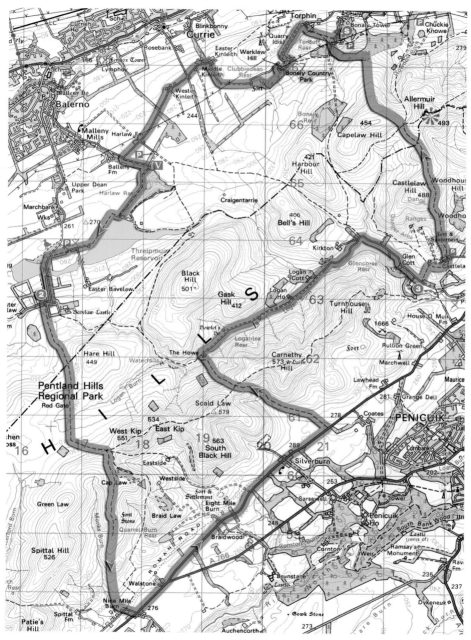

Around 500m after that take the singletrack down to the **L**, and through a gate. Turn immediately **R** after the gate on grassy path, climbing steadily up the northwest side of Capelaw Hill – this trail isn't marked on OS Landranger maps, but is on the Explorer.

Just as the trail drops off the shoulder it turns right, drops to a gate then passes through. Follow the track for around 500m, where it turns right. You want to follow the grassy path **L** here, keeping the forest on your left.

At the gate, lift your bike over then ride immediately up into the forest, keeping to the trail as it runs along the treeline for a while. This then drops through steep and technical in places choice of trail where the local downhillers practice (they all drop down, so choose your singletrack!) and finally spits you out onto the main Country Park trail that will drop back to the car park and finish.

Not Long Enough? If you want to add a bit of leg stretching distance, why not ride out from the centre of Edinburgh on the railway cycle path network, combined with the Union Canal and Water of Leith walkways.

Photo: Andy McCandlish.

More riding

Flotterstone Ride

A cracking ride for a sunny summer evening, this route takes you through a warm up of gentle tarmac climbing before diving onto the hill paths we all know and love in the Pentlands. Ultra-narrow hillside singletrack contours round the side of Black Hill, testing your balance and quick reactions, while steep grassy climbs test your lungs with Edinburgh as a spectacular backdrop later on. A final fast grass trail round Castlelaw Hill finishes the route off on a high note that will leave you searching the map for more.

Grade: **Red** » Distance: **21km** » Ascent: **590m** » Time: **2hrs+**
Start/Finish: **Flotterstone Inn Ranger Centre, NT 233631** » OS Map: **Explorer 344 Pentland Hills**

The Route » Ranger car park by Flotterstone Inn – tarmac climb to Glencorse reservoir – Loganlea reservoir – The Howe – continue on **R** side of glen – keep **R** on white gravel singletrack – **SA** at hut around Black Hill – **L** at Logan Cottage – **L** at NT 215640 – fork **R** towards Bonaly reservoir (not down to resr) – climb around north flank of Capelaw Hill to NT 225656 – southwest then south around Castlelaw Hill – turn **R** at NT 220641 – return to car park

Currie & Balerno

This is a cracking ride you can either choose as a specific challenge, or revert to it when the weather precludes you from going over the tops. Staying low above the villages of Currie and Balerno, it uses many of the little trails you would otherwise struggle to find on any map, many of which are superbly rooty and tricky to test your technical skills. Especially in the wet!

Grade: **Red** » Distance: **18km** » Ascent: **254m** » Time: **2hrs+**
Start/Finish: **Harlaw Car park, NT 181655** » Map: **Explorer 344 Pentland Hills**

The Route » Harlaw car park – Threipmuir Reservoir – East Rigg – Balerno – Malleny Mills – Poet's Glen – Harlaw car park

Photo: Andy McCandlish.

More information

Getting About

Edinburgh Waverley Station spits you out right in the centre of the city, handy for the main shopping streets if you fancy a poke around. Riding from the city centre is easily done via the Union Canal and Water of Leith walk/cycleways, hardly troubling tarmac the whole way. You can get to Edinburgh on sleepers from London that run seven days a week, or access from any major city. More train information can be found at the Edinburgh city website (www.edinburgh.org/traveltips/heretrain). By car just head north on the M6/M74, then peel off at Junction 13 M74 onto the A702. Alternatively Go-Where, based in Innerleithen, can pick you and your bikes up from Edinburgh Airport and transfer you wherever you like (www.go-where.co.uk).

Main Towns

Of course the main town is Edinburgh. Just a stone's throw away from the foot of the Pentlands it has everything a large tourist driven city would be expected to have. It is dripping in history, and the scope for evening entertainment is second to none.

Maps

Explorer 344 Pentland Hills, Penicuik & West Linton
Landranger 66 Edinburgh, Penicuik & North Berwick

Bike Shops

There are too many bike shops in Edinburgh to mention them all, but some of the most popular are
Edinburgh Bicycle Co-Op, 0131 228 3565
Alpine Bikes, 0131 225 3286
The Bike Chain, 0131 557 2801

Bike Hire

Most of the bike shops mentioned above will either hire or demo bikes – drop them a line before you leave to check on their hire status.

Accommodation

To get the most out of your trip, staying in the heart of Edinburgh has to be an option – see a bit of the town, sample the nightlife, then pedal out to the nearby hills for a ride when you recover. The city is absolutely crammed with all types of accommodation, including an SYHA hostel in the town centre (0131 524 2090, www.syha.org.uk) and a limitless number of B&Bs. If you are looking for something a bit closer to the hills, search around Balerno, Currie and Penicuik. As always, the tourist information at www.visitscotland.com is helpful.

Food & Drink

There are limitless options for eating in Edinburgh of course, but out towards the trails in the Pentlands we like:
Flotterstone Inn, 01968 673717 which is right at the foot of several ride options.
Juniper Green Inn, Currie is also a good option, 0131 458 5395

Tourist Offices

Edinburgh Tourist Information can be reached on 0845 2255 121, or look them up at www.edinburgh.org. Alternatively, pop in to see them at 3 Princes Street in the city centre, above the Princes Mall shopping centre.

Outdoor Shops

The nearest selection of outdoor shops is in Edinburgh, with Tiso at Ratho Climbing Centre on the west of the city (0131 333 1633) and in the centre at Rose Street (0131 225 9486). There are many more in and around the centre of the city.

Useful Websites

www.edinburgh.org – good for all round Edinburgh information
www.visitscotland.com – good for accommodation and other attractions

Guidebooks

Scotland Mountain Biking The Wild Trails, written by Phil McKane, published by Vertebrate Publishing

Photo: Andy McCandlish.

North Glasgow

There can be few cities quite as spoiled for riding choice as Glasgow. Overlooked by rolling hills to the north and south, you don't have to look far to find peaceful backcountry trails, easily swapping the vibrant hustle and bustle of this one-time City of Culture for some near wilderness riding in a few easy pedal strokes.

Here we have concentrated on the northwest of the city, taking in ancient tracks, long distance pathways and winding trails through country parks. We pass distilleries and snug pubs, and take on the wild hilltop singletrack of the Kilpatrick Hills.

The routes are just a flavour of what is out there though, so as you take on our suggested rides keep your eyes peeled and don't be afraid to follow your nose. Just don't forget to pack the map.

The Riding

There is a veritable spiders web of trails around the outskirts of Glasgow, with the volcanic cliffs and peaks of the Campsies and Kilpatricks to the north providing a wealth of more adventurous destinations for the local rider.

From beginner to advanced, there is plenty nearby for everyone. Novices can pedal out the West Highland Way, taking in the fabulous scenery only a few minutes ride from the suburban town centre of Milngavie, or they can venture up into Mugdock Park for a spin round the man-made walking trails there. More advanced riders can stick to the same area, but sniff out the technical singletrack that weaves between the more established trails.

Looking for something with a bit more distance? No problem, just head north. Ride out through to the Campsies or Kilpatricks where the little used trails turn to grassy paths and cut over the summits, taking you deep into the hills where it is hard to believe a city lurks just out of sight.

When to go

The best time is undoubtedly in the spring, between March and June. At this time there is often a prolonged dry spell, it is pre-midge season and the ferns in the low-lying areas haven't got out of control yet.

Photo: Andy McCandlish.

41 The Kilpatrick Hills

This rolling ride utilises some of the best routes in the area, combining a variety of riding with terrific views over the city and a good poke around the hills. You are onto back woods singletrack almost as soon as you nose out of Milngavie town centre, cutting over rooty trails through a golf course and on over open fields. After the climb up to Greenside Reservoir you are onto indistinct grassy trails for a while, and the same goes all the way across to Burncrooks Reservoir, so keep on top of your navigation. The return leg is pretty straightforward on well-established trails and the West Highland Way, easy to follow all the way back to that coffee and empire biscuit you deserve in Bullands.

Grade: **Red** » Distance: **30km** » Ascent: **649m** » Time: **2hrs+**	
Start/Finish: **Milngavie town centre** » Start GR: **NS 553745** » SatNav: **G62 8BX**	
OS Map: **Landranger 64 Glasgow, Motherwell & Airdrie**	
Parking: **Milngavie train station or other public car parks in town centre**	
Cafe: **Bullands Coffee House, Milngavie, T: 0141 956 6255** » Pub: **The Cross Keys, Milngavie, T: 0141 956 4211**	

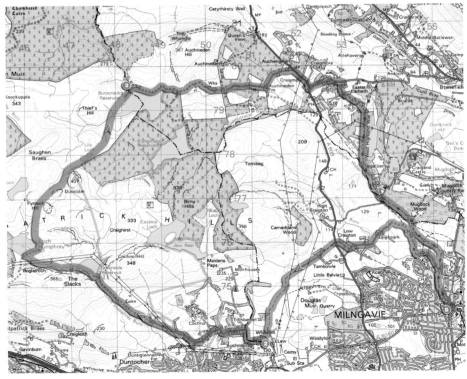

Directions

(S) Immediately opposite the West Highland Way obelisk on the main precinct, take the ramp down the side of Costa Coffee and follow the WHW markers down the narrow cutting of the pedestrian walkway. Follow this as it joins the riverbank, then where the WHW turns uphill on the right, fork **L** and continue on the riverside.

The path crosses a small bridge, at the far end of which you go immediately **R** and along a muddy singletrack trail. At the top of the river turn **R** over another small bridge and follow this trail up to the golf course clubhouse.

Through the car park and head north on the access road through the course. Follow this through Laighpark Farm and on up towards the A809. 300m short of the main road there is a **R** turn on to singletrack through the forest. Take this, then cross over the A809, through a gate fingerposted as Faifley.

Climb up the **R** side of the field as there is no real trail on the ground, aiming for the gate at the top. Go through this and follow the track southwest. This track turns to singletrack and continues over the moor and down to the road near Whitehill Farm.

(2) Turn **R** on the road and follow it for just short of 2km, then take a **R** turn up the hill towards Greenside Reservoir.

Cross the dam, then turn sharp **R** onto narrow singletrack contouring round the steep hillside. At the west point of the reservoir head on the faint path up the ridge at NS 468755. Cross under the pylons and follow the path to the track at Loch Humphrey.

Ride on wet trail round the east bank of the reservoir and strike north up Fynloch Hill on a visible grassy path. Cresting the top, follow the path round the north-west slopes of Duncolm and head for the junction of drystone walls at the far end. Climb over here and proceed along the wall line on wet path by Lily Loch.

Follow the trail as it leaves the wall and heads over the hill to the southwest point of Burncrooks Reservoir. The path is faint and non-existent at times, but just keep heading to this point of the reservoir and you will soon pick it up again.

(3) Pick up the track at the end of the reservoir dam and follow this water board road round the shore and on out to the A809. Turn **R** here and descend to turn **L** at the junction with the B821.

Climb up the road and just after the road starts to descend keep an eye out on the right. The second turn off **R** is the one you want, looping down and round through some huts and a ruined cottage. Just before the house gateposts, turn **R** up some muddy singletrack and follow over to rejoin the West Highland Way.

Descend gently on the West Highland Way past Craigallian Loch and on over the Khyber Pass road, following the white thistles of the WHW markers all the way back into your starting point in Milngavie.

Not Long Enough? If the weather is good and the summer days long, there is an excellent option of cutting left at Burncrooks Reservoir and riding up the hill past the Whangie. A fissure high up on Auchineden Hill that, story has it, was slashed out the landscape by the Devil's tail as he was on his way to a witch's coven on Stockiemuir. The Whangie is accessed by a stunning singletrack overlooking Loch Lomond and is a well worthwhile detour, but if the days are short you will probably be happy to head in and keep it for another day.

42 Dumgoyne Loop

Although on paper it looks very similar in length and height gain to the Kilpatricks route, the Dumgoyne Loop is a much less strenuous tour of the area. The trails are mostly hard packed with all-weather friendly surfaces and as a result the going is fast relative to the grind of the Kilpatrick singletrack. The West Highland Way, in the form of some wide and stony tracks, carries you out of town and down to the village of Dumgoyne where you can stop in at the Beech Tree Inn for refreshment or pop your head into the excellent Glengoyne Distillery visitor centre. More tracks take you back towards town, turning to enjoyable singletrack in places as you return via Mugdock Park. As you ride back in through Drumclog Moor, don't be afraid to just take to a singletrack that you fancy. Almost without exception they will not be a dead end and will spit you out somewhere useful, either on the West Highland Way or one of the other main paths cutting over the moor. It really is an area covered in excellent singletrack trails and the locals regularly just play in the area for hours, barely seeing the same trail twice in that time. Try it, just follow your nose!

Grade: **Blue** » Distance: **27km** » Ascent: **521m** » Time: **2hrs+**
Start/Finish: **Milngavie town centre** » Start GR: **NS 553745** » SatNav: **G62 8BX**
OS Map: **Landranger 64 Glasgow, Motherwell & Airdrie**
Parking: **Milngavie train station or other public car parks in town centre**
Cafe: **Bullands Coffee House, Milngavie, T: 0141 956 6255, Stables Tearoom in Mugdock Visitor Centre**
Pub: **The Beech Tree Inn, Dumgoyne, T: 01360 550 297**

Directions

S► Immediately opposite the West Highland Way obelisk on the main precinct, take the ramp down the side of Costa Coffee and follow the WHW markers down the narrow cutting of the pedestrian walkway. Follow this as it joins the riverbank, then follow the WHW as it forks **R** up the hill and out over the Khyber Pass Road. It continues on past Craigallian Loch to the top of the rise, where the WHW forks right.

Go straight on (leaving the WHW) to the muddy singletrack round the side of the house and join the tarmac driveway at NS 534792. Turn **L** and ride out to the B821, turning **R** for just over 200m then rejoining the WHW by turning **L** up the grassy Tinker's Loan.

Cross the stile, admiring the view north to Dumgoyne, then begin the descent past Arlehaven on the main WHW down to Dumgoyach Farm. Past the farm by 200m, the WHW turns **L** onto an abandoned railway path, well surfaced. Follow this all the way along to the Beech Tree Inn.

2 Turn **R** on the A81 for around 1km, turning **L** onto a track climbing steeply up to the **L** just before Dumgoyne Distillery. The track switchbacks up to meet the water board track contouring round the hillside. Turn **R** and follow it for around 5km where it drops into Blanefield.

At the road junction take a **R** then almost immediate **L** onto a walkway that cuts through to the football pitches. Follow it round the pitch then into the small residential estate. Go straight on to a T-junction and turn **R**, then after 20m take on the rocky and rough trail **L**, heading directly up the hill.

3 At the top of the hill stay **R** on the tarmac as it turns to rocky track and keeps climbing. This is known locally as the Gowk Stane track and it climbs almost relentlessly for a few kilometres.

Near the top of the climb the track goes straight on through a closed gate. A fingerpost points **L**, follow it onto some stony singletrack before turning **R** on the road for a few hundred metres and then **L** into Mugdock Country Park.

Follow the track past the gun emplacements on your left and descend past Mugdock Castle. Don't take any turn offs until you reach a car park on your left. Just 20m past the junction to the car park there is a singletrack path heading **L** down the riverside, on which you descend to the road. Turn **R** and drop down past the reservoirs.

At the 'Hole in the Wall' car park (NS 554760) turn **R** and follow the trail in. Just before the main path takes a sharp turn left, look on your **L** for a muddy section of fast singletrack that drops you down to the West Highland Way. Turn **L** at the riverside and follow the trail back into the town centre.

Photo: Andy McCandlish.

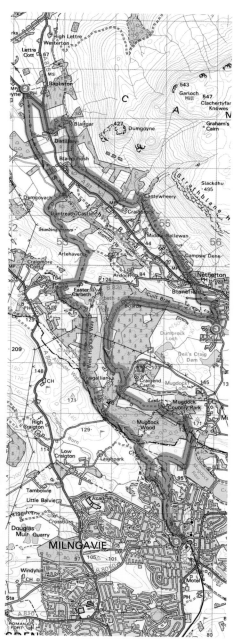

More riding

Earl's Seat

A real climber's route this one, leaving Glengoyne Distillery and climbing to the top of the highest peak of the Campsie Fells. A switchbacking stony track begins the height gain, before the water board track contours round and the climbing begins in earnest at High Lettre Farm. Turn right up the grassy track, before it turns to a more dirt-based surface and carries you up to grassy singletrack where the challenge is to stay on the bike to the skyline. The crest of the hill is grassy singletrack all the way to the top – hard going when wet, or when the wind is blowing. Then just enjoy it all again on the way back down!

Grade: **Red** » Distance: **19km**
Ascent: **711m** » Time: **2hrs+**
Start/Finish: **Glengoyne Distillery, NS 527827**
Map: **Landranger 64 Glasgow, Motherwell & Airdrie**

The Route » Glengoyne Distillery – Blairgar – High Lettre – Garloch Hill – Earl's Seat – Reverse

Photo: Andy McCandlish.

More information

Getting About

Milngavie is a well connected town with a train station right in the town centre and a main road all the way to the door. Step off the train and you are more or less at the start of the rides. By car get yourself into Glasgow city centre and take J16 off the M8, signposted to Aberfoyle. Follow the A879 signposted for Milngavie and heading out of town, before turning onto the A81 into Milngavie itself. Follow signs for the railway station and park in the station car park.

Main Towns

The nearest town to our trails is Milngavie. Now absorbed into the Glasgow sprawl, Milngavie is the official start of the West Highland Way and has plenty in the way of food shops, pubs and restaurants.

Maps

Landranger 64 Glasgow, Motherwell & Airdrie

Bike Shops

The nearest bike shop is Solid Rock Cycles on the road between Milngavie and Torrance (01360 622699, www.solidrockcycles.com) – good stock and good service. One of the best bike shops in the area, packed with character and building the best wheels in the west, is Wheelcraft in Clachan of Campsie. Dare to drink one of Big Al's coffees while you search through the mountain of stock (01360 312709, www.wheelcraft.net).

Bike Hire

Solid Rock Cycles hire bikes, as do Alpine Bikes in the centre of Glasgow (0141 353 2226) among many others.

Accommodation

In the Milngavie area there are a few good B&Bs catering for the West Highland Way tourists. A few of the more cycle friendly ones are Best Foot Forward (0141 956 3046, www.bestfootforward.eu.com) or Auchenhowe Cottage (0141 956 4003, www.auchenhowe.co.uk). Alternatively there is a local Premier Inn (08701 977 112, www.premierinn.com). Tourist information can help with more options.

Food & Drink

Bullands Coffee House (0141 956 6255) in the centre of Milngavie is very bike friendly and has a great selection of food, including home baking. For more of a pub meal, head for the Cross Keys in the precinct (0141 956 4211) or Burnbrae (0141 942 5951) half a mile or so back towards Glasgow.

Tourist Offices

Glasgow Tourist information, 0141 204 4400

Outdoor Shops

You will have to go further into Glasgow for an outdoor shop, with the huge Tiso Glasgow Outdoor Experience (0141 559 5450) having both outdoor equipment and a branch of Alpine Bikes under one roof, together with an excellent cafe.

Useful Websites

www.seeglasgow.com – good for all round stuff

Guidebooks

Scotland Mountain Biking – The Wild Trails, and Wild Trails Vol.2, both written by Phil McKane, published by Vertebrate Publishing
Bike Scotland Trails Guide, 40 of the Best Mountain Bike Routes in Scotland, written by Richard Moore and Andy McCandlish, published by Pocket Mountains

Photo: Andy McCandlish.

Loch Lomond & the Trossachs

Located barely 20 miles north of Glasgow, the Loch Lomond and Trossachs National Park could be forgiven for being a busy place. Of course it is on occasion, and particularly around the tourist hotspots of Loch Lomondside and Aberfoyle. But sneak into the woods even a short distance from the busiest car park and you will find yourself in a world of your own – it appears the bulk of Glaswegians don't range far from their cars.

With trails like the excellent West Highland Way cutting straight through the area, and a multitude of other paths leading up and around the nearby hills, it is an often overlooked goldmine of mountain biking. With the Highland Fault Line cutting right past Aberfoyle this is one of the more southerly locations where you can truly ride in Highland terrain.

The Riding

This is truly an area with a bit of something for everyone. If you fancy some long and scenic fire road trails, you will find plenty of that, but if you want some up-close-and-personal singletrack threading through the forest with technical descents and challenging climbs you will find that too. Even big mountains get a look in with the Ben Lomond tourist path a must try for every mountain biker who loves rocky descending. Just be prepared for some shouldering of the bike!

When to go

The Trossachs is a pretty sheltered area compared to other hilly spots and so, if you choose to, you can stay low and protected from the worst of the weather. That means you can ride pretty much all year round, although the Menteith Hills trail can get pretty muddy and slippy when it has been consistently wet. Take a ride in the wet, and bundle in to the Forth Inn for a drink and meal round the roaring fire.

Photo: Andy McCandlish.

43 The Menteith Hills

This excellent trail whisks you quickly out of the tourist hotspot of Aberfoyle and into the lesser trodden hills behind. As soon as you ride out of the town you are onto picturesque fire road, before climbing into the hills for some excellent and challenging grassy singletrack. Wind your way through rocks and splash through rivers before dropping steeply down to the secluded shore of Loch Venachar for an idyllic pedal through woodland. The final fire road climb and technical singletrack descent into Aberfoyle finish off a trail that has a bit of everything.

Grade: **Red** » Distance: **23km** » Ascent: **627m** » Time: **2hrs+**	
Start/Finish: **Aberfoyle Car Park** » Start GR: **NN 521009** » SatNav: **FK8 3UQ**	
OS Map: **Landranger 57 Stirling & The Trossachs; Explorer 365 The Trossachs**	
Parking: **Parking in the main Aberfoyle car park**	
Cafe: **Liz Macgregor's Restaurant and Coffee Shop, T: 01877 389 376; Wee Blether out at Kinlochard**	
Pub: **Forth Inn, Aberfoyle, T: 01877 382 372**	

Directions

S Starting at the Aberfoyle car park, turn **R** on the main street and carry along to the edge of town and a rough singletrack road on your **L** signposted *Dounans Outdoor Centre*. Take this and climb through the complex and onto fire road, taking a **R** turn at the T-junction at the top. Follow this along the top of the golf course, with great views south to the Campsie Fells. Pass one junction with a trail climbing off to the left before sweeping **L** at the next junction.

Climb from here for around 1.5km on track, watching carefully on the **L** for a dirt singletrack running parallel to the track for a short distance. Jump on to this and follow it through the forest before it opens out onto open moorland on mud singletrack. Stay on this trail all the way past the small loch on your right and turn **L** when you hit the fire road.

2 Follow this for around 1km before forking **L** at the junction. About 50m after this junction watch carefully on your **R** for a grassy trail heading steeply down the hill – careful here as it is very steep in places – and drop down it to the next fire road. Turn hard **R** there and follow the fire road down past some cottages on your left, before crossing a single track tarmac road and joining Sustrans Cycle Route 7 along the shores of Loch Venachar.

Just short of 2km along this path, keep an eye on your **L** for a narrow singletrack climbing up into the woodland. Take this up to the banks of Loch Drunkie, staying **R** on the trail to drop down to a little used fire road. Follow this out to the main fire road and turn **L**. Be careful of traffic here as it is a Forest Drive, and is pretty well used on holidays and weekends. Climb up the track, following the Cycle Route 7 signposts, round the shores of Drunkie, finally topping out at a wooden barrier over the track at a junction. Go around the barrier and continue on your way.

3 The track levels out and begins to drop down. At the first junction turn **R**, then get to a large open crossroads after some fast fire road descending. You can go straight on here to descend into Aberfoyle on Cycle Route 7, but we will go **L**, then after 100m, look on your **R** for a few excellent singletrack descents. The first you get to, by a large tree, is a downhill course and pretty technical in places; the second is more flowing – you choose your poison as they both drop out virtually at the same place. When you hit the track at the bottom turn **L** down the hill, then **R** at the next junction.

Around 50m after the junction keep an eye **L** for a small singletrack with rocks set in to the surface dropping down through the woods – take this past the small building, then on down to the track where you turn **L**, riding along to where you climbed out of the Dounans Centre back at the start.

Not Long Enough? You can get round this trail in less than two hours if you get your head down, so to extend it and get some glorious views at the same time, why not add a circuit of Loch Ard to the mix? Although largely fire road, this loop takes you through some great scenery with glimpses of Ben Lomond and Ben Venue close by.

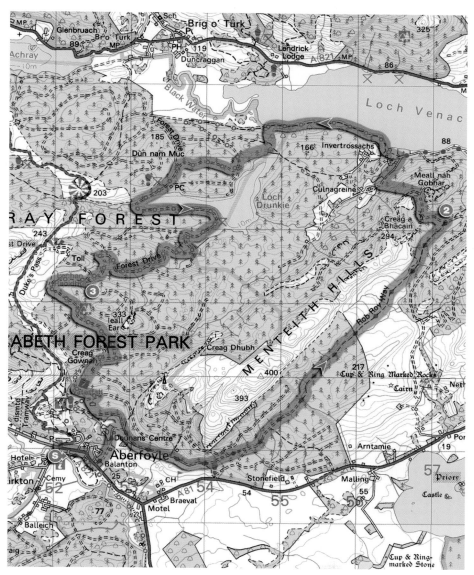

More riding

Loch Lomond Singletrack

If you love singletrack you are going to love this ride! Starting out on fire road to warm up the legs, the trail soon turns to tricky and steep trail over Conic Hill on the West Highland Way. Dropping off the hill, you veer off those thistle marker posts halfway down to take one of the fastest descents in the area off the grassy ridge and down to the lochside. The trail then picks up the WHW again and follows its singletrack all the way up to Rowardennan – sometimes fast, sometimes technical, but always enjoyable. It is deceptively tiring, as the 1,114m ascent spells out, as it is constantly undulating along the lochside. The return to Balmaha is via the same trail, but instead of reclimbing Conic Hill the route skirts the side and returns via more gentle fire road. A cracking route for a day out with amazing views of the loch.

Grade: **Red/Black** » Distance: **37km** » Ascent: **1,114m** » Time: : **4hrs+**
Start/Finish: **Garadhban Car Park nr Drymen, NS 480906** » OS Map: **Landranger 56 Loch Lomond & Inveraray**

The Route » Garadhban car park – West Highland Way west to Conic Hill – keep **R** at NS 424919 and descend ridgeline – cross road, through gate, turn **R** on WHW – refreshments at Rowardennan Hotel, then reverse route to where you joined WHW – continue around coast to pier and turn **L** on road – Milton of Buchanan – fork **L** after bus stop – fork first **R** in forest – rejoin outward route – car park

Inversnaid Loop

Starting from the shores of Loch Chon this trail warms you up with steep and sustained fire road climbing, but the result is spectacular views and wild countryside above Loch Lomond. Get a taste of challenging singletrack along the lochside before passing through lovely woodland and over the spectacular waterfalls by Inversnaid, before a quick drink in the hotel and a road ride return on classic highland singletrack roads. For refreshment, detour slightly off to Stronachlachar Pier where the excellent Pier Tea Room (01877 386 374) will welcome you with great coffee and a roaring wood stove. You can also dive back into the forest for a diversion on your return too.

Grade: **Blue/Red** » Distance: **32km** » Ascent: **850m** » Time: **2hrs+**
Start/Finish: **Lay-by by Loch Dhu, NN 433037** » OS Map: **Landranger 56 Loch Lomond & Inveraray; Landranger 57 Stirling & The Trossachs**

The Route » Lay-by at Loch Dhu – Gleann Dubh – Gleann Gaoithe – Cailness – Inversnaid – Glen Arklet – back to start

Ben Lomond

If you have a yearning for that big mountain feel, turn your wheels to Ben Lomond. Sections are rideable on the way up, but generally it is too steep. It is the immense views from the top of this Munro, and the technical, steep and rocky descent that are reward for all that toil though, and you will certainly have a ride to remember.

Grade: **Black** » Distance: **12km** » Ascent: **974m** » Time: **3hrs+**
Start/Finish: **Rowardennan, NS 359986** » OS Map: **Landranger 56 Loch Lomond & Inveraray**

The Route » Pick up the waymarked path from behind the information centre – climb to the summit – descend!

Photo: Andy McCandlish.

More information

Getting About

Unfortunately there are no train services to Aberfoyle or any of the trails we mention here, so you will need a car to get around the area properly. Aberfoyle can be found 20 miles north of Glasgow on the A81, and is actually signposted off the M8 in the city centre.

Main Towns

Aberfoyle is at the heart of a number of the trails, and at the centre of some excellent singletrack if you take the trouble to hunt it out. The hillside behind the town is literally covered with superb technical trails. It is a small town but has two pubs, a Co-op and numerous B&B and self-catering options.

Maps

Landranger 57 Stirling & The Trossachs
Landranger 56 Loch Lomond & Inveraray
Explorer 365 The Trossachs
Explorer 364 Loch Lomond North

Bike Shops

Wheels Cycling Centre (01877 331 100, www.scottish-cycling.com) have a stock of parts and accessories near Callander, and Big Al is always great for a superb wheel build or exotic bike part down at Wheelcraft at Clachan of Campsie (01360 312 709).

Bike Hire

Wheels Cycling Centre (01877 331 100) hire mountain bikes near Callander and have free parking and changing facilities, and Go Country out at Loch Ard, four miles west of Aberfoyle, also hire (01877 387 750).

Photo: Andy McCandlish.

Accommodation

With the Trossachs being a holiday hotspot, accommodation is plentiful and varied. Some options worth considering are the hostel over near Callander (on the cycleway along Loch Venachar) called the Trossachs Tryst Hostel (01877 331 200, www.scottish-hostel.com). It is tied in with, and at the same location as, the Wheels Cycling Centre who hire, sell and repair bikes. Alternatively go for the Oak Tree Inn at Balmaha (01360 870 357, www.oak-tree-inn.co.uk) for quality B&B right on the doorstep of a great pub. There is a 5 star campsite just outside Aberfoyle too, for 'glamping,' (01877 382 614, www.trossachsholidays.co.uk) and numerous sites up the coast of Loch Lomond north of Balmaha.

Food & Drink

Around Aberfoyle Liz Macgregor's cafe and restaurant (01877 389 376) is a well-known haunt after a ride, with the Forth Inn (01877 382 372) across the road being a good pub option for real ale and some good food. Otherwise the Co-op in Aberfoyle has a good bakery section for post ride blowouts. If you want to get out of the hustle of Aberfoyle, head three miles south to Gartmore for the Black Bull (01877 382 225) also owned by Liz, so the food is spot on. Round at Loch Lomond you can't beat the Oak Tree Inn in Balmaha (01360 870 357) for great pub food tied in with B&B accommodation right on the shore side trails. Callander has Mhor Bread (01877 339 518) a superb bakery, and numerous other restaurants and pubs, including the superb chippy Mhor Fish (01877 330 213).

Tourist Offices

Aberfoyle Trossachs Discovery Centre, 0870 720 0604

Callander Tourist Information Centre, 01877 330 342

National Park Gateway Centre, 01389 751 035

Outdoor Shops

The nearest outdoor shops are in Callander or Glasgow. Glasgow has the Tiso Glasgow Outdoor Experience (Tiso and Alpine Bikes under one roof – 0141 559 5450) among many others, and Callander has Caledonian Countrywear (01877 332 612) which has a lot of outdoor clothing and a limited selection of hardware.

Useful Websites

www.visitscottishheartlands.com – good for all round tourist information

www.lochlomond-trossachs.org – good for National Park information

www.trossachs.co.uk – good for local businesses, accommodation and other attractions

Guidebooks

Scotland Mountain Biking – The Wild Trails, and Wild Trails Vol.2, both written by Phil McKane, published by Vertebrate Publishing

Bike Scotland Trails Guide, 40 of the Best Mountain Bike Routes in Scotland, written by Richard Moore and Andy McCandlish, published by Pocket Mountains

Mountainbike Scotland, written by Kenny Wilson, published by Ernest Press

Pitlochry & Dunkeld

The Pitlochry and Dunkeld area, being on the main A9 corridor heading north, is an area often driven through and ignored. Riders heading for Aviemore, the Cairngorms and the north-west coast might admire the beautiful colours in autumn as they pass through, but not realise there is a mine of trails and wild countryside just perfect for mountain biking.

Dig deeper, leave the car parks behind and you will find the tree lined River Tummel, acres of woodland and open hillsides just begging to be explored. Of course that is in addition to the lochs, castles and picturesque villages.

The Riding

The Pitlochry and Dunkeld area is one of those locations where you can seek out just about any type of riding you want. From the downhill course in Dunkeld to the easy riverside singletrack up the Tummel, you can make life as easy or as epic as you like. Stick to the rivers and glens for easy family riding, or cast off the tree cover and head for the hills where you can go as far or as high as you like on lesser travelled grass trails or the more worn paths up to and around the local peaks.

When to go

As with many of the more easterly locations in Scotland, the Pitlochry area seems to suffer less from the weather than its more westerly equivalents. The glens are more sheltered, the rain doesn't make it this far east *quite* as much, and the winters tend to be colder rather than wetter. However, the Pitlochry area is simply stunning in the autumn when the large variety of trees turn to golden browns and reds, so it would have to be the top time to visit – the trails are quieter too!

Photo: Andy McCandlish.

44 Loch Bhac

This route climbs away from Garry Bridge, a few miles outside Pitlochry, initially on road, then on stony farm track and then forestry fire road once it hits the hilltop. At Loch Bhac, the trail turns to superb heather lined singletrack over the open moorland, splashing through the odd stream bed as it descends gently back towards Blair Atholl and the A9. From the bottom the trail turns to road as it follows the Sustrans Cycle Route 7 all the way to Killiecrankie where, at the visitor centre for the Pass of Killiecrankie, you can descend to the riverside and take this superbly scenic trail back to Garry Bridge.

Grade: **Red** » Distance: **35km** » Ascent: **630m** » Time: **3hrs+**	
Start/Finish: **Car Park at Garry Bridge** » Start GR: **NN 913610** » SatNav: **FK8 3UQ**	
OS Map: **Landranger 43 Braemar and Blair Atholl; Explorer 383 Pitlochry & Loch Tummel**	
Parking: **Large tourist car park at Garry Bridge** » Cafe: **Cafe Biba, Pitlochry, T: 01796 473 294**	
Pub: **The Moulin Hotel in Moulin, just northeast of Pitlochry centre, T: 01796 472 196**	

Directions

S Start from car park by the Garry Bridge, turning west on the B8019 for 3.5km. At a tight bend in the road, turn **R** up a minor road heading up Glen Fincastle.

Follow the Glen Fincastle road for 1.5km to where it forks – fork **L** to Edintian and follow this farm track as it climbs up. Just before the farmhouse there is a track heading off on your **L**, take this and follow it up and into the forest through a gate.

This forest track climbs steeply up before meeting the main forest track, where you turn **R**. Follow this for just over 3km to a junction where you turn **R**, following the fishing club and footpath signs. This takes you to the shores of Loch Bhac.

2 After soaking up the view, turn back up the track for 30m or so, looking for a post on your right which marks the start of the singletrack. Take this **R** through forest singletrack.

Climb over a stile on the edge of the forest, cross a burn and begin the 4km of excellent singletrack over the heather covered moor. Tremendous views ahead to Blair Atholl and the hills over the A9 glen.

At the bottom, join a farm track and turn **L**, continuing down the hill to cross the A9. Take care crossing this fast and furious main road and go through the gate on the far side onto a section of old road. Follow this along the riverside.

3 After passing under the A9 follow the minor road through Old Struan, Struan and Calvine. In Calvine stay **R** to head back east on the B8079 and begin this stretch of road that is the Sustrans Cycle Route 7.

Follow this for about 13km through Blair Atholl to Killiecrankie where, after a steep climb up through the village, you reach the Pass of Killiecrankie visitor centre. Turn into the visitor centre car park and stay hard **R**, where at the far end the trail takes you down to the riverside. Keep it dead slow here as there are always lots of pedestrians.

At the riverside stay **L**, heading south-east back towards Pitlochry. Enjoy this most scenic of riverside trails. After 1.5km on the riverside you will come to a small pedestrian footbridge on your **R**. Cross this and follow the path to the **L**. Shortly after crossing take the **R** fork path which climbs up to the Garry Bridge where you started.

Not Long Enough? Why not start the ride from Pitlochry itself, using the riverside trails that follow the River Tummel up past Loch Faskally and up to Garry Bridge. If you are really keen to add on 20 miles plus, you could also take a detour up Glen Tilt from Blair Atholl, and check out the Falls of Tarf before turning back down the glen for home.

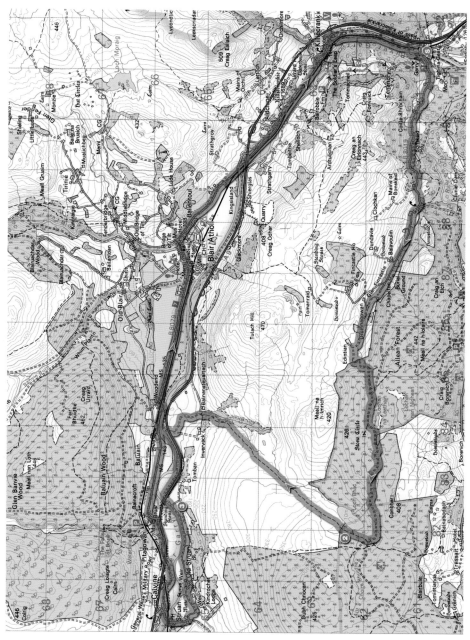

45 *Bankfoot to Dunkeld*

This lengthy ride is worth every step of the way, taking you through remote singletrack in wild glens, high fire roads and through some of the most historic spots of the area, including Macbeth's Birnam Wood, the Hermitage and Dunkeld. Be ready to be self-sufficient in the more open stretches of the ride as the only food stops are in the main towns, and dress for the weather if it is cold as you will be passing through some exposed areas. Other than that just be prepared to take a bit longer than the miles suggest as there is plenty to look at on the way!

Grade: **Red** » Distance: **46km** » Ascent: **839m** » Time: **4hrs+**
Start/Finish: **Bankfoot Main Street** » Start GR: **NO 068352** » SatNav: **PH1 4AB**
OS Map: **Landranger 52 Pitlochry & Crieff** » Parking: **Parking on street**
Cafe: **Palmerston's cafe in Dunkeld, T: 01350 727 231** » Pub: **Bankfoot Inn in Bankfoot, T: 01738 787 243,**
or The Taybank in Dunkeld, T: 01350 727 340

Directions

S From Bankfoot Main Street turn on to Prieston Road and follow the asphalt road for 5km to Upper Obney Farm. Pass through the **LH** side of the farm between the Steel building and brick/stone shed.

Take the farm track until reaching two gates. Cross the stile and head north through two fields. Bear **L** at the top of the second field to a gate, leading to the path through Glen Garr. Continue through Glen Garr on to the open moor. Continue on the rough Landover track for about 2km until it bends right towards the east. Look out for the narrow path to the **L** where the Landover track begins to bend right. Take this narrow path and follow the track across a small burn and three gates to meet the well made Balhomish Farm road. Turn **R** and descend towards the farm.

2 Just prior to the farm turn **L** and take the track through two fields towards Ladywell Forest. Follow the road round to the **R** and descend for 2km on the rough track which eventually emerges in Birnam. Turn **R** then immediately **L** on to the dirt track which runs behind the Birnam Hotel. Follow this road to the barrier across the road, turn **L** on to the path and descend the steps onto the riverside path. Turn **L** and follow the singletrack north for 2km until emerging at a T-junction beside the A9. Turn **R** and pass under the road bridge then turn **R** across the wooden footbridge. Turn **R** once more to regain the riverside path.

Follow the path north for some 4km until it passes first underneath the large road bridge (Jubilee Bridge) then the railway. The path ends at a minor road. Cross straight over this to the Forest Enterprise car park beyond.

Enter the forest. 50m further on turn sharp **L** up a very steep path. Follow the path through the trees to a forest fire road. Turn **R** then first **L**. Follow this forest fire road to a T-junction.

Ahead of you lies the path which takes you to the worthwhile diversion of the Hermitage. To continue on the trail however turn **R** and climb on the fire road for about 1km. Look for a little cottage situated on the left. Take the path which passes in front of this house. Follow the path through open land to a minor public road. Go straight ahead up the hill on reaching the public road and follow it all the way to its junction with the A822 at Trochry.

3 On reaching the A822 turn **R** and climb for 8km to the signpost for the right of way to Little Glen Shee at Little Findowie. Turn **L** and begin the demanding climb. Ignore the side tracks to the left and right and remain on the main track. Continue through Little Glen Shee for 6.5km to little Glenshee Farm. Join the public road and follow it south to a T-junction. Turn **L** and follow the signs back to your starting point at Bankfoot.

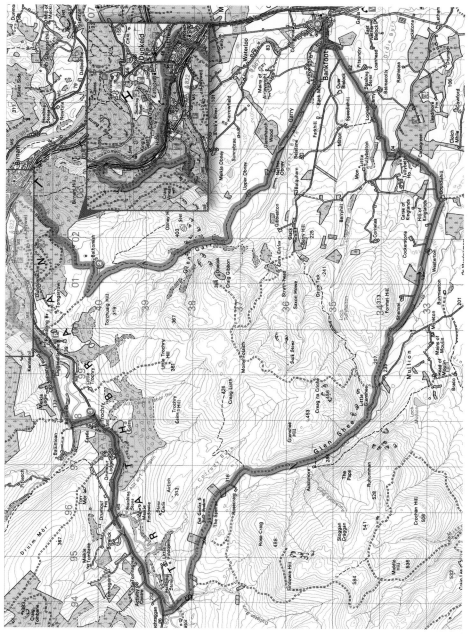

More information

Getting About

Pitlochry has to be one of the most accessible places in Scotland. It is bang on the fast A9 north so travel by car is a breeze, but it also has a train station right in the middle of town. Trains depart from Glasgow Queen Street and Edinburgh Waverley and in both cases the travel time is around 1½ hours. Most of the riding is within striking distance of Pitlochry, so the train is a viable option.

Main Towns

Pitlochry is a real tourist destination, so it gets pretty busy in the summer months. On the upside, this means it can support all sorts of interesting shops, accommodation and restaurants which line the main street, so it is a great place to base yourself from. It even has its own Pitlochry Festival Theatre just across the river for theatre, music and cinema. Dunkeld is around ten miles south, a little quieter on the tourist front but has some cracking pubs, a few interesting shops and trails just out of the back door. Both towns are very picturesque and lovely places with enough interest to keep the family busy if you are visiting en masse.

Maps

Landranger 43 Braemar and Blair Atholl
Landranger 52 Pitlochry & Crieff
Explorer 386 Pitlochry & Loch Tummel

Bike Shops

You have to visit Escape Route in Pitlochry (01796 473 859, www.escape-route.co.uk) at least once. Kevin and the staff are encyclopaedias of local knowledge when it comes to the trail network so while this guide will help with a few routes, he is your man to speak to if you want to dig deeper still. Apart from the knowledge, the shop is well stocked with parts, has an excellent workshop and serves great coffee.

Bike Hire

Escape Route, Pitlochry, 01796 473 859 – hires an excellent range of mountain bikes

Accommodation

Pitlochry is thick with accommodation, being a top tourist destination, but here are some bike friendly samples suggested by the local lads to get you started:

Atholl Villa Guest House (01796 473 820, www.athollvilla.co.uk), Almond Lee – two self catering cottages and B&B (01796 474 048, www.almondlee.com). The 300-year-old Moulin Hotel (01796 472 196, www.moulinhotel.co.uk) just above Pitlochry is an excellent choice too and even has its own microbrewery for you to sample before turning in for the night.

SYHA have a hostel in the town (01796 472 308) and there is an independent Pitlochry Backpackers Hotel (01796 470 044, www.pitlochrybackpackershotel.com) right on the main street.

Down in Bankfoot, the start of one of our rides, Blair House Guest House (01738 787 912) is also the home of a local mountain bike expert who can show you more in the area while you stay.

Food & Drink

With its roaring fires, cosy booths and great atmosphere, the Moulin Hotel in Pitlochry (01796 472 196, www.moulinhotel.co.uk) has to be one of our favourites in the country, so make sure you pay a visit – or even better – stay there on your trip. In Pitlochry, Cafe Biba on the main street (01796 473 294) is good for coffee, lunch or an evening meal, and Victoria's has long been a favourite if passing through (01796 472 670). In Dunkeld you have to pop into the Country Bakery for a Scottish breakfast (01350 727 343, www.countrybakerydunkeld.co.uk), and the best pub food we have come across are the stovies in the The Taybank (01350 727 340), formerly owned by folk legend Dougie MacLean.

Tourist Offices

Pitlochry Visitor Information Centre, 01796 472 215
Dunkeld Tourist Information Centre, 01350 727 688

Outdoor Shops

On the outskirts of Perth heading north there is a new Tiso Outdoor Experience (01738 634 464) which not only has a large selection of outdoor kit under one large warehouse roof, but also a branch of Alpine Bikes and the Fit Food Cafe. Escape Route in Pitlochry (01796 473 859) also does a good selection of outdoor kit.

Useful Websites

www.explore-highland-perthshire.com – good for all round tourist information
www.pitlochry.org – good for local information
www.perthshire.co.uk – good for tourist information

Guidebooks

Scotland Mountain Biking – The Wild Trails, and *Wild Trails Vol.2*, both written by Phil McKane, published by Vertebrate Publishing
Bike Scotland Trails Guide, 40 of the Best Mountain Bike Routes in Scotland, written by Richard Moore and Andy McCandlish, published by Pocket Mountains
Mountainbike Scotland, written by Kenny Wilson, published by Ernest Press
TrailMaps (trailmaps.biz) also do an excellent *Highland Perthshire Map Pack* of the area with some route suggestions

Photo: Andy McCandlish.

Ballater & Royal Deeside

Perhaps best known for its royal connections, Ballater lies around eight miles east of Balmoral Castle in some of the most picturesque countryside the UK has to offer. Everywhere you look in the village there are royal crests over the shop windows – butcher by appointment to HRH, Countrywear Supplier approved by the Prince of Wales, all that kind of thing.

The railway line runs from Aberdeen through the glens and terminates at Ballater, but that wasn't always intended to be the case. You can still ride on the track bed extending west from the town towards Balmoral, but the track was never constructed as Queen Victoria vetoed it, deciding it would impinge on her privacy at the castle.

The royals aren't the only ones that are drawn to this beautiful area, but it never feels too crowded no matter what time of year you choose to come. There are enough mountains, trails and forest for everyone to be swallowed up and disappear during the day, only to spark up the bars and restaurants in the evening for a pleasant bustle.

If you like high and rolling hills, ancient Scots pine forests, spectacular tumbling rivers and dry and sandy trails you have come to the right place.

The Riding

There is a bit of everything in Ballater. High mountain tracks take you right into the middle of nowhere if you choose, cresting the tops of the hills on estate routes more used to Land Rovers packed with shooting parties. Or you can stay low, buzzing through forest singletrack nearer town. If anything the trails are more flowing than technical, but everyone can appreciate them no matter what their regular riding type.

When to go

Winter can be a cold and snow blasted time of year up here, but then it can also be a magical frozen place as the east coast of Scotland is usually drier but colder than the west. Spring through to autumn is best if you want to go high of course. If you are there in stalking season (1st July to 20th October) be sensitive to the estate's stalking, using the Hillphones service to check where they are going to be shooting (www.snh.org.uk/hillphones).

Photo: Andy McCandlish.

46 Ballater to Glen Tanar

A great all-round route that takes you high into the surrounding hills on estate tracks before descending on cracking singletrack into remote Glen Tanar. You will need to brush up your navigation skills, particularly if the visibility isn't ideal, since a short section of trackless hillside in the middle needs some close attention. It is more than worth it though, soon developing into some of the best narrow singletrack in the area as it descends into Glen Tanar. The climb back out of the glen then takes you high above the Dee for a picturesque return to Ballater

Grade: **Red** » Distance: **29km** » Ascent: **798m** » Time: **3hrs+**
Start/Finish: **Cyclehighlands in Ballater town centre** » Start GR: **NO 370957** » SatNav: **AB35 5RA**
OS Map: **Landranger 44 Ballater & Glen Clova** » Parking: **Parking all round the centre of Ballater**
Cafe: **Bean for Coffee, Ballater, T: 01339 755 514** » Pub: **The Balmoral Bar, T: 01339 755 462**

Directions

S Starting at Cyclehighlands in Ballater town centre, pop out the front gate of the shop and turn **R**, **L**, then **R** again. This takes you out onto the main street, passing the shops and on over the old bridge. After the bridge turn **R** and follow the B976 for just over 1km.

Just as the main road swings right over the bridge, turn **L** up the estate road, beginning the climb up past Balintober. The track continues to climb for some time – keep **L** at the first fork and **R** at the second. Keep climbing until the summit is reached.

2 At the summit split **L**, following the signpost for Mount Keen. This descends a little before there is another signpost for Mount Keen pointing off into indistinct singletrack. Follow this as it pops over drainage ditches and climbs back up over a ridge to get to a gate with a big iron cross next to it. Go through the gate and start descending. Follow the trail as it descends to a burn, which you cross further down. Keep an eye on the right bank as it is easy to miss this crossing point. Continue down as the path gets more distinct and drops down to the valley floor.

When you get to the track turn **L** and follow it down the glen for around 4km, before turning sharp **L** back on yourself to climb another estate track onto the hillside.

3 This climbs relentlessly for 3km before beginning to descend to the north. As you descend and the track levels out slightly, you are looking to pick up a pass through a gate, and not long after are looking for the trail leaving on your **L**. Follow this through a boggy area before descending past shooting butts on your right. The trail drops down the side of Creag Mullach, splashing through the Pollagach Burn before turning into proper track and taking a sharp **R** into the trees for the final descent to the farm track.

Turn **L** and descend to the B976 where you take a **L** and ride on the road for just short of 1km. Take the track on your **R** here, forking off and passing through a gate. Stay **R** at the next junction and follow this track down to the Cambus O' May footbridge.

Here you can cross over and follow the railway line **L** back into Ballater, or if you have the energy, turn **L** just before the bridge and follow the singletrack down the south bank of the river back into town.

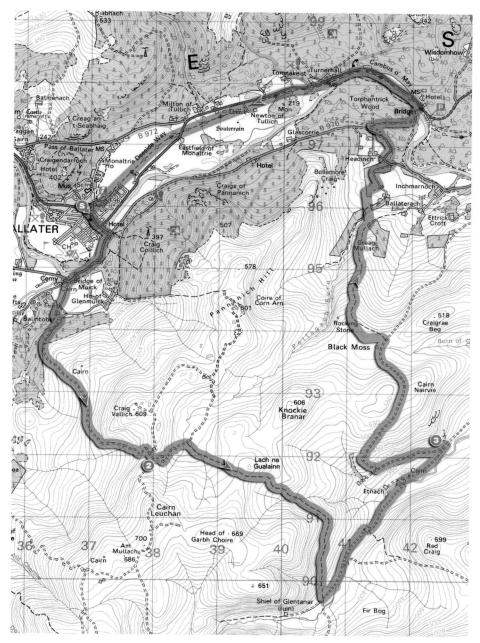

47 Morven Loop

A terrific route with a bit of everything thrown into the mix, from exposed hill tracks to nadgery forest singletrack winding through the Caledonian pines and local lochs. The Morven loop really does showcase the best of the area, and the return via Loch Kinord and the Burn O'Vat gives a great sample of this terrific area of singletrack, beloved of the local riders.

Grade: **Red** » Distance: **40km** » Ascent: **776m** » Time: **3hrs+**

Start/Finish: **Cyclehighlands in Ballater town centre** » Start GR: **NO 370957** » SatNav: **AB35 5RA**

OS Map: **Landranger 44 Ballater & Glen Clova; Landranger 37 Strathdon & Alford**

Parking: **Parking all round the centre of Ballater** » Cafe: **Bean for Coffee, Ballater, T: 01339 755 514**

Pub: **The Balmoral Bar, T: 01339 755 462**

Directions

S From Cyclehighlands, come out the front gate, turn **R**, then **R** again. Take the second **L**, just at the entrance to the golf course. Follow this road to where it swings left slightly, and you will see a footpath going straight ahead on the **R** side of the road – take this. It skirts round the riverside, past the golf course and up through a picnic area.

Follow the old railway line here for around 1km past the picnic area, keeping an eye out on your **R** for a narrow singletrack climbing the banking sharply back on yourself.

Climb this to the road and turn **L** for 200m, then take the singletrack road on your **R**. Follow this up Glen Gairn to Lary Farm, where the road turns to track and swings right up into the hills.

Go through the gate here and begin climbing. Around 1km short of Morven Lodge take the track on your **R**, splashing through the river before climbing steadily up the hill on the rocky surface. Stay on this track for 6km where you arrive at a wide open junction of several tracks.

2 Turn **R** here, up the hill again for a short time before beginning to descend to the east. Pass by the small wooden huts with the doves in and be careful on the loose surface. Drop down from here through a gate and onto the road. Turn **R**, then join the B9119. Turn right for 500m and look for a grassy trail forking off **L**.

Take this trail into the woodland. After 700m you will come to a trail cutting sharply back on yourself – take this. Beautiful woodland trail takes you to the Burn O'Vat visitor centre, so just follow the signs.

At the visitor centre you can either choose to continue the route, cutting out Loch Kinord, or ride the excellent singletrack round the loch.*

To ride the loch cross back over the road from the visitor centre onto the trail, and turn **R**. This takes you down through the trees and begins the circuit of the loch. The trail is sometimes on grassy singletrack, other times on old estate tracks, but is always excellent. Keep to the lochside where any options arise until the trail takes you to the small loch at Clarack. Here there is a little observation platform. The trail is a faint singletrack leading directly away from it, through the woods. It gets a little indistinct but eventually leads you to another track. Turn **L** here up to New Kinord Farm.

Go through the gate here and turn **L**, keeping an eye out on your **L** for a grass trail dropping steeply down to the loch. Follow this down and along through the silver birches before popping up and rejoining the track to Old Kinord. Turn **L** here – this is the junction you have been to before – and retrace your steps back to the visitor centre.

***Optional Route:** To cut out the Loch, jump to **point 3**.

3 At the visitor centre look for the obvious path heading steeply up the hill to the **R** of the buildings. Follow this all the way up until it meets another track. Turn **R** onto another trail. Follow this all the way through to meet the track climbing up to the quarry.

Turn **R** here and climb for 100m before taking the singletrack to your **L**, up a short climb and over a small burn. The trail then gets more defined and drops downhill past a small loch and into the back of Tullich Farm.

Go through the gate and onto the road, turning **R** for 500m then forking **R** onto the B972. Ride for just over 1km, taking the first small road on your **L**. Follow it down to where it swings right, then ends at a singletrack signposted *Ballater*. Take this along the side of the football fields then take the ramp to the **R**. Cross straight over the road through the path and onto the railway line. Turn **R** and you are back into town.

Not long enough? Ballater is at the heart of an amazing part of Scotland, with the southern Cairngorms a few miles down the road through Braemar for big adventures and short blasts alike. The glen that leads to Aberdeen from the town is also littered with locations and classic rides like the Fungle Road climbing out of Aboyne or, a munro baggers dream, Mount Keen just over the hill. You could stay for a fortnight and never ride the same trail twice.

Photo: Andy McCandlish.

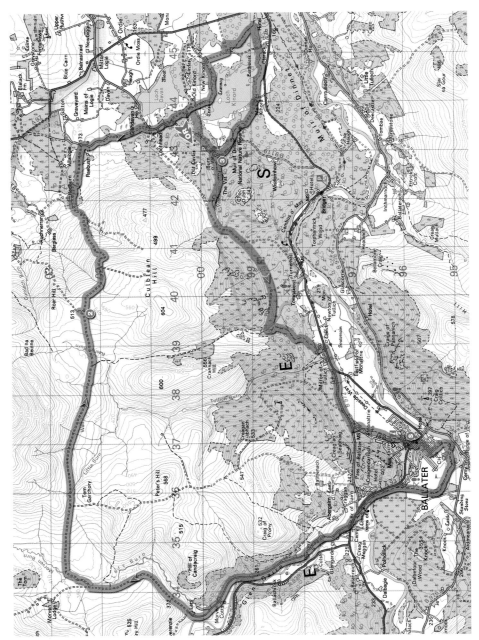

More riding

Deeside Railway Tour

This easy ride takes you on a short tour of the glen around Ballater, making good use of the excellent Deeside Way disused railway line, before returning with more of a challenging pedal through singletrack and forest trails. Perfect for an easy or family day out, it skirts the scenic River Dee for most of its length, where you can watch for leaping salmon and fishermen as you pedal the flat and even trail.

Grade: **Blue** » Distance: **13km** » Ascent: **151m** » Time: **1hr+**
Start/Finish: **Ballater, NO 370957** » Map: **Landranger 44 Ballater & Glen Clova**

The Route » Ballater – Cambus O'May Footbridge – Torphantrick Wood – Glascorrie – Ballater

Photo: Andy McCandlish.

More information

Getting About

Unfortunately there are no train services to Ballater, so you will need to access the town by car. The best approach from the south is through Glen Shee from Perth and Blairgowrie on the A93.

Main Towns

Ballater is the kind of Scottish town you can easily spend a week in and never get bored. Great shops, restaurants and picturesque surroundings all keep you busy when off the bike, and there is a dizzying selection of accommodation to choose from. Pop into the 'By Royal Appointment' butcher for some of the best meat in the land, or just chill out on one of the sunny outdoor tables at Bean for Coffee to watch the world drive by in its stalking hat and muddy 4x4.

Maps

Landranger 44 Ballater & Glen Clova
Landranger 37 Strathdon & Alford

Bike Shops

Cyclehighlands in Ballater (01339 755 864, www.cyclehighlands.com) is an excellent shop run by local enthusiasts and has a good stock of parts and accessories to keep you on two wheels. Take them in some lattes and they will love you for it.

Bike Hire

Cyclehighlands in Ballater (01339 755 864) also have an excellent hire fleet, including full suspension bikes. Braemar Mountain Sports (01339 741 242, www.braemarmountainsports.com) – sharing the same enthusiastic and knowledgeable owners – also offer bike hire.

Accommodation

As a popular tourist town, Ballater has a great selection of accommodation. Highlights would have to be the superb Habitat bunkhouse (01339 753 752, www.habitat-at-ballater.com) where an outdoor friendly approach is backed up by luxurious surroundings, and the Auld Kirk restaurant with rooms, where you can get some of the best food in the area (01339 755 762, www.theauldkirk.co.uk). The SYHA also have a hostel in Braemar just along the road (01339 741 659, www.syha.org.uk). There are numerous other hotels and B&Bs in the area.

Food & Drink

You are spoilt for choice in Ballater for good food options. We enjoy the cafe food in Bean for Coffee (01339 755 514) where you can get everything from a top class latte to some great cakes and lunch options. Otherwise the Brown Sugar Cafe is just down the main road (01339 755 388, www.brownsugarcafe.co.uk). For dinner you would struggle to beat the excellent Italian La Mangiatoia (01339 755 999) or the Auld Kirk (01339 755 762), both in Ballater itself.

Tourist Offices

Ballater Tourist Information Centre, 01339 755 306 » **Braemar Visitor Information Centre**, 01339 741 600

Outdoor Shops

Braemar Mountain Sports (01339 741 242, www.braemarmountainsports.com) is right in the heart of the village and is a mine of great kit and information. They also have a shop in Ballater, called The Outdoor Store (01339 753 878).

Useful Websites

www.aberdeen-grampian.com – good for all round tourist information
www.braemarscotland.co.uk – good for local information
www.visitballater.com – good for local information

Guidebooks

Scotland Mountain Biking – The Wild Trails, and *Wild Trails Vol.2*, both written by Phil McKane, published by Vertebrate Publishing
Bike Scotland Trails Guide, 40 of the Best Mountain Bike Routes in Scotland, written by Richard Moore and Andy McCandlish, published by Pocket Mountains
Mountainbike Scotland, written by Kenny Wilson, published by Ernest Press

Photo: Andy McCandlish.

Fort William

With the country's highest mountains dominating the skyline and some truly world class mountain biking on its doorstep, Fort William is certainly worth the journey north.

Nestling at the foot of the UK's highest mountain, it has existed in one form or another for centuries. The Fort itself was founded by Cromwell's army in 1654, who sailed into the Loch Linnhe with the express purpose of controlling the Highland clans. They thought it would only take a few years ...

In 1690 (yes, still there ...) the Fort was renamed Fort William after the king and in 1692 it played a part in the gruesome Glencoe massacre. Signs of history cover the landscape, and on the rides you will pass by ancient forts in the hills, overlook the spectacular Caledonian Canal and climb opposite the old pony track up the Ben, built in 1883 to service a summit observatory and hotel, now commonly known as the tourist route for hill walkers.

The Riding

It is easy to write off the riding in the area as purely epic grade, but especially with the arrival of the Nevis Range Witch's Trails – home of the legendary *10 Under the Ben* race – there are more 'wet weather' options in the sheltered forest for all levels of rider. Otherwise it is possible to seek out anything from an easy summer's evening potter along the banks of the Caledonian Canal, right through to a high mountain day out over hill walking routes and stalking paths – the choice is all there.

If you feel like leaving out the climbing there is also the new Nevis Red XC route – a 15-minute ride up the gondola leaves you standing at the top of 5.5 kilometres of tasty red grade downhill with 543 metres of vertical descent to come. A true 'must ride' if you visit the area.

When to go

The best time is undoubtedly in the spring, between April and June. At this time there is often a prolonged dry spell, it is pre-midge season and the tourists haven't arrived en masse yet.

North Face path, Ben Nevis. **Photo**: Andy McCandlish.

48 The West Highland Way

Taking in the excellent West Highland Way trail, this tour of the Fort William area takes a long fire road climb out of town along the picturesque Glen Nevis, warming legs up before the singletrack kicks in. Great riding is interspersed with the odd shouldering session up steep steps as you leave the Glen before descending on rough track and turning back towards town. The jink up Cow Hill is an excellent ride on its own, taking you to some breathtaking views right above the town before descending on the fast and furious (although careful, it is a shared trail with walkers!) Cow Hill trail that bobs and weaves round the hillside and eventually back into the Glen.

Grade: **Red** » Distance: **20km** » Ascent: **724m** » Time: **2hrs+**
Start/Finish: **Braveheart Car Park, Glen Nevis** » Start GR: **NN 121736** » SatNav: **PH33 6ST (general area)**
OS Map: **Landranger 41, Ben Nevis, Fort William and Glen Coe** » Parking: **Braveheart car park, Glen Nevis**
Cafe: **Cafe Beag, Glen Nevis, T: 01397 703 601** » Pub: **The Ben Nevis Inn, Glen Nevis, T: 01397 701 227**

Directions

S Starting in the well signposted Braveheart car park on the Glen Nevis road, leave the car park and turn **R** up the fire road and through the gate. Follow the track as it undulates and climbs steadily.

At the track fork, go **R** following the West Highland Way thistle marker posts. This track begins to climb more steeply before switchbacking further up as it reaches the head of the glen. Here there are new forest tracks not shown on the maps yet, but just follow the main track up and over the rise.

Glen Nevis. **Photo:** Andy McCandlish.

Just after you begin descending keep an eye out on your **L** for the singletrack heading off into the woods – again it is marked with a WHW thistle post. Follow this excellent singletrack through the trees; there are no other trails to go wrong on.

2 Pass through the gate and leave the forest, sticking to the WHW singletrack as it goes up the side of a small hill then down to another gate. Pass through this and begin the descent down to the road.

At the covered WHW information board turn **R** down onto the single track road (actually marked as an alternative WHW route into Fort William). Follow this road right to the outskirts of Fort William.

Just as you are reaching the first houses, and have passed down through some tight bends in the road, take the track on your **R**, climbing steadily back up onto Cow Hill.

3 At the high point of the stony track there is a cow's head on a sign marked to Glen Nevis. Take this **R** and descend initially on wide trail.

A sign on your left reads 'Multi-User trail' but isn't marked on any maps. Take this trail and descend an excellent flowing path all the way down towards Fort William.

At the first opportunity take the **R** turn and the trail turns back on itself to return you to the Braveheart car park.

Not long enough? Add as much distance as you like on the West Highland Way towards Kinlochleven. There are even options there for a much longer day out, returning via Loch Eilde Mor and the Lairig Leacach.

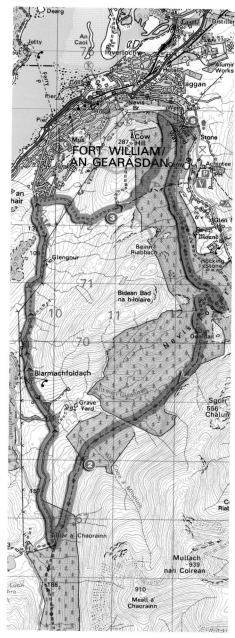

More riding

The North Face of Nevis Ride

For a real big mountain feel you really can't beat heading up Ben Nevis. This route follows the same trail that the winter climbers tread as they carry their gear up into exceptional winter routes on the north face of the mountain. A fire road climb soon reverts to technical singletrack as you follow the Allt a' Mhuilinn almost to its source. Rocks, stone culverts and steep gradients all challenge your power on the way up, and your nerve on the way back down. Sit and have a sandwich outside the CIC hut if you decide to go all the way. Link it up with a Gondola ride, the Nevis Red XC and forest singletrack for a great day out.

Grade: **Red/Black** » Distance: **14km** » Ascent: **619m** » Time: **2–4hrs**

Start/Finish: **The North Face car park, NN 145764** » OS Map: **Landranger 41 Ben Nevis, Fort William and Glen Coe**

The Route » North Face car park – climb on North Face path then **L** on 'Puggie Line' singletrack – sharp **R** on singletrack after 450m – turn **L** – turn **R** at T-junction – turn **L** on North Face mountaineers path towards Ben Nevis – CIC Hut (private, locked) – descend 3km back to track – take next **L** south-west – turn **R** down steep hillside – turn **R** at junction by pylons back on Puggie Line – after 1.5km turn **L** to car park

Glen Nevis

If the weather is wild – and it often is in the Fort William area – why not stay low and take in some of the spectacular scenery of Glen Nevis? Climb up the West Highland Way fire road up one side of the glen, descend on enjoyable singletrack through the forest and cross the river to hit the waterside singletrack all the way back to the car park.

Grade: **Blue** » Distance: **13km** » Ascent: **320m** » Time: **1–2hrs**

Start/Finish: **Braveheart car park, Glen Nevis, NN121736** » OS Map: **Landranger 41 Ben Nevis, Fort William and Glen Coe**

The Route » Braveheart car park – West Highland Way – Achriabhach – River Nevis – Ben Nevis car park – Braveheart car park

Heading for the Ben. **Photo**: Andy McCandlish.

The Trail Centres

Nevis Range & Witch's Trails

Home to World Championship and World Cup cross country and downhill trails, there's something for pretty much all riders at Nevis Range. The blue loop gives pleasant XC cruising – never too hard; the *10 Under the Ben* is a great XC loop with plenty of flowy singletrack (great black options, such as 'Nessie'); and the *World Champs* course has more great singletrack, with plenty of tricky riding. Or take the Gondola and descend one of the two trails from the top; the Red XC would probably be black anywhere in England or Wales, but it's all rollable with stunning boardwalk and granite slab sections before the final berms; or bring a big bike, a full facer and ride what is probably the best DH course on the world circuit ... and then stand in awe (with pumped arms) of the top guys who ride it in under five minutes ... !

Trail Count: **Broomstick Blue, 6km, Blue** » **10 Under The Ben, 10km, Red** » **World Champs XC, 8.5km, Red** » **Nevis Range XC, 5.5km, Red** » **Nevis Range World Cup DH, 2.8km, Orange**

Start: **Nevis Range, on the A82 seven miles north of Fort William, NN 170774** » SatNav: **PH33 6SQ**

More info: **www.bike.nevisrange.co.uk**

Photo: Andy McCandlish.

More information

Getting About
Fort William is well served with a good train station and excellent road access via the A82. The train station pulls you up right by the centre of town, handy for accessing Glen Nevis and the start of the riding. The A82 road comes all the way from Glasgow (around 2.5 hours), which is accessed by the motorway network – take junction 17 (signed A82 Dumbarton) from the M8 in the centre of Glasgow and stay on the A82 all the way to the Fort.

Main Towns
Fort William is the nearest town of course; not huge but it has just about everything you could want, from a plethora of outdoor shops, a supermarket, a cinema and some great pubs where you will always find a great mix of locals and outdoor sorts.

Maps
OS Landranger 41 Ben Nevis, Fort William and Glen Coe

Bike Shops
In the pedestrian precinct of Fort William is Alpine Bikes (www.alpinebikes.com, 01397 704 008) who carry a good stock of spares, bikes and clothing. They also have a branch at the Nevis Range centre (01397 705 825). Alternatively Nevis Cycles just outside the centre (www.neviscycles.co.uk) are similarly equipped.

Bike Hire
Both Alpine Bikes branches, Fort William and Nevis Range, are hire centres too, as is Nevis Cycles.

Accommodation
Fort William is absolutely packed with great value B&Bs, with some of the best value strung out along the A82 south of the town centre. If you want a touch of class the Distillery Guest House is a 4 star conversion of distillery workers cottages which is bike friendly and has a drying room for wet kit (www.stayinfortwilliam. co.uk, 01397 700 103). Alternatively, about two miles west of Fort William centre is the Ben Nevis Inn Hostel (www.ben-nevis-inn.co.uk, 01397 701 227), right by the tourist path for Ben Nevis – and a great place for food and drink too! There's also a Youth Hostel in Glen Nevis (01397 702 336).

Food & Drink
We very rarely visit Fort William without a visit to the Ben Nevis Inn (01397 701 227) for some food and real ale. It has a great atmosphere and cracking food and drink to boot. There are of course plenty of other options in and around town. The cafe in Nevisport (01397 704 790) is also a favourite for early breakfasts, lunch and coffees. There's also a cafe at Nevis Range.

Tourist Offices
Fort William, 0845 22 55 121, www.visithighlands.com

Outdoor Shops
Fort William has a number of outdoor shops, most notably Nevisport on the main street (01397 704 921) and Ellis Brigham near the train station (01397 706 220).

Useful Websites

www.visit-fortwilliam.co.uk – good for all round
www.outdoorcapital.co.uk – good for all things outdoor activity
bike.nevisrange.co.uk – info on riding at Nevis Range

Guidebooks

Scotland Mountain Biking – The Wild Trails, and *Wild Trails Vol.2*, both written by Phil McKane, published by Vertebrate Publishing
Bike Scotland Trails Guide, 40 of the Best Mountain Bike Routes in Scotland, written by Richard Moore and Andy McCandlish, published by Pocket Mountains
Mountainbike Scotland, written by Kenny Wilson, published by Ernest Press

Photo: Andy McCandlish.

Aviemore & Rothiemurchus

One of the great beauties of Scotland is the variety of terrain for mountain biking, and nowhere demonstrates this better than the Aviemore area.

Compared to the west coast you have a drier climate (although that can be hard to believe sometimes) and much sandier soils to ride on. The result is well-drained trails through large tracts of Caledonian Pine forest, something you just don't get in the more exposed and wet west.

The Riding

There are a number of riding choices in the area. First you have the old established mountain routes over wide stony tracks and trails through the glens. These cover large sections of the area, even going right into the heart of the mountains, and can be joined up to make superb long distance rides. These allow for some great extended trips in the area, particularly good for lightweight camping trips. There are also plenty of smaller singletrack trails in the forest, mostly around Aviemore and the other bigger towns, where the local riders, walkers and dog owners have beaten trail through the trees. These are terrific for stitching together into shorter but more challenging rides over smaller areas. In short, it has a bit of everything – great countryside, long routes and cracking shorter rides on woodland singletrack.

When to go

If you are staying low in Rothiemurchus and the surroundings, you can really ride at any time of year. It is sheltered, and in winter it could well be frozen – unless it is under two foot of snow! Of course spring is probably the best time to visit for all the usual reasons – no/less midges and good weather.

Photo: Andy McCandlish.

49 *Rothiemurchus Loop*

This ride can be seen as an introduction to a terrific area. While it doesn't explore many of the countless singletrack options in the area, it does take in some crackers and gives you the opportunity to get a taste for the terrain before investigating more on your own. The route is largely in the shelter of the beautiful Caledonian Pine forests of the area, so it is still an option if the weather is wild – it only crosses high exposed moorland for a short spell over Ryvoan Pass. At 52 kilometres it is a good day out, and there is a fair bit of climbing, but the riding isn't too taxing technically, so you can cover the ground pretty fast if you want to.

Keep your eyes peeled off to the sides of the trail – chances are if you see some trails going off into the undergrowth, they are heading somewhere. Particularly at Badaguish, there is the opportunity to split off the route and take in some of the best singletrack this side of Canada.

Grade: **Blue/Red** » Distance: **52km** » Ascent: **699m** » Time: **4hrs+**	
Start/Finish: **Inverdruie car park** » Start GR: **NH 901109** » SatNav: **PH22 1QH**	
OS Map: **Landranger 36 Grantown & Aviemore** » Parking: **Main car park at Inverdruie**	
Cafe: **The Glenmore Cafe in Glenmore is an essential stop, T: 01479 861 229**	
Pub: **The Lochain Bar in Glenmore Lodge is good for a drink and food, T: 01479 861 256**	

Directions

S▶ From Inverdruie take the road towards the ski area for 100m, then split **R**. After another 50m or so, keep an eye on your **L** for a gate – go through this and follow the wide singletrack to the next junction. Keep **R** here and follow this wide trail round the small loch until you reach a singletrack road. Turn **L** here then stay **R** round the car park for Loch an Eilein.

Follow the fire road round the loch, staying **L** at the T-junction, then take a **R** at Loch Gamhna. This is an optional spur off the route, but well worth it for the cracking rocky trail and wooden bothy at the end of it. Return to Loch an Eilein and this time turn **R** when you reach the lochside track. Follow this for 2km to the first track junction; turn **R**.

2 Follow this sandy fire road, staying straight on at the open junction and following cyclist signs heading for the Cairngorm Club footbridge. Cross the narrow bridge and follow the trail **R** up the riverside to 'Piccadilly,' a junction with a right turn option for the legendary Lairig Ghru. For this route stay straight on, following the wide singletrack to the junction with a wide track at Loch Morlich.

Turn **R** here, and follow the track round the loch, jumping on to singletrack at NH 970089. Follow this over the small bridge before turning hard **R** and up the riverside to the ski road. Turn **L** on the road for the Glenmore Cafe, and rejoin the route by turning up the single track road to Glenmore Lodge.

Follow the road past the lodge where it turns to sandy fire road again. This continues through the Glen (don't forget to stop for a look at the stunningly green An Lochan Uaine) before climbing steadily to Ryvoan Pass.

Follow the track **L** signed to Nethy Bridge and climb up past the bothy and on down stony fire road to Forest Lodge.

At the Lodge turn **L** and follow this wide fire road down to the single track road. **L** here, then down to Tulloch where you can turn **L** down the track just after the phone box. The road then undulates out to the B970.

3 Turn **L** on the B970 and ride for around 2km, looking on the **L** for signs to Milton Farm. Take this track up through the Caledonian Pines and over An Slugan pass. Stay straight on the track (or take the first track junction left into Badaguish for some singletrack fun) until the narrow single track road junction, where you turn **R** and descend to the ski road. Turn **R** onto the recent cycle trail back down toward Inverdruie, popping out on the road just above Coylumbridge. Skip down the road here, keeping an eye on your **L** just after the campsite for a last blast of singletrack parallel to the road, and pop back into Inverdruie.

Not long enough? There are countless options to extend this ride. Why not take a foray beyond the Inshriach bothy at the westernmost point of the ride, and head into the delights of Glen Feshie. Around the peak of Creag Dhubh (NN 823997) there are some excellent trails not marked on the map. Just get in there around the Uath Lochan and follow your nose. Otherwise join onto the Grantown route at (overleaf) Forest Lodge on the most easterly point of the trail, and descend the excellent singletrack there.

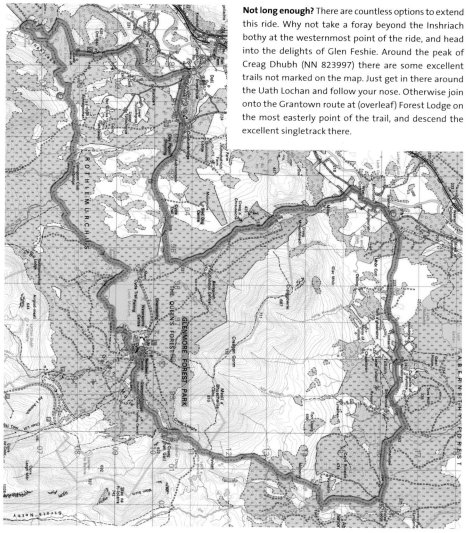

50 Grantown Loop

If you are looking to cover some of the local ground, see a bit of the scenery, but also dip into local singletrack, then this trail was designed for you. On the initial loop out of Grantown-on-Spey, you are heading into the hills behind the town. In an area known as Dreggie, the trails are short but technically great fun. Tight woodland trails, fast descents, roots and rocks are all there to test your legs, still fresh before the longer loop of the day. After dropping back into town, and maybe refuelling in the bakery, it is time to take in some of the surrounding area. Easy trails head towards Abernethy Forest on abandoned railway single track, shadowing the mighty Spey as it powers along in the opposite direction for the coast. A spin round the Abernethy Forest on wide and sandy tracks and a turn for home on cracking singletrack in the woods is finished with a pedal over wooded hills and glens back to Grantown-on-Spey for another bakery visit.

Grade: **Blue/Red** » Distance: **43km** » Ascent: **639m** » Time: **3hrs+**
Start/Finish: **Grantown-on-Spey town centre** » Start GR: **NJ 034280** » SatNav: **PH26 3HG**
OS Map: **Landranger 36 Grantown & Aviemore** » Parking: **Parking in Grantown centre**
Cafe: **Maclean's Highland Bakery on Grantown main street, T: 01479 873 827**
Pub: **Garth Hotel at north end of main square, T: 01479 872 836**

Directions

S Start at Basecamp MTB shop, turn SW on the main street, taking the first **R** turn up to the church. Turn **L** here then next **R** up past the campsite. Once you are by the old railway get onto the waymarked trail, following the

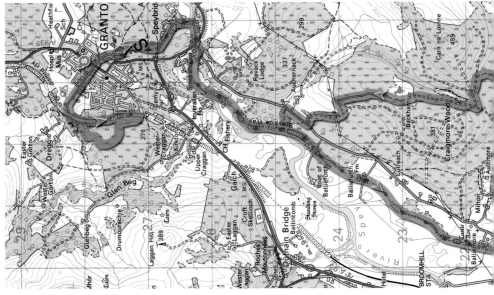

blue marker posts through the forest. Drop down to the railway again, then follow the trail back to Grantown. Instead of turning left to the church this time, go straight across the main street.

Follow this road down until it turns to track, where you can see on your **L** some forest singletrack bearing off. Take this to ride parallel to the main track. Pop back out and follow signs for the *Speyside Way* through Anagach and over the River Spey. Keep following the thistle signs as they shepherd you along the riverbank on the old railway. Keep following this to Nethy Bridge.

2 Pop up onto the single track road at Nethy Bridge and turn **L**. Climb up to the main street and turn **R**, then **L** just at the Spar shop. Keep an eye on the **L** for the riverside trail heading off after around 100m and follow that. After around 1.5km turn **R** before the narrow bridge, then **L** on the main track for 4km. At the T junction at the top turn **L** past Forest Lodge, then take the next available **R** over the bridge. Turn **R** again after 400m and climb up for around 2.5km, staying **L** at the junction. Look for the singletrack disappearing on your **L**, and follow that down.

3 Turn hard **R** at the bottom. Follow this through two river splashes and up onto some grassy track across moorland, staying **L** at the fork after the second river splash. Cross the moor to Bynackbeg, then turn **L** on the single track road and follow this for around 1.7km, taking a **R** turn past a cottage at Lettoch and up into the forest. Climb this pine needle fire road to a crossroads then turn **L** and descend to Blairgorm. Turn **R**, then sharp **L** down a track and over a bridge back into forest.

Climb steadily up Craigmore Wood, turn **L** then drop slightly and take the second **R** track down to Backharn before descending out the forest onto the B970. Turn **R** for 400m, keeping an eye out for a stile on the **L** onto singletrack. Drop down this trail – careful at the river splash it is deep! – and pop out onto the Speyside Way. Turn **R** and follow it back into town and the finish.

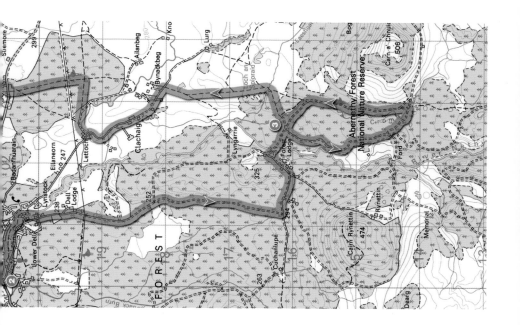

More riding

Carn Ban Mor from Glen Feshie

A real classic high mountain ride, with terrific and challenging singletrack along the River Feshie to get you warmed before a lung busting climb up to Munro height – and more – at the summit of Carn Ban Mor. Take in the views that come from being high on the Cairngorm plateau, and then gird your loins for a testing descent over rocks, loose stones and fast trail back down to the car park near Auchlean.

Note: Carn Ban Mor has been 'improved' so isn't as rocky and technical anymore but is still worth keeping in as a classic high mountain ride. The descent trail is now smoother ('improved!') with water bars so you have to be careful to avoid pinch punctures.

Grade: **Black** » Distance: **21km** » Ascent: **895m** » Time: **2hrs+**
Start/Finish: **Car park near Auchlean, on minor road south from Feshiebridge, NN 851984**
SatNav: **Feshiebridge** » OS Map: **Landranger 35 Kingussie & Monadhliath Mountains; Landranger 36 Grantown & Aviemore**

The Route » Car park near Auchlean – Auchlean – fire road by bridge over River Feshie – Carn Ban Mor – Auchlean – return to car park

The Burma Road

Another classic ride of the area, the Burma Road as it is known to locals, climbs steadily but relentlessly out of the Spey Valley and into the mountains west of Aviemore. Not technical, but the views are superb and dropping down to the River Dulnain very quickly feels like you are plunging into a wilderness excursion. Take to the trails down the Dulnain and you pick up General Wade's road back over, where the Speyside Way takes you rest of the way back into town.

Grade: **Red** » Distance: **38km** » Ascent: **824m** » Time: **4hrs+**
Start/Finish: **Car park in Inverdruie 1km SE of Aviemore, NH 901110**
SatNav: **Inverdruie** » OS Map: **Landranger 35 Kingussie & Monadhliath Mountains; Landranger 36 Grantown & Aviemore**

The Route » Inverdruie car park – Aviemore – Lynwilg – Burma Road – Caggan – Inverlaidnan – Sluggan Bridge – Kinveachy – Speyside Way – Aviemore – Inverdruie car park

Photo: Andy McCandlish

More information

Getting About

Aviemore is fortunate to be on the main train line north to Inverness, so you can literally step off the platform and into the town centre. There is plenty of accommodation close by too, so this is a real option for those coming up from the south (or indeed down form the north!). Otherwise you are driving up the main A9 from the central belt, the car giving you access to places like Grantown which is off the main rail link. The car is also useful for getting you into some of the best riding, such as Glen Feshie.

Main Towns

Aviemore is an excellent place to base yourself in the area. It has plenty of shops, cafes, train access and nightlife, if that is your bag. There is even a cinema in the McDonald's complex! It is always full of life, outdoor folks in cafes and climbers returning from forays into the Cairngorms. Grantown-on-Spey is a little more off the beaten track and therefore slightly quieter, but has nearly all the same amenities and is a very picturesque place to stay and soak up some Speyside atmosphere.

Maps

Explorer 403 Cairn Gorm & Aviemore
OS Landranger 35 Kingussie & Monadhliath Mountains
OS Landranger 36 Grantown & Aviemore

Bike Shops

The bike shops in the Aviemore area are all excellent, staffed by enthusiastic riders and a great source of information as well as parts and repairs. In Aviemore Bothy Bikes (www.bothybikes.co.uk, 01479 810 111) is a good first stop. BaseCamp Bikes in Grantown are equally helpful and well stocked (www.basecampmtb.com, 01479 870 050). There's also Mike's Bikes (www.aviemorebikes.co.uk, 01479 810 478) but these are just several of many in the area so keep your eyes peeled.

Bike Hire

There are more than a few bike shops in the area to choose from. Try BaseCamp Bikes in Grantown (01479 870 050), Bothy Bikes in Aviemore (01479 810 111) or Mike's Bikes in Aviemore (01479 810 478).

Accommodation

Aviemore and Grantown-on-Spey are saturated with accommodation, being the tourist magnets that they are. We have good experiences of the Aviemore Bunkhouse (www.aviemore-bunkhouse.com, 01479 811 181) on Dalfaber Road, right beside the excellent Old Bridge Inn. A small but really charming campsite and bunkhouse are just between Aviemore and Grantown in Nethy Bridge – the Lazy Duck (www.lazyduck.co.uk, 01479 821 642) is well worth a visit, if just for their solar powered bush shower! Craggan Bunkhouse, one mile south of outside Grantown, is also an excellent option if you want to base yourself over that way (www.cragganoutdoors.co.uk, 01479 873 283). A particularly good campsite is to be found at Coylumbridge – the Rothiemurchus campsite (www.rothiemurchus.net , 01479 812 800) is superbly sheltered in the Caledonian pines if the weather gets wild. Other than that there is a dizzying array of hotels, B&Bs and camping available in the area.

Food & Drink

For great cafe food in Aviemore we can't go past the Cairngorm Mountain Sports cafe, upstairs from the outdoor shop of the same name (www.braemarmountainsports.com, 01479 810 903). A more recent, but just as good, addition is the cafe in Active Outdoors at the opposite end of the main street (www.activeoutdoorpursuits.com, 01479 780 000). For something more substantial the Royal Tandoori makes a good curry (www.royaltandoorirestaurant.co.uk, 01479 811 199), and if you time it right you can dive into the 'all you can eat pizza and pasta' in La Taverna (01479 810 683) – perfect for a post ride refuel. There are plenty of eateries in Grantown-on-Spey too of course, the most notable being MacLean's Highland Bakery (01479 873 827) for cakes and carry out rolls for a lunch stop.

Tourist Offices

Aviemore, 01479 810 363 » **Grantown-on-Spey**, 01479 872 773

Outdoor Shops

There are a few outdoor shops to choose from in Aviemore, including Nevisport (01479 810 239), Ellis Brigham (01479 810 175), Cairngorm Mountain Sports with its excellent upstairs cafe (01479 810 903) and Active Outdoors with another excellent cafe upstairs (01479 780 000).

Useful Websites

www.visitcairngorms.com – good for all round

Guidebooks

Scotland Mountain Biking – The Wild Trails, and *Wild Trails Vol.2*, both written by Phil McKane, published by Vertebrate Publishing
Bike Scotland Trails Guide, 40 of the Best Mountain Bike Routes in Scotland, written by Richard Moore and Andy McCandlish, published by Pocket Mountains

Photo: Andy McCandlish.

Isle of Skye

As a climber, walker, sea kayaker or mountain biker – in fact any outdoors person –
Skye is just one of those places you have to visit at least once in your life. Off the west
coast of Scotland, with soaring alpine mountains, deep sea lochs and a rugged coastline,
it is a place of extremes.

The Cuillin hills have long been a training ground for alpine climbers, in fact many rate them as
technically more difficult in a lot of places than their continental counterparts – certainly the fickle
weather adds an element of uncertainty to your day!

History plays a large part in the landscape too. On some of the rides here you will pass through
peaceful abandoned villages – empty windows and missing roofs telling the story of their violent past.
The Highland Clearances were at their worst on Skye, with families literally being thrown out of their
homes to make way for sheep grazing, often in the middle of winter, only to watch their roofs being
burned off so they couldn't return. Give it a thought as you pass through the townships, especially
Boreraig where it doesn't require a lot of imagination for history to come alive.

The Riding

At first visit it appears Skye has little to offer the mountain biker. Every hill is an alpine style mountain
and every trail is rocky and steep. Dig around a little however, and you will find some real gems.
The riding does tend to the technical end of the scale, with most of the trails needing a keen eye and
nerve to ride the bulk of the route without reverting to Shank's Pony. You will need to polish your rock
riding technique and, if you don't want to get well acquainted with your puncture repair kit, practice
lifting your back wheel over culverts as soon as possible!

Regardless of how challenging and exciting the riding is, it is well worth taking a break and lifting
your eyes from the trail now and again to take in the spectacular views. The Cuillins are a magnet for
alpine climbers, with all the craggy cliffs and steep terrain that involves, and the coastal scenery is
second to none with cliffs dropping steeply down to fjord-style sea lochs. You won't get a more
spectacular riding spot in this country.

When to go

Skye can be a brutal place when the weather is bad, and it is bad quite frequently. The routes themselves
are mostly rock and firm singletrack, so don't suffer too badly in the wet, but you are going to be riding
into isolated spots so it would be wise to steer clear in the winter months. The best months for weather
and lack of midges would be May and June, traditionally a time when the weather settles into high
pressure for a while and is at its most reliable.

Photo: Andy McCandlish.

51 *Glen Sligachan*

If you set foot on Skye with a bike there is one route that you simply must turn your front tyre toward, and that is the Glen Sligachan route. Cutting through the deep Glen Sligachan in the Black Cuillin, it is a non-stop challenge of riding on rocks, picking lines through boulder fields and popping over drainage culverts. There are few places where you can let your concentration lapse, but when you do you will realise what a spectacular mountain location you are riding through and it is that which makes this ride a must-see. Although the ride through to the coast is only 13 kilometres on paper, be prepared for a hard shift in remote country. Popping out at the sea, take a while to stop for lunch and soak up the atmosphere at Camasunary bothy before deciding whether to head back the way you came, or tackle the big circuit.

Grade: **Black** » Distance: **26km (there and back)** » Ascent: **177m** » Time: **3hrs+**
Start/Finish: **Sligachan Hotel** » Start GR: **NG 485298** » SatNav: **IV47 8SW**
OS Map: **Landranger 32 South Skye & Cuillin Hills; Explorer 411, Skye – Cuillin Hills** » Parking: **Don't park in the Sligachan Hotel car park – it is usually busy enough – there are plenty of other roadside options nearby**
Cafe: **None** » Pub: **The Sligachan Hotel, T: 01478 650 204**

Directions

S Starting at the Sligachan Hotel – don't park in their car park – cross over the arched bridge and turn immediately **R** through the gate and onto the well signposted trail. Climb up the initial stone pitched rise and take in the views before setting off in earnest.

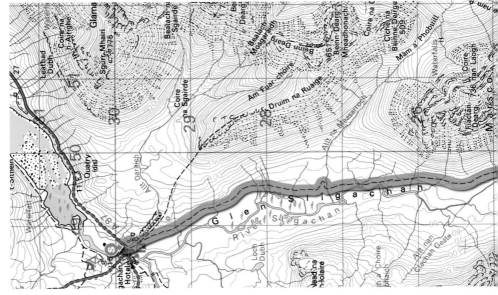

2 Approximately 8km along the trail there is a small cairn to mark a junction in the trail. Stay **L/straight on** for Camasunary (turn right to Loch Curuisk if you are on foot).

On the shores of Loch na Creitheach you will see another trail junction, with the left turn climbing steeply over a hill. Ignore this, staying **R** along the lochside.

At the end of Loch na Creitheach the path splits (not on the map) with one going right round the beach at the loch head and up the hill. Take either here – or vary them on the way out and back – as they both end up in the same place.

3 Drop down the gradual slope to the sea and turn **R** after the occupied, but isolated, farmhouse. Scoot along the beach to the bothy – a great place to sit and have lunch – before deciding whether to tackle the whole circuit or just return the way you came. We recommend the straight return as the circuit turns into a bit of a slog with little in the way of good riding once you hit the road at Kilmarie.

Extension (48km total):

This is part of a 48km loop, but it is by far the best part. If you want to do a circuit rather than an out-and-back, then take a left at Camasunary and climb steeply up the stony landrover track over the hill to Kilmarie. Turn **L** (north) on the B8083 here, continuing for 7km to the head of Loch Slapin. Cross the road bridge and turn immediately **L** and follow the often boggy and ill-defined trail through Srath Mor. At the township of Luib, turn **L** on the main road for 2km, then **R** on the minor road signposted to Moll. This takes you off the main road and round a lovely bit of coastline on single track road. Turn **R** back onto the A87 at Sconser and follow it back to the Sligachan Hotel.

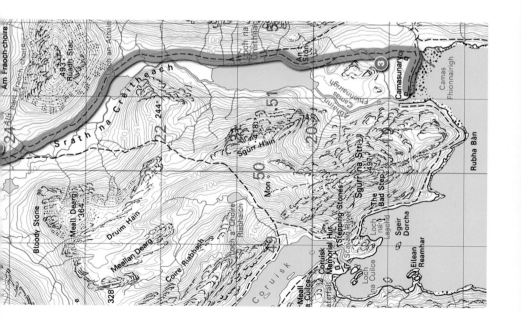

52 *Boreraig Coast*

This spin round the coastline of southern Skye gives some of the best riding in the country, combined with stunning views and a vivid chapter of Scottish history told as part of the bargain. Riding from Broadford you soon turn onto a roadside trail contouring the side of the glen. This was the line of the old railway, used to take Skye marble from the quarries in Strath Suardal to Broadford and the sea.

This historic theme continues as you climb over the hill on spectacular singletrack to the sea. After the descent you pass, on grassy trail, right by the door of ruined cottages by the shore. This is Boreraig, scene of some of the most brutal Highland Clearances.

The riding here turns quite technical along the coastline before mellowing out again as you reach the meadows near Suisnish and the track that returns you to the road and Broadford.

Grade: **Red** » Distance: **24km**

Ascent: **515m** » Time: **3hrs+**

Start/Finish: **Broadford car park next to petrol station**

Start GR: **NG 643235** » SatNav: **IV49 9AB**

OS Map: **Landranger 32 South Skye & Cuillin Hills**

Parking: **Parking on front at Broadford by fuel station**

Cafe: **Beinn na Caillich Cafe, T: 01471 822 616**

Pub: **The Broadford Hotel, T: 01471 822 204**

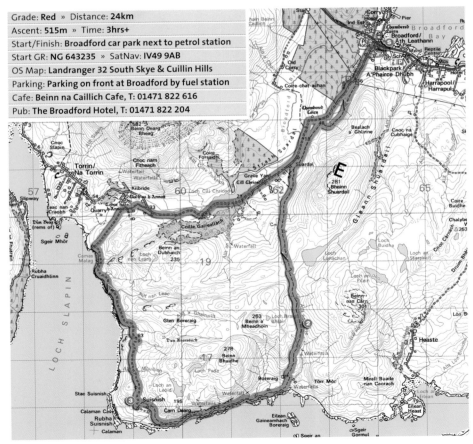

Directions

🅢 Start in the car park right next to the petrol station in Broadford. Turn up the B8083 towards Torrin and Elgol, keeping an eye on the **L** for a kissing gate after around 1km. Take this onto the wide gravelly singletrack. Follow this track for just short of 3km then pass through the gate and continue climbing the hill on the wide track.

② Descend to the coastline, where the path goes a little less distinct and grassy for a while. Aim for the large standing stone, then veer **R** through the abandoned houses where it becomes more defined. The trail becomes more technical here, following the rocky coastline. Climb the trail as it steepens up the front of the cliff, then flattens into excellent singletrack.

③ Skirt round to the **R** of the green shed at Suisnish and join the grassy track, following it round the coastline as it turns stony and undulating. It eventually turns to tarmac then drops you back out onto the B8083.
   Turn **R** here and follow the road back in to Broadford and your start point.

More riding

The Maidens

Another coastal classic for Skye, this is a short but technical ride out to spectacular maritime features. The trail is wet in places, fast in others, but almost always challenging as you climb and descend your way along the coastline. The reward at the end is a clifftop view of the Maidens, three sea stacks just offshore reputed to be named after the wife and daughters of the clan Macleod chief drowned there in a storm, their boat dashed on the rocks.

Grade: **Red** » Distance: **17km (there and back)** » Ascent: **320m** » Time: **2.5hrs+**
Start/Finish: **Orbost Farm, NG 257432** » SatNav: **IV55 8ZB** » OS Map: **Landranger 23 North Skye** » Parking: **The car park marked on the OS map seems to be the open farmyard as you get to the end of the public road. Park here, making sure not to obstruct any farm vehicles**

The Route » Orbost Farm – Loch Bharcasaig – turn **L** at NG 251423 – forest track then muddy singletrack then well-defined singletrack – Idrigill Point, NG 248364 (for the best view of the Maidens, take a left and ride down the grassy slopes toward Idrigill Point. Be especially careful near the edge here as we discovered the peat layer actually overhangs the drop in places and could give way easily if you stand too close to the edge) – cliffs above the Maidens (NG 244363) – Retrace route back to Orbost Farm

Quiraing

The riding at the Quiraing is spectacular (check out this book's cover!), but with one trail only a few kilometres long it is a short, sharp buzz. With steep drops off narrow singletrack you have to be on the ball, and every step of the way can be a challenge from the trail itself to the long singletrack road climb back up to the start if you choose to drop down to sea level on the path. Alternatively just do the trail as an out and back to save the climbing.

Grade: **Red/Black** » Distance: **10km** » Ascent: **375m** » Time: **1hrs+**
Start/Finish: **Car park on minor road, west of Brogaig, NG 446681** » SatNav: **IV51 9JY (nearby)**
OS Map: **Landranger 23 North Skye**

More information

Getting About

The train gets as far as Kyle of Lochalsh on the mainland side of the Skye Bridge, and you could theoretically pedal from there onto the island. Sligachan is 25 miles away though, so you would need to be fairly committed to public transport to consider this before the ride. As a result cars are pretty essential for getting around on Skye.

Main Towns

Portree is the nearest large town to the trails we have described. Built around a picturesque harbour, it has plenty of accommodation, great cafes and restaurants to keep you fed and watered on your trip. It is also steeped in history, being the last place where Bonnie Prince Charlie and Flora MacDonald met before he left for France.

Maps

OS Landranger 23 North Skye
OS Landranger 32 South Skye & Cuillin Hills
OS Explorer 407 Skye – Dunvegan
OS Explorer 411 Skye – Cuillin Hills
OS Explorer 412 Skye – Sleat

Bike Shops

There are no specialist mountain bike shops, so be prepared to be self-sufficient as far as possible. For spares and repairs you could try Island Cycles in Portree (www.islandcycles-skye.co.uk, 01478 613 121) or Fairwinds Bicycle Hire in Broadford (01471 822 270). Sshokwave have a demo centre in Dornie, around 10 miles short of the Skye Bridge (01599 555 739).

Bike Hire

Bikes can be hired at all the bike shops mentioned above, with Sshokwave (01599 555 739) being the one with the most specialist quality mountain bikes.

Accommodation

To get right on the doorstep of the main ride, why not opt for the classic Sligachan Hotel (01478 650 204). They offer everything from camping through self-catering, to a full-blown hotel stay. There is always plenty of life in the bar where climbers and walkers tend to congregate, and you could always partake in the alternative Cuillin traverse – the traverse of the bar's whisky selection, one end to the other!

Otherwise there are plenty of options to choose from on Skye. Portree is a busy harbour town with plenty of nightlife and accommodation to offer but there are plenty of hidden gem B&Bs on the island to choose from. Elgol is a particularly scenic fishing village overlooking the Cuillins.

Food & Drink

The Sligachan Hotel can't be beaten for good food and atmosphere after a ride, and if you are camped in the site you are a short walk from its hospitality. The Broadford Hotel is also a good choice for that end of the island (01471 822 204). Otherwise there is cracking cafe in Portree called Cafe Arriba (01478 611 830), always bustling and just above the harbour.

Tourist Offices

Portree, 01478 612 137 – very helpful too if you are in Portree

Outdoor Shops

There are surprisingly few outdoor shops in the area, given its heritage. The nearest is Cioch Outdoor Clothing Company in Struan (www.cioch-direct.co.uk, 01470 572 707). Alternatively pop into 914 Outdoor at Dornie (www.914outdoor.co.uk, 01599 555 362), on the way to the Skye Bridge.

Useful Websites

www.skye.co.uk – good for all round
www.isleofskye.com – good for accommodation and other attractions
www.visitscotland.com – good for accommodation and other attractions

Guidebooks

Scotland Mountain Biking – The Wild Trails, and *Wild Trails Vol.2*, both written by Phil McKane, published by Vertebrate Publishing
Bike Scotland Trails Guide, 40 of the Best Mountain Bike Routes in Scotland, written by Richard Moore and Andy McCandlish, published by Pocket Mountains
Mountainbike Scotland, written by Kenny Wilson, published by Ernest Press

Photo: Andy McCandlish.

Torridon & Applecross

If you are looking for the best of UK wilderness mountain riding, there can be few better places than the north-west of Scotland.

Tiny white painted villages nestle at the foot of some of the highest mountains in the country, a magnet for mountaineers in the summer and winter who flock here for the quality of terrain. With Torridonian sandstone being some of the oldest in the world, that terrain has been around a while too.

While there is little in the way of towns, the villages here are over endowed with great pubs, cafes and restaurants making full use of the local seafood and produce.

The Riding

Mountain biking is still a small part of the activities up here, partly because of the remote location, and partly because there are no 'easy' trails to take on in the area – you either hit the rocky paths head on and delve deep into the mountains, or you stick to the undulating coastal roads. Of course with mountains plummeting straight into the sea you know you are going to be at the sharp end of some serious climbing, so get your SPDs tightened, but at the same time every trail is technical to one degree or another so maybe not too tight ... The riding ranges from smooth mountainous singletrack you can blast through, to hair raising rocky trails you have to pick carefully down.

Because the trails are largely stalking or mountaineering paths, they tend to go up and over the mountains rather than sticking to the contours, and that also means they can be relatively fragile – so be realistic about what you can ride and be prepared to push rather than tear up the steeper sections.

When to go

Being situated on the north-west coast of Scotland, and high and rugged, you obviously can't come here in the winter – the snow cover regularly extends well below the height of the trails. Springtime is best for good weather and lack of midges, as is autumn.

Photo: Andy McCandlish.

53 *Torridon High Mountains*

This has to be one of the highest routes anywhere in the UK, taking you right into the peaks above Torridon village and almost to Munro height. It involves some shouldering of the bikes and a lot of rocky ground, but there are few trails in the country with the feeling of exposure and height this one gets, combined with some superbly rideable trails and challenging descents that will see you hanging off the back of the bike. It takes you into the heart of countryside that is very remote, but equally has a multitude of options, with breathtaking trails heading off in a number of directions from the Bealach na Lice. Descend from here to Annat to get a cracking ride, or follow this route up to the Coire Grannda for an 8 kilometres descent from over 680 metres to sea level. There is no doubt about it though, whichever route you choose you are going to have to work for it with rocky climbs and spells of hike-a-bike, but the enjoyment and the memories you'll have are even greater for it.

Grade: **Red/Black** » Distance: **22km** » Ascent: **808m** » Time: **2hrs+**

Start/Finish: **Coulags** » Start GR: **NG 957450** » SatNav: **IV54 8YH (gets you to the Lochcarron area, down the road)**

OS Map: **LExplorer 429 Glen Carron & West Monar** » Parking: **Large lay-by just west of the bridge at Coulags on the A890** » Cafe: **The Waterside Cafe in Lochcarron is good for a bacon roll, T: 01520 722 303**

Pub: **The Lochcarron Hotel, T: 01520 722 226**

Directions

S Follow the signposted right of way sign as it points you up the banks of the Fionn-abhainn, climbing on track at first then rough trail splashing through burns heading north. The trail is a challenging combination of gradient and rocky obstacles but is mostly rideable. Cross the open and narrow bridge over the river.

At Coulags bothy, stop for a while and drink in the scenery (or shelter if the weather is bad) before gearing up for the next part of the climb. The trail continues up the glen before skirting the shores of Loch Coire Fionnaraich and climbing again, this time more steeply. Shoulder the bike as you climb the last minutes up to the Bealach na Lice and take a well earned rest at the small cairn and path junction. Left for Annat, but we are going **R**.

2 From the Bealach junction the trail undulates along the contours before you will need to shoulder again for the Bealach Ban. Just over the top of the ridge is flatter however, and gives terrific riding on white quartzite trail with amazing views on your left down into Glen Torridon. Cut across the open floor of Coire Grannda before the shoulder comes into play yet again, for the last time.

3 At the small lochan you are now downhill all the way to Achnashellach on cracking trail. At times it is fast, at others more technical, so take your time and don't gather too much speed when dropping into blind corners where it has a habit of going technical when you least expect it. Remember you are a long way from help up here! Drop down next to the River Lair, going easy as the trail steepens up with some extensive rock pitching. There are some tricky turns here, so watch your step! At Achnashellach hit the A890, turn **R** and return to the start point.

Not long enough? There is a much longer route you can stitch onto this loop, and it still takes in some of the best descending anywhere so don't worry you aren't missing out! Continue on at the Bealach na Lice instead of turning right. This takes you through some simply stunning singletrack round Loch an Eion before the world class descent to Annat. Turn **R** there on the road and ride to Loch Clair where you turn **R** and return via Loch Coulin and path up the side of the Easan Dorcha. From the Drochaid Coire Lair drop down the rocky descent to Achnashellach station and turn **R** back to your start point.

54 The Applecross Peninsula

This route has so much more than the trail or views, it has one of the best pubs in the country to aim for!
As you climb away from the crofting community of Kenmore on the northern edge of the peninsula, keep your
eye on the half pint of prawns and real ale that awaits you at the excellent Applecross Inn, sitting outside over
a glittering sea. The trail cuts through some wild and remote countryside, which is why it is such a pleasure
to find it in such rideable condition. At times rocky, but always good fun, it cuts across to the River Applecross
where it turns to track and descends to the shore. Here you have the choice of returning the way you came,
or using the singletrack road that hugs the coast north as we have recommended here. It takes in an extra
section of superb and picturesque singletrack but, a word of warning, even though this road sticks to the
coast it undulates a lot and is far from an easy option.

Grade: **Red** » Distance: **41km** » Ascent: **950m** » Time: : **4hrs+**	
Start/Finish: **Parking place, near Kenmore** » Start GR: **NG 754577** » SatNav: **IV54 8XH (gets you to the general Kenmore area)** » OS Map: **Explorer 428 Lochalsh, Plockton & Applecross**	
Parking: **Parking place near Kenmore. Enough room for several cars**	
Cafe: **No specific cafe – get coffee in the Applecross Inn** » Pub: **The Applecross Inn, T: 01520 744 262**	

Directions

S Immediately opposite a parking lay-by on the roadside above Kenmore the trail passes through a signposted
gate and descends slightly before climbing up the slopes of Meall Dearg. There are few navigation issues as it is
the only trail anywhere near. Continue past the shores of Loch Gaineamhach on your right.

At the foot of Croic bheinn a faint trail comes in from your left – ignore this and continue around the shoulder
of Meall Arachaidh where the going gets occasionally rocky and challenging. Begin the descent to River Applecross
here. At the foot of the hill the narrow singletrack turns to track and continues down the glen.

2 Just short of 1km past the large house on your right, take the bridge on your **L**, turning immediately **R** after the
bridge onto more trails down the riverside. This pops you out at the coast where you can turn **L** to follow the
singletrack road round to the Applecross Inn for refreshment.

Arrive at the Applecross Inn and present yourself at the bar. Here you can either retrace your steps over the hill
to get back, or take the coast road north back to the start.

3 To take the coast road, at the opposite edge of the bay from Applecross village, climb up on the crofters trail
from the house marked as Cruarg on the OS map. This is a simply beautiful section of picture perfect trail that
climbs up and over the hill to the golden beach at Sand. Unfortunately from here it is a bit of a grind back round
the road to return to your car. The views are superb though and we have spotted everything from otters to whales
and even a submarine steaming down the Inner Sound between the mainland and Raasay. Take your time and
enjoy the experience.

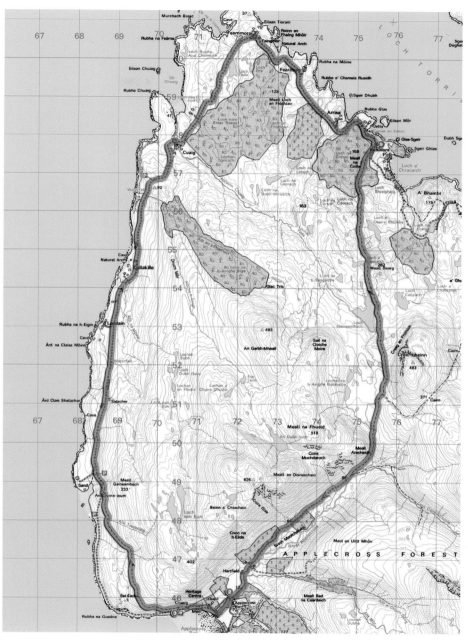

More riding

Loch Damh

A really enjoyable route that gives you a first taste of the area if you arrive too late in the day to try anything longer. Initial fire road around the fishing loch of Loch Damh soon gives way after the fishing bothy to singletrack. It is intermittently rocky but largely smooth and very rideable. The singletrack that climbs up the Srath a' Bhathaich is mostly rideable, except near the top where it deteriorates and steepens to the point of one needing to shoulder the bike for a short while. It is all worth it though; the mountain views that greet you over the top of the col above Coire Roill are stunning, as is the descent that sweeps you over fast trail and rocky drop alike to back down to – conveniently – the doors of the Torridon Inn.

Grade: **Red/Black** » Distance: **23km** » Ascent: **650m** » Time: **2hrs+**
Start/Finish: **Roadside car park, NG 866542** » SatNav: **IV22 2EY** » OS Map: **Landranger 24 Raasay & Applecross**

The Route » Roadside viewpoint car park – Loch Damh – Kinloch Damh – Srath a' Bhathaich – Coire Roill – Torridon Inn – Viewpoint car park

Photos: Andy McCandlish.

More information

Getting About

Torridon really is in the back end of nowhere as far as public transport goes. There is a bus service, but in general a car is by far your best mode of transport to get around the hills. To get to Torridon just head up the A87 to Skye, cutting north five miles before Kyle of Lochalsh on the A890. It is single track roads from Lochcarron over through Shieldaig to Torridon village, so take your time. The routes all start in either Torridon, or round the hills at Achnashellach.

Main Towns

The nearest village is Torridon, with a small shop, cafe, Youth Hostel, hotel and not a whole lot else. The nearest larger town would have to be Kyle of Lochalsh with a large Co-op, accommodation a-plenty and even a good chip shop.

Maps

OS Explorer 428 Lochalsh, Plockton & Applecross
OS Explorer 429 Glen Carron & West Monar
OS Landranger 24 Raasay & Applecross
OS Landranger 25 Glen Carron & Glen Affric

Bike Shops

There are no nearby cycle shops to Torridon, so be prepared to be self-reliant for spares and repairs. Sshokwave in Dornie (01599 555 739) is a bike hire and demo centre, but they may lend a hand if you ask nicely. Alternatively they would hire you a quality bike if the worst came to the worst.

Photo: Andy McCandlish.

Bike Hire

Sshokwave in Dornie (01599 555 739) hire some superb top-end mountain bikes; phone them to see what is available at the time.

Accommodation

Due to the proximity of climbing and mountaineering in the area, there are lots of budget options for accommodation. The excellent SYHA hostel in Torridon (www.syha.org.uk, 01445 791 284) is a great place to stay with top facilities, and Gerry's Hostel is at the foot of the trails on the south side of the mountains (www.gerryshostel-achnashellach.co.uk, 01520 766 232). There are also plenty of B&Bs to be found, and the Torridon Inn (www.thetorridon.com/inn, 01445 700 300) offers large rooms for up to six people at a very reasonable price – and they have the advantage of having the excellent pub and bar food right next door! For a more luxurious visit, take a look in The Torridon (part of the same group of buildings, so also on 01445 700 300). Otherwise there are several campsites with honesty boxes at Annat and Inveralligin with no facilities, and a free one in Torridon village with basic public toilet and shower facilities.

Food & Drink

In Torridon village itself, the Torridon Stores and Cafe (01445 791 400) offers some cracking cafe fare with a beautiful view out the large windows, and the chance to replenish your trail snack cache from the stores. Across the loch you will find the Torridon Inn for some excellent pub food and drink (01445 700 300) and nearby Shieldaig is well worth a visit for a larger store, the Shieldaig Bar and Kitchen (01520 755 251) and Nanny's cafe is superb for a takeaway coffee and cake to eat on the shore. Of course no trip would be complete without a visit to the Applecross Inn (01520 744 262) for a half pint of local prawns.

Tourist Offices

Kyle of Lochalsh, 01599 534 276

Outdoor Shops

The nearest outdoor shop is in Dornie, on the drive north; 914 Outdoor (www.914outdoor.co.uk, 01599 555 362) stocks most outdoor gear and the staff are very friendly and helpful.

Useful Websites

www.visithighlands.com – good for all round
www.visittorridon.co.uk – good for local knowledge and tourist info

Guidebooks

Scotland Mountain Biking – The Wild Trails, and *Wild Trails Vol.2*, both written by Phil McKane, published by Vertebrate Publishing
Bike Scotland Trails Guide, 40 of the Best Mountain Bike Routes in Scotland, written by Richard Moore and Andy McCandlish, published by Pocket Mountains
Mountainbike Scotland, written by Kenny Wilson, published by Ernest Press

Isle of Harris

You can't get much further afield in the UK than the Outer Hebrides off the north-west coast of Scotland. Of these islands there aren't many that shine as mountain biking destinations, but one that does is Harris. Where the other islands are either flat or slightly rolling moorlands, Harris has a combination of high craggy mountains (An Cliseam, the highest point, is 799 metres) dropping steeply to some simply amazing beaches on the west coast.

The east coast has a different character altogether with no beaches, but deep and heathery inlets perfect for mooring boats or watching otters.

It was probably brought to most people's attention with the 2000 programme Castaway when a community was marooned on the island of Taransay, just off the coast of Harris, for a year organised by BBC television. The programme gave a good feel for the remote location and idyllic beaches found in the area.

Traditionally a crofting area, Harris is also famous for its home spun Harris Tweed that graces some of the finest clothing in the world – more recently some Nike trainers! There are still some looms to heard clacking away in sheds all over the island, so keep your ears open.

The Riding

By an accident of history, the old crofters paths that criss-cross the island have turned out to be excellent for exploring the area by mountain bike. Built up out of the peat bogs on platforms of rock and stone as the highways between the isolated crofting communities, they have overgrown from their original one to two metre width into narrow walked-in singletrack with a cracking gritty surface in a lot of places. In others the grass has taken over, but they are still obvious on the ground and enjoyable to ride. The island's hilly nature means there is a lot of climbing and descending, but with a terrific view and chance of a paddle in clear blue sea to sooth hot feet at the end of a ride, it is all worthwhile.

When to go

Although the winters don't usually get as cold as the mainland, they can still be a bleak time with strong winds and very short days, so the best time would be May or June to escape the midges and get the best chance of some settled weather.

Photo: Andy McCandlish.

55 Rhenigidale Loop

It's hard to believe that the village of Rhenigidale only had its road to the outside world built in 1990, only beaten by electricity by ten years. Before the road you either sailed in by boat, or used the Postman's Path, which is part of our route here. For countless years the postman walked this trail three times a week to deliver mail, and was often joined by the village schoolkids as they completed the 10-mile round trip walk to school in Tarbert.

We have incorporated this trail into a 23-kilometre loop which, as it is Harris, involves a lot of climbing and descending. The beauty of it is that you are too busy marvelling at the scenery or the way the trail has been built to last into steep hillsides above crashing waves to notice. Shortly after leaving Rhenigidale, you pass through yet another abandoned village on the west coast of Scotland, Lingingis. The trail threads through the roofless houses on what would have been the main through 'road', so it isn't too hard to imagine life going on.

From here the trail is nothing short of spectacular. Clinging to the hillside on the built up crofters path, the going isn't too technical – although in places it can get tricky – but it is always amazing. A steep bike-on-the-shoulder climb sees you up at hilltop level before a grand and fast descent back towards Tarbert.

Grade: **Red** » Distance: **23km** » Ascent: **936m** » Time: **2hrs+**	
Start/Finish: **Tarbert car park** » Start GR: **NG 154999** » SatNav: **HS3 3DG**	
OS Map: **Landranger 14 Tarbert & Loch Seaforth** » Parking: **Main car park and bus station, Tarbert**	
Cafe: **The First Fruits Tearoom right next to the car park, T: 01859 502 439**	
Pub: **Hotel Hebrides, Tarbert, T: 01859 502 364; or Harris Hotel, Tarbert, T: 01859 502 154**	

Directions

S From the central car park climb the short hill and turn **R** in front of the general stores onto the Scalpay road. Follow this as it undulates along, then climbs steeply over to Lochannan Lacasdail.

2 Just as you reach the view over the loch, an obvious path leads **L** down a slope and onto the lochside on a wide track. This soon narrows before climbing up the Braigh an Ruisg saddle on an excellent trail then descending on rather more grassy and wet trail down to the shores of Loch Mharaig. Take the obvious path **R** just before reaching the river at the bottom and pass through a gate to emerge by the bridge and phone box.

Turn **R** on the road and climb over the hill towards Rhenigidale, passing Loch Mor on your right as you do. Keep an eye out for otters here as we have spotted them twice on the loch or road.

3 Don't descend too quickly as you will want to turn off to the **R** before reaching the bottom of the hill and the village. The trail drops sharp **R** off the road, dropping slightly at first before levelling out and dropping again through Linginis abandoned village. Follow the path around the coast, being careful not to fall to your left at all times, and eventually drop down some tricky bends to the bridge at Gleann Trolamaraig.

Cross this and shoulder the bike for a long hot climb up the zigzags. They are too steep and loose to ride, so just chill out and enjoy the view. Besides, it isn't long until you crest the summit and can really enjoy the superb descent down grass, mud and grit trails all the way back down to Lochannan Lacasdail and your return to Tarbert by road.

Not long enough? There are a few options for extending this ride, most of which involve stitching together the crofters paths mentioned in the 'More Riding' Crofters Paths ride (page 363). Overall though, this ride should be savoured and time taken, so you shouldn't have too much time on your hands before a pint in the Hotel Hebrides!

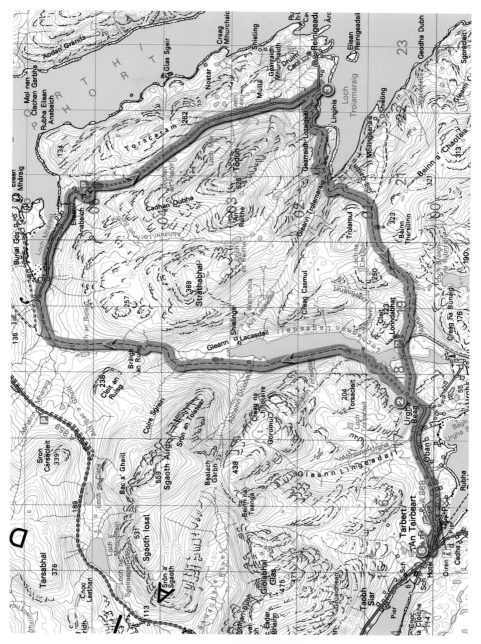

56 North Harris Tour

This is a long and sustained route with some quite tough riding in remote glens, far from the nearest road. There is little in the way of technical riding, but a lot in the way of tough, grassy and steep trail with energy sapping surfaces and the occasional wide river crossing to dice with. In other words, it is a cracking day out!

The trail up from the sea begins the route with a relatively easy surface, but it soon deteriorates into tougher stuff as you drop down and cross the Abhainn Langadail to toil up steep slopes of grassy path. Over the top and round the shores of Loch Chleistir the trail really opens out into a fast and gritty surface before dropping you down to the fast track gently descending Gleann Mhiabhaig. From here it is easy track or road – albeit sometime steep and taxing – back to the start.

Grade: **Red** » Distance: **38km** » Ascent: **1,108m** » Time: **4hrs+**	
Start/Finish: **Parking place, by the bridge over the Abhainn Bhioigadail** » Start GR: **NB 186116**	
SatNav: **HS3 3AB gets you to the nearby Scaladale Centre** » OS Map: **Landranger 14 Tarbert & Loch Seaforth**	
Parking: **Parking place, by the bridge over the Abhainn Bhioigadail**	
Cafe: **The First Fruits Tearoom right next to the car park, T: 01859 502 439**	
Pub: **Hotel Hebrides, Tarbert, T: 01859 502 364; or Harris Hotel, Tarbert, T: 01859 502 154**	

Directions

S Straight from the roadside the trail climbs away gently up the glen on a rough track surface. Follow this up and over the Bealach na h-Uamha, taking the rough trail down to the riverside.

2 Cross any way you can here; it can be a bit tricky. Climb on grassy trails up the side of Stulabhal, zigzagging in places as you gain height. The trail recovers into a harder surface here and is an enjoyable ride round the small loch. Drop down to the shores of Loch Bhoisimid and join the track by the small building.

3 Follow the track south from here all the way down to the B887 road and turn **L** to return to the main A859. Keep an eye on your right for the incongruous tennis court in the middle of nowhere and the chimney stack of the old whaling station.

At the main road turn **L** up the tortuous hill past the quarry entrance and continue on round until you reach your original start point.

Photo: Andy McCandlish.

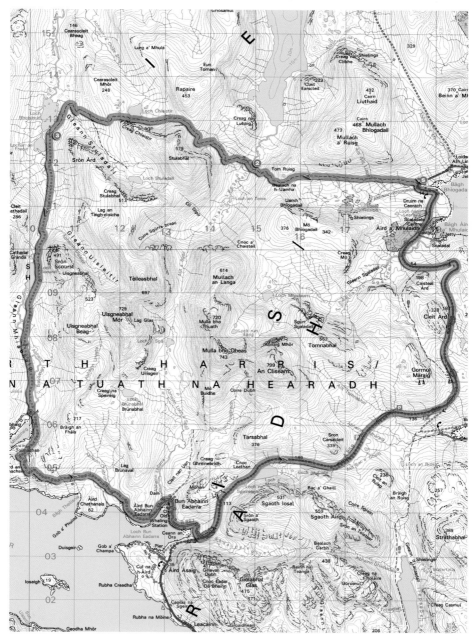

More riding

Coastal Crofters Paths, South Harris

This is really a patchwork of a few of the remaining crofters paths left on the rugged east coast of the island. Many of them have been swallowed up by tarmac, and others no doubt have just overgrown into oblivion. The ones that remain, however, are superb trails through the backcountry of the island, joining communities and crossing the island with ancient links. This route covers the island from west to east, leaving from the superb clean and fresh Luskentyre beach area (not to be missed) before crossing the island to the sharp contrast of far greener and boggy east coast at Aird Mhigh. The trails are tricky at times in boggy conditions, but open fast in others.

It continues round the coast, picking up trails where they exist, largely grassy and rideable, before recrossing the island on roads and tracks.

Grade: **Red** » Distance: **30km** » Ascent: **678m** » Time: **2hrs+**

Start/Finish: **Seilebost, NG 081969** » SatNav: **Seilebost** » OS Map: **Landranger 14 Tarbert & Loch Seaforth; Landranger 18 Sound of Harris**

The Route » Track at Seilebost up Bealach Eorabhat – Aird Mhighe – Caolas Stocinis – Ghreosabhagh – Drinisiadar – A859 – Return to start

Photos: Andy McCandlish.

More information

Getting About

You can fly into Stornoway on Lewis and hire a car to drive to Harris, with flights currently run by Flybe (www.flybe.com, 0871 700 2000). At time of printing the flights are around the £300 mark for a return trip from London, changing at a Scottish airport. Alternatively you will have to drive to the ferry port at Uig on Skye, and sail from there to Tarbert on Harris. Caledonian Macbrayne (www.calmac.co.uk, 0800 066 5000) run the ferry service most days of the week and a car with two passengers will currently cost around £70 return.

If you are happy to stick to the island of Harris, you can easily get away without bringing your car over. Bikes travel free on the ferry, so pack up your Bob trailer or rucksack and pedal on and it will only cost you just over £10 return. Get accommodation in Tarbert itself and you will only have a short ride or walk to drop your gear before setting out on a ride.

Main Towns

The nearest town is Tarbert where the ferry from Skye docks. It is the capital of Harris and home to the high school and bank, along with a few grocery and hardware shops and a cafe. If you time it right you might also get the travelling cinema parked up in the town centre when you arrive too! If you want a bigger town you will need to drive an hour north to Stornoway where you will find most facilities.

Maps

OS Explorer 455 South Harris
OS Explorer 456 North Harris & Loch Seaforth
OS Landranger 14 Tarbert & Loch Seaforth
OS Landranger 18 Sound of Harris

Bike Shops

There are no nearby cycle shops to Tarbert, or indeed any on the Isle of Harris that would cater for mountain bikes. Alex Dan's Cycle Shop in Stornoway (01851 704 025) would be your only chance of parts and repairs if you need them.

Photo: Andy McCandlish.

Bike Hire

Alex Dan's Cycle Shop in Stornoway (01851 704 025) hires basic mountain bikes under the name of Hebridean Cycle Hire.

Accommodation

There are a number of options in the immediate Tarbert area, handy for getting straight off the ferry and central for most of the rides. The Rock View bunkhouse is pretty basic but should cover your needs and is cheap (01859 502 626). A cracking option if you have the energy to ride round is the Gatliff Hostel at Rhenigidale – a converted croft house in a great location, it is packed with character. They don't accept advance bookings but it is unlikely you will be turned away. Am Bothan bunkhouse (01859 520 251) in Leverburgh on the south coast of Harris is another one well worth a look. Lastly, on the bunkhouse theme, there is the Scaladale Centre Hostel (01859 502 502) round at Ardvourlie.

A relatively recent addition to the accommodation options on Harris is the super-posh AA 4-Star Hotel Hebrides (01859 502 364). Renovated from the old Macleod Motel in Tarbert, it provides a real boutique hotel experience just where you wouldn't expect it! The Harris Hotel (01859 502 154) is also handy in Tarbert. Otherwise there are plenty of B&B and self-catering options throughout the island.

Food & Drink

For a quick snack and coffee, the First Fruits tearoom in Tarbert is a good bet (01859 502439) as is the Skoon Art Cafe (01859 530268) down the east side of the island at Geocrab. Skoon also has a terrific selection of original oil paintings and is a great place to unwind after a ride. For more substantial meals the Hotel Hebrides (01859 502364) in Tarbert is an excellent choice for bar food or their dedicated restaurant. The Harris Hotel (01859 502154) just up the road in the town also does good bar food.

Tourist Offices

Tarbert, 01859 502 011 – open April to October. (A handy tip is the toilets through the back of the information centre have a shower in the disabled toilets if you are camping.)

Outdoor Shops

There are no specialist outdoor shops on the Hebrides. You might find what you need in the hardware shops in Tarbert.

Useful Websites

www.visithebrides.com – good for all round
www.explore-harris.com – good for tourist attractions and activity ideas

Guidebooks

Scotland Mountain Biking – The Wild Trails, and *Wild Trails Vol.2*, both written by Phil McKane, published by Vertebrate Publishing
Bike Scotland Trails Guide, 40 of the Best Mountain Bike Routes in Scotland, written by Richard Moore and Andy McCandlish, published by Pocket Mountains
Mountainbike Scotland, written by Kenny Wilson, published by Ernest Press

MOUNTAIN BIKING GUIDEBOOKS

About the Great Outdoors

The great outdoors is not bottom bracket friendly; beautiful flowing singletrack can give way suddenly to scary rock gardens, hard climbs can appear right at the end of a ride and sheep will laugh at your attempts to clean your nemesis descent. Of course it's not all good news. You'll need a good bike to ride many of the routes in our set of mountain biking guides. You'll also need fuel, spare clothing, first aid skills, endurance, power, determination and plenty of nerve.

Bridleways litter our great outdoors. Our guides, written by local riders, reveal the secrets of their local area's best rides from 6 to 300km in length, including ideas for link-ups and night-riding options. Critically acclaimed, our comprehensive series of guides is the country's bestselling and most respected – purpose-built for the modern mountain biker.

The Guidebooks

Each guidebook features up to 28 rides, complete with comprehensive directions, specialist mapping and inspiring photography, all in a pocket-sized, portable format. Written by riders for riders, our guides are designed to maximise ride-ability and are full of useful local area information.

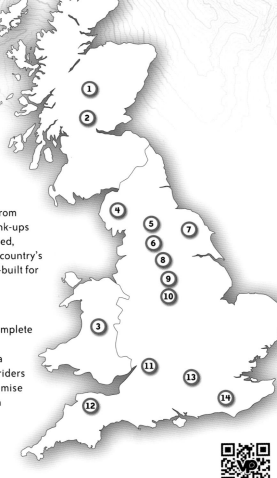

Available from bike shops, book shops or direct from:
www.v-publishing.co.uk